WEST ACADEMIC PUBLISHING'S LAW SCHOOL ADVISORY BOARD

INTELLECTUAL PROPERTY AND UNFAIR COMPETITION

IN A NUTSHELL®

EIGHTH EDITION

DAVID J. FRIEDMAN, ESQ.

WEST ACADEMIC

860 Blue Gentian Road, Suite 350
Eagan, MN 55121
1-877-888-1330

Published in the United States of America

ISBN: 978-1-63460-845-9

To Professor Charles McManis, whose impressive work created this book and sustained it for thirty years.

To my family, whose love and support brought me to where I am today.

And to you, the reader, whose interest in these fascinating legal areas helps make this knowledge available to everyone.

D.J.F.

PREFACE

This eighth edition of Intellectual Property & Unfair Competition in a Nutshell reflects significant legal changes since the 2013 edition. Congress created a federal cause of action for trade secret misappropriations, the Defend Trade Secrets Act of 2016 (P.L. 114–153). The Leahy-Smith America Invents Act (AIA) of 2011 (P.L. 112–29, 125 Stat. 284–341), substantially revised U.S. patent law and examination procedures and has significantly evolved since its initial passage. The Supreme Court decisions in *Matal v. Tam*, 582 U.S. 218 (2017) and *Iancu v. Brunetti*, 588 U.S. ___, 139 S. Ct. 2294 (2019) extended federal trademark protection to obscene, disparaging, immoral, and scandalous trademarks. Additionally, many sections of this book have been revised or expanded after Charles R. McManis shifted his focus to other works.

This publication's history bears remembrance at this transition point. Charles R. McManis originally published the first three editions of this book back in 1982 as "Unfair Trade Practices in a Nutshell." Each of these editions noted that "unfair trade practices" was merely one of many names for this emerging body of law and that other phrases such as "unfair competition" and "intellectual property" were also used to identify elements of it.

Following the third edition's 1993 publication, several important domestic and international developments in intellectual property and unfair competition laws highlighted the need for a more precise title. These events included actions by the American Law Institute and World Intellectual Property Organization, and the World Trade Organization's creation. From these developments, Charles R. McManis revised the title of the fourth and succeeding editions of this Nutshell to acknowledge both the laws of intellectual property and of unfair competition had come into their own.

The American Law Institute (ALI) published the Restatement of the Law, Third, of Unfair Competition in 1995. This was the ALI's first independent restatement of unfair competition law. The Restatement of Torts originally covered this subject, but it was omitted for the Restatement, Second, of Torts. Apparently unfair competition law had evolved to the point that it was no longer appropriately treated as a subcategory of tort law. The ALI noted "the term 'unfair competition' now describes an array of legal actions addressing methods of competition that improperly interfere with the legitimate commercial interests of other sellers in the marketplace, including actions for passing off, deceptive advertising, and the infringement of trademarks." The ALI also found a parallel increase in the significance of intellectual property law, including those laws defined through unfair competition law.

The 1990's saw two particularly important international intellectual property law developments. Global adoption of the Agreement on Trade Related Aspects of Intellectual Property

Rights ("TRIPS") occurred as part of the Marrakesh Treaty agreement bundle. These agreements also amended the General Agreement on Tariffs and Trade ("GATT") and created the World Trade Organization ("WTO"). TRIPS enforcement began on January 1, 1995, creating the first international agreement establishing minimum standards protecting all seven enumerated "intellectual property" categories: 1) copyrights & related rights; 2) trademarks; 3) geographical indications; 4) industrial designs; 5) patents; 6) integrated circuit designs; and 7) undisclosed information. Article 39 of TRIPS specified that undisclosed information protection was considered an essential element ensuring effective protection against unfair competition, as provided in Article 10*bis* of the older Paris Convention for the Protection of Industrial Property (1883).

The World Intellectual Property Organization (WIPO), the international agency long responsible for administering the Paris Convention and the Berne Convention for the Protection for Literary and Artistic Works (1886), reasserted its authority to guide international intellectual property policymaking in 1996. In doing so, it promulgated the WIPO Copyright Treaty (WCT) and the WIPO Performances and Phonograms Treaty (WPPT). These treaties sought to adjust the law of copyrights and related rights in the new digital age.

This basic framework remained in place as the seventh edition underwent revisions with Charles R. McManis assuming a co-authorship role. The seventh edition followed the evolution and growth of intangible property rights against a historic background shifting from local goods-oriented economies to a more global services-dominated economy. The growing digital marketplace gave rise to many new unfair competition and intellectual property law challenges meriting specific attention, including conflicts as geography-based jurisdictional limitations eroded further.

This eighth edition of Intellectual Property & Unfair Competition in a Nutshell focuses on the new laws and regulations of this decade and how they are interpreted. In addition to the updates already described, this edition expands its coverage of several vital subjects. Highlights include more developed discussions of legal defenses and remedies and greater detail discussing areas such as U.S. international trade regulations, privacy, and gaming and gambling-adjacent laws. This book is also revised to provide a more concise, and hopefully more enjoyable, reading experience.

Despite these changes, this book's underlying premise still asserts that understanding why the law creates specific intellectual property *rights* requires understanding how the law ultimately determines what constitutes unfair competition—i.e., a commercial *wrong*. Both historically and conceptually, intellectual property rights grew from laws governing fair and unfair competition. Likewise, both bodies of law seek to distinguish between fair and unfair trade practices.

Students of intellectual property and unfair competition laws should understand how these two conceptually distinct bodies of law nevertheless operate interdependently. The goal throughout this edition is to help provide a sense of both the distinctive policies underlying, and the linkages between, intellectual property and unfair competition laws. Contemporary jurisprudence has heightened the importance of this historical perspective.

On a personal note, I hope you join me in following Charles R. McManis's work and in wishing him the greatest success in his endeavors.

DAVID J. FRIEDMAN

March 2024

OUTLINE

PART 4. INJURIOUS PROMOTIONAL PRACTICES

TABLE OF CASES

References are to Pages

TABLE OF STATUTES

References are to Pages

TABLE OF AUTHORITIES

References are to Pages

1970–73 Transfer Binder CCH, Trade Reg.Rep. ¶ 20056 (1972), 450
Annotation, Francis M. Dougherty, Validity, Construction, and Application of State Statutory Provision Prohibiting Sales of Commodities below cost—Modern Cases, 41 A.L.R. 4th 612 (1985), 488
Areeda and Turner, Predatory Pricing and Related Practices Under Section 2 of the Sherman Act, 88 Harv.L.Rev. 697 (1975), 502, 518
Dougherty, Francis M., Validity, Construction, and Application of State Statutory Provisions Prohibiting Sale of Gasoline Below Cost, 26 A.L.R. 6th 249 (2007), 489
Holmes, Privilege, Malice and Intent, 8 Harv.L.Rev. 1 (1894), 34
Restatement of Torts § 731, 160
Restatement (First) of Torts § 757 (1939), 363, 368
Restatement (Second) of Torts § 623A, 410
Restatement (Third) of Torts § 717, 157
Restatement (Third) of Unfair Competition § 20, 157
Restatement (Third) of Unfair Competition § 21, 160
Restatement (Third) of Unfair Competition § 39, 363
Warren, & Brandeis, The Right to Privacy, 4 Harv.L.Rev. 193 (1890), 280

INTELLECTUAL PROPERTY AND UNFAIR COMPETITION

IN A NUTSHELL®

EIGHTH EDITION

CHAPTER 1

INTRODUCTION TO INTELLECTUAL PROPERTY AND UNFAIR COMPETITION LAWS

Suppose a company reacts to a competitor's online ridicule by establishing a rival website with a similar domain name. This new website duplicates much of the competitor's content and layout. The company lures away the competitor's webmaster and online advertisers with offers of higher wages or lower advertising and subscription rates respectively (all of which will be rescinded once the criticism is silenced). Ultimately, the offending website shuts down. Did the reacting company commit intellectual property infringement or actionable unfair competition? Was the responding company's reaction permissible? Could the competitor's often inaccurate ridicule itself be an act of unfair competition?

This hypothetical is a modern equivalent of *Beardsley v. Kilmer*, 236 N.Y. 80, 140 N.E. 203 (N.Y. 1923) which illustrates the principal topics this book covers. These topics include interference with prospective and existing contractual relations (Part I); product, service, and business misidentification (Part II); intangible business asset misappropriation (Part III); and injurious promotional and pricing practices (Part IV).

Intellectual property and unfair competition laws arise from numerous common-law (i.e., judicial) and statutory sources. These various legal sources may at first appear to be a patchwork of miscellaneous rules rather than a coherent body of law. However, these sources converge where they help businesses or consumers address commercial misbehavior or correct marketplace failures.

Understanding why the law creates specific intellectual property *rights* first requires understanding how the law identifies a commercial *wrong*. Intellectual property law is an outgrowth of unfair competition law, both historically and conceptually. Thus, the two parts of this book predominantly concerned with unfair competition laws (Parts I and IV) bracket the two parts concerned with intellectual property laws (Parts II and III).

A. SOURCES OF THE LAW OF INTELLECTUAL PROPERTY AND UNFAIR COMPETITION

1. COMMON-LAW SOURCES

Common law unfair competition affords businesses a private judicial remedy for various types of interference with trade relations. It is part of a larger body of tort law protecting advantageous business relations from harm.

Anglo-American unfair competition common law developed in a piecemeal fashion. Early English judges initially prioritized maintaining physical security for people and property. These judges did not protect trade or other relations and did not provide remedies for purely pecuniary harm. Parties to a damaged trade relation could only claim protection from direct physical injuries, threats to their persons, or direct trespasses to their property. For example, in the seminal *Schoolmaster's Case*, Y.B.Hen. IV, f, pL. 21 [1410], two schoolmasters had no cause of action against a third whose new competing school apparently attracted the plaintiffs' students through lower fees. Scholars cite this case as establishing a common-law competition privilege. However, it can more accurately be considered a simple judicial refusal to consider pecuniary harm claims without some form of physical injury.

A body of tort law gradually emerged to protect trading partners and those with other advantageous business relationships from economically injurious interference by third parties. This tort law branch protects advantageous relations generally and trade relations specifically. Tort law's growth in this area is similar to how contract laws emerged to prevent economic harm to trading partners or other advantageous relations from a promissory breach by the other party to the relationship.

a. Tortious Interference with Advantageous Relations Generally

Expanding protections for persons and property created the first relational interest protections. Nuisance laws were the first step in that expansion. These laws protect persons and property from direct and indirect physical interference causing only pecuniary harm.

Just as tort laws protect persons and property from direct and indirect physical interference, they can also shield people from injurious speech. Courts used these laws to remedy harm from threats, verbal harassment, deception, and falsehoods. Courts developed two distinct protections from such misconduct. The first protects persons deceived to their physical or economic detriment. The second protects those that would likely suffer economic harm from defamatory or disparaging statements made to others. *See* Ch. 2 & 8, *infra*.

In addition to the foregoing prohibitions against specific physical and verbal interference types, nineteenth century courts became concerned with protecting contractual relations specifically from virtually any active intentional interference. These courts also sought general protections for advantageous relations from certain specified non-physical and non-deceptive interference, particularly group interference. Out of this two-fold concern grew common-law prohibitions against both interference with contractual or confidential relations and coercion, conspiracy, and invasion of privacy. *See* Ch. 2, 3, and 7, *infra*.

English and American courts eventually viewed all contractual relations as a form of property. As such, intentional interference with these relations were prohibited as "malicious", even when the interference had sound commercial reasons. Nineteenth century equity courts were particularly concerned with protecting relationships of trust or confidence, and with preventing unauthorized use or disclosure of confidential writings or secrets made in these relations. Copyright and trade secrets common laws grew from this equitable relief. *See* Ch. 6 & 7, *infra*.

American courts first recognized tortious invasion of privacy in the twentieth century. Intrusive privacy invasions included eavesdropping, wiretapping, and other covert surveillance forms. Publicizing certain injurious or privileged information also invaded privacy rights, such as unauthorized commercial use of another's name or likeness. Where purely pecuniary harm occurred, as opposed to emotional harm, the latter became the common-law right of publicity. *See* Ch. 6, *infra*.

b. Unfair Competition

English and American courts specifically protect trade relations as well as generally protecting advantageous relations. Specific trade relations protections gave rise to unfair competition laws. Early cases first used the term "unfair competition" where merchants palmed off inferior goods as those from another more reputable merchant by using trademarks deceptively. *See* Ch. 4 & 5, *infra*. This differed from the previously mentioned misconduct types since it could involve commercial or non-commercial parties.

(1) Palming off and Trademark Infringement

Courts recognize many deceptive means of palming off goods. Early palming off involved deceptively using another merchant's trademark. Other palming off forms emerged, such as deceptive substitution for or alteration of requested goods. At the same time, certain particularly distinctive trademarks became accepted as a form of intangible property. Equity courts protected these "technical trademarks" from infringement, regardless of whether a subsequent trademark user had fraudulent intent or whether the merchant's customers were actually diverted. Trademark infringement torts are now distinguished from unfair competition.

The American legal lexicon adopted the term "unfair competition" for these deceptive torts over the term "palming off" despite the misleading implication that palming off requires a competitor's interference. Now, palming off is primarily associated with deceptive substitution or alteration of goods, or deceptively imitating product or business features whose identifying function was secondary to another commercial function. Manufacturers frequently bring these claims against retailers or wholesalers offering inferior quality goods as the manufacturer's own to protect the manufacturer's consumer relations. Whether the reseller directly competes with the manufacturer's customers does not affect these claims.

In the twentieth century, unfair competition laws expanded well beyond trademark infringement and palming off. Some courts apply the term to commercial interference with contractual relations and trade disparagement. Other courts apply it to the distinctly twentieth century commercial misappropriation tort and the more amorphous malicious competition torts.

(2) Misappropriation

Tortious misappropriation originated in *International News Serv. v. Associated Press*, 248 U.S. 215 (1918). The *INS* decision held a news service engaged in unfair competition when it copied or paraphrased another service's uncopyrighted stories as they were published and used those stories to compete with news services in other regions. This decision was the culmination of an era where the Supreme Court fashioned general common law principles for federal diversity-of-citizenship cases.

The *INS* Court characterized the defendant's misconduct as the converse of palming off: "Instead of selling its own goods as those of the complainant, it substituted misappropriation in place of misrepresentation, and sells complainant's goods as its own." The Court recognized uncopyrighted news could not be owned in any absolute sense after its first publication. Still, the Court held news could be considered a "quasi-property" because it could not be gathered without considerable investment of labor, skill, and money. The Court defined the misappropriation tort as diverting profits from those who have earned them to those who have not. More poetically, this is an attempt to reap where one has not sown, thereby appropriating another's harvest.

The nominate misappropriation tort may be considered an expansion of the conversion tort. Conversion was initially limited to appropriation of chattels, a tangible property with established ownership rules. Misappropriation, however, involves acquiring intangible assets, an "intellectual property", where courts are still defining ownership capacities. Notably, the individualistic labor theory of property implicit in misappropriation law gave way to a social utility theory. The social utility theory only values granting exclusive private rights to an intangible property to the extent the general public benefits from this grant. *See* Ch. 6, *infra.*

(3) Malicious Competition

We have seen how courts extended the unfair competition concept beyond trademark infringement and palming off to include the newer misappropriation tort (and to a lesser extent the torts of trade disparagement and interference with contractual relations). Courts label as "unfair competition" various commercial pecuniary interferences previously actionable as private or public nuisances. Meanwhile, nuisance laws began condemning virtually any purely malicious or predatory conduct, not only threats or physical violence. Put simply, otherwise lawful conduct undertaken purely to inflict economic injury on another became subject to nuisance laws. *See* Ch. 2, *infra.*

A classic malicious nuisance example regulates erection or removal of a residential "spite" fence, whose only purpose is to block another's light or air. This principle has commercial applications as well. For example, *Keeble v. Hickeringill*, 103 Eng.Rep. 1127 (1706) discussed how a commercial trapper had a cause of action against someone discharging guns nearby. The *Keeble* court emphasized the guns were "maliciously" discharged, purely to scare away wild fowl. The court indicated in dictum that no cause of action would exist if the defendant set up his own decoys to compete with the plaintiff.

The public's interest in encouraging competition makes courts reluctant to condemn competitive conduct undertaken partly for legitimate business reasons and partly for vindictive or spiteful ones. *See, e.g., Beardsley v. Kilmer*, 140 N.E. 203 (N.Y. 1923) (manufacturer running a newspaper critical of its products out of business was held not actionable).

Otherwise lawful commercial activity is only actionable if the disputed activity was done (at least primarily) for a malicious or predatory purpose. Only in rare cases will normal commercial activity by a single business operating under competitive conditions be actionable. Such rare cases require proof the business operated purely to cause economic harm to another and intended to terminate its operation after accomplishing this purpose. Actionable predatory misconduct will more readily be found where a single business dominates a market, or a group of businesses act in concert.

Even purely malicious commercial conduct may be privileged in some situations. A simple refusal by one person or business to deal with another person or business is not actionable, even though the refusal is motivated solely by whim, caprice, prejudice, or malice. *See Great Atl. & Pac. Tea Co. v. Cream of Wheat Co.*, 227 F. 46 (2d Cir. 1915). Individual freedom outweighs the interest in preventing economic injury—at least where competitive conditions prevail and there is no concerted group refusal to deal (i.e., group boycott) or violation of anti-discrimination laws.

c. Prima Facie Tort

From the foregoing nominate torts catalogue, some courts and commentators extrapolate that any intentional injury must be justified to avoid legal liability. Termed "prima facie tort," this principle amalgamates various unfair competition law branches and the entire nominate intentional tort body. Similarly, negligence principles synthesize accidental infliction of injury laws.

Under the prima facie tort theory, intentional tort laws balance the injurious conduct's utility against the invaded interest. This assessment does not consider malicious conduct. Thus, there is no general privilege for intentionally inflicting pecuniary harm for a purely spiteful purpose. This is true even when the injurious commercial conduct itself is justifiable, absent malice.

Likewise, there is no justification for using an improper means, even for the otherwise legitimate purpose of commercial gain. Improper means includes those threatening the physical security of persons or property. Improper means also includes those subverting competition or bargaining on the merits. Hence the special opprobrium attached to palming off, defamation, and disparagement. Such deceptive conduct has no more social value than purely spiteful conduct.

If a sufficiently great interest is invaded, there may be no justification for using an otherwise legitimate commercial means for a legitimate commercial end. Competitive freedom therefore may have less weight than the security of a person, property, or certain socially useful relations. Protected relations include contractual, confidential, and fiduciary ones.

The common law generally views non-deceptive but economically injurious commercial conduct as privileged for a single, non-monopolistic business. Examples include price cutting, hard bargaining, or refusing to deal with another business. However, this conduct cannot jeopardize personal, property, or certain socially useful relations. Even a purely malicious refusal to deal with another is likely privileged since free choice in one's business associates outweighs pecuniary harms. However, even a non-malicious refusal to deal can be actionable when a single business has market dominance or a group of businesses act in concert. In these cases, permitting such conduct creates more social danger than the inherent social interest.

Courts are generally reluctant to embrace a prima facie tort theory despite its value as a synthesizing principle. One court criticized requiring a defendant justify their conduct "requires too little of the plaintiff." *Leigh Furniture & Carpet Co. v. Isom*, 657 P.2d 293 (Utah 1982). *See also Tuttle v. Buck*, 119 N.W. 946 (1909) (dissent). The few jurisdictions expressly adopting the principle apply it only where the trade practice falls squarely within or just short of some nominate tort's traditional definition. *See Advance Music Corp. v. American Tobacco Co.*, 70 N.E.2d 401 (N.Y. 1946) where capriciously omitting songs from defendant's radio program without legitimate commercial justification was a prima facie tort. Arguably, intentionally or recklessly omitting the plaintiff's songs from a show called "Your Hit Parade" was a novel disparagement implying the songs were not "hits". The lawsuit in fact began as a disparagement case. However, the common law required special damages be pled and proved for disparagement, causing the claim's dismissal. *See* Ch. 8, *infra*.

The judiciary's limited use of the prima facie tort principle exposes an underlying unity in common law unfair competition. The principle removes nominate intentional torts from their definitional straitjackets. More importantly, the principle exposes two increasingly scrutinized assumptions central to developing private, judge-made unfair competition laws. The first assumption is that courts overseeing private litigation can adequately balance public interests in maintaining trade relationship freedom and stability. The second assumption is that courts adequately express the balance struck in conventional private judicial remedies where they find unfair bargaining or competitive practices.

These two assumptions are challenged by an emerging body of public law regulating interstate and international trade and a rapid expansion of state, federal, and international laws governing intellectual property protection. This creates tension between unfair competition common law and trade regulation and intellectual property's largely statutory and administrative laws.

2. STATUTORY, CONSTITUTIONAL, AND TREATY SOURCES

Trade regulation law supplements the common law private remedies and provides for public (i.e., government) regulation of trade practices. At points, it merges with the larger body of antitrust and consumer protection laws. Likewise, intellectual property law can be considered a separate and distinct body of laws combining judge-made unfair competition laws involving trademarks and trade secrets together with the federal statutory law of patents and copyrights. As we shall see, the term "intellectual property" is just as misleading as the term "unfair competition." "Intellectual property" suggests that the similarities among its various legal forms are more pronounced than the differences, when the opposite is more accurate.

Trade regulation law developed from perceived inadequacies in the common law of unfair competition. The common law, for example, proved unable to balance competing business and labor interests in labor disputes. Federal statutory labor relations law largely pre-empted this field.

Common-law courts (including federal courts in diversity-of-citizenship cases) too often simply assume a misappropriation was committed by any copying of a product, valuable business idea, or other scheme that cost another time, labor, or money to produce. These courts thus endowed the copied product, idea, or scheme with legal intangible property attributes. Unfortunately, these common-law courts fail to balance the utility of granting such a right against the competitive process costs in denying others free use of the product, idea, or scheme. That reflexive judicial response to commercial copying has drawn into question the matter's fitness for ad hoc judicial resolution, especially when federal statutory patent and copyright protection exists. *See* Ch. 6, *infra*.

Common-law courts also failed to provide adequate legal remedies for conduct that manifestly undermines the bargaining or the competitive process but causes no easily discernible private injury. At one time courts flatly stated businesses had no remedy for a competitor's consumer-aimed false advertising without evidence of palming off or commercial disparagement (i.e., deception which specifically identified its commercial victim). A few courts held a cause of action existed in the unusual case where one business can be shown to divert another company's customers by making false claims about its own product. In general, however, the common law cannot provide an effective remedy for false advertising that does not identify its commercial victim since the practice is often more a public than a private wrong. *See* Ch. 8, *infra*.

State legislation may be the most direct way to cure defects in state judge-made law, but lawmakers have not always proved equal to the task. At best, state legislation can only deal effectively with trade practices that are essentially local in scope. At worst, state legislative attempts to cure the common law's inadequacies can be even more harmful to healthy economic competition. Some state trade regulations are primarily concerned with protecting vested or politically powerful local commercial interests from the "harm" of competition. State legislation modifying unfair competition common laws thus generates a second point of tension between unfair competition and intellectual property laws—namely between state and federal law.

a. Federal Regulation

Congressional power to regulate trade relations and create intellectual property protections stems from two distinct constitutional sources. The patent and copyright clause of Article I, § 8 of the U.S. Constitution grants Congress power to "promote the progress of Science and useful Arts by reserving for limited times to Authors and Inventors the exclusive right to their respective Writings and Discoveries." This constitutional language explicitly authorizes federal creation of two distinct intangible property rights.

The commerce clause in that same section of the Constitution also authorizes Congress to regulate interstate and foreign commerce. While broadly construed, this power does not extend to purely local activity that does not affect interstate or foreign commerce.

Congressional and judicial power to invalidate state laws conflicting with federal statutes and the

Constitution derives from the Constitution's Supremacy Clause. This Clause declares the federal Constitution, along with the treaties and statutes enacted pursuant thereto, to be the supreme law of the land. The Supremacy Clause expressly authorizes Congress to preempt state law. The Clause also empowers courts to decide whether state laws, whether judge-made or legislative conflict with the federal Constitution, treaties, or statutes.

(1) Preemptive Federal Legislation: Patent, Copyright, and Labor Law

Federal legislation regulating trade relations and intellectual property has been both preemptive of and concurrent with state regulation. For example, § 301 of the Copyright Act of 1976 expressly preempts state laws granting exclusive rights to fixed works of authorship equivalent to the copyrightable subject matter categories specified in the Act. Before 1976, federal copyright law merely supplemented the common law of copyrights. Previously, federal copyright law extended the right to prohibit unauthorized copying to published works, just as the common law protected unpublished works.

The Supreme Court regularly evaluates how far states can extend the scope of federal patent or copyright protections or additional protections for writings or discoveries. *See, e.g., Brulotte v. Thys Co.*, 379 U.S. 29 (1964) (states may not enforce a patent license provision attempting to extend royalty payment beyond a patent's term).

In *Sears, Roebuck and Co. v. Stiffel Co.*, 376 U.S. 225 (1964) and *Compco Corp. v. Day-Brite Lighting, Inc.*, 376 U.S. 234 (1964) (known collectively as *Sears-Compco*), the Supreme Court determined federal patent laws prevent states from using unfair competition law to prohibit copying an unpatented and uncopyrighted article, or awarding damages for such copying. In both cases, lower courts granted relief against those copying articles whose patents were declared invalid for lacking the inventiveness federal patent law requires. Preventing such copying would interfere with federal policy found in the patent and copyright clause of the Constitution and implementing federal statutes. This policy allows unrestricted copying of whatever the federal patent and copyright laws leave in the public domain.

After *Sears-Compco,* but prior to when Congress expressly preempted state copyright law, the Court considered federal copyright law's implications for a state criminal statute prohibiting record piracy in *Goldstein v. California*, 412 U.S. 546 (1973). The *Goldstein* Court upheld the state statute, distinguishing *Sears-Compco. Sears-Compco* involved a federal patent statute with standards indicating what Congress wished to protect and what it wished to stay in the public domain. A state law protecting articles that federal patent law would leave in the public domain disturbed congressional intent. The 1909 federal copyright statute reflected no such congressional balancing for sound recordings. Rather, it merely left the area unregulated. Thus, states remained free to act until Congress expressly preempted state copyrights law.

Subsequent cases reflected the *Goldstein* reluctance to find preemption. In *Kewanee Oil Co. v. Bicron Corp.*, 416 U.S. 470 (1974), the Court held that state trade secret laws do not undermine federal patent policy, even where trade secrets protection was sought for clearly patentable inventions. Thus, no conflict requiring preemption existed. In *Aronson v. Quick Point Pencil Co.*, 440 U.S. 257 (1979), the Court held federal patent law did not preempt state contract law to preclude a royalty payment scheme. In this case, the patent applicant was to receive royalty payments as long as the contracting party sold articles embodying the putative invention. The patent application's later denial did not void this contract.

The trend away from further judicial preemption in favor of continued state regulation broke in *Bonito Boats, Inc. v. Thunder Craft Boats, Inc.*, 489 U.S. 141 (1989). Here, the Court held federal patent law preempted a state statute prohibiting unauthorized use of direct molding to duplicate for sale any manufactured boat hull made by another. Congress subsequently enacted a new *sui generis* form of federal protection for vessel hull designs. *See* Ch. 6.B.3, *infra*.

Congressional authority over interstate and foreign commerce, like its authority to grant patent and copyright protection, was exercised both exclusive of and concurrent with state regulation. Federal labor law, for example, preempted state law governing peaceful labor activity. This previously may have been treated as tortious interference with employment and commercial contracts. Now, states may only enjoin picketing marked by violence or physical intimidation. By contrast, while Congress enacted both trademark and antitrust legislation, states remained largely free to regulate these areas.

(2) Non-Preemptive Federal Legislation: Trademark and Antitrust Law

Federal trademark law, most recently embodied in the Lanham Act, manifests an overall congressional intent merely to supplement state trademark law, subject only to specific preemptive exceptions. *See* §§ 39(b), 43(c)(6), 15 U.S.C. §§ 1121(b), 1125(c)(6), discussed in Ch. 4(A)(1)(b), *infra*. This contrasts with federal patent, copyright, and labor legislation. Trademark law's limited legislative intent was mandated to some extent by the Supreme Court's decision in the *Trade-Mark Cases*, 100 U.S. 82 (1879), holding unconstitutional a Lanham Act predecessor that failed to evidence any intent to regulate only the interstate or foreign use of trademarks.

The *Trade-Mark Cases* Court held trademarks could not be considered a discovery or writing within the meaning of the patent and copyright clause. Where a trademark consisted of a common word or symbol, as it did in these cases, it lacked sufficient novelty, invention, or work of intellect. Thus, trademark regulation was beyond congressional patent and copyright powers. While recognizing trademarks might function as a useful and valuable aid or instrument of commerce, Congress failed to regulate only interstate or foreign commerce with these laws and thus exceeded its constitutional authority under the commerce clause. While the interstate commerce test broadened considerably since the Court decided the *Trade-Mark Cases,* federal authority nevertheless does not extend to purely local trademarks or trade names usage.

Similarly, illegal goods and services not subject to federal regulation may not receive federal protections. For example, while some states and certain circumstances permit cannabis cultivation, federal trademark protection for such products is not available as they are per se unlawful. *See, e.g., In re Stanley Bros. Soc. Enters., LLC,* 2020 USPQ2d 10658 (TTAB 2020) (Food, Drug, and Cosmetics Act); *In re Natn'l Concessions Group, Inc.,* 2023 USPQ2d 527 (TTAB 2023) (Controlled Substances Act).

The federal registration system created by the Lanham Act is an important supplement to the common law, notwithstanding these trademark protection power limitations. Federal trademark registration is not mandatory, only encouraged through incentives offering significant protection beyond that provided by state trademark law to businesses engaged in interstate or foreign commerce.

Section 43 of the Lanham Act provides merchants with a statutory cause of action prohibiting another's false designations of origin and false or misleading representations to consumers about one's own product or service. The latter is a form of false advertising that the common law of unfair competition has largely failed to reach. Section 43 also provides a federal cause of action for trade disparagement, famous trademark dilution, and "cybersquatting" trademarks as domain names.

Federal antitrust law, like federal trademark law, mainly runs concurrently with state law. Like the Lanham Act, antitrust laws may provide commercial parties with public and private remedies not available at common law. The Sherman Act prohibits joint efforts to restrain trade and unilateral abuse of market power. The Clayton Act prohibits certain anticompetitive acts, focusing exclusively on unreasonable restraints on trade. Certain other antitrust laws, notably the Federal Trade Commission Act and the Robinson-Patman Act, are arguably as concerned with prohibiting unfair diversions of trade as they are with prohibiting unreasonable restraints as such.

The Federal Trade Commission Act, as amended, gives the Federal Trade Commission broad authority over "unfair methods of competition in or affecting commerce and unfair or deceptive acts or practices in or affecting commerce". This includes broad power to protect both consumers and commercial parties from unfair competition. The FTC prohibits many trade practices where no effective private remedy may exist. Similarly, the Robinson-Patman Act's price discrimination prohibitions define a body of unfair competition largely beyond the common law's reach. *See* Ch. 9 *infra*.

(3) Constitutional Limits on State and Federal Regulation

In addition to express or implied legislative preemptions of state law, federal courts have long asserted autonomous power to invalidate state or federal law conflicting with the Constitution. For a time, the Supreme Court transformed the Fourteenth Amendment due process clause into a formidable weapon against state attempts to regulate commerce. The Courts did this by declaring its power to review not merely the fairness of the process by which states deprive persons of life, liberty, and property, but also the deprivation's fairness itself. Courts used this standard of review, known as substantive due process review, to strike down state economic regulation and further a judicially-developed national policy of unfettered economic development.

The Court ultimately abandoned the substantive due process standard of review for state trade legislation as unworkable. However, substantive due process appears to have a constitutional successor in the First Amendment to the Constitution. The Court seemed to draw a distinction between commercial and non-commercial speech in First Amendment cases. However, later cases held truthful advertising is entitled to constitutional protection just as other forms of expression. *See, e.g., Virginia State Bd. of Pharmacy v. Virginia Citizens Consumer Council, Inc.*, 425 U.S. 748 (1976) (states cannot prevent truthful prescription drug price advertising under the guise of protecting the public from unscrupulous price cutters).

The Court was also mindful in allowing states to regulate their own commercial affairs. This is a countervailing constitutional interest, implicit in the federal system itself. Just as the Court refused to preempt state legislation prohibiting record piracy and the common law of trade secrets, the Court found no First Amendment immunity for a television station charged with misappropriating a performer's human cannonball act by videotaping the entire act and broadcasting it on a television news program. *Zacchini v. Scripps-Howard Broad. Co.*, 433 U.S. 562 (1977). Similarly, a state statute prohibiting using a trade name to practice optometry did not violate the First Amendment. *Friedman v. Rogers*, 440 U.S. 1 (1979). Some state laws regulating trade relations may have been preempted or invalidated because of conflicts with federal statutory or constitutional policy. Still, a far more voluminous body of non-conflicting state trade regulation remains in force, supplementing both the common law of unfair competition and federal statutory and administrative trade regulation.

Two Supreme Court decisions demonstrate a renewed willingness to restrict the scope of federal regulatory power. *Florida Prepaid Postsecondary Educ. Expense Bd. v. College Sav. Bank*, 527 U.S. 627 (1999) held Congress may not utilize its Fourteenth Amendment enforcement clause power to waive state immunity to federal patent infringement liability, at least not without further congressional findings that other forms of relief are insufficient. The Court invalidated a similar congressional attempt to waive state immunity to federal false advertising claims in the companion case *College Sav. Bank v. Florida Prepaid Postsecondary Educ. Expense Bd.*, 527 U.S. 666 (1999). There, false advertising about one's own product did not implicate a property right protectable by Congress under the Fourteenth Amendment.

Conversely, *Eldred v. Ashcroft*, 537 U.S. 186 (2003) held the Copyright Term Extension Act of 1998 (extending existing and future copyright protection for twenty years) did not exceed Congress' power under the Copyright Clause or violate the First Amendment rights of prospective users of works that would otherwise have entered the public domain. Likewise, Congress did not exceed its authority under the Copyright Clause or violate the First Amendment by enacting 17 U.S.C. § 104A to extend U.S. copyright protection to works that lacked domestic protection but held existing copyright protection in member countries of the Berne Convention for the Protection of Literary and Artistic Works. *See Golan v. Holder*, 565 U.S. 302 (2012).

b. State Regulation

Many of the state statutory laws regulating trade are patterned after, analogous to, or specifically incorporate federal statutory laws or administrative trade regulation rules. This gives federal policy a local application. Some state statutory laws, however, protect trade relations in ways different from either the common law or federal statutory law.

For example, some states have long protected distinctive trademarks from "dilution" (i.e., non-deceptive imitation) and prohibited sales-below-cost.

State anti-dilution statutes specifically recognize and seek to protect the advertising value of particularly distinctive trade symbols. These statutes prohibit other businesses from using the same or similar marks even if it would not create consumer confusion, but rather merely dilute the original symbol's impact. Congress now provides federal anti-dilution protection through an amended § 43 of the Lanham Act. However, federal protection is limited to "famous" marks and thus may not be as extensive as state anti-dilution protection.

State sales-below-cost statutes likewise purport to supplement federal antitrust laws by prohibiting pricing practices that fall short of an antitrust violation. Such laws may in fact subvert federal statutes. *See* Ch. 9, *infra*.

c. International Regulation

Regulating international trade practices exceeds the domestic allocation of regulatory power among the various branches of federal and state government. The U.S. Constitution places this responsibility squarely with the federal government, declaring treaties to be the supreme law of the land just like federal statutes. However, applying federal statutory law to extraterritorial commercial activity raises challenges. Some international agreement provisions are self-executing (and so part of the supreme law of the according to the supremacy clause). Other provisions are not self-executing, requiring domestic legislation to become law.

(1) International Agreements

The United States has long been a member of the International Union for the Protection of Industrial Property (the Paris Union), established by the Paris Convention in 1883. This Convention is a multilateral treaty providing global protection to patents, trademarks, and other "industrial property" common in other parts of the world without an exact U.S. equivalent. The Convention also strives to prevent unfair competition in international trade.

Since 1967, the World Intellectual Property Organization (WIPO) administered the Paris Convention and the Berne Convention for the Protection of Literary and Artistic Works. The Paris Convention mainly ensures equal (non-discriminatory) patent and trademark protection is provided in each member country to citizens of all other member countries. Member country citizens includes all persons domiciled in or having business establishments in the member country. Note that the United States did not accept some later Paris Convention modifications.

The U.S. is party to many WIPO-administered treaties. The Madrid Protocol is the most important of the trademark treaties, as it facilitates international trademark registration via a single basic (i.e., home country) application. The United States is also party to the WIPO-administered Patent Cooperation Treaty. This Treaty, which came into force in 1978, establishes procedures facilitating parallel patent filings in signatory countries.

The United States is party to the UNESCO-administered Universal Copyright Convention of 1954 and many similar multilateral and bilateral treaties providing international copyright protection. Like the Paris Convention, the Universal Convention strives for "national" (i.e., non-discriminatory) treatment. The United States adhered to the older (WIPO administered) Berne Convention of 1886 in 1988. As most recently revised in 1948, this Convention generally requires member countries provide a very high level of copyright protection without requiring any prerequisite formalities. The Berne Convention also requires protection of an author's *droit moral* (i.e., author's moral right of attribution to the artwork in its original form).

The United States is a World Trade Organization ("WTO") member, which sets rules governing international trade. Created in 1994 as an outgrowth of the Uruguay Round of multilateral trade negotiations, the WTO is the successor to the stop-gap international agency that administered the General Agreement on Tariffs and Trade (GATT). The international agreements administered by the GATT/WTO regime provide a mechanism for reciprocally lowering tariffs and other non-tariff trade barriers. They also establish international standards for intellectual property right protections and regulations against discriminatory pricing practices.

The Agreement on Trade-Related Aspects of Intellectual Property Rights, Including Trade in Counterfeit Goods ("TRIPS") is particularly important to intellectual property and unfair competition law. TRIPS establishes a detailed set of substantive minimum standards governing the availability, scope, and use of intellectual property rights. It also establishes certain procedural requirements governing the administrative acquisition and maintenance of these rights. TRIPS specifies a detailed set of civil and criminal enforcement obligations, including border measures, which all WTO member countries must implement. TRIPS also incorporates, by reference, a GATT/WTO dispute-settlement process to resolve conflicts among WTO member countries in its implementation.

Regional free trade agreements comprise an increasingly important form of international law regulating intellectual property and unfair competition. The North American Free Trade Agreement (NAFTA) and European Union-based agreements are particularly important examples. However, the "plurilateral" Anti-Counterfeiting Trade Agreement (ACTA) attempt to strengthen intellectual property rights enforcement was a debacle. The European Parliament overwhelmingly rejected ACTA in 2012, even though the European Commission played a key role in its negotiation.

(2) U.S. Foreign Trade Legislation

Congress often enacts statutes regulating international trade practices pursuant to international treaties and its own power to regulate foreign commerce. This legislation may be concerned with regulating import or export trade. Import trade legislation should protect domestic enterprises from unfair trade practices of importers. The International Trade Commission (ITC) has specific authority to combat intellectual property infringement and unfair competition from imports. Export trade legislation should protect domestic exporters from both foreign government discrimination and unfair competition by domestic exporters. An important part of this international trade legislation directs the U.S. Trade Representative to identify and impose sanctions on countries not providing U.S. nationals with adequate or effective intellectual property protection.

Courts interpret legislation explicitly regulating international trade. They must consider the extent that domestic trade regulations apply to extraterritorial conduct by domestic and foreign companies. For example, the Supreme Court affirmed dismissal of an antitrust complaint alleging the defendants induced the Costa Rican government to seize plaintiff's rubber plantation and arrange a sale of the plantation to the defendant in *American Banana Co. v. United Fruit Co.*, 213 U.S. 347 (1909). Here, the Court held that the Sherman Act did not apply to actions occurring outside the United States that were lawful in the country where they were performed. The *American Banana* decision was later narrowed to matters applying U.S. law to extraterritorial conduct with heavy foreign government involvement.

Courts generally hold that U.S. law will apply to extraterritorial conduct affecting U.S. foreign or domestic commerce so long as the foreign government's involvement is sufficiently limited. *See Steele v. Bulova Watch Co.*, 344 U.S. 280 (1952); *International Bancorp v. Societe des Bains de Mer et du Cercle des Etrangers a Monaco*, 329 F.3d 359 (4th Cir. 2003); *Animal Sci. Prods., Inc. v. Hebei Welcome Pharm. Co.*, 585 U.S. ___, 138 S. Ct. 1865 (2018) (courts must respectfully consider a foreign government's statements about their laws, such as exporter price fixing, but must exercise independent review as a question of law rather than accepting such statements as conclusive).

Where foreign government involvement in foreign trade activity is sufficiently great, interested domestic persons or industries may petition the U.S. Trade Representative to investigate and recommend intervention by the U.S. Government. This may be done through formal dispute resolution processes, such as those provided by the WTO, that are only available to sovereign states as a matter of international law.

B. OBJECTIVES OF THE LAW OF INTELLECTUAL PROPERTY AND UNFAIR COMPETITION

The regulatory environment creating intellectual property and unfair competition laws includes the judicial and legislative branches of state and federal government, the Constitution binding those governments bodies together, and the international agreements governing U.S. relations with other nations. The very diversity of intellectual property and unfair competition laws reflects the variety in their underlying objectives.

Intellectual property and unfair competition laws protect a company's trade relations from undue interference by other businesses while promoting bargaining and competition among businesses. Trade relations protection is in constant tension with, and thus must be balanced against, the interest in promoting bargaining and competition. A useful approach to studying intellectual property and unfair competition law is first to identify the trade relations and broader relational interests subject to legal protection, and then distinguish interference forms prohibited as unfair from those privileged as legitimate bargaining or competitive practices.

1. TRADE RELATIONS AND RELATIONAL INTERESTS PROTECTED

A company's trade relations may be divided into internal relations (employment and owner) and external relations (commercial and consumer). Employment relations include management and labor relations. Where a business is co-owned and not a sole proprietorship, its owner relations will consist of either partner or shareholder relations. Business commercial relations include vertical (or bargaining) relations with customers and suppliers, and horizontal relations with businesses at the same level in the distributive chain for enterprises such as joint ventures and trade associations. Consumer relations include individual customer relations and more general public relations that companies establish and maintain through advertising and other promotional activities. Where such activity stimulates commercial and consumer relations, a company's public relations are more accurately viewed as a distinct trade relation rather than consumer relation.

With the exception of public relations, businesses may embody any or all of their trade relations in express or implied contracts. Whether or not a business reduces trade relations to enforceable contracts, the sum of its trade relations (including its public relations) constitutes a valuable intangible business asset known as "goodwill."

Goodwill is generally defined as the expectation of future patronage. One court said it is what makes tomorrow's business more than an accident. Goodwill derives from the good reputation or distinctive identity of the business, or its products or services. A distinctive identity may be created and maintained through identifying trademarks, trade names, and trade dress.

Goodwill is not the only intangible asset that adds to business value. In the course of employment or commercial relations, a company may create products of intellectual effort whose value depends on maintaining their secrecy while being exploited or in obtaining an exclusive legal right to publicly exploit such products.

Businesses have two distinct relational interests in trade relations. Businesses have an interest in pursuing purely prospective trade relations, including those trade relations being sought or already established by other businesses. Businesses also have an interest in maintaining established trade relations and fending off attempts by other businesses to divert them. New businesses, or businesses expanding horizontally or vertically, have a particular interest in being free to pursue trade relations. Established businesses are more interested in maintaining trade relations stability to preserve and expand their market share. Pursuing these interests often interferes with the prospective or existing trade relations of some other business. Intellectual property and unfair competition laws distinguish which interference forms are actionable wrongs and which forms are privileged.

2. ACTIONABLE AND PRIVILEGED INTERFERENCE WITH TRADE RELATIONS

Interference with another's relational interests is readily distinguished from interference with the physical security of another's person or property. Physical interference involves a party inflicting and another party suffering some form of physical harm. Relational interference requires at least three parties (i.e., two or more parties with a relationship and at least one party interfering with it), and some form of purely pecuniary harm to at least one party to the relationship.

Not every pecuniary harm is unlawful. Businesses may freely pursue trade relations and discourage their diversion, even when knowingly inflicting pecuniary harm on other businesses. As Mr. Justice Holmes remarked, "a man has a right to set up a shop in a small village which can support but one of a kind, although he expects and intends to ruin a deserving widow who is established there already." Holmes, Privilege, Malice and Intent, 8 Harv.L.Rev. 1, 117, 120–21 (1894). Deserving widows obviously can retaliate in kind, by lowering prices or rallying customers to their cause.

Intellectual property and unfair competition laws implicitly assume that bargaining and competition among businesses serves the larger public interest. These laws assume these practices promote lower prices and higher quality goods and services than either a privately or a publicly controlled economy, even though economically injurious to individual businesses who lose in this competition. Thus, economically injurious conduct should only be prohibited as unfair where it also injures some other private interest. These protected private interests include the physical security of persons or property and threats to the security and effectiveness of the bargaining and competitive process.

C. A SUGGESTED APPROACH: THE LAWS OF INTELLECTUAL PROPERTY AND UNFAIR COMPETITION IN FUNCTIONAL CONTEXT

A variety of trade practices can threaten bargaining and competitive process security. These practices are influenced by changing socio-economic conditions as well as (sometimes conflicting) judicial, legislative, and administrative perceptions when balancing competing interests in trade freedom and trade stability. Deciding what makes a trade practice unfair requires first determining who among the courts, legislatures, or government executive or administrative branches at the state or federal levels can best (1) decide what trade practices are fair or not and (2) can most effectively remedy unfair practices.

This book considers unfair competition and intellectual property laws in their functional context—as they relate to each phase of business efforts to establish and maintain advantageous trade relations at various distribution chain levels. This book first examines trade relations reducible to contract form and the applicable (and largely judge-made) law. Next, it reviews the judge-made and statutory laws governing public and confidential trade relations and other intangible assets of businesses. Finally, it examines the largely statutory laws governing promotional and pricing practices.

This progression presents intellectual property and unfair competition laws roughly in the order they developed. It starts with common law private remedies, then looks at both the public and private statutory remedies federal intellectual property laws provide and the essentially public remedies statutory and administrative trade regulation laws provide. This approach also approximates how an individual business establishes its various trade relations.

PART 1

INTERFERENCE WITH PROSPECTIVE AND EXISTING CONTRACTUAL RELATIONS

CHAPTER 2

INTERFERENCE WITH PRECONTRACTUAL AND NON-CONTRACTUAL RELATIONS

A functioning company must establish trade relations with its employees, suppliers, and customers. While some relations only become "established" by an expectation of ongoing relations, many are embodied in legally enforceable contracts.

Trade relations that a contract can embody have long been protected against interference, whether reduced to a writing or not. Common law courts regularly protected merchants from actual or threatened physical violence. From an equally early date the courts prevented interference with master-servant relations. These courts provided a civil remedy against any interference attempted by luring away another's servants. Physical violence or threats were not required. The common law developed in two directions from these antecedents.

Expanding on common law protections against direct or indirect physical injury, a line of cases began protecting trade and other advantageous relations from interference falling short of actual or threatened physical violence. These protected relationships do not require documentation. The other line of cases expanded the law's early master-servant relationship protections. These cases protect existing contractual relations from interference that would be wholly unobjectionable absent a contract.

This common law area remains largely intact despite subsequent state and federal legislation. Federal and state statutes generally focus on specific problems, such as preventing investment transaction misrepresentations or preventing monopoly or group interference with trade relations. Federal and state securities laws now largely govern shareholder relations. Federal labor laws and state and federal antitrust laws likewise largely govern group interference with trade relations. The common law still supplements federal labor laws to limit violent labor union activity and provides an alternative to statutory securities and antitrust laws in preventing deception, monopoly, and concerted group interference. State common law still mainly regulates individual interference with trade relations.

This chapter addresses common-law cases defining what constitutes actionable interference with pre-contractual and non-contractual relations. Chapter 3 addresses case law defining what constitutes actionable interference with trade relations reduced to contract. Consistent with Chapter 1's suggested approach, Chapter 2 first identifies protected trade relations and then distinguishes actionable from privileged interference.

A. TRADE RELATIONS AND RELATIONAL INTERESTS PROTECTED

All trade relations forms can be embodied in a contract, other than a company's public relations. This chapter focuses on trade relations a contract could embody that were not formally recorded. This includes both purely prospective (or pre-contractual) relations and existing but non-contractual relations.

Trade freedom is a company's freedom to pursue prospective trade relations without undue outside interference. This includes pursuing relations with employees and another company's customers. Since these laws also protect existing non-contractual trade relations from the same sort of interference, they may also promote trade stability.

B. ACTIONABLE AND PRIVILEGED INTERFERENCE

Common laws limiting unfair competition began by differentiating the various types of actionable economic interferences with advantageous relations. Applied to business conduct, these nominate torts catalogued improper business methods. Courts later prohibited certain otherwise unobjectionable interference with advantageous relations where the interference was purely malicious or solely intended to injure other trade relationships. These later became prohibitions against certain improper business objectives.

These common law prohibitions understood one party's interference with another's pre-contractual relations are presumed lawful. Actionable interference must be proven as accomplished by improper means or for improper ends. *See, e.g., Leigh Furniture & Carpet Co. v. Isom*, 657 P.2d 293 (Utah 1982) (Damages require proof (1) that the defendant intentionally interfered with plaintiff's existing or potential economic relations, (2) for an improper purpose or by improper means, (3) causing injury to the plaintiff); *Doliner v. Brown*, 489 N.E.2d 1036 (Mass.App.Ct. 1986) (No actionable interference with another's prospective contractual relations when the defendant "picked a deal off for himself" before a final contract formed).

Lawfulness is not presumed for concerted group interference with another's trade relations, or with a single party's interference with another's contractual relations. Such interference must be justified to avoid liability. *See Penna v. Toyota Motor Sales, U.S.A., Inc.*, 902 P.2d 740 (Cal. 1995).

The remainder of this chapter examines what constitutes improper business methods, what constitutes improper business objectives, and what constitutes improper concerted group conduct.

1. IMPROPER BUSINESS METHODS

Chapter 1 noted improper business methods include physical interference, injurious speech, and coercive conduct. Such interference generally must be proven intentional to make purely pecuniary harm actionable. Even where such interference is intentional, many defenses can defeat liability.

a. Physical Interference

Early common law protected merchants and others from unauthorized direct physical trespass to their persons or property. These laws also allowed pecuniary harm claims from direct physical injury to merchants or detention of their person or property. These simple common law extensions profoundly expanded relational security.

Private and public nuisance law developments mandated updated remedies. Courts awarded damages for indirect physical interference complaints, while equity courts granted injunctions protecting persons and property from indirect physical interference. This occurred even when the physical interference caused only pecuniary harm.

Private nuisance is an indirect interference with the peaceful use and enjoyment of land, including the land's commercial use. *See Garrett v. Taylor*, 79 Eng.Rep. 485 (1621) (threats and violent acts aimed at mason's workmen and customers impaired the mason's land lease); *Keeble v. Hickeringill*, 103 Eng.Rep. 1127 (1706) (firearm discharges maliciously scaring away wild fowl lured by another for commercial purposes interfered with the hunter's peaceful use and enjoyment of a pond).

Public nuisance laws extended legal protection beyond unreasonable interference with land use and enjoyment to virtually any conduct that substantially interferes with exercising public rights. Public nuisance laws were originally a low-level crime protecting public health, safety, and convenience. These laws became a private action available to individuals that could show specific harm beyond that suffered by the general public. Thus, commercial users of public areas could recover economic losses suffered from obstructions, pollution, or other interferences. *See Tarleton v. McGawley*, 170

Eng.Rep. 153 (1793) (firing on canoes to prevent slave transactions interfered with the public's right to use navigable waterways for trade); *Gregory v. Duke of Brunswick,* 134 Eng.Rep. 816 (1843) (conspiracy hiring hecklers to prevent an actor's performance was an actionable offense).

Actionable physical interference does not require malice. Any intentional and unreasonable physical interference with another, whether direct or indirect, may be actionable. *See Shamhart v. Morrison Cafeteria Co.*, 32 So.2d 727 (Fla. 1947) (cafeteria lines blocking neighboring drugstore entrance an actionable public nuisance); *Texas & Pac. Ry. Co. v. Mercer,* 90 S.W.2d 557 (Tex.Comm'n.App. 1936) (railroad's unauthorized highway obstruction preventing company's produce transport an actionable public nuisance). Similarly, aerial photography of a chemical plant construction site was not a proper means to discover manufacturing trade secrets. *E.I. DuPont deNemours & Co. v. Christopher*, 431 F.2d 1012 (5th Cir. 1970).

Old trespass laws have new uses on the internet, such as opposing bulk unsolicited commercial email messages or "spam". *See eBay, Inc. v. Bidder's Edge, Inc.*, 100 F.Supp. 2d 1058 (N.D.C.A. 2000) (likely trespass in accessing plaintiff's computer systems using an automated querying program without plaintiff's written authorization); *CompuServe, Inc. v. Cyber Promotions, Inc.*, 962 F.Supp. 1015 (S.D. Ohio 1997) (company intentionally using internet service provider's proprietary computer equipment an actionable trespass to chattels not protected by the First Amendment). *See* Ch. 8, *infra*.

The Computer Fraud and Abuse Act (CFAA), 18 U.S.C. § 1030, created analogous criminal prohibitions against intentional unauthorized access of a protected computer, transmission of harmful information to a computer, and related offenses. The CFAA was frequently used to threaten criminal prosecution in disputes about an employee's actions or a user's breaching the website's "Terms of Use" agreement. The Supreme Court narrowed this broad construction of the CFAA's "exceeds unauthorized access" clause for employment cases to only circumstances where the user accesses areas where they lack access privileges. *Van Buren v. United States*, 593 U.S. ___, 141 S. Ct. 1648 (2021) (permitted police database access used for an unauthorized purpose did not "exceed unauthorized access" under the CFAA). This decision's effect on accessing publicly available data remains uncertain. *See, e.g., Facebook, Inc. v. Power Ventures, Inc.*, 844 F.3d 1058, 1067 (9th Cir. 2016) ("[A] violation of the terms of use of a website—without more—cannot establish liability under the CFAA.").

Courts enjoin unreasonable interference where bona fide business operations are known to interfere with other businesses. Compensatory damages are available where an injured party establishes past pecuniary injury with sufficient certainty. Presently, the absence of malice merely bars punitive damage recovery.

Despite these rules, just negligently preventing a stranger from obtaining a prospective pecuniary advantage is not usually actionable. Negligent infliction of pecuniary loss remedies are often limited to cases where the interference either causes physical as well as pecuniary harm or when the parties had a "special relationship". Examples include contractual, professional, or fiduciary relationships.

Courts generally deny damages where negligent interference causes only pecuniary harm and no special relationship exists. In these cases, economic losses are either too unforeseeable, remote, or disproportionate compared to the defendant's fault. Thus, a negligent fire causing no physical damage but interrupting a neighboring business and causing layoffs does not give rise to an action for lost wages. *Stevenson v. East Ohio Gas Co.*, 73 N.E.2d 200 (Ohio App. 1946). Negligently damaging a chartered vessel does not create a pecuniary loss action for the charterer while the ship was repaired. *Robins Dry Dock & Repair Co. v. Flint*, 275 U.S. 303 (1927).

There are limitations to this policy of forgiving negligence. For example, commercial fishermen could sue an oil company for business losses due to a negligent oil spill. *Union Oil Co. v. Oppen*, 501 F.2d 558 (9th Cir. 1974). Even so, the *Union Oil* court apparently limited pecuniary injury actions to circumstances where the defendant had special reason to anticipate a limited class of persons conducting business nearby would be particularly vulnerable to economic injury from the defendant's negligence. *Accord, People Express Airlines v. Consolidated Rail Corp.*, 495 A.2d 107 (N.J. 1985).

b. Injurious Speech: Deceit, Defamation, and Disparagement

The common law protects businesses from various forms of economically injurious speech. Early protections focused on threats or verbal harassment aimed at employees or customers. *See Garrett v. Taylor, supra.* The common law later provided two distinct protections against deception and falsehood. These are protections for persons misled by another's misrepresentations (deceit) and protections for persons suffering pecuniary harm from defamatory or disparaging misrepresentations made to others.

Defamation laws initially focused on commercial reputations. Defamatory remarks about another's trade or business were considered sufficiently clear and financially dangerous enough to be actionable without requiring proof of actual pecuniary harm. Owners of real, personal, or intangible property had a right to freedom from negative false statements about the property's title (slander of title) or quality. Common law liability gradually extended to any injurious statement maliciously made about another's business as "trade disparagement". *See, e.g., Proctor & Gamble Co. v. Haugen*, 222 F.3d 1262 (10th Cir. 2000) (actionable tortious interference with business relations found where competing distributor alleged plaintiff financially supported the Church of Satan and placed the Devil's mark on its products).

Three prohibitions gave rise to much of the modern unfair competition common law. They are: (1) defamation of the merchant, (2) disparagement of the title or quality of goods, and (3) palming off inferior quality goods as those of another merchant. These prohibitions protect public relations and prospective contractual relations. Common law protections against economic injury from communications made to third persons are discussed in Parts II and IV.

c. Coercive and Other Improper Conduct

Nineteenth-century English and American courts protected express or implied contractual relations, to the point of tolerating a degree of economic heavy-handedness in arms-length transactions. American courts were equally concerned with preventing coercive superior bargaining power used in forming, modifying, terminating, or refusing to form contracts. The greatest concerns were market dominance by a single business or concerted conduct by groups of businesses. Hence, the law condemned coerced or otherwise unconscionable contracts and contracts in restraint of trade. The law also targeted oppressive group conduct, particularly conspiracies restraining trade, group boycotts, and similar combinations.

While some forms of economic coercion are actionable, the common law favors protecting individual efforts to derive maximum economic advantage from bargaining and competition. Thus, in *Katz v. Kapper*, 7 Cal. App. 2d 1, 144 P.2d 1060 (1935), the court dismissed a wholesale fish dealer's complaint that a rival promised the dealer's customers substantial price reductions for their business and threatened them with financial ruin otherwise. The court held threatening a company's customers with lawful competition was not unlawful, even when coercing them to change trading partners.

The law intervenes where coercion is exerted by improper means or for improper ends. Early improper means examples include direct or indirect physical interference and deceptive or otherwise injurious speech. later improper means examples include initiating groundless litigation, employee bribery, or violating established trade or professional standards. *See Coleman v. Whisnant*, 35 S.E.2d 647 (N.C. 1945) (alleged groundless litigation threats); *Adler, Barish, Daniels, Levin and Creskoff v. Epstein*, 393 A.2d 1175 (Pa. 1978) (departing attorney soliciting clients while still in law firm's employment improperly interfered with firm's client relations). *See* Ch. 8, *infra* for more on employee bribery.

Actionable coercion cases absent improper conduct generally involve abuse of unequal bargaining power or business relationships not at "arm's length". Such transactions often pursue improper business objectives as well. One must understand how to identify an improper business objective to determine what might constitute actionable coercion without improper physical interference or deceptive speech.

2. IMPROPER BUSINESS OBJECTIVES

Businesses cannot knowingly inflict pecuniary harm on others. Likewise, they may not restrain or destroy competitive marketplace conditions or actively inflict pecuniary harm for an entirely malicious purpose. Ambiguity arises where malicious refusal to deal with another business, rather than affirmative business conduct, causes pecuniary injury.

a. Anticompetitive Conduct

The common law has long condemned misuse of market dominance, contracts, combinations, and conspiracies to restrain or destroy market competition. Anticompetitive conduct generally involves an improper business objective and either some market dominance misuse or concerted group conduct.

The marketplace permits some concerted group conduct. For example, a single patent holder's invention can become an industry standard fostering product compatibility. To be lawful, however, the patent's owner must license the patent to industry participants under fair, reasonable, and non-discriminatory ("FRAND") terms. Using such a patent for any perceived unfair monopolistic advantage may be actionable. *See also, NCAA v. Alston,* 594 U.S. ___, 141 S. Ct. 2141 (2021) (Applying "rule of reason" analysis to uphold injunction and finding rules by a monopolistic joint venture regulating amateur sports that limited education-related benefits schools may provide to student-athletes violated federal antitrust laws).

Federal and state antitrust statutes generally supersede common law prohibitions against anticompetitive conduct. The Sherman Antitrust Act,

15 U.S.C. §§ 1–2, broadly prohibits (1) contracts, combinations, and conspiracies that restrain interstate or foreign trade and (2) monopolization, attempts to monopolize, or combinations or conspiracies to monopolize any part of interstate or foreign trade. State antitrust statutes avoid federal preemption by focusing on activities within state regulatory authority, such as controlling retail prices and limiting other unfair business practices. *Oneok, Inc. v. Learjet, Inc.*, 575 U.S. 373 (2015) (no Federal Energy Regulatory Commission preemption authority existed when state law claims addressing pipelines' index manipulation only sought damages for excessive prices).

From these broad legislative prohibitions, courts deem certain conduct unjustifiably harmful to the competitive process. This conduct is unlawful *per se*, regardless of its purpose or effect. *Per se* Sherman Act violations historically included horizontal and vertical price-fixing, horizontal market division, and group boycotts. Courts frequently prohibit tying a product's sale to purchasing another unwanted product. Courts evaluate other trade restraints using a rule of reason. The rule of reason analysis establishes a burden-shifting process for showing antitrust violations. *See, e.g., Ohio v. American Express Co.*, 585 U.S. ___, 138 S. Ct. 2274 (2018) (anticompetitive effects of anti-steering provisions must be shown harmful for both merchants and cardholders before the plaintiff had to prove pro-competitive benefits). For this, courts consider whether a practice promotes, merely regulates, suppresses, or destroys competition.

The Clayton Act and the Federal Trade Commission Act supplement the Sherman Act. Both target anticompetitive practices diminishing competition or causing market monopolization. The Clayton Act, as amended by the Robinson-Patman Act, prohibits four specific misconduct types: (1) price discrimination and sales at unreasonably low prices, (2) exclusive dealing and tying arrangements, (3) anticompetitive mergers and acquisitions, and (4) interlocking directorates.

Clayton Act 15 U.S.C. § 15(a) states "any person who shall be injured in his business or property by reason of anything forbidden in the antitrust laws may sue. . .". This covers consumers buying goods or services priced above competitive levels from a monopolistic retailer, although indirect purchasers two or more steps removed from the distribution chain may not sue. *Apple, Inc. v. Pepper*, 587 U.S. ___, 139 S. Ct. 1514 (2019).

The FTC Act broadly prohibits conduct violating the spirit, if not the letter, of antitrust laws. The FTC Act also prohibits business conduct that is deceptive or otherwise unfair to consumers or other businesses. (*See* Ch. 8 and 9, *infra.*) For U.S. antitrust laws applied to extraterritorial conduct, particularly foreign government conduct, *see* Ch. 1, *supra.*

b. Malicious or Predatory Conduct

Like anticompetitive business activities, purely malicious or otherwise unjustified noncompetitive actions are unlawful. To encourage bargaining and competition, courts distinguish between cases with a primarily malicious motive and those where some legitimate motive exists. To state a claim, an otherwise lawful business activity must be proven to be undertaken solely, or at least primarily, to cause another party's economic loss. *But cf. Leigh Furniture & Carpet Co. v. Isom*, 657 P.2d 293 (Utah 1982) (deliberate contract breach to ruin another business held tortious). This conduct or activity applies to purchasing and sales decisions as well. *Weyerhaeuser Co. v. Ross-Simmons Hardwood Lumber Co.*, 549 U.S. 312 (2007).

Pleading and proof guidelines limit predatory conduct claims resulting from bargaining or competition injuries. *Brooke Group Ltd. v. Brown & Williamson Tobacco Corp.*, 509 U.S. 209, 222–224 (1993) (predatory pricing claims require showing market condition changes adverse to the injured party's interests, pricing below the competitor's costs, and a "dangerous probability" the competitor will recoup any lost profits).

Conclusively proving "disinterested malevolence" shows a business acted out of pure malice. Specious competition, for example, occurs where a company plans to exit the market after destroying another's business or gratuitously injures a business with which it is *not* in a competitive or bargaining relationship.

Vindictive statements, selling below cost, or operating at a loss may be evidence of malice. However, none exclude a potential accompanying legitimate competitive purpose. For example, in *Tuttle v. Buck*, 119 N.W. 946 (Minn. 1909), a banker who allegedly circulated "false and malicious reports and accusations", threatened existing customers, and set up a rival barbershop that ran at a loss still had to answer the injured barber's complaint as the banker could have justification for entering an unrelated business and taking these actions.

Acquisition of new or growing companies by those with market dominance has come under increasing regulatory scrutiny. These cases focus on new entities with innovative products or services that have yet to generate significant revenue getting purchased by an entity dominating the market segment the new company is poised to disrupt. These acquisitions may stifle potential competition for the dominant company by eliminating a future threat. From the dominant company's perspective, such acquisitions are asserted as a cost-effective way to innovate and may benefit the market by speeding public access to these new products or services.

A complaint should be summarily dismissed when a competitive justification is clear on the face of the plaintiff's pleading. *See Katz v. Kapper, supra,* (defendant fishmonger competed with the plaintiff and was not charged with using any improper means or market dominance to attract plaintiff's customers); *Beardsley v. Kilmer*, 140 N.E. 203 (N.Y. 1923) (no cause of action where defendant started a newspaper in response to plaintiff's published attacks and continued operations after driving plaintiff out of business).

There are circumstances where business activity lacks justification even in the absence of subjective malice. For example, capricious omission of a musician's songs from defendant's radio program without commercial justification amounted to a prima facie tort. *Advance Music Corp. v. American Tobacco Co.*, 70 N.E.2d 401 (N.Y. 1946). Here, the absence of competition between the parties arguably made the defendant's conduct an improper business method (i.e., a disparagement of plaintiff's songs).

c. Refusals to Deal with Another Business

Sometimes individual conduct causing economic harm is privileged despite the worst motives. Simply refusing to deal with another, for example, has long been held not actionable at common law even if motivated solely by spite or whimsy. The U.S. Constitution protects this liberty regardless of justification. *See Great Atl. & Pac. Tea Co. v. Cream of Wheat Co.*, 227 F. 46 (2d Cir. 1915).

The rule against unjustified malicious conduct apparently does not address refusals to deal with others. The judiciary and legislature are increasingly concerned with promoting both economic opportunity equality and legal control of economic power. Still, such refusals will not likely cause others serious economic injury or give individual businesses undue advantage. This theory assumes normal competitive conditions with readily available alternative sources of goods, services, labor, and employment. Significantly, the common law has long restricted the refusal to deal rights available to public utilities and industries regulated as monopolies or quasi-monopolies.

Many statutes limit rights to refuse to deal with others in the marketplace. For example, federal antitrust laws limit these rights where the refusal is a part of monopolization attempt or a combination in restraint of trade. *But cf., Verizon Commc'ns Inc. v. Law Offices of Curtis V. Trinko, LLP*, 540 U.S. 398, 410 (2004) (no obligation to provide rivals with "sufficient" service where no antitrust duty to deal with rivals exists); *Pacific Bell Tel. v. Linkline Comm.*, 555 U.S. 438 (2009) (company without antitrust duty to deal with rivals may set a high wholesale price and a low retail services price, thereby "squeezing" competitors' profit margins).

Various civil rights statutes limited the right to refuse to deal with persons based on their race, religion, gender, or national origin. *See, e.g., Newman v. Piggie Park Enter., Inc.*, 390 U.S. 400 (1968); *Bob Jones Univ. v. United States*, 461 U.S. 574 (1983); *Pittsburgh Press Co. v. Pittsburgh Comm'n on Human Relations*, 413 U.S. 376 (1973); but see *303 Creative LLC v. Elenis,* 600 U.S. ___, 143 S. Ct. 2298 (2023) (the First Amendment prevents states from requiring a business to publish a message for which the creator disagrees, which was passed in the context of sexual preference matters but lacked any limiting language). State and local rules may regulate decisions based on sexual preference or gender identity, so long as they adequately respect speech and religious freedoms. *See Masterpiece Cakeshop Ltd. v. Colorado Civil Rights Comm'n*, 584 U.S. ___, 138 S. Ct. 1719 (2018). Federal labor laws limit business refusal to deal rights when they are applied to unions or employee union members.

Federal statutes limit food processors and others' rights to refuse to deal with farmers belonging to agricultural associations.

Federal and state statutes purport to limit circumstances where a franchisor can terminate contractual relations with a franchisee. Franchising is a common licensing method for distributing branded goods and services. As a distribution system, franchises fall midway between a company-owned (i.e., vertically integrated) distribution system and the traditional three-tiered (i.e., manufacturer-wholesaler-retailer) distribution system.

There are three distinct franchise operation types: (1) Manufacture franchises, where the franchisor exploits a trade secret or other business knowledge by licensing product manufacturing and distribution to others; (2) distribution franchises, where the franchisor distributes its branded products through others' facilities; and (3) style-of-business franchises, where the franchisor licenses a developed brand and associated business standards to others who operate retail outlets for a product or a service.

Theoretically, both franchisors and franchisees benefit from the arrangement. The franchisor maintains many sources or outlets for its product or service with limited additional capital and other resources invested. The franchisee operates an independent business with the franchisor's technical and advertising assistance. In reality, many franchise relationships reflect vastly inequitable bargaining power. This is particularly true in distribution and style-of-business franchises, where franchisees are often merely terminable-at-will employees substantially invested in the business.

Laws grant certain franchisees additional protections since a franchisor's termination decision frequently destroys the franchisee's business. Auto dealers can fight a franchisor's termination in federal court if the termination was not "in good faith and without coercion" under the Automobile Dealers' Franchise Act, (ADFA) 15 U.S.C. § 1221. Likewise, the Federal Petroleum Marketing Practices Act, (FPMPA) 15 U.S.C. §§ 2801–2841, strictly limits permissible termination reasons for motor fuel distributors or dealer franchises and specifies certain franchise termination procedures. *Cf. Mac's Shell Serv. v. Shell Oil Prods.*, 559 U.S. 175 (2010) (no constructive franchise termination claim under FPMPA unless the franchisor's wrongful conduct forced the franchise's abandonment). The FPMPA expressly preempts conflicting state statutes. While the ADFA lacks a preemption provision, many state statutes extending franchisee protections beyond the ADFA were held unconstitutional. *See, e.g., U.S. Brewers' Ass'n v. Nebraska*, 220 N.W.2d 544 (Neb. 1974) (As the ADFA generally applies to franchise termination, the court ultimately found a state statute regulating liquor distributor termination to be unconstitutional).

The Federal Trade Commission promulgated rules establishing certain disclosure requirements and prohibitions concerning franchising and business opportunity ventures in 1979. *See* 16 C.F.R. §§ 436.1–11. *See also* Ch. 8.

Unlike unconditioned refusals, a company's conditioned refusal to deal with another business or a prospective employee amounts to a threat. Improper threat objectives may make the refusal to deal actionable. For example, a business inducing another to breach a contract by conditioned refusal to deal may be liable for actionable interference with contractual relations. Even using a conditioned refusal to deal with another to induce a contract modification might be condemned where superior bargaining power is involved. *See* Ch. 3, *infra*.

3. CONCERTED GROUP CONDUCT

Concerted group conduct may make refusals to deal with another actionable, whether conditioned or unconditioned. Group interference with another's trade relations is presumed unlawful and requires justification to avoid liability. Group interference includes concerted group refusals to deal (i.e., boycotts). Group interference with another's trade relations can eliminate alternative sources of goods, services, labor, or employment. Both the greater potential for serious economic injury received by those targeted and undue economic advantage enjoyed by those businesses acting together mandate this more aggressive position.

Common-law civil conspiracy and federal antitrust laws embody this presumption against lawful economically injurious concerted group conduct. These laws distinguish between a single company's acts, which are only illegal under antitrust laws if attempting to monopolize any part of trade or commerce, and concerted acts which are illegal under antitrust laws wherever they constitute an unreasonable restraint of trade. Still, distinguishing individual and concerted action can be difficult. *See, e.g., American Needle, Inc. v. National Football League*, 560 U.S. 183 (2010) (single licensing entity created by separately-owned teams violated § 1 of the Sherman Antitrust Act as it was a vehicle for concerted activity since teams compete with each other for entertainment revenue and the joint entity restrained the teams' individual intellectual property rights marketing).

Most litigation concerning concerted commercial conduct occurs under federal or state antitrust laws since treble damages are available. The common law civil conspiracy tort may apply where antitrust laws do not, or where antitrust laws lack remedial advantages. Most common-law conspiracy cases therefore either predate federal and state antitrust laws or rely heavily on cases decided by those acts.

As with individual interference with others' trade relations, those acting in concert are liable for civil conspiracy only where they use an improper means or pursue improper ends. Any improper interference by an individual will be improper for a group. Civil conspiracy cases pose a unique question: whether lawful individual conduct is unlawful for a group.

Improper group conduct findings often merely condemn a series of group practices that would be improper for an individual business. For example, *Evenson v. Spaulding*, 150 F. 517 (9th Cir. 1907) affirmed an injunction forbidding a business association from continued systematic interference with a peddler's buggies and wagons. Association agents harassed the peddler, accosted and diverted customers without offering their own goods, and even carried arms and were deputized to enforce invalid laws. Some of these individual actions might not have been tortious if a single actor performed them. However, this systematic group harassment using improper means to restrain competition or destroy another's business was clearly unlawful conduct.

Some group conduct is condemned solely because it is a group activity, such as the prohibition against concerted group refusals to deal (i.e., group boycotts). An illegal boycott is a group refusal to deal with a business without adequate justification. Justifying a group boycott can be difficult. The difficulty increases for a "secondary" boycott, where the conditioned refusal to deal with a business derives from its relations with another business.

Jackson v. Stanfield, 36 N.E. 345 (Ind. 1894), a common law conspiracy case, found coercion and intimidation by a lumber retailer association. The association boycotted manufacturers or wholesalers selling lumber directly to consumers or supplying non-retailers who did. The association circulated lists of offending business and penalized member violations. The court observed that "it is not a mere passive, let-alone policy. . . that creates liability but the threats and intimidation shown in the complaint." Recall similar threats and intimidation were lawful when a wholesale fish dealer threatened to ruin retailers if they continued purchasing from a rival. *See Katz v. Kapper, supra. Katz* and *Jackson* suggest that, unlike business groups, an individual business (without market dominance) may use threats inducing another business to terminate third-party relations, including a conditioned refusal to deal.

A boycott can unreasonably restrain trade without coercion or intimidation. Generally, a business combination's actions are unreasonable if its operation tends to prevent competition, raise prices, or create a monopoly without justification. In *Grillo v. Board of Realtors of Plainfield Area*, 219 A.2d 635 (N.J. Super. Ch. 1966), a listing service operated exclusively for board members created an unlawful trade restraint. The comprehensive statutory scheme licensing real estate brokers countered the board's claims that these restrictive practices established and improved professional membership standards.

Other private policing schemes met similar fates even where comprehensive public regulation was lacking. *See, e.g., Fashion Originators' Guild of Am., Inc. v. FTC*, 312 U.S. 457 (1941), where a dress designer and manufacturer association violated federal antitrust laws by conditioning sales on agreements not to deal with design pirates even though common-law cases held design piracy was tortious misconduct. (For more on design piracy, *see* Ch. 6, *infra*).

Privately administered policing schemes are upheld when they utilize objective standards, fair policing procedures, and lack any element of an explicit group boycott. An individual member's decision not to deal with a disfavored business may be based on an association ruling, but may not result from "concerted" association action. However, collusion through group use of a common algorithm or technology platform is receiving additional scrutiny as price fixing through an intermediary.

One early antitrust case illustrates this difficulty determining when conduct is concerted or unilateral. In *United States v. Colgate & Co.*, 250 U.S. 300 (1919), the Court affirmed Colgate could attempt retail price maintenance by refusing to deal with wholesale and retail price cutters. A business can exercise independent discretion in deciding to deal with others, which includes advanced announcements of conditions where it will not sell. Others' unilateral decisions to comply with those conditions would not be concerted action. While *Colgate* has questionable antitrust precedent authority, it may reflect the common law view dividing unilateral and concerted conduct. (For more on price cutting, *see* Ch. 9, *infra*).

Non-commercial group boycotts are privileged despite the general prohibition against concerted commercial conduct, so long as they do not utilize improper means. Examples include boycotts for political, religious, or social purposes. Obviously, courts are alert for sham purposes when a company's competitors sponsor a "non-commercial" boycott. A combination of businesses presumably could agree to refuse to deal with a business engaged in illegal activities. Whether a group of businesses could use economic coercion inducing another's refusal to deal with a competitor whose conduct was politically or morally objectionable remains unresolved.

C. AFFIRMATIVE DEFENSES AND REMEDIES

In actions alleging interference with pre-contractual and non-contractual relations, there are affirmative defenses in addition to the justifications and privileges already mentioned. Common affirmative defenses include the statute of limitations, laches, estoppel, unclean hands, and speculative or absence of damages. More specialized privileges or justifications include legitimate or fair competition, absence of tortious or otherwise wrongful conduct, protection of contractual or financial interests (absent improper means), directing business policy, or responsibility for another's welfare. *See, e.g., Chaves v. Johnson,* 335 S.E.2d 97 (1985); *Richardson v. La Rancherita* 98 Cal.App.3d 73, 81 (1979). Truth of a statement may refute claims alleging defamatory or spiteful statements. *See C.R. Bard, Inc. v. Worldtronics Corp.*, 561 A.2d 694, 235 N.J. Super. 168 (1989). A defendant may also challenge the relationship of the pre-contractual parties. *See, e.g., CBS, Inc. v. Ahern,* 108 F.R.D. 14 (S.D.N.Y.1985) (questioning whether a contract would have been created absent the defendant's actions); *A.S. Rampell, Inc. v. Hyster Co.,* 3 N.Y.2d 369 (N.Y. 1957) (relation of confidence between a manufacturer and distributor supported a cause of action for interference with an "at will" relationship).

Remedies for interference with pre-contractual and non-contractual relations include damages, restitution, and injunctive relief. Compensatory damages are recoverable where the extent of past pecuniary injury is established with sufficient certainty. Where the interference was malicious, either punitive damages or restitution of the defendant's profits may be allowed. Injunctive relief is available where monetary damages will not adequately protect the plaintiff.

CHAPTER 3

INTERFERENCE WITH CONTRACTUAL RELATIONS

Common laws protect contractual relations from virtually any form of intentional interference. While early English common laws remedied interference with master-servant relations, the modern origin of interference with contractual relations torts is *Lumley v. Gye*, 118 Eng.Rep. 749 (1853). *Lumley* held an opera company manager liable for inducing a singer to breach a rival's exclusive contract.

The *Lumley* case is important for several reasons. First, the court expanded common law contractual relation protections beyond master-servant relations to service contracts. This laid the foundation for protecting all contractual relations forms. Second, *Lumley* had no evidence of malicious conduct and mentioned no improper means for inducing the singer's contract breach (such as coercion, intimidation, or deceit). The singer voluntarily breached their contract and the defendant manager had sound commercial reasons to employ the singer. Apparently the "malice" found was merely the defendant manager's intentional offer to the singer that induced her breach of contract. *Lumley* therefore protects contractual relations even from bona fide competitive interference. Finally, the exclusive dealing provision the singer was induced to breach itself restrained trade. The court's protection of this contract showed even agreements restraining trade may be protected from competitive interference.

Judicial decisions since *Lumley v. Gye* refined the case's basic conclusions to identify (1) what contractual relations are protected and (2) what interferences with those relations are actionable.

A. CONTRACTUAL RELATIONS PROTECTED

As we have seen, trade relations that can be embodied in a contract include a retail company's individual consumer relations and any company's ownership, employment, and commercial relations. Since the principal threat of economic harm to partner, shareholder, and consumer relations comes from conduct likely to be tortious even without a contract, this chapter focuses on employment and commercial contracts.

As with employment relations themselves, employment contracts may include management and labor contracts. Commercial contracts cover parties at various distribution chain positions. Contracts among similar businesses often involve joint ventures, trade association activities, or business asset sales (including intangible assets such as business goodwill or intellectual property). Contracts between businesses of different types or at different distribution chain positions often involve financial transactions, selling or leasing goods or real estate, selling or licensing intellectual property, service performance, or some combination of these.

Contracts may range from elaborate written documents to agreements entirely implied from the parties' course of dealing. A contract may contain post-contractual covenants, such as warranties of title or merchantability, covenants not to compete, or confidentiality agreements. The Statute of Frauds requires that certain contract types be in writing, such as those that transfer an interest in land, sell goods priced at $500 or more, that cannot be performed within one year, or where one entity guarantees another's debt or other obligation.

Today, virtually any contract qualifies for protection against interference, whether express or implied, term or terminable at will, enforceable or unenforceable. Courts will imply contract terms when none are expressed, prevent interference with contracts terminable at the parties' will, and protect contractual relations where the contract itself is unenforceable or voidable. This judicial position indicates the protected interest is not merely contractual interests in the performance of promises, but rather a larger commercial interest in the stability of existing advantageous relations.

1. EXPRESS CONTRACTS: TERM, TERMINABLE AT WILL, AND UNENFORCEABLE CONTRACTS

Most courts hold that a contract terminable at the will of the parties, no less than a term contract, is protected against various forms of "improper" interference. This is so even though technically one cannot induce "breach" of such a contract. On the other hand, mere promissory fraud may not be actionable interference with a terminable at will contract unless the promise is part of an actionable scheme to defraud or is one element in a pattern of fraudulent acts. *Speakers of Sport, Inc. v. ProServ, Inc.*, 178 F.3d 862 (7th Cir. 1999) (affirming summary judgment against a sports agency suing a competitor for fraudulently inducing an athlete to end a terminable at will contract, as promises to secure endorsements were held mere "puffery," i.e., an expression of hope rather than a commitment).

Some courts hold that unenforceable or voidable contracts may still be protected against third-party interference when both parties would have otherwise performed. Apparently the trade relation is still valuable even if the contract itself cannot be enforced. When determining what constitutes actionable interference with such contracts, however, courts treat these contracts like pre-contractual or non-contractual trade relations.

Unenforceable and voidable contracts are distinguished from enforceable contracts, as well as contracts considered altogether void as illegal or contrary to public policy. Void contracts receive no legal protection. Thus, usurious or gambling contracts and contracts that unreasonably restrain trade do not receive legal protection.

As *Lumley v. Gye* illustrates, actions for interference with contractual relations often involve contractual terms restraining trade. Of course, contracts naturally restrain some trade. Some constraints are reasonable as they bring order and stability to existing trade relations. Exclusive dealing contracts and post-contractual covenants not to compete require greater scrutiny. Today, federal or state antitrust laws generally determine an exclusive dealing contract's validity. The validity of covenants not to compete, by contrast, may be determined in the context of a common-law tort claim for contractual interference. *See, e.g., Imperial Ice Co. v. Rossier*, 112 P.2d 631 (Cal. 1941).

Covenants not to compete often accompany contracts for employment or for sale of a business. Employers and business purchasers may require these covenants to protect their business goodwill from subsequent appropriation. Express noncompetition covenants that are ancillary to a valid employment or commercial contract and are necessary to protect a contracting party may be upheld if the covenant has a reasonable scope. Reasonableness requires the covenant not be unnecessarily broad in time or geography, not so extensive as to be oppressive to the covenanting party, and not inimical to the public interest. State laws often regulate these provisions. Particularly in the employment context, reasonableness determinations vary significantly by location. *Compare,* Tex. Bus. & Com. Code Ann. § 15.50(a) (reasonable non-compete agreements allowed), *with* Cal. Bus. & Prof. Code §§ 16600 *et seq.* (generally prohibiting such contracts).

A contract's subject matter determines whether a non-compete agreement's temporal and territorial scope is reasonable. A citywide territorial competitive restriction might reasonably protect a large retail business owner but is too broad for a neighborhood barbershop. A two-year competition restriction may reasonably protect a purely commercial enterprise owner having many competitors and producing goods or services in plentiful supply. However, the same restriction is unreasonable for a regulated business when licensed professionals are in short supply.

Covenants not to compete are generally presumed valid for business sale contracts that clearly transfer goodwill. A majority of courts hold, for example, that lack of a time limit does not render the covenant not to compete *per se* unreasonable. *Cf. Imperial Ice Co. v. Rossier, supra.*

Limitations on a former employee's post-termination freedoms are much harder to justify. Courts generally only enforce an employee's express covenant not to compete in situations where the employee had either: (1) close personal relations with a significant number of their employer's customers or (2) access to the employer's confidential customer information or other trade secrets. *See, e.g., Reed, Roberts Assocs. v. Strauman*, 353 N.E.2d 590 (N.Y. 1976). In these situations, a former employee could divert a significant portion of the employer's goodwill or other intangible business assets. Even then, courts will not enforce a former employee's covenant not to compete (as opposed to a simple covenant not to disclose trade secrets) if it lacks definite temporal and territorial limits or imposes undue hardships. See, *e.g., Milwaukee Linen Supply Co. v. Ring*, 246 N.W. 567 (Wis. 1933) (covenant with physically-impaired former route manager not to call customers of a linen supply business or otherwise compete within a given metropolitan area for two years held invalid, even when held reasonable for a route driver who had closer customer relations).

In addition to these common law measures, most states have antitrust statutes rendering void every contract which restrains one from engaging in a lawful profession, trade, or business. Courts in some states hold employee covenants not to compete or work for competitors are void and unenforceable, regardless of the scope. *See, e.g., Golden State Linen Serv. v. Vidalin*, (1977) 69 Cal.App.3d 1, 137 Cal.Rptr. 807 (so construing Cal. Bus. & Prof. Code §§ 16600 *et seq.*); *Edwards v. Arthur Andersen LLP*, 81 Cal. Rptr.3d 282 (Sup. Ct. 2008) (rejecting a requested narrow-restraint exception to § 16600, as non-competition agreements are invalid in California unless they fall within the applicable statutory exceptions for sale or dissolution of corporations, partnerships, and limited liability corporations).

Most jurisdictions having such a statute have created a narrow class of exceptions to the "void per se" rule, either by the courts or legislature. Some statutes set out the maximum permissible temporal and territorial restrictions. In others, courts construe the statute to except contractual provisions if the employee promises not to solicit former customers.

2. IMPLIED CONTRACTS AND THE OBLIGATION OF FAIR DEALING

Even without an express contract, courts often imply certain contractual terms from the trade relation's mere existence. These terms are often implied regardless of whether a tacit meeting of the minds actually existed. These implied terms let courts impose an obligation of good faith and fair dealing on parties to a trade relation. *See, e.g.*, U.C.C. § 1–203 (imposing a "good faith" obligation on parties for contracts governed by the U.C.C.). A third party inducing breach of this implied obligation can be held liable for their actions, or enjoined from interfering with the contractual relation. This is similar to the consequences when a third party induces breach of an express contractual provision.

When parties bargain for the sale of a business, courts usually imply a good faith covenant from the bargaining relationship itself. The prospective buyer is expected not to share or exploit information disclosed in confidence if the sale does not occur. After selling a business, the seller is expected not to interfere with the company's goodwill by soliciting former customers. *See, e.g., Mohawk Maint. Co. v. Kessler*, 419 N.E.2d 324 (N.Y. 1981) (rights acquired by purchasing a company's goodwill through the implied covenant to refrain from soliciting customers are logically permanent, not subject to divestiture after a reasonable time).

The seller's implied covenant not to detract from the value of the goodwill sold is narrower than an express covenant not to compete. This implied covenant does not prevent sellers from engaging in a competing business. The implied covenant merely prohibits directly soliciting former customers. Courts will not imply terminated employees have an analogous obligation to avoid soliciting their former employer's customers. Courts do imply an employee has a duty of loyalty to their employer during their employment, and covenants not to use or disclose a former employer's trade secrets—including confidential customer lists—may survive termination.

B. ACTIONABLE AND PRIVILEGED INTERFERENCE

Not all interferences with contractual relations are necessarily actionable. Likewise, actionable interference does not require a contract breach. Wrongful interference is, of course, clearly actionable, even without causing a contract breach. *See, e.g., McNary v. Chamberlain*, 34 Conn. 384 (Conn. 1867), finding actionable interference where the defendant intentionally damaged a road the plaintiff was hired to repair which raised the plaintiff's performance costs. Had the plaintiff been unable to perform, the road's owner could claim both trespass damages and interference with the contractual relation. *But see Price v. Sorrell*, 784 P.2d 614 (Wyo. 1989), finding no actionable interference where an attorney wrote to another's client questioning the plaintiff attorney's reputation, making the plaintiff's performance more expensive and burdensome but not causing a contract breach. In such cases, other causes of action such as libel, defamation, or slander may be appropriate.

The principles on which *McNary* is based were well established long before *Lumley v. Gye. See* Ch. 2 *supra*. *Lumley* remains important as it established contractual interference need not be independently wrongful to be actionable. "Maliciously" inducing the contract breach is sufficient.

1. INDUCING CONTRACT BREACH

Where a contract lasts for a definite term, as in *Lumley,* "malice" comes from mere knowledge of the contract while offering an inducement. Where the contract is voidable or terminable at the parties' will (thus capable of non-performance or termination without actionable breach), "malicious" interference requires interference by improper (i.e., deceptive or coercive) means or for an improper (i.e., anticompetitive or predatory) purpose.

The term "malice" has various meanings. Some courts, likely influenced by the prima facie tort theory, altogether abandoned malice as a concept and instead consider justifiable or unjustifiable contract interference. Where contractual stability interests are strong (as with valid term contracts), even interference for bona fide business reasons may be unjustified and thus actionable. Here, freedom to pursue trade relations has less (or at least no more) social utility than trade relation stability. Justifiable interference with such contractual relations requires defending an interest with greater countervailing social utility than contractual stability. For example, in *Brimelow v. Casson,* 1 Ch. 302 (1923), a company that severely underpaid chorus line women (forcing some into prostitution) justified an actors' association official's request that theatres cancel the troupe's performance contracts unless the women received higher wages. Here, the interference defended public health, safety, or morality. Modern labor laws also assume improving working conditions is socially important and sufficiently justifies peaceful concerted activity.

Freedom to interfere with contracts increases as contractual stability diminishes (as with voidable and terminable-at-will contracts). These freedoms include interference for bona fide business reasons. Actionable interference requires proof the disruptor either employed improper means or lacked bona fide business reasons for interfering. *See Doliner v. Brown*, 489 N.E.2d 1036 (Mass. App. Ct. 1986) (no actionable interference with prospective contractual relations where defendant "picked a deal off for himself" before the plaintiff's contract finalized).

Some courts balance whether intentional interference with contractual relations is actionable or privileged. This approach either fictionalizes malice requirements or fully displaces them. As with most general legal rules, however, limiting actions for contractual relations interference to only those featuring intentional misconduct requires many exceptions to avoid unjust results.

Courts generally will not extend liability beyond intentional or reckless interference with contractual relations. Mere negligence in contract interference is rarely actionable. This refusal reflects judicial efforts limiting tort liability and reluctance to extend negligence liability beyond conduct physically injuring a person or property. Otherwise, such laws would burden a company's freedom to contract with a duty of care to avoid inducing others to breach existing agreements. A negligent actor may be strictly liable for a likely intentional contract breach by the induced party.

Different considerations apply where negligent interference creates an unreasonable risk of harm to a contracting party's person or property that results in injury. Should the contracting parties be blameless and their contractual relation foreseeable to the interfering party, the interfering party may be liable for any physical injuries they cause. One court even awarded consequential damages for economic loss where the injury basis was strict liability rather than negligence. *See Hales v. Green Colonial, Inc.*, 490 F.2d 1015 (8th Cir. 1974). Courts may even let one contracting party recover pecuniary damages for negligent physical injury to *another* party.

Courts struggle with what "induces" a contract breach. Since inducement injuries ultimately result from the breaching party's intentional intervening acts, an inducement should be sufficiently overt to justify treating it as a concurring cause of injury. Liability therefore arises when an entity actively and affirmatively induced a contract breach.

2. COERCING MODIFICATION OF CONTRACTS AND ABUSE OF TRUST OR CONFIDENCE

Inducement to breach a contract must be affirmative and active to be actionable. However, the cause of action for contractual relation interference is not so limited. Likewise, neither an inducement nor a resulting contract breach is necessary to file a lawsuit. Physical interference or deception were considered actionable interference even before *Lumley v. Gye,* regardless of whether a contractual relationship existed or a contract breach occurred. *See* Ch. 2, *supra.* Cases following *Lumley* extended the contractual interference cause of action to cases involving coerced contract modification, abuse of trust or confidence, and concerted group interference with contractual relations.

In *Hannigan v. Sears, Roebuck and Co.*, 410 F.2d 285 (7th Cir. 1969), for example, a retailer actionably interfered with contractual relations between a distributor and manufacturer through economic coercion. The *Hannigan* court found this coerced contract between the manufacturer and distributor to reduce the retailer's commission obligations was functionally equivalent to an induced contract breach. The retailer's conduct when forcing a price concession exploited unequal bargaining powers and could also have been an antitrust violation (i.e., inducing price discrimination). *See* Ch. 9.

The common law opposition to abusing either unequal bargaining power or a relationship of trust or confidence may explain its protection of terminable-at-will contractual relations. For example, *A.S. Rampell, Inc. v. Hyster Co.*, 144 N.E.2d 371 (N.Y. 1957) found a cause of action for interference with manufacturer's employment relations when the accused dealer and one of the plaintiff's own salesman allegedly fomented dissention and lured away certain employees before the manufacturer ended the relationships. The court emphasized that the manufacturer-distributor arrangement involves bargaining power inequality and, in this instance at least, also a relationship of trust and confidence. Similarly, the salesman allegedly violated their duty of fidelity. *Rampell* illustrates the principal common-law theories franchisees use for relief from coercive or oppressive franchisor conduct. *See also Roberts v. Sears, Roebuck & Co.*, 573 F.2d 976 (7th Cir. 1978) (upholding a jury verdict awarding profits and damages against an employer for fraud, negligent misrepresentation, and breach of a confidential relationship when it secured patent assignment of an invention created while the employee was off-duty).

3. CONCERTED GROUP INTERFERENCE WITH CONTRACTUAL RELATIONS

Concerted group conduct increases the likelihood that economic coercion or oppression will constitute actionable interference with contractual relations, even without a contract breach. While some courts allow organized group activities the same latitude as individuals, other courts consider such group conduct actionable even when individual conduct would be privileged. The latter perspective considers the greater potential for coercion or oppression in concerted group conduct and may be influenced by the common law's distaste for contracts and conspiracies restraining trade.

Concern over concerted group conduct largely explains judicial willingness to protect contractual relations terminable at the parties' will. *See, e.g.*,

Wear-Ever Aluminum, Inc. v. Townecraft Indus., Inc., 75 N.J. Super. 135 (Ch. Div. 1962), holding a manufacturer actionably interfered with a competitor's contractual relations by hiring many of the competitor's terminable-at-will sales team and decimating the competitor's sales efforts. Liability principally rested on how the organized mass exodus crippled the plaintiff's operations and how the competitor benefited from the plaintiff's investment in training its sales team. The latter basis for imposing liability amounts to finding the competitor misappropriated the plaintiff's sales organization. (For more on misappropriation, *see* Ch. 6–7 *infra.*) *A.S. Rampell v. Hyster Co., supra*, upheld a similar concerted interference claim along with alleged abuse of special relationships.

4. OTHER IMPROPER INTERFERENCE

Conduct that would be improper without a contract remains improper where it interferes with an existing contractual relation. *See, e.g., Associated Press v. International News Serv.*, 245 F. 244 (2d Cir. 1917) (bribing an employee); *Adler, Barish, Daniels, Levin and Creskoff v. Epstein*, 393 A.2d 1175 (Pa. 1978) (violating established standards of a profession or trade). *See generally,* Ch. 2 *supra.*

C. AFFIRMATIVE DEFENSES AND REMEDIES

The principal affirmative defenses to an action for interference with contractual relations are that the contract is void and the interference is justified.

Contracts are void if they are illegal or contrary to public policy. Interference is justifiable if it intends to defend public health, safety, or morals.

Other defenses may include privilege or absolute immunity (such as for true but harmful statements made during a judicial proceeding), lawful or fair competition, responsibility for another's welfare, financial interest, lack of a valid business expectancy (for anticipated business relationships), lack of knowledge of the contract or of interference with its performance, lack of intent to interfere, lack of causation, or lack of duty owed to the complainant. A defendant may also assert the plaintiff's conduct caused the contract breach, or deny any damages were caused by the alleged interference. Sometimes a defendant may challenge existence of contractual relations.

The remedies available for an actionable interference with contractual relations include damages, restitution, and injunctive relief. Recoverable damages could include all damages proximately caused by the misconduct, regardless of foreseeability, general damages, attorney's fees, and even punitive damages in egregious cases. Economic losses may include lost earnings, lost profits, or professional expenses (including medical) incurred. Future economic damages may also be contemplated. In some cases, physical pain or mental anguish may be considered as well.

Rules governing special damages availability vary significantly between contract and tort actions. Special damages flowing from the contract breach may be recoverable if such damages can be proven with sufficient certainty and are not too remote. Special damages for contract breach are limited to those within the contemplation of the parties when the contract formed. Special damages in tort actions are usually more generous, especially in intentional misconduct cases. Likewise, punitive damages and restitution awards (i.e., defendant's profits) are not often available in contract actions but may be awarded in intentional tort actions.

These variations between tort and contract remedies mean a plaintiff's monetary claims against the party inducing a contract breach may be considerably greater than that against the party breaching a contract. A successful plaintiff also may recover general contract damages (i.e., the plaintiff's reasonable expectation of profit under the contract) from either the breaching party or the inducer.

Damages awards are often sufficient to make a plaintiff whole. Such awards may encompass contract damages claims against the breaching party and tort damages claims against the inducer. Courts generally let plaintiffs pursue both claims, but will prohibit recovery of the same damages more than once. If a contract cannot be enforced against the breaching party, the plaintiff may look to the party inducing the breach for all their injuries.

Injunctive relief may be available if financial remedies are inadequate. Many contracts are subject to specific performance. However, an employee cannot be forced to perform an employment contract. Such a remedy would constitute involuntary servitude in violation of the Thirteenth Amendment of the Constitution. Even so, there are circumstances where a former employee and a competitor may be enjoined from working together.

PART 2

PRODUCT, SERVICE AND BUSINESS MISIDENTIFICATION

CHAPTER 4

USE OF SIMILAR TRADEMARKS AND TRADE NAMES

In an increasingly impersonal market, businesses often invest considerable time, money, and effort promoting public awareness and ongoing recognition of their products, services, or company. The type and nature of protectable trademarks have expanded greatly along with developments in technology and communications. Even if a business does not take deliberate efforts to develop distinctive branding, the company should still limit customer confusion and diversion. Consumers also gain value from a company's marks. These benefits include reasonable expectations about a service or product's attributes and the expected ability to seek redress from a known source if a dispute arises. Protecting business and consumer expectations are often complimentary objectives in trademark law. When these objectives conflict, identify the business or consumer protection priority to understand the case or rule logic.

Trademark law covers a broad range of tangible subject matter. A trademark can be a word, phrase, symbol, design, or other device that identifies and distinguishes the source of a particular good or service. *See* 15 U.S.C. § 1127. Trademarks frequently comprise brand names, logos, or slogans used either by a single entity or cooperatively under certain conditions. Trademarks can also encompass a variety of other sensory inputs, such as sounds, colors, motions, textures, scents, and potentially even flavors. Since trademarks can potentially receive endless protection, many limitations overlap with other intellectual property protections to preserve others' abilities to describe their goods and services and otherwise compete in the global marketplace.

The laws protecting identification of products, services, and companies began as an offshoot of common law deceit. In the unreported sixteenth-century *Clothier Case,* the English Court of Common Pleas apparently found a cause of action where one clothier deceptively used another clothier's mark on inferior cloth. Later cases indicated the *Clothier Case* was brought by either a deceived purchaser or the clothier that owned the falsified mark. *See, e.g., Southern v. How*, 79 Eng. Rep. 1243 (1617) (clothier as the plaintiff). A purchaser would have a cause of action for deceit. The clothier's claims would be for trade diversion and reputational injury to their business and goods. Regardless, the *Clothier Case* was subsequently cited as authorizing an actionable commercial tort for attempts to palm off one's goods as those of another merchant. *See, e.g., Blanchard v. Hill*, 2 Atk. 484, 26 Eng. Rep. 692 (1742).

From this beginning, laws governing identification of products, services, and businesses developed in different directions. One legal branch focused on trademark and trade name infringements that did not necessarily involve conscious palming off. Another branch considered forms of conscious palming off that did not necessarily involve deceptive use of another's trademark or trade name. This chapter focuses on actionable and privileged interference with distinctive trade symbols. Chapter 5 reviews other forms of palming off.

A. TRADE RELATIONS AND TRADE SYMBOLS PROTECTED

The public relations, or goodwill, of a product, service, or business are protectable trade relations. This chapter focuses on goodwill embodied in two types of distinctive trade symbols—namely, trademarks and trade names.

1. MARKS AND NAMES PROTECTED

Merchants have identified their goods using distinctive marks for centuries. Some marks indicated the goods' ownership, such as branded livestock. Other marks identified the goods' source or origin. Individual artisans first used the latter form, which is a precursor of the modern-day trademark. Powerful (and monopolistic) trade guilds required these marks as a regulatory tool that identified foreign (i.e., non-member) goods and poorly crafted member goods.

Marks on certain durable goods eventually became sufficiently well-established, and more an asset than liability for the producer. While still limited to contacts between the producer and consumer, these marks began symbolizing the product's accrued goodwill. These marks particularly benefited cutlery and cloth products as they were often transported great distances before sale. Still, trade symbols only truly transformed into business assets after the

Industrial Revolution significantly stratified and depersonalized the marketplace.

As trademarks became business assets, unscrupulous merchants abused trademarks and the goodwill they symbolized by using reputable merchants' marks to palm off inferior quality goods. Hence, common-law palming off actions received early recognition.

Trademark law's growth continued following the series of cases referencing the *Clothier Case* that confirmed trademark infringement required showing some form of deception. The first reported trademark case after this series of cases was *Blanchard v. Hill*, 2 Atk. 484, 26 Eng. Rep. 692 (1742), where the court would not enjoin a competitor from using a mogul's stamp on the competitor's playing cards. The *Blanchard* court distinguished the *Clothier Case,* stating merely using a mark could not support legal action unless the competitor was "doing it with a fraudulent design, to put off bad cloths by this means, or to draw away customers from the other clothier."

As the Industrial Revolution progressed, courts shifted focus from the accused's deceptive conduct to the complaining company's rights in the trade symbol. Thus, what started as deceit law became part of intellectual property law. During the transformation, the terms "trademark" and "trade name" took two distinct meanings—an older, common-law meaning and a more modern statutory meaning.

a. Common-Law Trademarks and Trade Names

Common-law courts distinguished technical trademarks from trade names. Technical trademarks were any fanciful, arbitrary, unique, distinctive, or non-descriptive mark, word, letter, number, design, or picture designating goods and affixed to them. Essentially, technical trademarks were inherently distinctive trade symbols that identified a product. One obtained technical trademark rights merely by adopting a mark or word and using it as a trademark. Afterwards, trademark infringement lawsuits could vindicate trademark rights.

Trade names are words that describe a product, service, or business, or names of persons, partnerships, corporations, or a geographic location. This classification recognizes trade names' common use in commercial discourse. A trade name could only receive protection in palming off cases (or unfair competition as the United States eventually named the tort) where there was proof the name acquired a "secondary meaning". Secondary meaning requires the public perceive the mark as designating a particular merchant's goods, services, or business rather than merely being a descriptive word or common name. Eventually other product or service attributes capable of acquiring secondary meaning (outside of names or logos) received analogous common-law protections. These attributes include product features, packaging, other trade dress forms, and literary or artistic titles and characterizations.

For a time, courts distinguished both the scope of and rationale for trademark and trade name protection as well as trademark rights acquisition methods. A few courts, for example, enjoined substantial technical trademark copying without evidence of either deceptive intent or likelihood the public would be deceived as to the goods' origin. Recognized trademark infringement harm expanded from deceptively diverting customers to misappropriating the trade symbol itself. While most courts required proving at least some likelihood of consumer confusion as to the goods' origin, plaintiffs received the benefit of the doubt in these cases.

Courts still resisted finding unfair competition where a merchant used another's trade name or trade dress without sufficient evidence of actual public confusion over the goods' origin. Trade names were regularly common commercial terms, so even injunctive relief generally required strong inference of deceptive intent and actual diversion of a plaintiff's trade. Injunctive relief for trade name infringement was much more limited than for technical trademark infringement. Courts protected the plaintiff's trade, not the trade name or trade dress. When granted, injunctive relief for trade name infringement regularly just mandated additional identifying words to eliminate confusion.

The distinctions between technical trademarks and trade names eventually disappeared. Courts began granting the same protection to technical trademarks and to trade names that acquired a secondary meaning. Secondary meaning exists where an otherwise unprotectable mark can identify a good or service's source or origin. Marketing, long-term trademark use, and other public exposure frequently establishes secondary meaning. Establishing infringement required likelihood of public confusion as to the goods or services' attributes. Meanwhile, fraudulent intent helps determine available trademark infringement remedies or contest unfair registration practices. Courts now use the terms "trademark" and "trade name" as defined in the Lanham Act and state registration statutes modeled on the Lanham Act.

b. Statutory Trademarks, Service Marks, and Trade Names

Federal trademark law established common-law distinctions between technical trademarks and trade names in *Standard Paint Co. v. Trinidad Asphalt Mfg. Co.*, 220 U.S. 446 (1911). In *Standard Paint*, the Supreme Court limited federal trademark registration under the 1905 Trade Marks Act to common-law technical trademarks. The Lanham Trademark Act of 1946, 15 U.S.C. §§ 1051–1127, and similar state statutes later redefined the terms "trademark" and "trade name." Section 45 of the Lanham Act, for example, defines a trademark as any word, name, symbol, device, or any combination thereof adopted and used by a person to identify *goods*, and a trade name as any name used by a person to identify their *business or vocation. See* 15 U.S.C. § 1127. The Lanham Act makes federal registration available to a trademark having either inherent or acquired distinctiveness. Trade names, however, were not originally eligible for federal registration. To fill a gap these definitions created, the Lanham Act specifically permits federal registration for "service marks" that advertise or sell services.

The Supreme Court held the Lanham Act construes potential trademark subjects "in the broadest of terms." *Qualitex Co. v. Jacobson Prods. Co.*, 514 U.S. 159 (1995). While limitations exist, trademarks and service marks may take virtually any form, whether *verbal* (i.e., words, names, numbers, slogans, titles, or character names), *audio-visual* (i.e., symbols, pictures, designs, colors, devices, holograms, animations, distinctive sounds, product configurations or packaging, trade dress, advertising formats, or artistic characterizations), or *unconventional* (i.e., scents, textures, or tastes).

The Lanham Act provides for "certification marks" and "collective marks" designating a relationship between the mark's actual owner and other entities using a mark. Collective marks are limited to use by certain group members, while certification marks are available to anyone complying with the trademark owner's defined standards. Collective marks come in two forms: collective trademarks or service marks, and collective membership marks. The former identifies goods or services from a particular group, while the latter identifies group membership. *See* 15 U.S.C. § 1127; *Aloe Creme Labs., Inc. v. Am. Soc'y for Aesthetic Plastic Surgery, Inc.*, 192 USPQ 170, 173 (TTAB 1976). Certification marks tend to designate geographic origin, certain good or service attributes, or certain creation-related attributes (such as labor union membership).

Unlike business names, trademarks could receive federal registration due to the different functions trademarks and trade names play. Manufacturers and franchisors generally use trademarks and service marks to establish the product or service's identity with consumers independently of a retailer or franchisee. As consumer relations are increasingly depersonalized and franchising proliferates, trademarks and service marks are gradually shifting function. Rather than identifying a single known good or service source, these marks often assure uniform good or service quality originating from one or more unknown sources. Some businesses even use marks as an advertising device to *create* goodwill for new products and services.

While trademarks and service marks generally enjoy national scope and are subject to federal regulation, state and common law protections remain important. States have considerable latitude in regulating local trademark and name use, so long as they do not conflict with federal law. *See, e.g., Friedman v. Rogers*, 440 U.S. 1 (1979) (no First Amendment violation by state statute prohibiting optometry practices using a trade name due to public deception concerns, as it only incidentally affected commercial speech content). *But see Sambo's Rests., Inc. v. Ann Arbor*, 663 F.2d 686 (6th Cir. 1981) (city's refusal to permit signage featuring a racial stereotype violated the First Amendment).

Lanham Act § 39(b), 15 U.S.C. § 1121(b), prohibits requirements by states or other political subdivisions that would alter a registered federal trademark or require display of any additional mark different from the federal registration certificate. Congress enacted the new § 39(b) in 1984 to legislatively overrule *Century 21 Real Estate Corp. v. Nevada Real Estate Advisory Comm'n*, 448 F.Supp. 1237 (D. Nev. 1978) which held the Lanham Act did not preempt a state regulation requiring licensed real estate brokers modify federally-registered trademarks so 50% of any advertisement displayed the local franchisee's name. *But cf. Blockbuster Videos v. City of Tempe*, 141 F.3d 1295 (9th Cir. 1998) (zoning ordinances can preclude certain trademark displays, such as storefront installation of Blockbuster's distinctive awning).

The Federal Trademark Dilution Act of 1995, amended in 2006, contains a similar limited preemption provision. This provision specifies that owning a valid federal trademark registration on the principal register completely bars any state law action for dilution by blurring, tarnishment, or harm to the distinctiveness or reputation of a mark, label, or advertisement form. *See* 15 U.S.C. § 1125(c)(6).

c. A Note on Nomenclature

Given the difference between the common-law and statutory definitions of the terms "trade-mark" and "trade name," a uniform nomenclature system must be specified. Hereafter, these terms are used in their modern sense unless otherwise specified. The term "mark" normally refers to trademarks, service marks, certification marks, and collective marks as defined in the Lanham Act. The terms "trademark" and "service mark" are also used in their modern sense as defined by the Lanham Act. When used together, the terms "trademark" and "service mark" implicitly include certification and collective marks as well. As we have seen, certification and collective marks are simply specialized trade or service mark types. The term "trade name" normally refers exclusively to business names. The phrase "mark or name" is used as a shorthand reference to trademarks, service marks, and trade names.

2. ACQUIRING RIGHTS IN A MARK OR NAME

a. Federal, State, and Common Law Trademark Prosecution

The trademark rights acquisition process varies based upon the rights conferred. While this chapter focuses predominantly on federal trademark law and principles, state and common law trademark rights acquisition and scope bear consideration as well.

(1) Federal Trademarks

Federal trademark protection requires registration with the U.S. Patent and Trademark Office ("USPTO") of the U.S. Department of Commerce. Federal statutory infringement proceedings require a federal registration as well.

The federal trademark registration process usually begins with a USPTO trademark examiner's *ex parte* examination of an application. The Trademark Trial and Appeal Board ("TTAB") handles trademark registration decision appeals, oppositions, expungement or reexamination proceedings, and certain other matters. Before 1958, the Commissioner of Patents heard *ex parte* proceedings appeals and *inter partes* proceedings. Since the TTAB's formation, appeals to the Commissioner only occur in unusual circumstances. The Trademark Modernization Act of 2020 codified procedures allowing third-party evidentiary submissions during trademark examination. Due to an increase in filing system abuse from abroad, the USPTO now requires a U.S.-licensed attorney represent foreign-domiciled trademark applicants, registrants, and parties to TTAB hearings.

The USPTO maintains two registries. The Principal Register is for trademarks with sufficient inherent or acquired distinctiveness to identify and distinguish the source of goods or services. Either the mark's unique characteristics or exclusive and ongoing use create this distinctiveness. Principal Register trademark protections include, without limitation, presumed trademark validity, prima facia evidence of the mark's ownership, and acknowledgement of continuous and exclusive use. Following five years continuous and uninterrupted use after the registration date, a trademark on the Principal Register can become "incontestable". Incontestability limits the grounds another party can assert against its validity.

The Supplemental Register is for marks merely capable of identifying and distinguishing the source for goods or services. Such marks would be no more than "merely descriptive" of the source for goods or services and require assertion the applicant actually uses the mark in commerce. Ordinarily, marks appear on the Supplemental Register either when diverted from the Principal Register due to an examiner's descriptiveness finding or when an applicant accepts their trademark is descriptive but continued use may make it distinctive. Supplemental Register trademarks appear in USPTO database trademark searches, have priority over later registration of similar marks, receive priority or registration in certain foreign countries and regions that do not require actual use or secondary meaning but do require domestic registration, and may still use the "®" symbol denoting a registered trademark.

For a Supplemental Register trademark to appear on the Principal Register, the owner must file a new application asserting acquired distinctiveness. Five consecutive years on the Supplemental Register, notoriety, advertisement activities, and third-party declarations associating the trademark with the registrant's goods or services may all contribute to meeting the Principal Register's distinctiveness requirements.

Any person or entity likely to be commercially damaged by a trademark's registration on the Principal or Supplemental Register may seek an *inter partes* proceeding before the TTAB in its trial capacity. 15 U.S.C. §§ 1063, 1064, 1092. The intervening party must have a reasonable basis for believing the registration will damage them and must show a "real interest" in the matter through a direct and personal stake in the outcome or a legitimate personal interest in the proceedings. *See, e.g., Ritchie v. Simpson,* 170 F.3d 1092, 1095 (Fed. Cir. 1999); *Meenaxi Enter., Inc. v. Coca-Cola Co.*, 38 F.4th 1067 (Fed. Cir. 2022) (foreign distribution of branded products sufficient for standing to challenge domestic trademark registrations, but lack of lost sales or reputational injury within the U.S. precludes § 14(3) reputational injury or a § 43(a) cause of action). Neither the claim itself nor actual damages must be proven to establish standing. *Enbridge, Inc. v. Excelerate Energy L.P.*, 92 USPQ2d 1537, 1543 n.10 (TTAB 2009).

A contested hearing may be held as an opposition, cancellation, interference, or concurrent use proceeding. An opposition proceeding contests a trademark's registration after publication for opposition in the USPTO's *Official Gazette* but before the mark is registered. Cancellation proceedings are brought against registered marks. Interference proceedings are brought by owners of conflicting trademark applications to determine whether either may be registered. Concurrent use proceedings are similar to interference proceedings but may allow more than one party to register the same or similar trademarks under certain conditions or limitations.

The TTAB has jurisdictional limits as an administrative law body. For example, the TTAB cannot declare any portion of the Lanham Act or other statute unconstitutional. *See, e.g., In re District of Columbia,* 101 USPQ2d 1588, 1602 (TTAB 2012).

Likewise, the TTAB cannot adjudicate trademark infringement or unfair competition claims.

There are two ways a TTAB final administrative decisions on a registration receives judicial review. The first is through direct appeal to the U.S. Court of Appeals for the Federal Circuit. This court was created in 1982 to assume the old Court of Customs and Patent Appeals and Court of Claims' jurisdiction. It essentially reviews the closed USPTO administrative proceedings record, much as an appellate court reviews a trial court's record. Another review path is through filing a civil action in federal district court for a de novo proceeding. This path also allows infringement litigation and permits entering new evidence into the record. A TTAB decision may establish the basis for issue preclusion in federal courts, depending on other requirements and if the TTAB used the same material factors to evaluate a likelihood of confusion. *B&B Hardware v. Hargis Indus.*, 575 U.S. 138 (2015). Federal district court proceedings may be appealed to the federal courts of appeals.

The Trademark Modernization Act of 2020 created an *ex parte* reexamination protocol allowing Lanham Act § 1(a) use-base registration challenges. The Act also created an *ex parte* expungement protocol allowing challenges to trademarks never used in commerce under § 44(e) or § 66(a). The USPTO Director may also instigate a nonuse proceeding on their own initiative. Any party can make these challenges, but the opportunity expires if the trademark was registered for at least five years. A registrant's successful defense will have preclusive effect against further *ex parte* challenges. A registrant's loss means the challenged goods or services are be stricken from the registration, subject to appeal before the TTAB.

Federal registration confers many benefits. Acceptance to the Principal Register constitutes nationwide constructive notice of trademark usage, and thus confers nationwide protection. Principal Register registration also constitutes prima facie evidence, in any subsequent proceedings, of the registrant's exclusive right to use the mark in commerce. After five years the prima facie right can become incontestable with compliance with certain formalities, with some limitations. Federal courts have jurisdiction over infringement actions involving federally registered marks, regardless of the amount in controversy. The registrant has the right to *ex parte* seizure of goods bearing a counterfeit mark, which the Act defines as "a spurious designation that is identical with or substantially indistinguishable from a registered mark." 15 U.S.C. § 1127 (2006). A registrant also has the right to treble damages and attorney's fees against those intentionally using a counterfeit mark, absent extenuating circumstances. There are also severe criminal penalties for using counterfeit marks. *See* 18 U.S.C. § 2320. Finally, the Principal Register gives a registrant the right to have the Bureau of Customs exclude imports bearing marks that would infringe upon the registered mark.

While one may not secure a federal trademark registration for a trade name, the Lanham Act provides trade names with certain other protections. If a trade name identifies goods or services as well as a business, it can be registered as a trade or service mark. A trade name owner may also: oppose a confusingly similar mark's registration, § 2(d), 15 U.S.C. § 1052(d); prevent a trademark that received federal registration from becoming incontestable, § 15, 15 U.S.C. § 1065; prevent importation of articles which copy or simulate the name, § 42, 15 U.S.C. § 1124; or bring a federal civil action against anyone using in commerce a false designation of origin or a false or misleading description or representation of fact, § 43, 15 U.S.C. § 1125. *See* Ch. 8, *infra*. Section 44 of the Lanham Act provides explicit protection for trade names owned by nationals of certain treaty participants.

(2) State Trademarks

State trademark registration statutes generally follow the Model State Trademark Bill, drafted by the U.S. Trademark Association (now the International Trademark Association). The Model Bill in turn is largely based on the Lanham Act. These statutes are for trademarks not used in interstate or foreign commerce and therefore not eligible for federal registration. Most states do not register trade names.

In contrast to federal registration, state registration may or may not confer advantages over common-law protection. *See, e.g., Burger King of Florida, Inc. v. Hoots*, 403 F.2d 904 (7th Cir. 1968) (state trademark registration did not give more protection than the common law and could not enlarge the common law to prohibit statewide use of a federally-registered mark). *But see Noah's, Inc. v. Nark, Inc.*, 560 F.Supp. 1253 (E.D. Mo. 1983) (senior user and prior federal registrant who abandoned nationwide rights still entitled to statewide trademark protection due in part to its registration under Iowa state law, holding registration constitutes "prima facie evidence of the . . . registrant's right to use the mark throughout the state"); *National Ass'n for Healthcare Commc'ns v. Central Arkansas Area Agency on Aging, Inc.*, 257 F.3d 732 (8th Cir. 2001) (injunction for state trademark infringement limited to a six-county area of actual use, but stating in dictum that a state registrant's expansion decision could oust defendant from the state).

At one time, the Model Bill's most important feature was the optional protection for registered and unregistered distinctive marks and trade names against "dilution." The Federal Trademark Dilution Act of 1995, as amended in 2006, now provides federal protection against dilution to "famous" marks. The Lanham Act's registration provisions allow opposition to or cancellation of a registration where a subsequent trademark may cause dilution under § 43(c). *See* 15 U.S.C. §§ 1052, 1063–64, 1092. *See also* Ch. 4(B)(2), *infra*.

State dilution statutes still provide important protections beyond federal law. Federal dilution laws have limited their preemption of state dilution law. *See* 15 U.S.C. § 1125(c)(6). Even so, state laws still risk preemption under the U.S. Constitution's Supremacy Clause if they undermine federal dilution policy. State laws must also avoid abridging free speech in violation of the First Amendment and so may require narrow construction.

(3) Common Law Trademarks

Common-law trademark or trade name rights creation is a default process providing limited protections. Establishing and maintaining common-law rights in a trademark, service mark, or trade name, requires the mark (1) be in actual use and associated with a good, service, or business; (2) possess sufficient inherent or acquired distinctiveness to identify the good, service, or business; and (3) be otherwise suitable for use as a trademark, service mark, or trade name. The Lanham Act adopts the same general requirements, with two limited exceptions: 1) an intent-to-use application establishes a constructive use date to determine ownership priority, and 2) a trademark registered in a country party to any trademark convention or treaty the U.S. joined can apply its foreign filing date for federal registration priority, whether or not the trademark was previously used in the U.S. *See* Paris Convention, Art. 4.

Common law trademarks create fact-intensive challenges for federal trademark registration holders. The United States recognizes senior user's common law trademark claim priority based upon the trademark's usage time rather than mere adoption. *See, e.g., Hannover Star Milling Co. v.*

Metcalf, 240 U.S. 403, 415 (1916); *United Drug Co. v. Theodore Rectanus Co.*, 248 U.S. 90, 97 (1918). Section 43(a) of the Lanham Act provides an analogous federal vehicle protecting unregistered trademarks from infringement, codifying the decision in *Two Pesos, Inc. v. Taco Cabana, Inc.*, 505 U.S. 763, 768 (1992).

Even an incontestable federal trademark registration holder may have challenges contending with a senior common law trademark holder. Section 15 of the Lanham Act, 15 U.S.C. § 1065, provides that a trademark registered and supported by the proper affidavits is incontestable "except to the extent, if any, to which the use of a mark registered on the Principal Register infringes a valid right acquired under the law of any State or Territory by use of a mark or trade name continuing from a date prior to the date of registration. . ." *See also Cuban Cigar Brands NV v. Upmann Intern., Inc.*, 457 F.Supp. 1090 (S.D.N.Y. 1978) (common law trademark holder can cancel an incontestable federal trademark that misrepresents the goods' source).

The common law usually limits its trademark protection to the region where the trademark is actually used, plus territories of natural expansion. *See, e.g., Dawn Donut Co. v. Hart's Food Stores, Inc.*, 267 F.2d 358 (2d Cir. 1959) (per se rule against injunctive relief where two businesses do not compete in the same geographic market because there is no likely confusion); *Food Fair Stores, Inc. v. Square Deal Market*, 206 F.2d 482 (D.C. Cir. 1953). The Internet eroded the importance of geographic remoteness, so long as the services offered are not tied to a geographic location. *Compare, Guthrie Healthcare Sys. v. Context Media, Inc.*, 826 F.3d 27 (2d Cir. 2016) (remanding to determine whether injunctive relief should include Internet use as online trademark use sufficient to cause likelihood of confusion), *with Tana v. Dantanna's*, 611 F.3d 767 (11th Cir. 2010) (restaurants can coexist in remote markets, as both websites show unrelated businesses).

(4) Foreign Trademarks

Foreign trademark registrations can receive federal registration when the United States and the owner's country of origin are party to an international trademark convention. The mark's foreign filing date will be the constructive U.S. filing date for priority. *See* 15 U.S.C. § 1126.

Foreign trademarks or trade names may obtain domestic registration on the Principal Register without proof of actual use in the United States or anywhere else in the world. This frequently applies to both the mark itself and the international classes of goods or services the mark protects. The foreign mark must, however, possess sufficient inherent or acquired distinctiveness to identify a specific product or service and must otherwise be suitable for trademark use. The latter provision implements Article 4 of the International Convention for the Protection of Industrial Property (the Paris Convention) and similar treaties where the U.S. is a signatory.

Addressing the numerous inactive U.S. trademarks registrations caused by these practices, the Trademark Modernization Act of 2020 now requires foreign and domestic registrants maintain their trademarks by making sworn statements of ongoing use in commerce or excusable nonuse under § 8 or § 71 of the Act. Excusable nonuse is not applicable for business decisions to discontinue use of a trademark, but does apply where trademark usage must cease due to government sanctions. *ARSA Distributing v. Salud Natural Mexicana,* 2022 USPQ2d 887 (TTAB 2022).

b. Actual or Intended Use

Acquiring and maintaining trademark or trade name rights requires actual and continuous use of the mark to identify goods, services, or a business. Prior use of an inherently distinctive mark dictates priority in rights—even for common-law marks that qualify for federal registration. Intent-to-use and foreign applications, however, can start a race to the USPTO.

While the Trademark Act does not define the term "service", courts determined that services eligible for trademark protection must be (1) a real activity, (2) performed to benefit someone other than the applicant, and (3) qualitatively different from activities necessarily performed in connection with selling the applicant's goods or performing other services. *In re Canadian Pac. Ltd.*, 754 F.2d 992, 224 USPQ 971 (Fed. Cir. 1985); *In re Advertising & Mktg. Dev., Inc.*, 821 F.2d 614, 2 USPQ2d 2010 (Fed. Cir.

1987) (considering a service as "the performance of labor for the benefit of another"). The key question is whether the service activity primarily benefits the trademark applicant or another person or entity. *Compare In re Venture Lending Assocs.*, 226 USPQ 285 (TTAB 1985) (granting protection for activities that primarily benefit others but incidentally benefit the trademark applicant) *with In re Dr. Pepper Co.*, 836 F.2d 508, 5 USPQ2d 1207 (Fed. Cir. 1987) (contest promoting applicant's goods not a protectable service, even though contest winners benefit). Note that a usage specimen for a service mark "must show an association between the mark and the services." *In re Keep A Breast Found.*, 123 USPQ2d 1869, 1876 (TTAB 2017).

Services considered routinely offered or expected when selling one's own goods or services are not eligible for trademark protection. *In re Landmark Commc'ns, Inc.*, 204 USPQ 692, 695 (TTAB 1979) (requiring a service "be qualitatively different from anything necessarily done in connection with the sale of goods" to be protectable). Therefore, advertising one's own goods or services is not itself a protectable service. *In re Reichhold Chems., Inc.*, 167 USPQ 376 (TTAB 1970). This principle applies to a variety of activities. *See, e.g., In re Alaska Nw. Publ'g Co.*, 212 USPQ 316 (TTAB 1981) (periodicals); *In re Dr. Pepper Co., supra,* (contests); *City Nat'l Bank v. OPGI Mgmt. GP Inc. / Gestion OPGI Inc.*, 106 USPQ2d 1668 (TTAB 2013) (operating an internal website).

A trademark or name's extent and duration of use need not be great, so long as it is used in the United

States and the good or service's sales are not just token or sporadic. The Trademark Revision Act of 1988 amended the Lanham Act to clarify "use in commerce" means bona fide trademark use in the ordinary course of trade. *See* 15 U.S.C. § 1126. So, token use no longer qualifies trademarks for federal registration by reserving rights in the mark. Likewise, another's token prior use of a mark cannot defeat federal registration priority. *See Zazu Designs v. L'Oreal, S.A.*, 979 F.2d 499 (7th Cir. 1992); *Paramount Pictures Corp. v. White*, 31 USPQ2d 1768 (TTAB 1994), *aff'd,* 108 F.3d 1392 (Fed. Cir. 1997) (advertising fliers insufficient to register a game); *Procter & Gamble Co. v. Johnson & Johnson, Inc.*, 485 F.Supp. 1185 (S.D.N.Y. 1979) (fifty product case shipment is nominal and not a bona fide attempt to establish meaningful trade). On the other hand, a "use in commerce" need not be a commercial use. *See Planetary Motion, Inc. v. Techsplosion, Inc.*, 261 F.3d 1188 (11th Cir. 2001) (open-source software distribution sufficient "transport" to be "use in commerce" for § 45 of the Lanham Act).

Courts may allow trademark holders to "tack" an earlier trademark's first use onto a subsequent mark. To do so, the marks must create the same continuing commercial impression and the later mark cannot materially differ from or alter the earlier mark's character. *Brookfield Commc'ns v. West Coast Ent. Corp.*, 174 F.3d 1036 (9th Cir. 1999). Courts also let mark holders claim priority based on "analogous use"—*e.g.*, prior use as a trade name, prior use analogous to a trademark or service mark, or any other use that sufficiently establishes proprietary rights. *Herbko Int'l. Inc. v. Kappa Books, Inc.*, 308 F.3d 1156 (Fed. Cir. 2002). *See also Aktieselskabet AF 21 November 2001 v. Fame Jeans*, 525 F.3d 8 (D.C. Cir. 2008) (activities other than sales themselves can establish "analogous use" for opposition, so long as analogous use is "of such a nature and extent as to create public identification of the target term with the opposer's product.").

In 1988, Congress amended the Lanham Act to create intent-to-use trademark applications for those with a bona fide intention to use a mark in commerce. Previously, federal trademark applicants had to establish they actually used a mark in commerce to receive protection. The intent-to-use filing offers applicants federal trademark review, potential approval, and some protection for a new trademark before the applicant commits substantial resources to the mark's development and use. An intent-to-use applicant must still show actual use for registration, but the initial application date remains the filing date for priority. *See* 15 U.S.C. §§ 1051, 1057. Domestic trademarks that can distinguish goods or services may also be registered in foreign countries despite not being used in the United States or having acquired a secondary meaning at the time of registration, just like foreign trademarks.

An accepted federal intent-to-use application gives the applicant six months to file a verified statement of use in commerce. This period can be extended by right for an additional six months and, upon good cause shown, may be extended for successive six-month periods aggregating not more than 24 months.

This allows the applicant a maximum of 36 months to begin using the mark in commerce. A junior user cannot prevent an intent-to-use trademark applicant from using the trademark by preliminary injunction even if the junior user first used the mark in commerce. *WarnerVision Ent. v. Empire of Carolina, Inc.*, 101 F.3d 259 (2d Cir. 1996).

c. Inherent and Acquired Distinctiveness

Where a trademark or name acquires distinctiveness (i.e., secondary meaning), priority of rights in the mark or name comes from priority in establishing secondary meaning rather than use. A trademark or name that is inherently unsuitable for use as a product, service, or business identifier will not receive protection even if it has acquired secondary meaning.

Trademarks and names have varying degrees of distinctiveness. This distinctiveness spectrum ranges from inherently distinctive to the completely generic. Trademarks and names that are fanciful or arbitrary receive the broadest protection. This protection diminishes for suggestive marks and diminishes further for merely descriptive marks that must acquire distinctiveness for protection. Trademarks or names inherently unsuitable for use receive no protection. These include generic or deceptive terms and functional product features. *See Abercrombie & Fitch Co. v. Hunting World, Inc.*, 537 F.2d 4 (2d Cir. 1976).

(1) Inherently Distinctive Marks and Names

Inherently distinctive trademarks (known at common law as "technical trademarks") are marks and names that are either *fanciful* (i.e., made-up terms) or *arbitrary* (i.e., common terms used in an uncommon way to identify a product, service, or business). Securing rights to fanciful or arbitrary terms should have little impact on competitors describing their own goods or services. Examples include the created term "Clorox" for bleach or using "Apple" for computers which are unrelated to fruit. An inherently distinctive mark or name receives common-law protection upon use. Inherently distinctive marks used in the U.S. or having a foreign registration may receive a federal registration.

Only "technical" (i.e., inherently distinctive) trademarks received federal registration under the 1905 Act. However, federal courts often strained to avoid classifying marks as descriptive (and hence not federally registrable). Courts thus developed a third category of inherently distinctive trademarks that were subsequently recognized by implication in the Lanham Act—namely marks which are suggestive rather than merely descriptive.

Suggestive trademarks hint at a product or service's characteristics without actually describing them. Lanham Act § 2(e), 15 U.S.C. § 1052(e) only denies federal registration to "merely descriptive" marks without proof of distinctiveness. *Compare, Franklin Knitting Mills, Inc. v. Fashionit Sweater Mills, Inc.*, 297 F. 247 (S.D.N.Y. 1923) ("Fashion Knit" not entitled to registration under the 1905 Act as descriptive of knitted sweaters) *with Minnesota Mining and Mfg. Co. v. Johnson & Johnson*, 454 F.2d 1179 (CCPA 1972) ("Skinvisible" suggestive rather than "merely descriptive" of bandage tape and thus registrable under the Lanham Act without proof of secondary meaning). *See also Investacorp, Inc. v. Arabian Inv. Banking Corp. (Investcorp) E.C.*, 931 F.2d 1519 (11th Cir. 1991) (competitors' commercial usage is relevant to the distinctiveness inquiry).

(2) Descriptive Marks and Names

Descriptive trademarks now receive federal and common-law protection. The distinction between suggestive and descriptive marks remains an important separation between inherently distinctive marks and names and those that must prove distinctiveness. Inherently distinctive marks and names, including suggestive ones, receive legal protection and priority merely upon proof of use in identifying goods, services, or a business. Descriptive marks and names, however, receive protection and priority only upon showing they acquired a "secondary meaning"—that is, the consuming public associates the mark with a particular company, product, or service.

The term "secondary meaning" can be misleading. A trademark or name's meaning is secondary only in that it is a new meaning given to a trademark or name with an older "primary" meaning. To receive trademark protection, the mark or name's new or "secondary" meaning must be the primary meaning the public usually attaches to the mark. Due to the inherent ambiguity in the term "secondary meaning," § 2(f) of the Lanham Act simply requires a descriptive mark "become distinctive" of the applicant's products in commerce for registration. 15 U.S.C. § 1052(f).

The line between suggestive and descriptive marks and names can be difficult to draw. Courts test whether the mark "requires imagination, thought and perception to reach a conclusion as to the nature of the product or service." *Compare Maidenform, Inc. v. Munsingwear, Inc.*, 195 USPQ 297 (S.D.N.Y. 1977) ("Underneath It All" for undergarments requires such imagination) *with Zatarains, Inc. v. Oak Grove Smokehouse, Inc.*, 698 F.2d 786 (5th Cir. 1983) ("Fish-Fri" and "Chick-Fri" for fried food batter mixes does not require such imagination).

Another approach considers the burden that trademark protection would place on others describing their own goods, services, or business. The secondary meaning requirement essentially protects company and consumer rights to use common descriptive words and symbols. A merely descriptive trademark may describe the product itself or the intended use or purpose of the product which includes other goods associated with the product's use. *In re Zuma Array Ltd.*, 2022 USPQ2d 736 (TTAB 2022).

Established secondary meaning is a factual question the trademark applicant must prove. Direct or circumstantial evidence may show proof of secondary meaning. The most comprehensive (and expensive) direct evidence form is a consumer survey, properly designed and conducted. Expert testimony, and even testimony from random purchasers can be sufficient proof. Circumstantial evidence can also establish secondary meaning, such as through advertising expenditures and the duration of the trademark's use. *See, e.g., International Kennel Club of Chicago, Inc. v. Mighty Star, Inc.*, 846 F.2d 1079 (7th Cir. 1988) (upholding preliminary injunction upon finding a good chance that a descriptive mark acquired secondary meaning through substantial advertising and publicity, industry activities, and fifty years of use). *But see Aromatique, Inc. v. Gold Seal, Inc.*, 28 F.3d 863 (8th Cir. 1994) (consumer association of a trademark or trade dress with a source cannot be inferred from the product's success or a competitor copying the original product; other circumstantial evidence is required). The USPTO may accept proof of a trademark or name's substantially exclusive and continuous use for five years prior to applying for protection on the Principal Register as prima facie evidence that a mark became distinctive. *See* 15 U.S.C. § 1052(f).

The descriptive trademarks and names category covers many terms that cannot identify a product, service, or business on their own. A descriptive mark may allude to the intended use, users, merit, or experience of using the product, services, or business. Descriptive trademarks often invoke a specific characteristic, component, or geographic origin a good, service, or business. Personal names are not considered inherently distinctive and so must show secondary meaning to receive trademark protection.

Geographically descriptive marks can be distinguished from other descriptive marks only insofar as the Lanham Act draws a meaningful distinction between "merely" descriptive marks and "primarily" geographically descriptive marks. The terminology suggests trademarks are geographically descriptive if their primary (but not necessarily sole) function describes or invokes a particular location. A geographic mark should be rejected as descriptive when the U.S. public generally knows the location, the term's geographic significance is its primary significance, and the goods originate from the geographic region. *In re Handler Fenton Ws., Inc.*, 214 USPQ 848, 849 (T.T.A.B. 1982). An acceptable geographic mark's geographic meaning is minor, obscure, remote, or ordinarily unconnected in the public mind with the goods or services. *See In re Newbridge Cutlery Co.*, 776 F.3d 854 (Fed. Cir. 2015) for a history of geographic mark protection. When a term is primarily geographically descriptive and does not identify a particular company, local businesses may bring a false advertising lawsuit against a company that falsely represents its products as coming from that locale. (*See* Ch. 8, *infra*.)

Connecting a personal name with a product, service, or business does not inherently connect it with a single source since more than one person may use the same name. Accordingly, the common law does not grant trademark protection to personal names without proof of secondary meaning. *But cf. Peaceable Planet, Inc. v. Ty, Inc.*, 362 F.3d 986 (7th Cir. 2004) ("Niles" for toy camels is a suggestive term rather than a personal name). Similarly, § 2(e) of the

Lanham Act, 15 U.S.C. § 1052(e), denies Principal Register protection for a name that is "primarily merely a surname" without proof of distinctiveness. *See In re Rath*, 402 F.3d 1207 (Fed. Cir. 2005) (foreign registration that is primarily merely a surname not "eligible" for registration under Lanham Act § 44(e) unless it satisfies the §§ 2(e) and (f) requirements). *But see* concurring opinion of Judge Bryson, offering a more plausible interpretation of § 44(e) by suggesting "eligible" refers to § 44(b) eligibility. Although applicants must establish a surname acquired secondary meaning, the USPTO must first prove a word is in fact "primarily merely" a surname.

Statutory language sheds no light on how a name can be both "primarily" and "merely" a surname. The purchasing public's perception of a word's primary significance determines whether the word is merely a surname. *See, e.g., Ex parte Rivera Watch Corp.*, 106 USPQ 145 (Comm'r Pat. 1955) (the average consuming public member would not consider "Rivera" merely a surname). Where a surname predominates a trademark, the mark will lack inherent distinctiveness and thus require proof of secondary meaning for federal registration. *But see, e.g., In re Hutchinson Tech., Inc.*, 852 F.2d 552 (Fed. Cir. 1988), where despite the USPTO examiner's telephone directories citations containing over 200 "Hutchinson" surname entries and assertion that "technology" was merely descriptive, the "Hutchinson Technology" mark for a Hutchinson, Minnesota company's goods was found not primarily merely a surname. Generally, adding a first name to a surname or hyphenating two surnames may allow registration without proof of secondary meaning. Merely adding initials to a surname is less successful.

Historical names, such as "Benjamin Franklin", may be used as a trademark, service mark, or trade name without proof of secondary meaning so long as the mark neither disparages nor falsely suggests a connection with a living or deceased person. *See* Lanham Act, § 2(a), 15 U.S.C. § 1052(a); *Lucien Piccard Watch Corp. v. 1868 Crescent Corp.*, 314 F.Supp. 329 (S.D.N.Y. 1970) ("Da Vinci" for jewelry); *In re Pyro-Spectaculars*, 63 USPQ 2d 2022 (TTAB 2002) ("Sousa" for fireworks). Apparently recognized historical names are understood to function as a trademark, trade name, or service mark.

Failure to secure another living person's consent to use their name or likeness as a mark may constitute common-law invasion of privacy or publicity. *See, e.g., In re Hoefflin*, 97 USPQ2d 1174, 1176 (TTAB 2010); *Hirsch v. S.C. Johnson & Son, Inc.*, 280 N.W.2d 129 (Wis. 1979) ("Crazylegs" trademark an actionable appropriation of a famous athlete's nickname and common-law trade name); *but see In re Hearst Commcn's State Right of Publicity Statute Cases,* No. 21–cv–8895 (RA) (S.D.N.Y. Dec. 19, 2022) (non-trademark case where selling subscriber lists does not infringe consumers' rights of publicity or misappropriate their identities). *See generally,* Ch. 6, *infra*.

The Lanham Act explicitly mentions slogans as entitled to Supplemental Register registration only in the § 23 trademark definition and the § 45 service mark definition. Still, courts hold even lengthy slogans may appear as trademarks on the Principal Register. A sufficiently imaginative slogan (*e.g.*, having a double entendre) may be registered without proof of distinctiveness. Purely laudatory or descriptive slogans, however, require proof of secondary meaning.

A "family" of trademarks can acquire distinctiveness through a familiar pattern of terms. To be a family, the trademarks must (1) have a recognizable common characteristic, (2) be distinctive, and (3) be promoted in such a way as to create "recognition among the purchasing public that the common characteristic is indicative of a common origin of the goods or services." *In re LC Trademarks, Inc.*, 121 USPQ2d 1197 (TTAB 2016). *See also J & J Snack Foods Corp. v. McDonald's Corp.*, 932 F.2d 1460, 18 USPQ2d 1889 (Fed. Cir. 1991). If third parties often use the common characteristic in their own trademarks, an applicant cannot claim it as a family of marks. *See, e.g., Land-O-Nod Co. v. Paulison*, 220 USPQ 61 (TTAB 1983). The TTAB previously held that while asserting the family of marks doctrine was permissible in *inter partes* proceedings, it was barred from *ex parte* proceedings since the USPTO lacked resources to determine how the alleged family of marks was used in the marketplace. *In re Hitachi High-Technologies Corp.*, 109 USPQ2d 1769 (TTAB 2014). The TTAB later allowed this doctrine as evidence to help show acquired distinctiveness of new family members under § 2(f). *In re LC Trademarks, Inc., supra.*

(3) Misdescriptive Marks and Names

While treated as descriptive marks, some trademarks and names *misdescribe* a product, service, or business in a nonobvious but harmless way. Lanham Act § 2(e) refers to these trademarks as "deceptively misdescriptive" marks. *See* 15 U.S.C. § 1052(e). These marks are distinguished from "deceptive" marks that are not suitable for use as trademarks and thus not federally registrable. *See* Lanham Act, § 2(a), 15 U.S.C. § 1052(a).

A deceptively misdescriptive mark may receive trademark protection if the misdescription does not affect a consumer's decision or preference and is thus not materially deceptive. Unlike an obviously misdescriptive (and hence arbitrary) mark, however, a deceptively misdescriptive mark *appears* to describe a product or service. Thus, the mark is no more distinctive than an accurate description and must acquire secondary meaning before it can be protected or registered. Deceptively misdescriptive marks must also show secondary meaning for registration. *See, e.g., Gold Seal Co. v. Weeks*, 129 F.Supp. 928 (D.D.C. 1955) (refusal of "GLASS WAX" for substance containing little or no wax upheld as it was deceptively misdescriptive without showing acquired secondary meaning).

There is a similar distinction between arbitrary, deceptively misdescriptive, and deceptive geographic terms. Geographic terms that are either obviously misdescriptive or primarily deceptively misdescriptive may receive trademark protection. *Compare, In re Amerise*, 160 USPQ 687 (TTAB 1969)

("Italian Maide" not obviously misdescriptive as to constitute an arbitrary geographic term use, nor deceptive, without proof of a discernible consumer preference for Italian vegetables) *with In re Nantucket, Inc.*, 677 F.2d 95 (CCPA 1982) (reversing denial of "Nantucket" as primarily geographically deceptively misdescriptive trademark without indication that the public expects men's shirts originate from Nantucket Island).

International trade agreement compliance subsequently limited this principle. TRIPS Agreement Articles 22 and 23 require certain geographical origin indicator protections, particularly for wines and spirits. The North American Free Trade Agreement contains similar provisions. Congress therefore amended Lanham Act § 2(a), prohibiting geographical indication registrations used on or in connection with wines or spirits that identify a place other than the goods' origin. Congress also amended Lanham Act §§ 2(e) and (f) to altogether prohibit registering primarily geographically deceptively misdescriptive marks. *But see In re California Innovations, Inc.*, 329 F.3d 1334 (Fed. Cir. 2003) (USPTO must deny registration if 1) the mark's primary significance is a generally known geographic location, 2) the consuming public likely believes the identified place indicates the goods' origin when the goods originate elsewhere, and 3) the misrepresentation was a material factor in the consumer's purchasing decision).

Notwithstanding the CAFC's decision, the Lanham Act §§ 2(e) and (f) amendments arguably were not designed to safeguard consumers. Rather, the amendments reserving geographic terms for use as geographical origin indications should prospectively bar deceptively misdescriptive geographical terms regardless of whether consumers find the deception material. For example, neither the foregoing changes in the Lanham Act nor Articles 22 and 23 of the TRIPS Agreement apply to using European geographic indications (*e.g.*, "champagne") that have long been used as generic terms in the U.S. The amended §§ 2(e) and (f) merely recognize European efforts (predominantly French) to secure international protection for geographical origin indications, including those for wines and other agricultural products.

The United States provided indirect protection for geographical indications even before the Lanham Act §§ 2(e) and (f) amendments. Section 4 of the Lanham Act, 15 U.S.C. § 1064, permits descriptive geographic term registrations certification marks without proof of secondary meaning. *See Community of Roquefort v. William Faehndrich, Inc.*, 303 F.2d 494 (2d Cir. 1962). Certification marks may be canceled, however, if they do not continuously meet the Lanham Act's strict standards. Section 14(5) of the Act, 15 U.S.C. § 1064(5), allows any individual who believes they will be damaged by a certification mark registration to petition for the mark's cancellation if the registrant (1) does not control or cannot legitimately exercise control over the mark, (2) produces or markets any goods or services where the certification mark is applied, (3) permits the certification mark's use for purposes other than to certify, or (4) discriminately refuses certification (new or ongoing) to any goods or services that maintain the standards or conditions the mark certifies.

(4) Trade Dress and Other Protections for Distinctive Product and Business Features

Trade dress is a symbol or device that conveys a product or service's source or origin. Trade dress protection usually requires proof of secondary meaning. Common trade dress examples include distinctive product designs, packaging, service uniforms, vehicles, business premises, or literary or artistic titles or characters. Trade dress protections balance protectable elements identifying the good or service's source or origin against functional elements that must remain generally available for market competition.

Functionality tests distinguish protectable products and business features from competitively necessary ones. *See generally, Inwood Labs. v. Ives Labs.*, 456 U.S. 844 (1982); *Qualitex Co. v. Jacobson Prods. Co.*, 514 U.S. 159 (1995) (dictum); Lanham Act § 1052(e)(5). Even utilitarian or aesthetic product features can be functional. For example, a red, heart-shaped box for Valentine's Day candy is just as functional as a wrench's shape. *Compare, Int'l Order of Job's Daughters v. Lindeburg & Co.*, 633 F.2d 912 (9th Cir. 1980) (fraternal organization insignia on jewelry a functional aesthetic component not subject to trademark protection) *with In re Morton-Norwich Prods., Inc.*, 671 F.2d 1332 (C.C.P.A. 1982) (spray bottle shape that also held a design patent not *de jure* functional). *See also, In re Palacio Del Rio, Inc.*, 2023 USPQ2d 640 (TTAB 2023) (drawings of a common hotel building design are not inherently distinctive and lacked secondary meaning).

As the Supreme Court noted in *Inwood Labs.* and *Qualitex,* a product feature is functional if it is "essential to the use or purpose of the article or if it affects the cost or quality of the article—that is, if exclusive use of the feature would put competitors at a significant non-reputation-related disadvantage." In *Qualitex,* the Court cited the Restatement (Third) of Unfair Competition (§ 17, Comment c) that a design is functional if the design's aesthetic value lies in its ability to confer a significant benefit that alternative designs cannot practically duplicate. *See also, Ezaki Glico v. Lotte Int'l Am. Corp.,* 977 F.3d 261 (3d Cir. 2020) (partial chocolate covering on snack useful and therefore functional). While many sensory inputs receive trademark or trade dress protection, functionality limitations generally preclude trademarks for flavors. *See, e.g., In re N.V. Organon,* 79 USPQ2d 1639 (TTAB 2006); *New York Pizzeria, Inc. v. Syal,* 56 F.Supp.3d 875 (S.D. Tex. 2014).

Historically, trade dress rarely fits well within the common law's technical trademark and trade name definitions. Courts previously treated trade dress protection as an unfair competition law branch. The USPTO and the federal courts were likewise slow to grant trade dress federal trademark protection.

This conservative position changed following a series of Supreme Court decisions. In *Two Pesos, Inc.*

v. Taco Cabana, Inc., 505 U.S. 763 (1992), the Supreme Court rejected previous lower court decisions requiring proof of secondary meaning in all trade dress cases. Instead, the Court held trade dress could be inherently distinctive under Lanham Act § 43(a) when granting protection for a particular restaurant design. In *Qualitex Co. v. Jacobson Prods. Co.*, 514 U.S. 159 (1995), the Court held color alone can meet trademark registration requirements after noting valid trademark registrations existed for sound, product packaging, and scent.

Lower court responses to these trade dress cases likely led to subsequent Supreme Court decisions encouraging greater attention to functionality limitations. In *Wal-Mart Stores v. Samara Bros. Inc.*, 529 U.S. 205 (2000), the Court unanimously held product design (as opposed to packaging) is distinctive and thus protectable under Lanham Act § 43(a) only upon showing secondary meaning. The Court added that in close cases, courts should err towards classifying trade dress as product design to prevent conflict with federal patent and copyright law policies. Thus, trade dress frequently requires proof of secondary meaning. *But see, In re Seminole Tribe of Florida*, 2023 USPQ2d 631 (TTAB 2023) (guitar-shaped building similar to product packaging and eligible for registration without proving acquired distinctiveness). Likewise, in *TrafFix Devices, Inc. v. Mktg. Displays, Inc.*, 532 U.S. 23 (2001), the Supreme Court held one seeking trade dress protection for a product feature subject to an expired patent claim, "must carry the heavy burden of showing that the feature is not functional, for instance, by showing that it is merely an ornamental, incidental, or arbitrary aspect of the device."

Common-law courts have long struggled with how much to protect product features from duplication. Some tried balancing public protection from deception against allowing duplication of unpatented and uncopyrighted product features. Other courts, influenced by the emerging misappropriation tort (*see* Ch. 6, *infra*) were less willing to protect copying. The Supreme Court eventually considered whether federal patent law conflicted with state unfair competition law, when the latter imposes liability for or prohibits copying an article protected by neither a federal patent nor a copyright. *See Sears, Roebuck & Co. v. Stiffel Corp.*, 376 U.S. 225 (1964) (unpatented article may be freely copied, but state laws may require precautions preventing source deception); *Compco Corp. v. Day-Brite Lighting, Inc.*, 376 U.S. 234 (1964) (state law cannot prevent copying an article unprotected by patent or copyright); Ch. 1, *supra*.

As sweeping as the *Sears-Compco* decisions appeared, they left considerable room for continued state protection of distinctive product features. The Court noted in dictum, for example, that just as a state "may protect businesses in the use of their trademarks, labels or distinctive dress in the packaging of goods," so it "may, in appropriate circumstances, require that goods, whether patented or unpatented, be labeled or that other precautionary steps be taken to prevent customers from being misled as to the source of goods and may impose liability on those who violate such requirements." This dictum also suggests a distinction between preventing product copying and preventing copying a container or packaging. However the *Sears-Compco* cases may have affected common law misappropriation (*see* Ch. 6, *infra*), the cases merely placed *remedial* limitations on state powers to prevent palming off. They did not altogether abolish state power protecting distinctive product features.

The *Sears-Compco* cases also let states protect distinctive product and packaging features where such protection did not in fact conflict with federal law. While the 1976 Copyright Act expressly preempted state law granting equivalent copyright protections, it expressly permitted state protection with respect to (1) subject matter not covered by the Act or (2) extending rights not equivalent to those created by the Act. *See* Ch. 6, *infra*.

The *Sears-Compco* also permit federal trademark protection for distinctive product and business features. For a time, some lower courts viewed *Sears-Compco* as asserting the Constitution's patent and copyright clause limited any government's powers—federal or state—to prevent simulation of unpatented articles. The prevailing view holds federal patent law preempts state unfair competition law where they conflict. The Supreme Court adopted this perspective in *Goldstein v. California*, 412 U.S. 546 (1973). Thus, the federal government may prohibit or otherwise regulate product and business imitation. Such regulation must be within the government's constitutional powers to grant patents and copyrights or regulate commerce and cannot conflict with other constitutional limitations like the First Amendment. The *Goldstein* ruling led the way for the Supreme Court's federal trade dress protection rulings in *Two Pesos* (1992) and *Qualitex* (1995).

Guided by the Supreme Court's trade dress rulings in *Qualitex* (1995), *Wal-Mart* (2000), and *TrafFix Devices* (2001), the USPTO required proof of secondary meaning before registering a product design. *But see, In re Forney Indus.*, 955 F.3d 940 (Fed. Cir. 2020). Courts consider various elements such as whether the trade dress is a basic shape or design, unique or unusual in the industry, whether it is a common ornamentation, and whether the trade dress can create a commercial impression distinct from the accompanying words. *See, e.g., Seabrook Foods, Inc. v. Bar-Well Foods Ltd.*, 568 F. 2d 1342 (C.C.P.A. 1977).

The USPTO will also deny federal registration for "functional" product or packaging features. However, the USPTO has long held proof of such secondary meaning unnecessary where a container configuration or other trade dress form obviously only identifies the product or service's source. *See, e.g., In re Int'l Playtex Corp.*, 153 USPQ 377 (TTAB 1967).

(5) Literary Works and Characters

The USPTO was slow to permit trademark registrations for literary or artistic titles. No matter how arbitrary or fanciful the title of a single book, drama, movie, record, song, or broadcast radio or television program may be, acquired secondary meaning (i.e., an established association with the particular work) must be shown to register a title as a federal trademark or service mark. *See, e.g., Application of Cooper*, 254 F.2d 611 (CCPA 1958).

The CCPA indicated a greater willingness to grant trademark registration of literary or artistic *series* titles without proof of secondary meaning. Here, a series name more clearly functions as a trademark or service mark by indicating that each unit in the series has the same source. For similar reasons, the USPTO permitted registrations for fictitious performer and musical group names as service marks identifying the entertainment services rendered. *See, e.g., In re Folk*, 160 USPQ 213 (TTAB 1968); *In re Ames*, 160 USPQ 214 (TTAB 1968). Lanham Act § 45 specifically allows service mark registration for titles, character names, and other distinctive radio or television program features. *See* 15 U.S.C. § 1127. Following a determination that the Internet has significantly changed the marketplace for news, the TTAB determined newspaper column titles now constitute "separate goods in trade" that may receive trademark protection where before they were only considered portions of a publication. *In re The New York Times Co.*, 2023 USPQ2d 392 (TTAB 2023).

States can provide legal protection for individual literary and artistic titles through unfair competition common law. For the most part, that protection was a form of the common-law prohibition against palming off. Since common-law protection against palming off is not equivalent to federal copyright protections, states currently can protect authors from copying *per se* just as they can prevent dilution of distinctive trademarks and trade names. Where a literary or artistic title consists of a personal name, the title may also be subject to common-law publicity rights along with any First Amendment defenses. *See* Ch. 6, *infra*. Since trademark law protects literary work series titles, they likely are not eligible for common-law protections.

Literary and artistic characters, like literary and artistic titles, also receive common-law protection as a literary or artistic work's distinctive identifying features. *See, e.g., Fisher v. Star Co.*, 132 N.E. 133 (N.Y. 1921) (cartoon strip title and characters protectable upon showing acquired secondary meaning). This trademark protection extends to prominent show elements, and the artist need not file a trademark to receive this protection. *See Viacom Intern. v. IJR Capital Inv., LLC,* 891 F. 3d 178 (5th Cir. 2018) (Animated show established trademark ownership and distinctiveness of "The Krusty Krab" through sales and licensing in unrelated outlets, so another's use of the phrase would create likelihood of confusion).

Literary and artistic characters may also receive federal copyright protection. Cartoon characters in particular are clearly entitled to such protection. So long as it does not affect an object's operability, adding a cartoon character design to a product can even secure design patent protection for the character. (*See* Ch. 6, *infra.*) States may protect characters eligible for copyright or patent protection against deceptive imitation through unfair competition common law. However, the state protection against deception may not grant a right equivalent to copyright. States may thus require labeling, even if they may not prohibit copying.

d. Inherently Unsuitable Marks and Names

Trademarks and names requiring proof of secondary meaning are distinguished not only from inherently distinctive marks and names but also from those words, symbols, designs, and devices deemed wholly unsuitable for use as a trademark, service mark, or trade name. A mark or name may be unprotectable because it is confusing, or because it is a generic term, functional product, or business feature.

15 U.S.C. § 1052, which outlines statutorily prohibited subject matter, has undergone increased scrutiny and many historic prohibitions have been reversed as unconstitutional. Among the surviving prohibitions that are noted but not analyzed here is a refusal to register insignias of the United States, a State or municipality, or foreign nation.

(1) Generic Terms

Generic terms are nouns functioning as names for whole classes of products, services, or businesses. These terms cannot serve as trademarks or names since they do not identify a single source of origin. Lanham Act § 14(3), 15 U.S.C. § 1064(3), originally called these terms "common descriptive names." These terms were sometimes confused with § 2(e)'s reference to "merely descriptive" or "primarily geographically descriptive" terms. The Trademark Revision Act of 1988 addressed the problem by amending § 14(3), changing the term "common descriptive name" to "generic name."

Generic terms are usually distinguishable from descriptive terms. Descriptive terms are adjectives that commonly characterize a product, service, or business. These terms can acquire secondary meaning even though they still perform their descriptive function. However, a descriptive term can become a part of a larger generic term and thus become altogether unsuitable for trademark use. *See, e.g., A.J. Canfield Co. v. Honickman*, 808 F.2d 291 (3d Cir. 1986) ("chocolate fudge" generic rather than descriptive for soda so competitors can communicate that their product possesses a functional flavor characteristic); *Miller Brewing Co. v. G. Heileman Brewing Co., Inc.*, 561 F.2d 75 (7th Cir. 1977) ("light" and phonetic equivalent "Lite" are generic or common descriptive terms as applied to beer); *Genesee Brewing Co. v. Stroh Brewing Co.*, 124 F.3d 137 (2d Cir. 1997) ("honey brown" generic as applied to ales). *Cf. In re Seats*, 757 F.2d 274 (Fed. Cir. 1985) ("Seats" not generic as applied to ticket reservation service); *with Eastern Air Lines, Inc. v. New York Air Lines, Inc.*, 559 F.Supp. 1270 (S.D.N.Y. 1983) (while "shuttle" may have gained a specialized meaning denoting plaintiff's air services, the term retains its principal, generic, or descriptive meaning).

Geographic terms may likewise become part of a generic name and thus incapable of obtaining trademark protection. Examples include "French fries", "English horns", or "Danish pastries".

Website domain name trademarks have weakened some rules limiting generic trademarks. Companies selling goods and services online favor generic words as domain names to attract consumers and provide website addresses that are easy to remember. Some companies argue that the combination of a top-level domain name (TLD) such as ".com" with a generic or descriptive word or phrase can create a unique commercial source impression in the minds of consumers. The Trademark Trial and Appeal Board (TTAB) long held that generic TLDs do not have source-identifying significance. *See, e.g., In re Martin Container, Inc.*, 65 USPQ2d 1058 (TTAB 2002); *In re CyberFinancial.Net, Inc.*, 65 USPQ2d 1789 (TTAB 2002). Rather, TLDs were analogous to business forms and merely adding "company" or "corporation" to a generic term did not create trademark eligibility. *Goodyear's India Rubber Glove Mfg. Co. v. Goodyear Rubber Co.*, 128 U.S. 598 (1888).

Subsequent case law rejected this position. The Federal Circuit first created an "exceptional circumstance" carveout to the USPTO's rule. The Federal Circuit held the USPTO must evaluate a trademark's commercial impression as a whole, including the TLD indicator, as the TLD may render an otherwise descriptive term sufficiently distinctive for trademark registration. *In re Oppedahl & Larson LLP*, 373 F. 3d 1171, 1177 (Fed. Cir. 2004). While trademark applicants frequently claimed exceptional circumstances existed, such findings were rare.

Compare, In re Hotels.com, LP, 573 F.3d 1300 (Fed. Cir. 2009) (upholding refusal to register) *with In re Steelbuilding.com*, 415 F. 3d 1293 (Fed. Cir. 2005) (vacating registration refusal).

The Supreme Court took a broader view, holding a compound term is only generic if, taken as a whole, the term signifies a class of goods or services to consumers. *USPTO v. Booking.com B.V.*, 591 U.S. ___, 140 S. Ct. 2298 (2020) (finding a generic TLD combined with a generic term can create a protectable trademark, relying heavily on post-rejection consumer survey results). The Court rejected the USPTO's proposed *per se* generic rule for generic TLDs, favoring a fact-intensive inquiry. However, the dissent noted businesses could likely use generic domain name trademarks for anti-competitive purposes since trademarks prevent others from using substantially similar names, thereby granting a much stronger penumbra of protection that is ripe for abuse. *See also Advertise.com, Inc. v. AOL Advertising, Inc.*, 616 F. 3d 974 (9th Cir. 2010) (vacating preliminary injunction that prohibited use of ADVERTISE.COM or other designations confusingly similar to the ADVERTISING.COM mark). The majority asserted other trademark principles can offset such abuses.

Generic terms can sometimes originate as inherently distinctive (i.e., technical) trademarks and later acquire a generic meaning. This happens when the consuming public uses the trademark term as a synonym for the product or service rather than as an adjective to describe the source. Such use destroys the trademark's ability to identify a product or service's source or origin, ultimately limiting or ending the owner's trademark rights. *Compare, Kellogg Co. v. National Biscuit Co.*, 305 U.S. 111 (1938) ("Shredded Wheat" generic rather than descriptive) *with King-Seeley Thermos Co. v. Aladdin Indus., Inc.*, 321 F.2d 577 (2d Cir. 1963) (trademark rights in "Thermos" limited to exclusive right to use the word with its first letter capitalized). Other examples of original coined trademarks for new products that became generic include "aspirin", "cellophane", "escalator", "trampoline", and "yo-yo".

"Genericide" is the loss of a trademark's ability to designate the source or origin of a good or service. Genericide usually when a trademark owner does not take adequate steps to protect their rights in a particularly distinctive mark or name. Even so, genericide may occur despite the owner's diligent efforts. *See, e.g., The Murphy Door Bed Co. v. Interior Sleep Sys., Inc.*, 874 F.2d 95 (2nd Cir. 1989) (plaintiff's trademark policing held inconsequential when finding "Murphy bed" was a generic term to a majority of the public).

Unique patent-protected inventions bearing a single trademark originally experienced genericide once the patent expired, although these rules have since changed. In *Singer Mfg. Co. v. June Mfg. Co.*, 163 U.S. 169 (1896) the Court held a patent expiration made the term "Singer" enter the public domain along with the protected invention. This *Singer* doctrine created an irrebuttable presumption that where only one product brand was on the market, the public would necessarily use the trademark as a generic term for the product. Lanham Act § 14(3) originally provided for cancelling a registered mark if it became the "common descriptive name of an article or substance on which the patent has expired."

More recent cases and Lanham Act amendments now recognize the sole genericide question is how the consuming public views the trademarked term. In 1962, Congress endorsed this view by deleting the words specifying cancellation of a product trademark "on which the patent has expired" from the original Lanham Act § 14(c). Trademark management and policing enabled manufacturers of formerly patented products to retain or regain trademark rights after a patent expired. The most notable "recapture" example was the very trademark that created the *Singer* doctrine. *See Singer Mfg. Co. v. Briley*, 207 F.2d 519 (5th Cir. 1953) (manufacturer's efforts to re-educate the consuming public enabled trademark recapture from the public domain).

The Trademark Clarification Act of 1984 added the following language to what is now Lanham Act § 14(3), 15 U.S.C. § 1064:

> A registered mark shall not be deemed to be the common descriptive name of goods or services solely because such mark is also used as a name of or to identify a unique product or service. The primary significance of the registered mark to the relevant public rather than purchaser motivation shall be the test for determining whether the registered mark has become the

common descriptive name of goods or services in connection with which it has been used.

The definitions of "trade-mark" and "service mark" in § 45 of the Act, 15 U.S.C. § 1127, were likewise amended to explicitly include marks that identify a unique product or service. This legislatively overruled the decision in *Anti-Monopoly, Inc. v. Gen. Mills Fun Group, Inc.*, 684 F.2d 1316 (9th Cir. 1982), which invalidated registration of the "Monopoly" trademark for board games by finding a majority of consumers said the board game's maker would not affect their purchase, even though a majority of consumers linked the game with its single producer.

(2) Unrelated Registration of Expired Marks

A term or name may be held unsuitable for trademark protection because its resemblance to another previously used mark or name would likely cause confusion, mistake, or deception. *See* Lanham Act § 2(d), 15 U.S.C. 1052. Some judges and commentators assert § 2(d) grants greater protection to private property in a previously used trademark or trade name than granted by § 2(e) for publicly owned descriptive words or phrases. *See, e.g., Minn. Mining & Mfg. Co. v. Johnson & Johnson*, 454 F.2d 1179 (CCPA 1972) (opinion of Rich, J.). A majority of the court, however, asserted an opposer's § 2(e) right to protect their and the public's interest in using the allegedly descriptive term is no weaker than the § 2(d) right to protect a private property interest in a previously used mark or name. *See id.*, (opinions of Baldwin, J., Almond, J., and Lane, J.).

(3) Functional Product and Business Features

Functional products and business features, like generic terms, are deemed wholly unsuitable as trademarks or names. *But see U.S. Golf Ass'n v. St. Andrews Sys., Data-Max, Inc.*, 749 F.2d 1028 (3d Cir. 1984) (device calculating a golfer's handicap using a golfing organization's formula did not employ a false origin designation violating Lanham Act § 43(a), despite the public associating the formula with a golfing organization, since the formula was "functional"). *See also Wallace Int'l Silversmiths, Inc. v. Godinger Silver Art Co.*, 735 F.Supp. 141 (S.D.N.Y. 1990) (the aesthetic functionality doctrine prohibits trademark protection for basic silverware patterns, as finding otherwise would hinder competition by limiting the range of alternate designs).

Congress amended the Lanham Act in 1998 to explicitly state functional features are not registrable as trademarks (15 U.S.C. § 1052(e)(5)), that functional trademark registrations can be canceled at any time (15 U.S.C. § 1064(3)), and that functionality remains a defense even where a trademark is incontestable (15 U.S.C. § 115(b)(8)). The last amendment legislatively overruled *Shakespeare Co. v. Silstar Corp.*, 9 F.3d 1091 (4th Cir. 1993), which interpreted the Supreme Court's *Two Pesos* decision to hold a fishing rod's functional color scheme was an incontestable trademark.

A feature's functionality may depend on whether a product feature or some other trade dress is involved. Many businesses file product, service, or business feature trademarks on the Supplemental Register to resolve functionality questions before making expenditures to develop secondary meaning. Supplemental registration, it will be recalled, merely requires that a trademark or name be *capable* of distinguishing the applicant's goods or services. A USPTO finding of capacity to distinguish is equivalent to a non-functionality finding. If granted, the trademark will be eligible for the Principal Register after establishing secondary meaning.

Colors present unique functionality challenges. At one time, product color could not receive trademark protection as courts felt there are too few colors to reserve any one for a company's exclusive use. For example, a match manufacturer could not prevent another from using the same colors for fear that a few companies could appropriate the remaining colors and thus monopolize the industry even without a patent. *Diamond Match Co. v. Saginaw Match Co.*, 142 F. 727 (6th Cir. 1906). *See also Radio Corp. of Am. v. Decca Records, Inc.*, 51 F.Supp. 493 (S.D.N.Y. 1943) (no protection for red record label; *Application of David Crystal, Inc.*, 296 F.2d 771 (CCPA 1961) (no protection for red and blue bands on white socks). Product color cases at the time often hinged upon whether nonfunctional design elements added to the color element qualified for protection. However, registrations for colors used on packaging, business vehicles, and buildings faced less opposition.

Later cases held non-functional colors could receive trademark protection upon showing secondary meaning. *See, e.g. In re Owens-Corning Fiberglas Corp.*, 774 F.2d 1116 (Fed. Cir. 1985) (color pink for insulation). Multi-color marks used on product packaging may be inherently distinctive and so registerable without proof of acquired distinctiveness depending on the character of the color design, and no association with a specific peripheral shape is needed for a multi-color mark to be inherently distinctive. *In re Forney Indus., Inc.*, 955 F.3d 940 (Fed. Cir. 2020). Even so, functional colors remain unprotectable. *See Brunswick Corp. v. British Seagull, Ltd.*, 35 F.3d 1527 (Fed. Cir. 1994) (black is *de jure* functional for outboard motors); *Inwood Labs. v. Ives Labs., Inc.*, 456 U.S. 844 (1982) (affirming brand name drug capsule's color lacked secondary meaning and was functional). The Supreme Court's *Qualitex* decision in 1995 affirms this approach.

(4) Deceptive, Immoral, or Disparaging Marks and Names

The USPTO previously did not grant trademark protection to marks falsely suggesting a connection with, or bringing into contempt or disrepute, persons living or dead, institutions, beliefs, or national symbols. Lanham Act § 2(a), 15 U.S.C. § 1052(a). *Compare, In re Anti-Communist World Freedom Cong., Inc.*, 161 USPQ 304 (TTAB 1969) (refusing registration for mark disparaging a Soviet Union national symbol) *with In re Old Glory Condom Corp.*, 26 USPQ2d 1216 (TTAB 1993) (neither the word mark nor a condom resembling the U.S. flag were scandalous). *See also* Ch.4(A)(2)(b)(2), *supra*.

Section 2(a) of the Lanham Act prohibited registration of disparaging, deceptive, immoral, or scandalous matter. However, the Supreme Court determined that the prohibition against disparaging trademarks violated the First Amendment as viewpoint discrimination in *Matal v. Tam*, 582 U.S. 218 (2017). The prohibitions against registering immoral and scandalous trademarks suffered the same fate soon thereafter. *Iancu v. Brunetti,* 588 U.S. ___, 139 S. Ct. 2294 (2019). Even so, widespread use of scandalous terms erodes their suitability for trademark use creates challenges for establishing their ability to indicate the source of a good or service. *Compare, In re Erik Brunetti,* 2022 USPQ2d 764 (TTAB 2022) (denying common epithet), *with In re Lizzo LLC*, 2023 USPQ2d 139 (TTAB 2023) (popular lyric not a common expression).

(5) Living Persons or Deceased Presidents

Previously, unauthorized use of names or parts of names, portraits, or signatures of either living persons or deceased presidents whose spouses are still alive could not receive federal registration. *See* Lanham Act, § 2(c), 15 U.S.C. § 1052(c), *In re Masucci,* 179 USPQ 829 (TTAB 1973) (Rejecting "EISENHOWER" mark). However, a series of Supreme Court decisions favoring First Amendment rights over trademark restrictions beginning with *Matal v. Tam, infra,* indicated this law was disfavored.

Following this indication, the Federal Circuit reversed the USPTO's denial of a trademark utilizing a living president's name. *In re Elster*, 26 F.4th 1328 (Fed. Cir. 2022). The court held 15 U.S.C. § 1052(c) unconstitutional as the applicant's First Amendment interests regarding a public official (including parody, criticism, commentary on matters of public importance, or artistic transformation) outweighed the official's rights to control public expression about them in the marketplace. The court did, however, note in dicta that publicity and certain privacy right implications are limited by § 2(a) of the Lanham Act for false suggestion of a connection between the official and the source of a good or service.

3. TERMINATION OR TRANSFER OF RIGHTS IN A MARK OR NAME

Once obtained, trademark rights are perpetual and may be transferred from one party to another. The Lanham Act specifies trademark registrations may be canceled if a mark is abandoned or loses its distinctiveness. This can happen through misuse or non-use of a trademark by the owner, a transferee, or unauthorized users.

Federal and state courts adjudicate trademark infringement actions. Trademark owners may use USPTO administrative opposition or cancellation proceedings to contest federal registration of similar marks, while applicants may challenge the owner's rights and use of the mark. For arguably infringing foreign marks or names, a trademark owner may seek to bar importation of the goods. Such goods would bear trademarks or names that simulate a federally registered mark or copy a trade name of any domestic company or foreign company located in a country having trademark treaties with the U.S.

a. Termination by Non-Use or Misuse

Trademark abandonment occurs through non-use of the trademark or name or by its misuse causing the mark or name to lose its distinctiveness. Abandonment is essentially a trademark user's conduct that cancels a prerequisite for acquiring rights in the mark. In compliance with Article 19(1) of the TRIPS Agreement, Lanham Act § 45 specifies non-use for three consecutive years (prior to 1994, two) is prima facie evidence of abandonment. 15 U.S.C. § 1127.

Abandonment through non-use requires clearly manifested intent to permanently abandon rights in the trademark or name. Mere suspension in using a mark or name does not cause abandonment, such as temporary withdrawal from the marketplace due to business delays or difficulties. As one court put it, "We reject the view that the slightest cessation of use causes a trademark to roll free, like a fumbled football, so that it may be pounced upon by any alert opponent." *Cont'l Distilling Corp. v. Old Charter Distillery*, 188 F.2d 614 (D.C. Cir. 1950). Abandonment intent can be inferred from trademark non-use coupled with a failure to enforce rights against infringers, or from an extended non-use period.

While residual goodwill is not an abandonment defense, severely diminished but ongoing business operations may maintain trademark ownership rights. For example, a business closed for nine years avoided trademark abandonment by showing the business premises remained intact, pending sale as a going business, and that trademark use could resume on short notice. *Sterling Brewers, Inc. v. Schenley Indus., Inc.*, 441 F.2d 675 (CCPA 1971). *But see Exxon Corp. v. Humble Exploration Co., Inc.*, 695 F.2d 96 (5th Cir. 1983) (trademark use cessation for three years except for limited arranged product sales either bearing both old and new marks or on product invoices did not rebut abandonment presumption). *See also ITC Ltd. v. Punchgini, Inc.*, 482 F.3d 135 (2d Cir. 2007). *Compare, Major League Baseball Props., Inc. v. Sed Non Olet Denarius, Ltd.*, 817 F.Supp. 1103 (S.D.N.Y. 1993) (no preliminarily injunction against restaurant's use of "Brooklyn Dodger"), *with Indianapolis Colts v. Metropolitan Baltimore Football Club*, 34 F.3d 410 (7th Cir. 1994) (Baltimore Colts move to Indianapolis did not entitle the Canadian Football League to use "Colts" for its new Baltimore team).

Once a challenger establishes a *prima facie* abandonment case, the original trademark owner must prove they either used the trademark during the statutory period or intended to resume using it. *Crash Dummy Movie LLC v. Mattel Inc.*, 601 F.3d 1387, 94 USPQ2d 1315 (Fed. Cir. 2010). The *Mattel* case also notes the challenger ultimately must prove abandonment by a preponderance of the evidence. Subsequent trademark usage does not retroactively cure past abandonment. *Hornby v. TJX Co. Inc.*, 87 USPQ2d 1411, 1422 (TTAB 2008).

The Lanham Act abandonment presumption often requires *nationwide* non-use for the prescribed period. *See Dawn Donut Co. v. Hart's Food Stores, Inc.*, 267 F.2d 358 (2d Cir. 1959) (failure to license federal trademark in a given market area for over 30 years did not abandon the mark). Common-law trademark or trade name rights, on the other hand, may be abandoned through non-use in that area.

Trademark abandonment may also occur through misuse of a mark or name. Unlike abandonment through non-use, misuse need not be intentional. Abandonment through misuse may arise with substantial changes to the underlying product, service, or business. It can also come when the trademark owner or a competitor uses the mark as a generic product designation. *Bayer Co. v. United Drug Co.*, 272 F. 505 (S.D.N.Y. 1921).

Trademark misuse may also derive from changes in the format of the mark or name itself. Not every minor variation will constitute abandonment, though. The law allows for periodic modifications in the underlying product, service, or business. So long as these changes are not so extreme as to defraud the consuming public, they will not result in abandonment.

Modernizing a trademark may not lead to abandonment due to the "tacking" doctrine. This doctrine lets a trademark owner claim the same priority in a mark based on its prior use. The new trademark or name must create the same, continuing commercial impression and cannot materially differ from or alter the original one's character. Tacking is a question of fact reserved for a jury. *Hana Fin., Inc. v. Hana Bank*, 574 U.S. 418 (2015). A trademark applicant cannot establish priority for every good or service in their application using tacking from a single good or service. *Bertini v. Apple Inc.*, 2023 USPQ2d 407 (Fed. Cir. 2023).

The Lanham Act is particularly stringent in insisting that certification marks are not misused. Section 14(5) of the Act provides for cancelling a certification mark if the registrant does not control the mark's use, produces or markets any goods or services on which the mark is used, permits the mark's use for purposes other than certification, or discriminately refuses to certify goods or services meeting the registrant's standards. 15 U.S.C. § 1064.

b. Transfers

Trademarks and names cannot be transferred without the goodwill of the product, service, or business they symbolize. An attempt to transfer a mark or name without the symbolized goodwill is termed an "assignment in gross". Assignments in gross do not pass trademark rights to the assignee. The subject trademark may be considered abandoned by the assignor if they cease using the trademark after the assignment in gross.

The test of a valid trademark assignment is whether the assignee's products, services, or business substantially shares the same characteristics as those of the original mark or name. *See Sugar Busters LLC v. Brennan*, 177 F.3d 258 (5th Cir. 1999) (retail store featuring diabetic products and supplies and plaintiff's diet book not sufficiently similar). *But cf., Marshak v. Green*, 746 F.2d 927 (2d Cir. 1984) (management continuity a factor for determining assignment validity).

Assignments in gross are valid in some other nations, such as Japan. Article 21 of the TRIPS Agreement specifies "the owner of a registered trademark shall have the right to assign his trademark with or without the transfer of the business to which the trademark belongs." Whether this provision merely recapitulates or reverses the U.S. rule on assignments in gross remains to be seen.

Trademark licensing was initially inhibited by a view that trademarks designated a particular physical source of goods. Under that early view, trademark rights could not be transferred without transferring the source—i.e., selling the underlying business. Thus, assignment was the only proper way to transfer trademark rights. The law eventually recognized that trademarks and names can also function as a symbol of quality regardless of the product or service's source. Trademarks can now be licensed if the licensor exercises adequate quality control over the licensee's branded goods or services. Uncontrolled (or "naked") licensing, like assignments in gross, may cause the trademark to lose its significance and become abandoned.

There is no formal quality control standard to avoid naked licensing. Some courts find merely retaining quality control rights is sufficient, even if the licensor exercises no actual control. Others upheld licenses when the licensor simply relied on the licensee's voluntary quality control efforts. Most courts, however, hold a valid trademark or service mark license depends on the licensor's actual quality control. In addition to setting product specifications, a prudent trademark licensor enables and conducts periodic inspections to ensure consistent product quality. *See, e.g.*, *Barcamerica Int'l USA Trust v. Tyfield Imps., Inc.*, 289 F.3d 589 (9th Cir. 2002) (naked license found where the registrant played no meaningful role in holding licensee to any standard of quality—good, bad, or otherwise).

Too much quality control can create antitrust law challenges. A licensor who designates a specific source of supplies or ingredients to maintain quality control over the protected product risks charges for illegally tying a product's purchase to the trademark license. *See, e.g.*, *Siegel v. Chicken Delight, Inc.*, 448 F.2d 43 (9th Cir. 1971) (illegal tie-in where a fast food franchisor required franchisees purchase all equipment from the franchisor).

Bankruptcy often poses a challenge for trademark licensing agreements. A bankruptcy declaration allows a debtor to reject "executory" contracts, where both parties have continuing obligations and either's failure to perform would be a material breach excusing the other's performance. 11 U.S.C. § 365. This grants the debtor relief from unfavorable deals. The other contracting party receives an unsecured claim against the debtor as of the date just before the bankruptcy filing.

Intellectual property licensees receive certain protections under 11 U.S.C. § 365(n), such as retaining their rights to use the licensed intellectual property in return for continually making any required payments. This is particularly important for licenses requiring a substantial initial payment. However, a bankrupt licensor no longer needs to update or develop the intellectual property. Congress passed this provision to overturn *Lubrizol Enters. v. Richmond Metal Finishers*, 756 F.2d 1043 (4th Cir. 1985).

The 11 U.S.C. § 365(n) bankruptcy definition includes U.S. patents and patent applications, mask works, copyrights, and trade secrets, but glaringly omits trademarks. Even if intellectual property rights were bundled (conveying patent or copyright protections along with associated trademarks), the trademark license could still be stripped out in bankruptcy. *See, e.g., In re Centura Software Corp.*, 281 B.R. 660 (Bankr. N.D. Cal. 2002). Even so, the Supreme Court rejected any negative inference from this, holding a trademark licensee retains the right to either continue licensing the bankrupt licensor's mark by making payments or consider the contract breached based on 11 U.S.C. § 365(g). *Mission Prod. Holdings, Inc. v. Tempnology, LLC*, 587 U.S. ___, 139 S. Ct. 1652 (2019).

Courts generally will not allow a bankrupt licensee to assign a trademark license as part of an asset sale without the licensor's consent. *See, e.g., In re Rupari Holding Corp.*, 573 B.R. 111 (Bankr. D. Del. 2017); *In re Trump Ent. Resorts, Inc.*, 526 B.R. 116, 123–24 (Bankr. D. Del. 2015). The Bankruptcy Code prohibits such assignments based on applicable non-bankruptcy laws which include federal trademark law, although the parties may contractually avoid this requirement. 11 U.S.C. § 365(c)(1).

B. INFRINGING AND NON-INFRINGING USES

A prima facie trademark infringement case requires proof of: (1) plaintiff's priority in using the mark or name as a trademark, service mark, or trade name and (2) defendant's infringing use of an identical or confusingly similar mark or name. The Lanham Act's definition of "use in commerce" governs both plaintiff's and defendant's use in commerce, and "commerce" is broadly defined to mean all commerce which may lawfully be regulated by Congress. *See* Lanham Act §§ 32, 43(a), 15 U.S.C. §§ 1114, 1125(a). *Compare, International Bancorp, LLC v. Société des Bains de Mer et du Cercle des Etrangers a Monaco (SBM)*, 329 F.3d 359 (4th Cir. 2003) (Lanham Act's "use in commerce" requirement satisfied by the sale and advertising of gambling services to U.S. citizens, as Congress may lawfully regulate foreign trade), *with DaimlerChrysler AG v. Bloom*, 315 F.3d 932 (8th Cir. 2003) (defendant licensing a toll-free telephone number, without more, is not a "use in commerce" per the Lanham Act). However, §§ 1114(1) and 1125(a)(1) lack extraterritorial reach, so the relevant use in commerce is only domestic conduct and does not include foreign activities. *Abitron Austria GmbH v. Hetronic Int'l, Inc.*, 600 U.S. ___, 143 S. Ct. 2522 (2023).

Trademark infringement also requires the mark be used "in connection with" goods or services. Using a trademark to enhance Internet search results raises a difficult "use" question, as such trademark use is invisible to and thus does not confuse the consumer. Metatags are computer code elements on a website, not visible to users, that provide information to search engines categorizing the website. Using trademark-protected words or phrases as metatags may divert website traffic from the trademark owner's website to a competitor, but with a diminished likelihood of confusion among Internet users that never see the metatag.

Brookfield Commc'ns v. West Coast Ent., 174 F.3d 1036 (9th Cir. 1999) invoked "initial interest confusion" as a concept (an unfair promotional practice more popularly known as "bait and switch"—*see* Ch. 8 *infra*) to prohibit using another's trademark in metatags. *Brookfield* stated a consumer's potential diversion to another website created an actionable harm, even though the consumer was never confused about the diverting website's source since the diversion itself "misappropriates" the trademark owner's goodwill. *But cf.*, concurring opinion of Judge Berzon, criticizing failure to distinguish between confusing a consumer and simply offering the consumer an additional choice; *Bihari v. Gross*, 119 F.Supp.2d 309 (S.D.N.Y. 2000) (no initial interest confusion possible where trademark owner did not have a website). *See also Lamparello v. Falwell*, 420 F.3d 309 (4th Cir. 2005) (initial interest confusion doctrine should not apply to non-commercial "gripe sites").

Courts also disagree as to whether using trademark-protected words or phrases as keywords that trigger advertisements constitutes a trademark's "use in commerce" satisfying a "likelihood of confusion" analysis. *See North Am. Med. Corp. v. Axiom Worldwide, Inc.*, 522 F. 3d 1211 (11th Cir. 2008) (using another's mark as a metatag and website search results description is a use in commerce); *Rescuecom Corp. v. Google Inc.*, 562 F.3d 123 (2d Cir. 2009) (display, offer, and sale of another's mark as an Internet search term is a use in commerce); *but see Playboy Enter., Inc. v. Netscape Commc'n Corp.*, 55 F.Supp.2d 1070 (C.D. Cal. 1999) (no liability as protected words not "used" as trademarks).

Trademark use priority, as we have seen, has both temporal and territorial dimensions. Temporal priority in a trademark or name depends on whether the trademark's distinctiveness is inherent or acquired. Territorial priority depends on whether common-law or federal rights are asserted.

For inherently distinctive common-law marks and names, the first business using the trademark or name in a market area has priority of rights there. For common-law marks and names lacking inherent distinctiveness, the business whose mark or name first acquires secondary meaning in a market area has priority of rights in that area. Federal trademark registrations having inherent or acquired distinction establish nationwide rights in the mark. The registrant presumptively owns the mark throughout the country. However, senior common-law trademark owners can create limited exceptions to the registrant's priority by showing acquired priority in the same or a similar mark before the federal registration.

State trademark statutes may also consider whether dilution of a trademark or name occurs. Dilution occurs where another's use of the same or a similar trademark or name will likely diminish another trademark or name's distinctive quality, even when there is no likelihood of confusion. Congress amended the Lanham Act to provide federal protection against dilution of "famous" marks in 1996. Congress further amended the Lanham Act to provide protection against "cyberpiracy" in 1999, namely registering, trafficking, or using a website domain name that is dilutes or is confusingly similar to a trademark or personal name. *See*, 15 U.S.C. § 1125(d). Unlike ordinary trademark infringement, neither dilution nor cyberpiracy requires proving likelihood of consumer confusion. The following section separately discusses confusion and non-confusion-based trademark infringement theories.

Not every use of another's mark or name constitutes an infringement. Certain "collateral" (or "fair") uses are recognized as privileged. For example, a business that repackages or reconditions another company's products may leave the original product trademark on the altered goods so long as no deception results. *See, e.g., Champion Spark Plug Co. v. Sanders*, 331 U.S. 125 (1947) (refurbisher not required to cover original trademark where product is adequately identified as used); *Prestonettes, Inc. v.*

Coty, 264 U.S. 359 (1924) (repackaged products allowed to describe contents using the original designation, so long as the trademark in no way stands out from that statement of fact).

Similarly, one may use another's trademark in comparative advertising or advertising replacement parts for another's product. *See Smith v. Chanel, Inc.*, 402 F.2d 562 (9th Cir. 1968) (competitor's trademark can be used in comparative advertisements so long as the use is not a misrepresentation or create likelihood of confusion); *Am.-Marietta Co. v. Krigsman,* 275 F.2d 287 (2d Cir. 1960) (replacement sponge producer may advertise their product fits competitor's mops).

One may also make "nominative" fair use of another's trademark to identify the owner's product or service. In *The New Kids on the Block v. News Am. Publ'g, Inc.*, 971 F.2d 302 (9th Cir. 1992) a commercial user was entitled to a nominative fair use defense where 1) the product or service in question was not readily identifiable without using the mark; 2) only so much of the mark was used as reasonably necessary to identify the product or service; and 3) the user did nothing to suggest sponsorship or endorsement by the trademark holder. *Compare, Playboy Enter., Inc. v. Welles*, 279 F.3d 796 (9th Cir. 2002) (using trademarks as metatags, website masthead, and banner ads "nominative uses" when identifying "Playmate of the Year 1981"), *with Align Tech., Inc. v. Strauss Diamond Instruments, Inc.*, Case No. 18–cv–06663–TSH (N.D. Cal. Feb. 22, 2019) (using competitor's trademarks in hashtags not nominative fair use).

One may use another's trademark in good faith to identify or describe one's own product. *See* 15 U.S.C. § 1115(b)(4); *KP Permanent Make-up, Inc. v. Lasting Impression, Inc.*, 543 U.S. 111 (2004) (claimant must prove likelihood of confusion in prima facie case, while accused has no independent burden to negate the likelihood of confusion in raising fair descriptive use defense under § 33(b)(4); *International Stamp Art, Inc. v. United States Postal Serv.*, 456 F.3d 1270 (11th Cir. 2006) (no trade dress infringement as greeting cards made good faith descriptive use of only design feature able to evoke postage stamps).

Whether a nominative fair use defense is legally distinguishable from a descriptive fair use defense has split the courts. Courts have particular difficulty determining whether the nominative fair use defense is an affirmative defense or merely challenges a prima facie case of likely confusion. *Compare, New Kids, supra* (defenses distinguishable) *with Century 21 Real Estate Corp. v. Lendingtree, Inc.*, 425 F.3d 211 (3d Cir. 2005) (for both defenses, defendant must merely prove use of some portion of the plaintiff's marks is necessary to describe the defendant's own product or service and that the defendant's conduct or language reflects the true and accurate relation between the products or services).

Where a marketplace operates as a neutral intermediary between third-party vendors and consumers, courts generally do not find the operator liable for sales of infringing goods. *See, e.g., Tiffany*

(NJ) Inc. v. eBay Inc., 600 F.3d 93, 103 (2d Cir. 2010); *Multi Time Mach., Inc. v. Amazon.com, Inc.*, 804 F.3d 930 (9th Cir. 2015); *but see Lorillard Tobacco Co. v. Amouri's Grand Foods, Inc.*, 453 F.3d 377, 381 (6th Cir. 2006) (physical retail store directly selling trademark-infringing counterfeit items to consumers may be liable for Lanham Act violations). A company's greater participation in the marketplace weakens this protection. *See, e.g.*, *Lockheed Martin Corp. v. Network Solutions, Inc.*, 194 F.3d 980 (9th Cir. 1999) (innocent printer of infringing goods may be enjoined from future infringement); *H-D U.S.A., LLC v. SunFrog, LLC,* 282 F.Supp. 3d 1055 (E.D. Wis. 2017) (print-on-demand, advertising, and shipping service for third-party designers uploading infringing designs acted knowingly or in reckless disregard of infringing activities); *Ohio State Univ. v. Redbubble, Inc.,* 989 F. 3d 435 (6th Cir. 2021) (company contacting independent artists and arranging manufacturing, shipping, customer service, and marketing for goods including trademark-infringing images may be liable for direct trademark infringement); 15 U.S.C. § 1114.

1. USES CREATING A LIKELIHOOD OF CONFUSION

The common-law trademark infringement test requires an offending trademark or name be "identical with or confusingly similar to" the plaintiff's mark. *See* Lanham Act § 43(a)(1)(A), 15 U.S.C. § 1125(a)(1)(A); 3 Restatement, Torts § 717; Restatement (Third) of Unfair Competition § 20. A plaintiff claiming infringement of a federal trademark registration must show use of a reproduction, counterfeit, copy, or colorable imitation of their registered mark is "likely to cause confusion, mistake or to deceive" under Lanham Act § 32, 15 U.S.C. § 1114.

Proving likelihood of confusion is both necessary and sufficient to establish trademark infringement. A trademark or name owner need only show that the relevant marks are sufficiently similar, and that the product, service, or business the marks identify are sufficiently related as to create a likelihood of confusion. Neither specific intent to cause consumer confusion nor actual consumer confusion should be required. It is also unnecessary to establish that the accused user actually used the prior user's trademark or name to identify an identical product, service, or business.

a. Proof of Likelihood of Confusion

Fraudulent intent is no longer necessary to prove trademark infringement, but it remains a relevant factor and may be dispositive to show likelihood of confusion. *See, e.g., Kemp v. Bumble Bee Seafoods, Inc.,* 398 F.3d 1049 (8th Cir. 2005) (likelihood of confusion found in part due to clear intent to use the goodwill and brand equity in previously assigned mark). Courts often assume an intentional attempt to create consumer confusion regarding a trademark will likely succeed. Thus, proof of intent to confuse is often sufficient evidence of a likelihood of confusion.

Proof of intent to confuse also affects trademark infringement remedies. Showing fraudulent intent provides a basis for awarding punitive or compensatory damages or an accounting of the infringing party's profits. Without evidence of a fraudulent intent, relief may be limited to an injunction prohibiting future infringement.

Likelihood of confusing an appreciable number of actual or prospective customers is apparently sufficient to create trademark infringement liability. This does not mean a majority of consumers. At least one court suggests even a small number of actual mistakes made by average consumers can establish confusing similarity. *See McCormick & Co. v. B. Manischewitz Co.*, 206 F.2d 744 (6th Cir. 1953).

Likelihood of confusion is no longer limited to confusion by potential purchasers. Congress struck out language in the Lanham Act limiting the likelihood of confusion, mistake, or deception to "purchasers as to the source of origin of such goods and services" in 1962. Likelihood of confusion now may arise either where buyers are likely to confuse products after their purchase, or where subsequent sellers are likely to confuse products either before or during their sale. *See, e.g., American Cyanamid Co. v. United States Rubber Co.*, 356 F.2d 1008 (CCPA 1966) (upholding trademark application denial due to likelihood a user may confuse the existing fungicide with applicant's insecticide and damage crops with the wrong product); *Syntex Lab., Inc. v. Norwich Pharmacal Co.*, 437 F.2d 566 (2d Cir. 1971) (confusion among physicians and pharmacists, rather than source confusion among drug purchasers, sufficient for infringement finding).

Likely post-sale confusion by the non-purchasing general public is sufficient to support a Lanham Act § 43(a) claim. *See Ferrari S.P.A. v. Roberts*, 944 F.2d 1235 (6th Cir. 1991) *See also Beacon Mut. Ins. Co. v. OneBeacon Ins. Group,* 376 F.3d 8 (1st Cir. 2004) (Confusion relevant for parties who can influence purchasing decisions or whose confusion presents a significant risk to trademark owner's sales, goodwill, or reputation).

In *Polaroid Corp. v. Polarad Elecs. Corp.*, 287 F.2d 492 (2d Cir. 1961), the Second Circuit elaborated an extensive list of factors to consider when assessing whether another's trademark use constitutes an infringement. These factors include the strength of the plaintiff's mark, the degree of similarity between the two marks, product similarity, the likelihood that the plaintiff will expand into the defendant's market, evidence of actual confusion, defendant's good faith or lack thereof, the quality of the defendant's product, and the sophistication of buyers of the two products. The *Polaroid* factors parallel the Restatement of Torts § 731 and Restatement (Third) of Unfair Competition § 21 as the common-law test for determining whether the goods, services, or business of one party are likely to be viewed as associated with another's. Other courts adopted similar standards. *See Application of E.I. DuPont de Nemours & Co.*, 476 F.2d 1357 (CCPA 1973); *AMF Inc. v. Sleekcraft Boats*, 599 F.2d 341 (9th Cir. 1979). Additional factors often considered include the amount of care consumers spend selecting the products or service (often based on price), trade channels, and advertising expenditures.

The degree of similarity between trade symbols is based on the overall impression they provide under actual market conditions. Focusing on the degree of similarity of their "sound, sight, and meaning", small trivial differences between two marks are uncompelling. Two marks may be visually distinguishable but sound identical or confusingly similar. *See, e.g., Esso, Inc. v. Standard Oil Co.*, 98 F.2d 1 (8th Cir. 1938) ("Esso" v. "S.O."); *Brown-Forman Distillery Co. v. Arthur M. Bloch Liquor Importers, Inc.*, 99 F.2d 708 (7th Cir. 1938) ("Old Forester" v. "Old Foster"). Likewise, two trademarks may have confusingly similar meanings. *Cf.*, *Hancock v. Am. Steel & Wire Co.*, 203 F.2d 737 (CCPA 1953) ("Tornado" for wire fencing denied registration due to confusing similarity with "Cyclone").

Courts usually consider whether an ordinary purchaser is likely to be confused under actual market conditions in these likelihood of confusion inquires. This test element considers the general commercial impression a trademark or name creates, not a side-by-side comparison of the marks. An ordinary purchaser is generally expected to exercise a degree of care appropriate to the kind of choice being made. Cheap or impulse buys involve much less care than expensive goods. Likewise, a child is not expected to use the same degree of care as an adult. On the other hand, professional buyers are expected to show considerable discrimination.

A discriminating purchaser's possible ability to notice differentiation on product labels will not negate an infringement claim if an ordinary purchaser would not be so discriminating. As one English decision succinctly put it in a brewery dispute: "Thirsty folk want beer, not explanations." *Montgomery v. Thompson*, [1891] A.C. 217. *See also Univ. of Ga. Athletic Ass'n v. Laite*, 756 F.2d 1535 (11th Cir. 1985) ("Battlin' Bulldog Beer" infringed service marks despite differentiation, no competition between defendant's product and plaintiff's services).

Actual market conditions and "streams of commerce" are relevant to likelihood of confusion inquiries. Identical products sold on the same shelves require greater differentiation than those marketed in different places or ways. Similar trademarks or names are more likely to be found confusing if a mark or family of marks are inherently distinctive (*e.g.*, "Kodak", "Kodachrome"). Likewise, trademarks or names are less likely to be confusing if the trademark or family uses a common generic or descriptive element.

b. Use of Marks and Names on Related but Non-Competing Goods, Services, or Businesses

The common law originally only found trademark infringement where a confusingly similar marks or names appeared on a competing product, service, or business. The harm to avoid was sales diversions, so there could not be harm without product competition. *See, e.g., Borden Ice Cream v. Borden's Condensed Milk Co.*, 201 F. 510 (7th Cir. 1912).

The Trademark Act of 1905 stated the test both for denying a trademark registration and for finding infringement was use of a confusingly similar mark on goods having the "same descriptive properties". The Lanham Act removed the "same descriptive properties" language, ultimately broadened the protective scope for federal trademark registrations still further.

Influenced by the first of these federal legislative developments, the common law recognized identity confusion can cause economic harm to the reputation or goodwill of a product, service, or business even without competition between them. In *Aunt Jemima Mills Co. v. Rigney & Co.*, 247 F. 407 (2d Cir. 1917) the court held, apparently as a matter of common law, that using the "Aunt Jemima" mark on pancake syrup infringed the plaintiff's identical mark for pancake batter. The court concluded that the goods, though different, were so related that complainant's reputation was effectively in the defendant's hands.

The Second Circuit used the *Aunt Jemima* "related goods" rule in federal trademark cases as well as common-law infringement. For example, the court upheld denial of "Yale" for flashlights, given the opposer's prior use of the word on many other types of hardware such as locks. *See Yale Elec. Corp. v. Robertson*, 26 F.2d 972 (2d Cir. 1928). *See also L.E. Waterman Co. v. Gordon*, 72 F.2d 272 (2d Cir. 1934) (denying "Waterman" for razors due to a likelihood of confusion with federal registration of "Waterman" for fountain pens). In the Lanham Act of 1946, Congress eliminated the "same descriptive properties" language of the 1905 Act, approving the Second Circuit's use of the *Aunt Jemima* "related goods" rule in federal trademark cases.

Private contractual arrangements can be utilized to resolve non-competing goods cases. For example, in *E.I. duPont deNemours & Co. v. Christopher*, 431 F.2d 1012 (5th Cir. 1970) the original applicant sold its car wax business trademark, application, and goodwill to DuPont while retaining the mark for detergent. The CCPA affirmed the USPTO's authority to independently review likelihood of confusion concerns, but required substantial weight be given to detailed agreements designed to avoid such confusion. The court noted companies have a pecuniary interest in avoiding confusion, and that refusal to register a trademark does not prevent confusion as it does not prevent use of the mark.

Trademark infringement claims for using similar marks on non-competing goods or services are often joined with claims of unfair competition (Ch. 1 *supra*), dilution (Part B.2. *infra*), false or deceptive advertising (Ch. 9 *infra*), or invasion of right of publicity where similar names or likenesses of individuals are involved (Ch. 6 *infra*).

c. Marks and Names Used in Different Geographic Markets

Common law trademark or name protections are limited to geographic markets where the mark is actually used. *See* Part A(2) *supra*. Federal registrations (including intent-to-use applications) constitute nation-wide constructive notice of the exclusive right to use a mark. A federal trademark registrant may usually prevent further domestic use of confusingly similar marks. However, common law marks in continuous use prior to the federal registration often may continue operating in their region.

A federal trademark owner must establish likelihood of confusion to enforce their rights against a senior common law user. The federal trademark must be used in the contested region to receive a remedy for likelihood of confusion. *See, e.g., Dawn Donut Co. v. Hart's Food Stores, Inc.*, 267 F.2d 358 (2d Cir. 1959). The same principle applies for two common law trademark holders. *Hannover Star Milling Co. v. Metcalf,* 240 U.S. 403 (1916). This policy assumes the federal registration can stand against the senior user's rights. *See Cuban Cigar Brands NV v. Upmann Intern., Inc.,* 457 F.Supp. 1090 (S.D.N.Y. 1978) (incontestable trademark cancelled as infringing common law mark and not used in good faith).

The equitable defense of laches for unreasonable delay in asserting one's rights (*see* Part C. *infra*) does not apply until a federal trademark owner knows or should have known a provable infringement claim existed; merely knowing a potential future likelihood of confusion claim exists is insufficient to trigger a laches defense. *What-A-Burger VA v. Whataburger, Corp. Corpus Christi, TX*, 357 F.3d 441 (4th Cir. 2004).

Private agreements often resolve geographic trademark use disputes. The Lanham Act encourages such agreements by letting either party file a concurrent trademark registration. The USPTO may issue concurrent use registrations for the same or similar marks in different geographic areas of the country under Lanham Act § 2(d). *See, e.g.*, *Application of Beatrice Foods Co.*, 429 F.2d 466 (C.C.P.A. 1970) (allowing contractual territorial division despite no actual use in certain areas, as federal registration grants nationwide privileges and agreements may be disregarded only when necessary to prevent likelihood of confusion). Without such an agreement, a junior user who first seeks federal registration may retain nation-wide protection subject only to the first user's territory. *See, e.g.*, *Weiner King, Inc. v. Wiener King Corp.*, 615 F.2d 512 (C.C.P.A. 1980).

National territorial limits of trademark protection are particularly stringent given the Paris Convention's territoriality principle. *See, e.g.*, *Person's Co., Ltd. v. Christman*, 900 F.2d 1565 (Fed. Cir. 1990) (company that popularized "Person's" in Japan but did not use or seek U.S. trademark registration under Lanham Act § 44 has no claim under U.S. law against a U.S. citizen who encountered the "Person's" mark in Japan and subsequently adopted, used, and registered the mark in the U.S.); *McBee v. Delica Co.*, 417 F.3d 107 (1st Cir. 2005) (no Lanham Act jurisdiction or claim against a Japanese company adopting a famous musician's name without showing U.S. commerce was substantially affected).

On the other hand, Article 6*bis* of the Paris Convention requires that members refuse or cancel a trademark registration and prohibit a mark's use where it constitutes a reproduction, an imitation, or a translation used on identical or similar goods and therefore is liable to create confusion with a well-known mark in a member country. *See, e.g., Grupo Gigante v. Dallo & Co.*, 391 F.3d 1088 (9th Cir. 2004), recognizing a famous mark exception to the national territoriality principle, but dismissing as duplicative plaintiff's Article 6*bis* unfair competition claim on the dubious ground that Article 10*bis* does not itself create substantive rights and that the interaction between Lanham Act § 44 and Paris Convention Article 10*bis* simply results in treating foreign and domestic parties equally in trademark disputes. *But see* Paris Convention, Article 10*bis*(3), stating the "following acts in particular shall be prohibited: [thereafter enumerating the acts of passing off, trade disparagement, and deceptive advertising]"; Lanham Act § 44(b), 15 U.S.C. § 1126(b), stating any person whose country of origin is party to any convention or treaty relating to trademarks, trade or commercial names, or the repression of unfair competition "shall be entitled to benefits of this section . . . to the extent necessary to give effect to any provision of such convention or treaty . . . *in addition to* the rights to which any owner of a mark is otherwise entitled by this chapter" (emphasis added); and § 44(h) "Any person designated in subsection (b) of this section as entitled to the benefits and subject to the provisions of this chapter shall be entitled to effective protection against unfair competition. . ."

U.S. courts are remarkably reluctant to recognize any specific court obligation to protect foreign marks that are well-known in the U.S. under either Article 6*bis* of the Paris Convention, the Lanham Act itself, or the common law of trademarks. *See, e.g., ITC Ltd. v. Punchgini, Inc.*, 482 F.3d 135 (2d Cir. 2007), finding no legal obligation under either the Paris Convention or federal law to protect the well-known Paris Convention member trademarks. The unique U.S. approach that bases trademark priority on first use rather than first registration may explain this judicial myopia. U.S. courts never needed to develop a domestic well-known mark exception, and thus have little domestic precedent to recognize the international principle.

Based on the Paris Convention, apparently implemented by Congress in Lanham Act § 44(b), a well-known mark should receive federal protection rather than depending on state trademark common law. *See also In re Rath*, 402 F.3d 1207 (Fed. Cir. 2005), *supra*, where the concurring opinion suggests registrants should be considered "eligible" to register their foreign marks under § 44(e) of the Lanham Act if they meet § 44(b) eligibility requirements, as opposed to the § 2 domestic eligibility requirements.

d. Resale of Protected Goods

Trademark rights should not give the holder perpetual ownership or control over a good. Rather, the first sale should exhaust the owner's right to control distribution of their product. *See, e.g., Inwood Labs. v. Ives Labs.*, 456 U.S. 844, 854 n. 14 (1982) (first sale rule satisfies source designation requirements of trademark law while preserving competition by limiting a producer's ability to control the resale market). This "first sale" doctrine protects those reselling genuine branded products from trademark infringement accusations since there can be no confusion as to the original source of a product. This principle applies to other intellectual property rights as well.

The first sale doctrine frequently challenges trademark owners benefitting from distribution agreements. Reselling trademark-protected goods or services often has an international element. Parallel imports, also called "grey market" goods, are genuine goods purchased abroad and brought into the United States by an importer not licensed to distribute the goods by the entity holding domestic rights.

The Supreme Court originally held that parallel importation infringes an authorized trademark owner's rights after a foreign company sold its U.S. business, trademarks, and goodwill and could no longer do domestic business under that same trademark. *A. Bourjois & Co. v. Katzel*, 260 U.S. 689 (1923). Soon afterwards, the Supreme Court clarified that foreign goods could be repackaged or resold under the same trademark in the U.S. so long as the trademark correctly designated their source or origin. *Prestonettes, Inc. v. Coty*, 264 U.S. 359 (1924).

Around this time, Congress enacted § 526 of the Tariff Act, 19 U.S.C. § 1526, making it unlawful "to import into the United States any merchandise of foreign manufacture if such merchandise . . . bears a trademark owned by a citizen of . . . the United States." The 1946 Lanham Act § 42, 15 U.S.C. § 1124, prohibits merchandise entering the U.S. that copies or simulates either a federally registered mark, the domestic company name, or a foreign company name located in a country which by treaty, convention, or law accords certain rights to U.S. citizens. To aid customs officials, § 42 authorizes parties to record facsimiles of their name or federally registered marks with the Department of Treasury for distribution to customs officials.

Later decisions clarified that the relevant distinction lies in the relationship between the foreign and domestic company, as an unrelated entity becomes the new source of origin. *See, e.g., Champion Spark Plug Co. v. Sanders,* 331 U.S. 125, 128 (1947). *Compare, Weil Ceramics and Glass, Inc. v. Dash*, 878 F.2d 659 (3d Cir. 1989) (§§ 32 and 42 of the Lanham Act do not provide a U.S. subsidiary relief against genuine goods produced by a foreign subsidiary without material differences) *with Lever Bros. Co. v. United States*, 877 F.2d 101 (D.C. Cir. 1989) (§ 42 of the Lanham Act bars third party goods importation marked identically to a valid U.S. trademark where the goods are physically different from the U.S. goods, regardless of whether the trademark is genuine or the producers are affiliated). *See also Lever Bros. v. United States*, 796 F.Supp. 1 (D.D.C. 1992), *aff'd* 981 F.2d 1330 (1993), holding on remand that § 42 bars unauthorized foreign good importation bearing identical branding to a valid U.S. mark that is materially different from the U.S. goods, regardless of affiliation between the foreign manufacturer and the U.S. trademark owner; the U.S. Customs Service's affiliate exception to § 42's unauthorized imports ban is enjoined in these cases.

Similarly, the U.S. Department of Justice successfully argued that § 526 does not authorize a U.S. company in a close relationship with a foreign trademark owner to bar parallel imports, and that any such attempt constitutes a trade restraint violating the Sherman Act. *United States v. Guerlain, Inc.*, 155 F.Supp. 77 (S.D.N.Y. 1957). *Guerlain* was later vacated and dismissed by federal request, which then unsuccessfully sought legislative codification of the *Guerlain* ruling. The Bureau of Customs revised its internal regulations to preclude exclusion of parallel imports. The preclusion applies where either the same entity owns the foreign and domestic trademarks, the foreign and U.S. companies are subject to common control or have a parent/subsidiary relationship, or where a recorded mark or name is applied to the goods by the U.S. mark owner's authorization (i.e., a licensing arrangement). *See* 19 C.F.R. § 133.21.

The Supreme Court held the Customs Service regulation is consistent with § 526 by exempting from the importation ban goods manufactured abroad by the same entity who holds the U.S. trademark, or has common control with the U.S. trademark holder. *K Mart Corp. v. Cartier, Inc.*, 486 U.S. 281 (1988) However, the *K Mart* Court also found the regulation invalid in permitting goods importation bearing a recorded trademark or name due to a licensing arrangement with a U.S. owner.

The "first sale" doctrine does have limitations, such as where the goods are materially different, quality controls set by the manufacturer have been violated, or there is a false representation of an affiliation between the distributor and the trademark owner. Merely stocking, displaying, or reselling a product does not violate the Lanham Act. *Sebastian Intern. v. Longs Drug Stores*, 53 F. 3d 1073, 76 (9th Cir. 1995). However, the reseller may not use another's trademark (such as through display or advertising) to give the false impression that they are authorized or favored dealers of the product. *See, e.g., Australian Gold, Inc. v. Hatfield,* 436 F. 3d 1228 (10th Cir. 2006) (applying principle to Internet use).

Trademark owners frequently invoke the "material difference" exception in distribution conflicts due to its lack of an established rule. Any difference between authorized and unauthorized goods could be material if the consumer would consider it relevant when making a purchase. *Societe Des Produits Nestle, S.A. v. Casa Helvetia, Inc.*, 982 F.2d 633, 641 (1st Cir. 1992). Since these differences do not need to be physical, goods manufacturers frequently create this material difference through post-sale service plans, warranties, or related policies. *See, e.g., SKF USA Inc. v. ITC*, 423 F.3d 1307 (Fed. Cir. 2005) (material differences need not be physical, but manufacturer's post-sale services rejected as insufficiently provided to be a material difference).

Section 337 of the Tariff Act gives the International Trade Commission ("ITC") authority to prohibit unfair competition methods for U.S. imports. The ITC generally follows the principle prohibiting parallel imports that are materially different from

U.S. goods using the same trademark. *See generally, Gamut Trading Co. v. ITC*, 200 F.3d 775 (Fed. Cir. 1999) (upholding a material physical differences finding); *but cf. Duracell, Inc. v. ITC*, 778 F.2d 1578 (Fed. Cir. 1985) (presidential rejection of ITC grey market good determination need not detail rationale; general policy reasons, such as avoiding conflicting administrative interpretations of parallel imports laws are sufficient).

2. DILUTION

The federal trademark dilution statute offers an extraordinary remedy preventing others from using a "famous" trademark in a way that likely diminishes the trademark's unique association with a particular product or service in the public mind. To prove dilution, a trademark owner must show their trademark meets the statutory fame requirement, another party made unauthorized commercial use of the trademark after it became famous, and this misuse will likely dilute the famous mark's distinctive quality.

Dilution protection evolved appreciably since it was originally provided by some state statutory laws. The 1995 Federal Trademark Dilution Act ("FTDA") provided federal dilution protection for "famous" marks by amending § 43 of the Lanham Act, 15 U.S.C. § 1125. The Trademark Dilution Revision Act ("TDRA") made further amendments in 2006.

In its current form, § 43(c)(2) of the Lanham Act, 15 U.S.C. § 1125(c)(2), defines a famous mark as one "widely recognized by the general consuming public of the United States as a designation of source of the goods or services of the mark's owner." The injunctive relief the Act authorizes to prevent a famous mark's dilution is considered "extraordinary" as it is available regardless of actual or likely confusion, competition, or actual economic injury. Ordinary trademark owners have no such right or remedy. *See, e.g., Advantage Rent-A-Car Inc. v. Enterprise Rent-A-Car Co.*, 238 F.3d 378, 381 (5th Cir. 2001).

There are potentially significant differences in how federal and state dilution statutes are worded which can yield inconsistent results in their protective scopes. Federal protection is expressly limited to "famous" marks, while state statutes modeled on the 1964 Model State Trademark Act contain no such express limitation. State statutes, and now the amended FTDA, use a "likelihood of dilution" test. The original FTDA required that the use "causes dilution". Unlike state dilution statutes, the FTDA is significantly limited in its specific exclusion for nominative or descriptive fair use (including comparative advertising, parodies, and critical commentary), news reporting, and non-commercial uses. While state dilution statutes only authorize injunctive relief, the FTDA provides for damages and destruction of infringing articles where there is willful intent to trade on the owner's reputation or to cause dilution.

The Supreme Court's decision in *Moseley v. V Secret Catalogue, Inc.*, 537 U.S. 418 (2003) resolved a circuit split as to whether economic damages must be shown for dilution under the FTDA by holding proof of actual dilution could be shown by surveys or other circumstantial evidence of dilution.

The Trademark Dilution Revision Act of 2006 legislatively overruled *Moseley*, changing the statutory language from "causes dilution" to "is likely to cause dilution by blurring or dilution by tarnishment of the famous mark." This change liberalized the federal dilution standard of proof, but substantively limited federal dilution to blurring and tarnishment cases. *See* Lanham Act § 43(c)(1), 15 U.S.C. § 1125(c)(1). The TDRA also 1) modified the "famous" definition by clarifying that a famous mark must be "widely recognized by the general consuming public" of the U.S.; 2) provided separate multi-factor lists to determine fame and dilution by blurring; and 3) defined dilution by tarnishment. *See* Lanham Act § 43(c)(2), 15 U.S.C. § 1125(c)(2).

The FTDA, as amended by the TDRA, explicitly bars dilution claims for 1) any nominative or descriptive fair use other than as a designation of source for the person's own goods or services, including comparative advertising, parodies, or critical comment; 2) all forms of news reporting and commentary, and 3) any noncommercial use of a mark. *See* 15 U.S.C. § 1125(c)(3). The TDRA also amends the FTDA's limited state law preemption provision by specifying a federal trademark registration completely bars state law dilution claims, whether alleging blurring, tarnishment, or other harm to a mark's distinctiveness or reputation. *See* Lanham Act § 43(c)(6), 15 U.S.C. § 1125(c)(6).

"Nominative fair use" exists when the protected word or phrase must be used to identify a good or service and the user has no claimed connections to the source, such as ownership, sponsorship, or endorsement. "Fair use", by comparison, permits good faith use of a protected word or phrase to describe a product or service. *See KP Permanent Make-Up, Inc. v. Lasting Impression I, Inc.*, 543 U.S. 111 (2004) (possible consumer confusion between trademarks does not preclude the fair use doctrine).

The First Amendment, as well as the Lanham Act, protects news reporting, commentary, parody, and certain other non-commercial use of words or phrases receiving trademark protection. *See New Kids on the Block v. News Am. Publ'g, Inc.*, 971 F.2d 302 (9th Cir. 1992) (newspaper could use band's name to conduct commercial telephone poll as nominative fair use); *Mattel, Inc. v. MCA Records, Inc.*, 296 F.3d 894 (9th Cir. 2002) (production and distribution of "Barbie Girl" song nominative fair use, albeit parody, and "noncommercial use" within the meaning of the FTDA by doing more than merely proposing a commercial transaction).

Some courts find parody defenses non-dilutive or fair use even for commercial use of another's famous trademark or as a source designation for the defendant's own product. *See Louis Vuitton Malletier S.A. v. Haute Diggity Dog LLC*, 507 F.3d 252 (4th Cir. 2007) (dog toy parodies of fashion trademark caused no likelihood of confusion or dilution); *Mattel, Inc. v. MCA Records, Inc., supra*. However, the Supreme Court since held that use of another's trademark to designate the source of one's own goods is dilution and does not receive First Amendment protection. *Jack Daniel's Props. Inc., v. VIP Prods. LLC,* 599 U.S. ___, 143 S. Ct. 1578 (2023) (where an alleged infringer uses another's trademark as a designation for their own goods, there is no First Amendment protection as an alleged infringer may not market its own products using a trademark owner's goodwill).

The TDRA added a new provision to the FTDA regarding unregistered trade dress dilution. In such cases, the trade dress owner asserting dilution must prove the trade dress is famous, not functional, and, for cases where the trade dress includes a federally registered mark, that the unregistered matter is famous separate and apart from the registered mark. *See* Lanham Act § 43(c)(4), 15 U.S.C. § 1125(c)(4).

A potential international dispute over trademark dilution protection may result from ambiguous wording in Article 16(3) of the TRIPS Agreement. It states Article 6*bis* of the Paris Convention (which requires well-known marks receive protection against confusing uses on "identical or similar goods") shall apply to goods or services not similar to those covered by a registered trademark, provided using the mark "would indicate a connection" between those goods or services and the registered mark's owner. According to the Federal Trademark Dilution Act's legislative history, the TRIPS Agreement "includes a provision designed to provide dilution protection to famous marks." *See* H.R. Rep. No. 104–374, at 4 (1995).

Blurring impairs a famous trademark's distinctiveness by using it to signify products in other markets. *Cf.*, *Mead Data Cent., Inc. v. Toyota Motor Sales, U.S.A., Inc.*, 875 F.2d 1026 (2d Cir. 1989) ("Lexus" for automobiles does not dilute "Lexis" for computerized legal research service). Courts consider the similarity between the marks, the famous mark's distinctiveness, whether the famous mark owner makes exclusive use of the mark, recognition of the famous mark, and whether there was an intent to create an association with the famous mark. 15 U.S.C. § 1125(c)(2)(B).

Tarnishment harms a trademark's reputation by associating a mark with inferior products or unsavory or unwholesome activities (such as pornography or violence). *See Dallas Cowboys Cheerleaders, Inc. v. Pussycat Cinema Ltd.*, 604 F.2d 200 (2d Cir. 1979) (pornographic film utilizing branded uniform diluted cheerleading squad's reputation). *But cf., Girl Scouts of the U.S.A. v. Personality Posters Mfg. Co.*, 304 F.Supp. 1228 (S.D.N.Y. 1969) (without any likelihood of confusion evidence, poster of a pregnant woman in a Girl Scout uniform did not violate New York's anti-dilution statute). If another party's use of the mark does not cause negative associations for the trademark owner, then there is no dilution by tarnishment. *See Hormel Foods Corp. v. Jim Henson Prods.*, 73 F.3d 497 (2d Cir. 1996) (Muppet character "Spa'am" did not dilute "Spam" for meat).

3. DOMAIN NAMES AND CYBERSQUATTING

Courts strain to apply the Federal Trademark Dilution Act ("FTDA") and Lanham Act to "cybersquatting" or "cyberpiracy"—registering another's famous trademark as a website domain name. Mere domain name registration does not constitute using another's mark "in connection with" goods or services under Lanham Act §§ 32 or 43(a), a "commercial use" within the meaning of the FTDA, nor proof the registrar had sufficient knowledge of trademark infringement to make the domain name registry a contributory infringer. *Lockheed Martin Corp. v. Network Solutions, Inc.*, 985 F.Supp. 949 (C.D. Cal. 1997). *See also, Bird v. Parsons*, 289 F.3d 865 (6th Cir. 2002) (company auctioning infringing domain names does not "use" the infringing names in the meaning of the Lanham Act). *But cf., Panavision Int'l, L.P. v. Toeppen*, 141 F.3d 1316 (9th Cir. 1998) ("Panavision" registration sufficient commercial use of mark to constitute dilution under federal and state dilution statutes). *See also Nissan Motor Co., Ltd. v. Nissan Computer Corp.*, 89 F.Supp.2d 1154 (C.D. Cal. 2000) (likelihood of confusion and clear trading off goodwill where 90% of computer services website revenue was from automotive industry advertisements).

Congress enacted the Anticybersquatting Consumer Protection Act (ACPA) in 1999. Trademark likelihood of confusion or dilution principles do not always apply to cybersquatting, so the ACPA created a civil cause of action against those who register, traffic in, or use a domain name that is identical or confusingly similar to a trademark or dilutive of a famous mark where there is "bad faith intent to profit from that mark." 15 U.S.C. § 1125(d). Note that mere domain name application is not sufficient for ACPA protection. *Del Monte Intern. GMBH v. Del Monte Corp.*, 995 F.Supp. 2d 1107 (C.D. Cal. 2014) (also questioning whether top level domains should receive ACPA protection).

The ACPA provides a non-exhaustive list of factors to consider when determining if a defendant acted with "bad faith". *See, e.g., Sporty's Farm v. Sportsman's Mkt. Inc.*, 202 F.3d 489 (2d Cir. 2000); *Shields v. Zuccarini*, 254 F.3d 476 (3d Cir. 2001); *Virtual Works, Inc. v. Volkswagen of Am., Inc.*, 238 F.3d 264 (4th Cir. 2001); *PETA v. Doughney*, 263 F.3d 359 (4th Cir. 2001). The ACPA applies to second and top-level domain names but not subdomains (ex. www.subdomain.secondlevel.tld) since a domain name registrar does not register or assign subdomains. *GoForIt Ent., LLC v. DigiMedia.com LP*, 750 F.Supp. 2d 712 (N.D. Tex. 2010).

The ACPA also limits trademark infringement liability for domain name registrars. Companies that administer domain name registration, transfer, or cancellation must have a reasonable policy, consistent with trademark laws, and provide some protection to domain name registrants against overreaching trademark owners to receive this protection. *See* 15 U.S.C. § 1114(2)(d).

Private arbitration proceedings permit quick and relatively cheap resolution of domain name ownership disputes. Domain name registrations or renewals contractually subject applicants to the Internet Corporation for Assigned Names and Numbers (ICANN)'s Uniform Dispute Resolution Policy (UDRP) in specified circumstances. *See* UDRP, § 4(a), adopted Aug. 26, 1999. Even so, one filing an UDRP proceeding may also sue in federal court before, during, or after this filing. *BroadBridge Media, L.L.C. v. Hypercd.com*, 106 F.Supp.2d 505, 508–09 (S.D.N.Y. 2000). Courts do not grant UDRP proceedings the deference other arbitrations receive under the Federal Arbitration Act. *Parisi v. Netlearning, Inc.*, 139 F.Supp.2d 745, 746 (E.D. Va. 2001). Trademark owners prefer litigation when seeking compensation or injunctive relief in addition to domain name ownership.

Trademark holders can commit cyberpiracy too. "Reverse domain name hijacking" occurs where a trademark owner makes a bad faith attempt to seize a domain name incorporating a protected trademark, where the domain is used in good faith and without likelihood of confusion or dilution. *See, e.g., Goldline Int'l, Inc. v. Gold Line*, Case No. D2000–1151 (WIPO, Jan. 4, 2001). The ACPA grants domain name registrants some protection against these overreaches where another's knowing and material misrepresentation causes a domain registrar action against the registrant. *See,* 15 U.S.C. § 1114(2)(d)(iv)–(v). Access to this equitable remedy requires the registrant did not act in bad faith or inequitably. *Ricks v. BMEzine.com, LLC*, 727 F.Supp. 2d 936, 965 (D. Nev. 2010).

ACPA protections against overreaching trademark owners may provide a cause of action for domain name registrants to challenge adverse decisions by World Intellectual Property Organization (WIPO) dispute panels pursuant to the ICANN UDRP. *See, e.g., Sallen v. Corinthians Licenciamentos LTDA*, 273 F.3d 14 (1st Cir. 2001); *Dluhos v. Strasberg*, 321 F.3d 365 (3d Cir. 2003); and *Barcelona.com, Inc. v. Excelentisimo Ayuntamiento De Barcelona*, 330 F.3d 617 (4th Cir. 2003) (also holding the ACPA and not foreign law applied as WIPO proceedings are not jurisdictional, and WIPO panel decisions receive no deference under the ACPA).

"Gripe sites" are websites incorporating another's trademark into their website's domain name to draw attention to the website's criticism of the trademark owner's product, service, business, or other activities. These websites often fare poorly in domain name disputes. Although the criticism itself exercises protected free speech, courts disfavor letting gripe sites use their target's trademarks as part of their domain name. While likelihood of confusion claims are tenuous given the clear hostility toward the trademark owner's business, product, or activities, courts often find gripe sites create either a likelihood of consumer confusion, dilution, or have a bad faith intent to profit from the use of the mark. *Jews for Jesus v. Brodsky*, 993 F.Supp. 282 (D.N.J. 1998) (Ideological critic's registration of "jewsforjesus.org" found likely to confuse even with disclaimer and links to opposing organizations).

Courts are particularly hostile to any commercial activity on gripe sites, such as an offer to sell the domain name to the trademark owner, the sale of merchandise, or advertising space. *See e.g. Planned Parenthood Fed'n of Am., Inc. v. Bucci*, 42 USPQ2d 1430 (S.D.N.Y. 1997) ("plannedparenthood.com" registration diverted website traffic and sold anti-abortion books, infringing plaintiff's trademark); *PETA v. Dougherty, supra* (finding both trademark infringement and an ACPA violation by initial interest confusion and bad faith intent to profit from the plaintiff's mark where defendant requested an offer to buy the website). *But see Bosley Med. Inst., Inc. v. Kremer*, 403 F.3d 672 (9th Cir. 2005) [noncommercial trademark use as gripe site domain name does not constitute a use "in connection with" the sale of goods or services under Lanham Act § 43(a), 15 U.S.C. § 1125(a) (likelihood of confusion), or a "commercial use in commerce" under § 43(c) (likelihood of dilution), but noting commercial use is not required for a § 43(d) (ACPA) claim as the defendant need only have a bad faith intent to profit from the trademark's use]; *Lucas Nursery & Landscaping, Inc. v. Grosse*, 359 F.3d 806 (6th Cir. 2004)(gripe site operator had no bad faith intent to profit from trademark used as a domain name).

4. CONTRIBUTORY INFRINGEMENT AND VICARIOUS LIABILITY

Contributory trademark infringement holds manufacturers or distributors liable for harm caused by either intentionally inducing another's trademark infringement or supplying products to another that the supplier knows or has reason to know engages in trademark infringement. *See Inwood Labs., Inc. v. Ives Labs., Inc.*, 456 U.S. 844 (1982). Such conduct amounts to knowingly or recklessly aiding or inducing trademark infringement. There is also liability for knowingly or recklessly contributing to or inducing another to pass off goods or services as those of the complaining party. *See* Ch. 5 *infra.* The doctrine targets direct infringement enablers, as direct infringers may either not be easily identified or may conduct business from foreign jurisdictions.

On the other hand, it is not enough that one can merely foresee another might use the instruments supplied to infringe a trademark or name. *See Inwood Labs., supra* (generic drug manufacturer not liable for contributory infringement without evidence it continued supplying pharmacists whom it knew or had reason to know mislabeled the generic drug as a brand name drug); *cf. Tiffany (NJ) Inc. v. eBay Inc.*, 600 F.3d 93 (2d Cir. 2010) (contributory trademark infringement liability requires more than general knowledge or reason to know one's service is used to sell counterfeit goods, as liability requires some contemporary knowledge of particular listings that do or will infringe a mark).

Contributory infringement liability requires direct infringement evidence. This liability is a judicial doctrine derived from a common law tort. *Georgia Pac. Consumer Prods., LP v. Von Drehle Corp.*, 618 F.3d 441 (4th Cir. 2010). Courts developed it by analogy to contributory patent infringement law, which has a statutory basis and is better developed. *See* Ch. 6(B)(1), *infra*.

Trademark cases restrict vicarious liability more than copyright cases. *See* Ch. 6 (B)(2), *infra*. Vicarious trademark infringement liability requires the defendant and direct infringer have either an apparent or actual partnership, authority to bind each other in transactions with third parties, or exercise joint control over the infringing product or services. *See Hard Rock Cafe Licensing Corp. v. Concession Servs., Inc.*, 955 F.2d 1143 (7th Cir. 1992). Contributory liability for infringing online services does not apply to companies offering data processing services, services processing credit card payments, or affiliated banks even when notified of alleged copyright or trademark infringement by specified websites as these activities do not constitute material contribution to infringement. *See Perfect 10, Inc. v. Visa Int'l Serv. Assoc.*, 494 F.3d 788 (9th Cir. 2007). The *Perfect 10* court also did not find vicarious liability without the accused directly controlling and monitoring the direct infringer's instrumentality.

C. AFFIRMATIVE DEFENSES AND REMEDIES

A prima facie trademark infringement case alone may preclude certain types of relief. Certain remedies require willful infringement. Likewise, fairness concerns or plaintiff misconduct could bar or limit the available relief. Policy reasons alone may also limit or deny trademark infringement relief as well.

1. AFFIRMATIVE DEFENSES

A defendant may prove certain affirmative defenses to create additional grounds for denying or limiting relief. However, a plaintiff must prove priority and likelihood of confusion or dilution. A complete or absolute defense fully extinguishes a plaintiff's trademark or name rights. Equitable defenses establish judicial discretion to decide whether and what relief to grant.

There are several principal affirmative defenses to trademark, service mark, or trade name infringement (i.e., defenses notwithstanding likelihood of confusion or dilution evidence). Absolute defenses include abandonment, collateral or fair use, loss of distinctiveness (i.e., genericide), and functionality (*See* Part A., particularly § A(2)(c)(2) and A(3) *supra*). Equitable defenses include laches, estoppel, acquiescence, and unclean hands (including trademark misuse).

The Lanham Act purportedly limits available defenses where a federal trademark registration becomes "incontestable." Section 15 of the Act, 15 U.S.C. § 1065, specifies that a federally registered mark becomes incontestable if (1) the mark has been in continuous use for five consecutive years after registration, (2) there have been no final decisions adverse to the registrant's claim of ownership or right to register, (3) there are no pending USPTO or court proceedings, (4) the registrant files a "five year affidavit" with the USPTO, and (5) the mark is not the generic name of an article or substance.

Even so, abandonment, functionality, and loss of distinctiveness may be raised "at any time" as grounds to cancel a federal trademark registration. *See* Lanham Act § 14, 15 U.S.C. § 1064; *AmBrit, Inc. v. Kraft, Inc.*, 812 F.2d 1531 (11th Cir. 1986) (a trademark registration may be cancelled at any time after abandonment, even if the trademark holder resumed the mark's use). While § 33(b), 15 U.S.C. § 1115(b), states that an incontestable registration is conclusive evidence of the registrant's exclusive right to use the registered mark, it goes on to list applicable defenses. Section 33(b) also lists various equitable defenses (including, but apparently not limited to, laches, estoppel, and acquiescence) available against an incontestable mark's claimed infringement. An incontestable mark cannot be contested for mere descriptiveness. *Park 'N Fly, Inc. v. Dollar Park and Fly, Inc.*, 469 U.S. 189 (1985).

Section 33(b) of the Lanham Act, 15 U.S.C. § 1115(b), enumerates misconduct that creates defenses to an "uncontestable" federal registration. These are: (1) fraudulently obtaining the registration or incontestable rights, (2) misrepresenting the source of goods or services the incontestable mark identifies, and (3) using the mark to violate antitrust laws. Amendments to § 33(b) add equitable principles such as laches, estoppel, and acquiescence. Section 19 of the Lanham Act, 15 U.S.C. § 1609, expressly provides that equitable principles of laches, estoppel, and acquiescence are available in all *inter partes* proceedings before the U.S. Patent and Trademark Office.

Fraud requires a TTAB finding that the registrant's or applicant's intent to deceive was clear and convincing by knowingly making a false, material representation with the intent to deceive the USPTO, rather than a mere negligence standard of making material representations of fact it knew or should have known were false or misleading. *In re Bose Corp.*, 580 F.3d 1240 (Fed. Cir. 2009). Statements made in reckless disregard for the truth are considered "willful" and therefore meet this fraud standard. *Chutter, Inc. v. Great Management Group, LLC,* 2021 USPQ2d 1001 (TTAB 2021).

Sections 34 and 35 of the Lanham Act, 15 U.S.C. §§ 1115–1116, state that "principles of equity" govern judicial relief for infringement of federally registered marks. This arguably includes the traditional equitable defenses of laches, acquiescence, and unclean hands. Each of these defenses, if successful, function as an estoppel—i.e., they preclude the trademark holder from asserting an otherwise valid claim or obtaining otherwise available relief. Estoppel is distinguishable from absolute defenses which, when successful, deprive the owner of all rights in a trademark or name.

The laches defense seeks to prevent unreasonable (i.e., inexcusable and prejudicial) delay in asserting rights. Latches requires an *inexcusable* delay by the trademark owner that is unduly *prejudicial* to the accused. *Armco, Inc. v. Armco Burglar Alarm Co.*, 693 F.2d 1155 (5th Cir. 1982). There is no precise rule defining an unreasonable delay. Instead, the defense requires a fact-intensive inquiry considering the parties' competing interests and equities and protecting the consuming public against deception, confusion, and mistake.

A laches finding usually ends a trademark holder's demand for an accounting or damages, but on its own does not bar injunctive relief since unreasonable delay implies consent to the conduct similar to a revokable license. *See, e.g., Menendez v. Holt,* 128 U.S. 514, 524 (1888). A defendant's actual reliance on the trademark holder's affirmative act bars injunctive relief. *See, e.g., Saratoga Vichy Spring Co. v. Lehman,* 625 F.2d 1037, 1041 (2d Cir. 1980).

An acquiescence defense seeks to prevent rights assertion after the holder makes express or implied assurances not to assert their rights. *See, e.g., Sweetheart Plastics, Inc. v. Detroit Forming, Inc.,* 743 F.2d 1039, 1046 (4th Cir. 1984). Acquiescence estops a senior user's trademark claim against a junior user unless the trademarks will create inevitable confusion. *Coach House Rest. v. Coach and Six Rest.*, 934 F.2d 1551, 1564 (11th Cir. 1991).

An acquiescence finding places a legal duty upon the trademark holder to respect the junior user's mark and avoid creating confusion, creating an equality between the marks. *SunAmerica v. Sun Life Assurance Co.*, 974 F.2d 1348 (11th Cir.1992). Where the acquiescence defense is not based on a trademark owner's delay, it can be an assertion of express or implied acquiesced to the defendant's trademark or name use, but this does not extend to other uses not already occurring or not foreseeable. *See Conan Props., Inc. v. Conan's Pizza, Inc.*, 752 F.2d 145 (5th

Cir. 1985) (acquiescence to single restaurant's cartoon character use based on one creator's visit and encouragement did not extend to later franchise expansion plans).

The acquiescence and laches defenses effectively merge when acquiescence is implied by a trademark holder's delay in asserting rights. *But see Kellogg Co. v. Exxon Corp.,* 209 F. 3d 562 (6th Cir. 2000) (reversing laches and acquiescence findings and invoking the progressive encroachment doctrine, as the trademark holder may delay its lawsuit until the "likelihood of confusion looms large").

The unclean hands defense bars relief based on the trademark holder's own trademark misuse or other misconduct related to the litigation's subject matter. Unclean hands defenses include any relevant immoral or illegal conduct. *See, e.g., Clinton E. Worden & Co. v. Cal. Fig Syrup Co.*, 187 U.S. 516 (1903) (trademark misrepresenting product's ingredients unenforceable); *Carl Zeiss Stiftung v. VE.B. Carl Zeiss, Jena,* 298 F.Supp. 1309 (S.D.N.Y. 1969) (antitrust violations negate trademark enforcement); *Werts Novelty Co. v. Chandler*, 30 F.Supp. 774 (W.D. Mo. 1939) (illegal lottery), *Knights of Ku Klux Klan v. Strayer*, 34 F.2d 432 (3d Cir. 1929) (hate group); *Sega Enter. Ltd. v. Accolade, Inc.*, 977 F.2d 1510 (9th Cir. 1992) (using trademark as part of a software security system scheme to prevent unauthorized games).

Courts generally prefer not to allow a trademark holder's misconduct completely defeat injunctive relief against infringement, at least where it leaves the public unprotected from two wrongs. A court may deny monetary relief to a trademark holder with unclean hands, but issue injunctive or condition relief to end the trademark's misuse.

The federal dilution statute, as amended in 2006, creates exceptions to federal dilution claims. These exceptions include fair use, news reporting, and noncommercial trademark use. The fair use exception includes nominative or descriptive fair use, comparative advertising, parody, and both news and critical commentary.

The federal dilution statute also bars actions against valid federal trademarks on the Principal Register for claims brought under state statutory or common law to prevent blurring, tarnishment, or any likely or actual harm to the distinctiveness or reputation of the mark, label, or advertisement form. *See Mattel, Inc. v. MCA Records*, 296 F.3d 894 (9th Cir. 2002) (song's dilution of Mattel's "Barbie" mark a noncommercial expression form, such as parody or satire, that was not part of a commercial transaction). *See also ETW Corp. v. Jireh Publ'g, Inc.*, 332 F.3d 915 (6th Cir. 2003) (commemorative painting was noncommercial speech protected by the First Amendment where athlete's image or likeness had not consistently been used on specific goods); *Rogers v. Grimaldi*, 875 F.2d 994 (2d Cir. 1989) (First Amendment speech interests prevail unless the trademark's use has no artistic relevance to the underlying work or explicitly misleads as to the work's source or content); *AM Gen. LLC v. Activision Blizzard, Inc.*, 450 F.Supp. 3d 467 (S.D.N.Y. 2020)

(First Amendment permits military combat video game provider to include branded vehicles in campaign unless the trademark usage has no "artistic relevance to the underlying work whatsoever" and "explicitly misleads as to the source or content of the work"); *but see Jack Daniel's Props. Inc. v. VIP Prods. LLC,* 599 U.S. ___, 143 S. Ct. 1578 (2023) (*Rogers* First Amendment and fair use considerations are not applicable where an alleged infringer uses another's trademark as a designation for their own goods); Ch. 6, *infra.*

Issue preclusion prevents a party from relitigating an issue decided in a prior case so long as the issue was necessary to the judgment. Claim prelusion prevents a party from later raising issues it could have raised in a prior action but did not. Any preclusion or defense must, at minimum, satisfy issue preclusion or claim preclusion requirements in sharing a "common nucleus of operative facts". *See Lucky Brand Dungarees, Inc. v. Marcel Fashions Group, Inc.*, 590 U.S. ___, 140 S. Ct. 1598 (2020) (separate lawsuits asserting different misconduct regarding different trademarks at different times did not permit claim preclusion foreclosing assertion of a past settlement agreement).

Even while a lawsuit is pending, a covenant not to sue may extinguish an action. In *Already, LLC v. Nike, Inc.*, 568 U.S. 85 (2013), Nike sued a competitor alleging two designs infringed its trademark. The defendant's counterclaims included trademark invalidity. During the lawsuit, Nike issued a covenant not to sue for trademark or unfair competition claims based on the defendant's existing designs or future designs constituting a "colorable imitation" of the defendant's current products. Over the defendant's objections, the case and counterclaims were dismissed as moot. The defendant claimed it had new lines to market, investors that required the trademark invalidated before acting, and an affidavit that Nike was intimidating retailers to block their products. Nevertheless, the Supreme Court affirmed the lower court holdings that the case was moot due to the voluntary cessation doctrine. The voluntary cessation doctrine states a lawsuit becomes moot when there are no longer issues to resolve pursuant the U.S. Constitution's "case or controversy" requirement in Art III, § 2, cl. 1. Usually, a defendant cannot voluntarily cease a challenged practice to avoid federal court scrutiny of the practice's legality. *City of Mesquite v. Aladdin's Castle, Inc.*, 455 U.S. 283, 289 (1983). In *Already*, however, Nike's covenant encompassed all the allegedly unlawful conduct, the defendant could not establish concrete plans or current activities outside the covenant's scope, and third-party decisions based upon "hypothetical speculation" did not establish standing.

The Trademark Remedy Clarification Act of 1992 (TRCA) purportedly made states, or state employees or instrumentalities, liable for Lanham Act violations. However, the Supreme Court confirmed the Act was unconstitutional unless applied to a property right Congress has 14th Amendment authority to protect, such as freedom from false advertising. *College Sav. Bank v. Florida Prepaid*

Postsecondary Educ. Expense Bd., 527 U.S. 666 (1999).

2. CRIMINAL SANCTIONS AND CIVIL AND ADMINISTRATIVE REMEDIES

a. Criminal Sanctions

The Trademark Counterfeiting Act of 1984 (as amended), 18 U.S.C. § 2320, now authorizes federal criminal penalties up to $2,000,000 for an individual ($5,000,000 for repeat offenders and non-individuals, $15,000,000 for non-individual repeat offenders) and imprisonment up to five years (15 years for repeat offenders) for intentionally trafficking in goods or services known to bear a counterfeit mark. A counterfeit mark is a spurious mark 1) used in connection with trafficking in any goods, services, labels, etc.; 2) "identical with or substantially indistinguishable from" a federally registered mark in use, regardless if the defendant knew the mark is registered; 3) applied or used in connection with goods or services for which the mark is registered; and 4) likely to cause confusion, mistake, or deception. The Act explicitly excludes parallel imports (grey market goods) as violative of this prohibition. *See* 18 U.S.C. § 2320(e)(1).

It is unconstitutional for the government to seize collective membership trademarks or transfer them to a third-party pursuant to an organization's criminal conviction. A District Court held a motorcycle club's conviction under the Racketeer Influenced and Corrupt Organizations Act, 18 U.S.C.

§§ 1961 *et seq.*, lacked the requisite nexus between the criminal offense and the collective membership marks making such seizure an "unjustified and grossly disproportionate" action violating the Eighth Amendment's Excessive Fines Clause. *United States v. Mongol Nation,* 370 F.Supp. 3d 1090, 1098 (C.D. Cal. 2019). The *Mongol Nation* decision also held such a forced trademark transfer would violate the First Amendment by chilling members' continued rights to wear or otherwise use the marks without fear of legal retaliation or licensing fees.

b. Civil and Administrative Remedies

Judicial remedies available to trademark, trade name, or trade dress infringement, willful dilution, or cybersquatting victims can include injunctive relief, damages, an accounting of the defendant's profits, and attorney's fees in exceptional cases. Administrative remedies such as federal trademark registration cancellation and barring importation of goods bearing an infringing mark or name are also available. *See* 19 U.S.C. § 1526.

Courts routinely make injunctions available as equitable remedies in trademark and trade name infringement cases, recognizing the difficulty of proving money damages and the inherent inadequacy of these damages to remedy continuing infringement. Injunctive relief awards are subject to equitable principles. *See N. Am. Med. Corp. v. Axiom Worldwide, Inc.*, 522 F.3d 1211 (11th Cir. 2008). After the Supreme Court eliminated presumed permanent injunctive relief grants for patents upon finding irreparable harm in *eBay, Inc. v. MercExchange*, 547 U.S. 388 (2006), the circuits split over applying this presumption to trademarks. The Trademark Modernization Act of 2020 amended the Lanham Act, creating a rebuttable presumption of irreparable harm if a trademark owner establishes infringement at the proof stage or shows a likelihood of liability when seeking a temporary restraining order or preliminary injunction. *See, e.g., Nichino Am. Inc. v. Valent USA LLC,* 44 F.4th 180 (3d Cir. 2022).

The scope of available injunctive relief depends on the trademark type involved. An injunction may prohibit use of an inherently distinctive mark or name, or place conditions on using a geographically descriptive term, personal name, or distinctive product feature. *See, e.g., Taylor Wine Co. v. Bully Hill Vineyards, Inc.*, 590 F.2d 701 (2d Cir. 1978) (modifying order prohibiting Walter S. Taylor from using "Taylor" with his business).

Similarly, the *Sears-Compco* decisions should limit injunctive relief in common-law product imitation cases to requiring distinguishing labels or trade dress. *But cf. Truck Equip. Serv. Co. v. Fruehauf Corp.*, 536 F.2d 1210 (8th Cir. 1976) (upholding injunction preventing copying a semi-trailer configuration, where the designer and defendant's engineers testified that the configuration was "useless"). *See also Boston Prof'l Hockey Ass'n, Inc. v. Dallas Cap & Emblem Mfg., Inc.*, 510 F.2d 1004 (5th Cir. 1975) (unauthorized, intentional duplication of a professional team's symbol sold as a clothing patch was an infringement under the Lanham Act and common law; the district court erred in limiting relief to require the patches be labeled as unauthorized and not from team). The *Boston Hockey* case is criticized as giving a trademark owner complete monopoly over a trademark's use, including functional uses. *See International Order of Job's Daughters v. Lindeburg & Co.*, 633 F.2d 912 (9th Cir. 1980). However, today a dilution claim would cause a similar result for a sufficiently famous mark.

In addition to injunctive relief, victims of trademark infringement, willful dilution, or cybersquatting may receive damages for provable losses. In appropriate cases, the plaintiff may also recover a defendant's profits. *See, e.g.*, Lanham Act § 35, 15 U.S.C. § 1117; *Romag Fasteners, Inc. v. Fossil, Inc.*, 590 U.S. ___, 140 S. Ct. 1492 (2020) (unlike trademark dilution cases, trademark infringement plaintiffs need not show willfulness to receive the defendant's profits); *Synergistic Int'l, LLC v. Korman*, 470 F.3d 162 (4th Cir. 2006) (trial court erred by awarding damages without referencing relevant equity principles; proof of willfulness is relevant but not essential for awarding damages).

A trademark infringer's profits can be evidence of a trademark owner's losses where the infringing mark competed with the owner's business. Even without competition or diversion of sales, an infringer's profits may become restitution for unjust enrichment. *See, e.g., Maier Brewing Co. v. Fleischmann Distilling Corp.*, 390 F.2d 117 (9th Cir. 1968). An accounting is an equitable remedy, not a right, so courts usually require evidence the infringement was deliberate and willful to grant it.

To receive punitive damages, a trademark owner often must prove an infringer's deliberate and willful misconduct. Most courts refuse punitive damage awards if there are no compensatory damages awarded. While the Lanham Act does not specifically provide for punitive damages awards, it does let courts award up to treble the owner's actual damages. In fact, Lanham Act § 35 has two trebling provisions, a type of statutory liquidated damages provision and a punitive one. *See* 15 U.S.C. § 1117.

Lanham Act § 35 was amended in 1975, enabling the prevailing party to receive attorney's fees in exceptional cases. An exception case requires the trial court determine 1) whether the accused engaged in any culpable conduct; and 2) whether circumstances are sufficiently exceptional in light of other factors, such as the closeness of the liability question and whether plaintiff suffered damages warranting attorney's fees award. *Green v. Fornio*, 486 F.3d 100 (3d Cir. 2007). Culpability is a necessary, but not a sufficient, condition for an attorney's fees award. *See also K & N Eng'g, Inc. v. Bulat*, 510 F.3d 1079 (9th Cir. 2007) (election to receive statutory damages under 15 U.S.C. § 1117(c) precludes an attorney's fees award under § 1117(b)).

The Trademark Counterfeiting Act of 1984 authorizes virtually mandatory treble damages and attorney's fees awards in civil counterfeiting cases. *See* 15 U.S.C. § 1117(b) ("the court shall, unless the court finds extenuating circumstances, enter judgment" for such awards). Where the accused is likely to destroy, conceal, or render inaccessible any instrumentalities of the counterfeiting, the Act also authorizes courts to enter, as interim relief, *ex parte* orders to seize the goods, counterfeit marks, the means of making such marks, and any records documenting the items' manufacturing, sale, or receipt. *See* 15 U.S.C. § 1116(d).

The Anti-Counterfeiting Consumer Protection Act of 1996 makes statutory damages available to trademark owners for losses attributable to trademark counterfeiting. *See* 15 U.S.C. § 1117, authorizing statutory damages between $500 and $100,000 per counterfeit mark for each type of goods or services, and up to $1,000,000 per counterfeit mark for willful misconduct.

Courts generally award compensatory damage measures liberally. Courts also require less certainty when proving the extent of claimed damages as they require to show the damage occurred. For example, in *Big O Tire Dealers, Inc. v. Goodyear Tire & Rubber Co.*, 561 F.2d 1365 (10th Cir. 1977) the plaintiffs received damages recouping corrective advertising costs incurred to dispel the "reverse confusion" created by the infringer's advertising (i.e., an impression that plaintiffs were passing off their "Big Foot" tires as the defendant's rather than the reverse). The award was 25% of the infringer's national advertising costs, reduced by geography, based on the Federal Trade Commission's misleading advertising penalty requiring 25% of the offender's advertising budget be spent on corrective advertising. Dispelling confusion in the consuming public's mind does not require a dollar-for-dollar expenditure. *See also Sands, Taylor & Wood v. Quaker Oats*, 34 F.3d 1340 (7th Cir. 1994) ($10.3 million dollar award reasonable in a reverse confusion case, but remanding to clarify the rationale for doubling this amount pursuant to Lanham Act § 35(a)). *But cf. Illinois High Sch. Ass'n v. GTE Vantage, Inc.*, 99 F.3d 244 (7th Cir. 1996) (high school basketball tournament's "March Madness" trademark not infringed when the media used it to reference the NCAA college basketball tournament, which the NCAA later adopted).

The federal trademark dilution provision, 15 U.S.C. § 1125(c)(5), limits a famous mark's owner's remedies to injunctive relief through 15 U.S.C. § 1116 unless the injunction target willfully intended to trade on the owner's reputation or dilute the famous mark. Showing such willful intent entitles the famous trademark's owner to 15 U.S.C. §§ 1117(a) and 1118 remedies (namely profits, damages, costs, attorney fees, and destruction of infringing articles) subject to equity principles and the court's discretion.

The Anticybersquatting Consumer Protection Act authorizes court-ordered forfeiture, cancellation, or transfer of a domain name. *See* 15 U.S.C. § 1125(d)(1)(C). The Act also creates an in rem civil action against the domain name. *See* 15 U.S.C. § 1125(d)(2); *Harrods Ltd. v. Sixty Internet Domain Names*, 302 F.3d 214 (4th Cir. 2002) (in rem provision constitutional, not limited to § 1125(d)(1) violations, and authorized for certain federal infringement and dilution claims). The injunctive and monetary remedies for trademark infringement under Lanham Act §§ 34–35, 15 U.S.C. §§ 1116–1117, were extended to violations of 15 U.S.C. § 1125(d) too.

For business names, federal trademark registration holders and qualifying foreign users may register their mark with the Customs Service to bar infringing imports. *See* Lanham Act § 42, 15 U.S.C. § 1124. 19 U.S.C. § 1526(e) authorizes such seizures and forfeitures. Customs seizure of goods believed counterfeit but ultimately returned to the owner is not considered a "taking" under the U.S. Constitution's Just Compensation Clause. *Acadia Tech., Inc. v. United States*, 458 F.3d 1327 (Fed. Cir. 2006).

The International Trade Commission ("ITC") may issue exclusion or cease and desist orders (subject to presidential review) to prevent an unfair competition method under § 337 of Tariff Act of 1930, 19 U.S.C. § 1337, as subsequently amended in 1974, 1979, 1984, and 1988. Such unfair competition may include importation or subsequent sale of goods bearing an infringing trademark. *See, e.g., Bally/Midway Mfg. Co. v. ITC*, 714 F.2d 1117 (Fed. Cir. 1983). Whether ITC findings in trademark cases have preclusive effect on district court proceedings is not settled. *See, Union Mfg. Co. v. Han Baek Trading Co.*, 763 F.2d 42 (2d Cir. 1985), *Swagway, LLC v. ITC*, No. 18–1672 (Fed. Cir. Aug. 14, 2019) (vacating portion of May 9, 2019 decision finding no preclusive effect without comment).

A party may also petition The Office of the U.S. Trade Representative to impose sanctions on foreign countries that give inadequate or ineffective protection to a U.S. national's intellectual property. *See* Ch. 1, *supra*. The Office annually reviews intellectual property protection and enforcement by U.S. trading partners pursuant to § 182 of the Trade Act of 1974, as amended by the Omnibus Trade and Competitiveness Act of 1988, the Uruguay Round Agreements Act, and the Trade Facilitation & Trade Enforcement Act of 2015. *See* 19 U.S.C. § 2242.

CHAPTER 5

PRODUCT SUBSTITUTION OR ALTERATION

While the earliest palming off form deceptively used another's trademark, there are many ways to palm off inferior or unfamiliar goods or services as those of another more reputable or recognized source. Distinctive product or business features can be imitated to deceive the consuming public. The common law condemns many "palming off" forms—such as deceptively imitating distinctive product or packaging designs, advertising slogans, or literary or artistic titles and characters. This chapter focuses on deceptive actions. Even so, reviewing legitimate ways to resell refurbished, substitute, or complimentary goods helps clarify the boundaries between permitted and deceptive business activities.

Deceptive product substitutions or alterations are forms of palming off that offer unknown or inferior goods in the place of reputable or higher quality goods. This does not necessarily require deceptive use of another's trade symbol or imitation of a distinctive product or business feature. It is sufficient to sell used goods as new ones or adulterated goods as the original. Consumer deception is possible precisely because some products are typically distributed without accompanying trade symbols or trade dress. Consumer may not easily discern the unbranded goods requested and those provided.

A. TRADE RELATIONS PROTECTED

The common law governing product substitution and alteration protects a company's existing public relations or goodwill. This performs essentially the same role as common law trademarks and trade names. While common law trademarks and trade names specifically protect any goodwill generated by using distinctive trade *symbols*, product substitution and alteration laws protect *product* goodwill regardless of whether it uses a symbol. A retailer who deceptively offers a substitute or altered product from the one requested both deceives the customer and interferes with the goodwill of the product, its manufacturer, or its distributor.

B. ACTIONABLE AND PRIVILEGED PRODUCT SUBSTITUTION OR ALTERATION

Not every product substitution or alteration is actionable. A seller may persuade a customer to accept substitute or altered products so long as they make no false or deceptive representations. Unannounced substitution or alteration of goods is a long-standing form of unfair competition, even when goods are accurately marked. Nevertheless, the most common product substitutions or alterations are unmarked goods or goods sold outside their original containers.

1. PRODUCT SUBSTITUTION

Product substitution takes three primary forms: (1) substituting a less well-known product for a recognized one, (2) substituting a lower-quality product, and (3) substituting another's product as one's own (reverse palming off).

Substituting lesser-known products for recognized ones commonly occurs in the drugs, food, and beverages industries. In fact, the Coca-Cola Company created much of the early case law governing such unannounced substitutions. Services may be deceptively substituted as well, but this often involves a deceptively similar trademark. *See, e.g., Dial-A-Mattress Franchise Corp. v. Page*, 880 F.2d 675 (2d Cir. 1989) (prohibiting a deceptively similar customized telephone number). *But cf. Holiday Inns, Inc. v. 800 Reservation, Inc.*, 86 F.3d 619 (6th Cir. 1996) (deceptively similar phone number acceptable when promptly informing callers of the number's owner and proposing an alternative reservation service).

Trademark owners can seek relief from the manufacturer or distributor supporting a retailer that substitutes lesser-known goods, as well as from the retailer itself. A trademark owner must show the manufacturer or distributor induced the substitution either explicitly, by suggestion or insinuation, or provided the substituted product knowing the retailer would or could be expected to perform unannounced substitutions. The latter amounts to contributory palming off and is a form of unfair competition like contributory trademark infringement. *See William R. Warner & Co. v. Eli Lilly & Co.*, 265 U.S. 526 (1924).

Substitution cases are less straight-forward where a trademark is weak, whether highly descriptive or generic. Nearly descriptive or generic trademarks may have more than one meaning or simply fail to provide source-identifying information about a product or service. *See* Ch. 4, *supra*. Since a weak or generic trademark does not clearly indicate a particular brand or product was ordered, there is doubt whether to hold a retailer liable for palming off. After all, the requesting customer received a product with the same descriptive qualities or that fell within the same generic classification.

Palming off cases involving ambiguous trademarks are fact intensive. For example, where two different hat brands are sold under the "Stetson" surname but only one hat maker is responsible for the "Stetson" hat reputation, the ambiguity is more apparent than real; a second hat maker named Stetson who fails to distinguish their goods from the original will be liable for palming off. *See John B. Stetson Co. v. Stephen L. Stetson Co., Ltd.*, 14 F.Supp. 74 (S.D.N.Y. 1936). In such cases, the junior user must assume that the ambiguous surname is used as a trademark and, where necessary, clarify any confusion about the brand.

Where there is real ambiguity between products or services and the trademark owner either created or failed to protect against ambiguity, courts allow retailers greater latitude. *See, e.g., DuPont Cellophane Co. v. Waxed Prod. Co.*, 85 F.2d 75 (2d Cir. 1936), holding the trademark "Cellophane" became generic and a retailer merely needed to state the product's producer. In such cases, a retailer need not provide free advertising by asking if the originator's product was requested.

A substituted product's quality is irrelevant because sales diversion is the prevented harm. In practice, the lesser-known product is often of inferior quality. Another substitution type occurs where "seconds" (i.e., a particular brand's flawed goods) are palmed off as that brand's top-quality goods. Unsurprisingly, courts find misrepresenting the quality of a brand's goods to be a deceptive substitution that constitutes palming off. There is no prohibition against dealing in seconds, of course, so long as the purchaser is notified.

Cases involving palming off "seconds" as higher-quality goods require proof that multiple classes of the brand's goods exist. For example, in *Harris v. Warren & Phillips*, 35 RPC 217 (1918) a publisher sought to enjoin republication of a popular songwriter's earlier works recorded before she became famous. The publisher argued the early works lacked merit and should not be published in a way that could create the belief that it was the songwriter's recent work. The court, refusing to compare the relative merits of the songwriter's earlier and later compositions, denied the plaintiff relief.

Reverse passing off, or passing off another's product as one's own, is an actionable offense. *See, e.g., International News Serv. v. Associated Press*, 248 U.S. 215 (1918) (dissenting opinion of Mr. Justice Holmes) ("The ordinary case, I say, is palming off the defendant's product as the plaintiff's, but the same evil may follow from the opposite falsehood—from saying, whether in words or by implication, that the plaintiff's product is the defendant's, and that, it seems to me, is what happened here [where one news service copied or paraphrased another news service's stories as they were published on the east coast and then used those stories to compete with the other news service on the west coast]").

"Reverse passing off" frequently involves plagiarizing another's literary work. In such cases, the passing off claim often accompanies claims of copyright infringement, misappropriation, or invasion of publicity rights. *See, e.g., Bajpayee v. Rothermich*, 372 N.E.2d 817 (Ohio App. 10 Dist. 1977) (research laboratory president presented an employee's unpublished article as his own without authorization, violating the employee's right to recognition and giving rise to a cause of action—whether a claim for relief for plagiarism, invasion of a publicity right, or prima facie tort—even though the employee claimed no common-law copyright interest in the article and discovery revealed the article was the employer's property).

In *Dastar Corp. v. Twentieth Century Fox Film Corp.*, 539 U.S. 23 (2003), the Supreme Court recognized an important limitation to "reverse passing off" claims under Lanham Act § 43(a). The Court held releasing videos of a previously copyrighted TV series that had entered into the public domain, without attribution to the original producer, did not constitute reverse passing off or a false designation of origin violating § 43(a). To avoid conflict with federal copyright laws, the "origin of goods" under Lanham Act § 43(a) should mean the origin of the tangible product sold in the marketplace, not the origin of ideas or communications the product embodies or contains. To read § 43(a) as creating a cause of action for plagiarism, said the Court, would be hard to reconcile with *Wal-Mart Stores v. Samara Bros.*, 529 U.S. 205 (2000). The *Wal-Mart* case held that otherwise unprotected product design features are distinctive, and thus protectable under § 43(a), only if the feature acquired secondary meaning.

At least one post-*Dastar* decision questioned whether there is anything wrong with reselling someone else's goods under your own mark if you first buy the goods at retail. *Bretford Mfg., Inc. v. Smith Sys. Mfg. Corp.*, 419 F.3d 576 (7th Cir. 2005) held that an unannounced substitution of plaintiff's unique table-leg assembly on one of defendant's own display tables did not amount to reverse passing off when the purchaser was happy with the final product. While conceding the *Dastar* finding that "'reverse passing off' can violate the Lanham Act if a misdescription of origin causes commercial injury," the *Bretford* court determined:

> Businesses often think competition unfair, but federal law encourages wholesale copying, the better to drive down prices. Consumers rather than producers are the objects of the law's solicitude.

2. PRODUCT ALTERATION

Two primary unannounced substitution types are selling reconditioned goods as new or adulterated goods as originals. Both forms of unannounced alteration of goods strongly resemble substitution of "seconds" (a particular brand's flawed goods) for primary goods.

There is no law against reconditioning and reselling used goods, just as a customer may legitimately be convinced to accept substitute goods or deal in seconds. One can resell used goods using the original trademark as long as the customer is notified. There is, however, an inherent danger that reconditioned used goods may be palmed off as new ones on an unsuspecting consumer. Those who recondition and resell used goods must take steps to avoid retail customer confusion over whether the goods are new or used. This is similar to how manufacturers and distributors must anticipate their goods being deceptively substituted for another, better known or higher quality brand.

In *Champion Spark Plug Co. v. Sanders*, 331 U.S. 125 (1947), the Supreme Court upheld trademark infringement and unfair competition claims against a refurbisher selling goods under their original "Champion" mark without adequate reconditioning notices. Champion only won a partial victory, however, as the reconditioner merely had to clearly and distinctly stamp "Repaired" or "Used" on the plugs and did not need to remove the original trademark. The Court held that, while used, the plugs were still Champion-brand plugs and the refurbisher was entitled to identify them as such. *See also Nitro Leisure Prod., LLC v. Acushnet Co.*, 341 F.3d 1356 (Fed. Cir. 2003), upholding denial of preliminary injunctive relief against a refurbisher that removed the original producer's mark and then reapplied it to the product. *But see* Judge Newman's dissenting opinion arguing trademark owners should have a right to prevent their trademark's reapplication to damaged goods.

Goods may be altered so substantial that identifying them by the original trademark would be deceptive. Changes to a product's size or configuration may preclude adequate notice of the alteration. In such cases, courts may order the original trademark obliterated before resale.

Selling an adulterated form of the original product is a palming off type that usually occurs when goods are sold outside their original containers. Drugs, cosmetics, foods, and beverages are the most common targets.

Remanufacturers and refurbishers have a right to contest an original manufacturer's false or misleading claims, just like any other competitor. Section 43(a) of the Lanham Act, 15 U.S.C. § 1125(a), creates a federal cause of action against anyone using a false designation of origin, description, or representation in connection with any goods or services put into commerce.

A competitor has § 1125(a) standing to sue so long as the injury flows directly from a deception caused by the defendant's advertising and occurs when the deception causes consumers to withhold trade from plaintiff. *Lexmark Int'l, Inc. v. Static Control Components, Inc.*, 572 U.S. 118 (2014). *See also* Ch. 8, *infra*. The Court designated "zone of interests" and "proximate cause" requirements as better guidance for determining standing than the multi-factor balancing, the direct competitor, or the reasonable interest tests. The "zone of interests" test examines whether the legislature made a cause of action that includes a particular claim (here injury to a commercial interest in reputation or sales). The proximate cause requirement reviews whether the alleged harm is sufficiently connected to the challenged conduct.

Preventing unannounced alteration of a literary or artistic product may be similar to the right to prevent a physical product's adulteration. In *Gilliam v. American Broad. Cos., Inc.*, 538 F.2d 14 (2d Cir. 1976), artists were entitled to a preliminary injunction restraining broadcast of an edited version of their shows. The court concluded the artists stated a cause of action under 15 U.S.C. § 1125(a).

Interestingly, the *Gilliam* court held the edited program constituted an actionable mutilation (or "deformation") of the underlying work. American copyright law had not recognized an equivalent of the European civil law concept of *droit moral* at the time (i.e., an artist's right to have his work attributed to them in the original form). Despite the broadcasting license granted, the *Gilliam* court found substantial likelihood that the broadcaster's editing infringed upon the artists' copyrights in the underlying script.

The artists prevailed as U.S. courts had long granted common-law relief based either on a theory of breach of implied contractual obligation, or unfair competition for misrepresenting an artist's work. A legend disclaiming the artists' approval of the edited version was not considered adequate relief. Viewers could not compare the truncated version with the original, and may begin viewing the broadcast after the disclaimer was displayed. *But cf. Dastar Corp. v. Twentieth Century Fox Film Corp.*, 539 U.S. 23 (2003), discussed in Part B(1), *supra*.

C. AFFIRMATIVE DEFENSES AND REMEDIES

The affirmative defenses and remedies for product substitution and alteration claims are essentially the same as those available in trademark or trade name infringement cases. Product substitution or alteration defendants may establish the asserted trademark or name was abandoned or lost its distinctiveness. The defendant should demonstrate adequate warning or labeling, good faith, and lack of fraud in their practices. A defendant may also claim laches, acquiescence, or unclean hands defenses. Where the claim involves use of a product or service, the manufacturer and end user should be parties to the lawsuit.

Defendants may respond to customer claims asserting responsibility for the product's shortcomings by assigning blame to the original source's failure in design, manufacture, or marketing. When challenging the customer, the defendant may examine whether the injury was proximately caused by the substitution or alteration, whether the consumer misused or negligently used the product, or whether the alleged defect could be adequately cured. For certain products, federal labeling or other regulatory requirements may undermine some customer claims. Conversely, First Amendment challenges to controls of or requirements for commercial speech are also increasingly common. *See* Ch. 8 *infra*.

Commercial victims of an unannounced product substitution or alteration may recover provable compensatory damages or obtain injunctive relief. A prevailing commercial victim may also attempt to prevent further substitutions or alterations by seeking a cease and desist order from the Federal Trade Commission or either an exclusion or cease and desist order from the International Trade Commission. Sometimes a plaintiff may recover punitive damages or restitution of the defendant's profits. The commercial victim's damages and seller's profits may be difficult to prove in product substitution and alteration cases, highlighting the importance of injunctive relief and punitive damages. Additional remedies are available where strict liability or other statutory regulations apply. Consumer remedies may include repair or replacement of the challenged goods or services as well as compensatory, punitive, or statutory damages.

For public sector trade, the federal government commonly uses the Civil False Claims Act, 31 U.S.C.

§§ 3729 *et seq.*, to combat fraud, waste, and abuse in government contracts. This includes unauthorized product or service substitutions or mislabeling. Originally enacted in 1863 to punish contractors defrauding the Union Army, the Act was since amended to target knowing submissions of false claims for government funds, creating false records material to such claims, falsely creating financial obligations owed by the government, improperly avoiding financial obligations owed to the government, or conspiracy to commit any of these offenses. The scienter element is evaluated based on the defendant's knowledge and subjective beliefs (including deliberate ignorance or recklessness) at the time of the activity rather than what an objectively reasonable person might believe. *United States ex rel. Schutte v. Supervalu Inc.*, 598 U.S. ___, 143 S. Ct. 1391 (2023). Statutory damages or criminal penalties may apply as well.

A *qui tam* provision allows individual whistleblowers to initiate claims under this Act. The § 3731(b) statute of limitations is different for a U.S. official and the private person ("relator") who is not considered an "official of the United States", but the relator may take advantage of the government knowledge tolling provision even when the government does not intervene. *Cochise Consultancy, Inc. v. United States ex rel. Hunt*, 587 U.S. ___, 139 S. Ct. 1507 (2019). If the federal government intervenes in the suit, it may dismiss the action over the relator's objection so long as the relator received notice and a hearing opportunity. *United States ex rel. Polansky v. Executive Health Resources, Inc.*, 599 U.S. ___, 143 S. Ct. 1720 (2023).

PART 3

APPROPRIATION OF INTANGIBLE BUSINESS ASSETS

CHAPTER 6

APPROPRIATION OF PUBLICLY DISCLOSED INTANGIBLE ASSETS

A company's intangible assets may include any legally protectable intellectual property, including inventions, trademarks and related goodwill, literary or artistic works, or any other commercially valuable ideas or information. These intangible assets are products of intellectual effort that often entail substantial investment of time and money.

Federal and state laws protect products of intellectual effort. For example, Article I, § 8 of the U.S. Constitution specifically empowers Congress to "promote the progress of science and useful arts, by securing for limited times to authors and inventors the exclusive rights to their respective writings and discoveries." Pursuant to that authority, Congress has long provided and periodically expanded federal patent and copyright protections. Like other federal laws enacted pursuant to constitutional authority, the Supremacy Clause of the Constitution declares U.S. patent and copyright laws to be the supreme law of the land. Inconsistent state laws may not undermine them.

Federal patent and copyright laws should secure intellectual labors for the public benefit, not simply reward inventors and authors. A patent may be considered a contract between an inventor and the public (represented by the federal government): in return for an invention's full public disclosure, the public grants an inventor the time-limited right to exclude others from making, using, offering for sale, selling, or importing the invention (or the product of a patented process) in the United States. Similarly, federal copyright laws encourage public dissemination of literary or artistic works by conferring a bundle of intangible rights upon the work's "author" at the moment the work is reduced to tangible form. These rights grant the author domestic control, for a limited time, over copying, publishing, adapting, or distributing a literary or artistic work, and for some works publicly performing or displaying them as well.

Patent and copyright laws are limited by national boundaries. A foreign patent or copyright does not necessarily confer rights in the United States, and a domestic patent or copyright often lacks authority abroad. An inventor must file separate patent applications in each country where they desire protection [facilitated by the Patent Cooperation Treaty—*see* Ch. 1(A)(2)(c) *supra*]. Likewise, authors must meet national legislation requirements to protect their works abroad. Article 5 of the Berne Convention minimizes the multinational filing burden, as authors who are citizens of a Convention member nation enjoy reciprocal exclusive copyrights for protected artistic works. Article 5 requires that no formalities may limit the exercise or enjoyment of these rights.

General patent protection is the exclusive method for retaining rights in publicly disclosed inventions in the United States. However, there are other ways to protect an invention. State contract laws govern patent assignment and licensing. Federal and state laws also protect trade secrets, covering certain non-publicly disclosed inventions, ideas, or information from unauthorized acquisition, use, or disclosure. *See* Ch. 7, *infra*.

A dual system protected U.S. literary and artistic works until 1976. State common law originally protected literary and artistic works prior to general publication. Federal statutory law protected specified classes of literary and artistic work after publication. The Copyright Act of 1976, 17 U.S.C. §§ 101, *et seq*., modified this system. Today, federal copyright protection extends to specified classes of works reduced to tangible form, regardless of public disclosure. Common-law copyright protection still covers unfixed works and tangible works outside federal protection subject matter.

The Leahy-Smith America Invents Act (AIA) of 2011 (P.L. 112–29, 125 Stat. 284–341) substantially revised U.S. patent law. In 2013, the U.S. changed from a "first to invent" to a "first inventor to file" priority system, aligning U.S. patent law more closely (albeit not completely) with foreign patent systems. Another amendment expanded prior art to include publication anywhere in the world rather than merely domestic disclosures. Other amendments included expedited examination capability, a third-party right to submit and explain relevant prior art, and curtailment of certain abusive practices.

One of the AIA's most visible changes lay in conducting administrative review proceedings instituted by a third party to challenge a patent's validity: *inter partes* review (35 U.S.C. § 311) and post-grant review (35 U.S.C. § 321). The underlying intention was to improve patent quality and address challenges created by non-practicing entities asserting dubious patents.

Any third party may initiate a patent review within nine months following a patent grant. After this time, any third party may initiate an *inter partes* review to cancel any patent claim that might be unpatentable in light of the prior art. The USPTO must decide whether to institute an *inter partes* review request upon receipt. 35 U.S.C. § 314. The decision "whether to institute an *inter partes* review . . . shall be final and non-appealable" 35 U.S.C. § 314(d). However, the Patent Act bars instigating an *inter partes* review if requested more than a year after a patent infringement lawsuit was filed against it. *See* 35 U.S.C. § 315(b); *Thryv, Inc. v. Click-To-Call Techs., LP*, 590 U.S. ___, 140 S. Ct. 1367 (2020) (USPTO application of § 315(b) time bar cannot be appealed under § 314(d)). Once accepted, the USPTO must render a final written decision on *all* challenged claims. *SAS Inst. Inc. v. Iancu*, 584 U.S. ___, 138 S. Ct. 1348 (2018). Since the unreviewable authority an Administrative Patent Judge wields during an *inter partes* review is not compatible with their appointment by the Secretary of Commerce to an inferior office, the Director of the USPTO must have ultimate authority to review an *inter partes* review proceeding's final outcome and may issue decisions on the Patent Trial and Appeal Board's behalf.

United States v. Arthrex, Inc., 594 U.S. ___, 141 S. Ct. 1970 (2021).

Patent holders have raised many unsuccessful challenges to the *inter partes* review process. Challenges to *inter partes* review require clear and convincing indication that Congress intended to bar review of the determination, or where the challenge is tied to statutes related to the determination. *Cuozzo Speed Techs., LLC v. Lee*, 579 U.S. 261 (2016) (*inter partes* review granted the broadest possible applicability as it protects the public's "paramount interest in seeing that patent monopolies . . . are kept within their legitimate scope"). *Inter partes* review is constitutional and does not violate either Article III or the Seventh Amendment. *Oil States Energy Servs., LLC v. Greene's Energy Group, LLC*, 584 U.S. ___, 138 S. Ct. 1365 (2018). State sovereign immunity does not bar *inter partes* review proceedings. *Regents of the Univ. of Minn. v. LSI Corp.*, 926 F.3d 1327 (Fed. Cir. 2019). Similarly, tribal sovereign immunity does not bar *inter partes* review proceedings as the review is more of an agency enforcement action than a private civil suit. *Saint Regis Mohawk Tribe v. Mylan Pharm. Inc.*, 896 F.3d 1322 (Fed. Cir. 2018) (rejecting patent licensure to Native American tribe to avoid *inter partes* review). However, the federal government is not considered a "person" that can challenge a patent's validity. *Return Mail v. United States Postal Serv.*, 587 U.S. ___, 139 S. Ct. 1853 (2019).

Federal patent and copyright laws also impact common law misappropriation. Originating in the famous news piracy case of *International News Serv. v. Associated Press*, 248 U.S. 215 (1918), (*see* Ch. 1, *supra*), misappropriation laws purportedly supplement federal and state laws by protecting publicly disclosed products of intellectual effort (*e.g.* the news). Common laws protecting privacy emerged contemporaneously. From these privacy laws emerged a body of state statutory and common laws forming the "right of publicity." These laws grant an exclusive right to prohibit or authorize commercial exploitation of an individual's own name or likeness. State laws also provide residual protection against misappropriation of certain publicly disclosed trade values not protected by federal law.

Several other bodies of federal law supplement federal patent and copyright law. They create *sui generis* intellectual property protections for intangible assets such as new plant varieties, semiconductor chip designs, and vessel hull designs. Likewise, state contract laws still govern intellectual property assignment and licensing, subject to specific federal requirements. However, the AIA amended various federal judicial code provision to deny state courts jurisdiction over legal actions relating to patents, plant variety protection, or copyrights. *See, e.g.*, 28 U.S.C. § 1338(a). State courts also retain subject matter jurisdiction over malpractice claims related to patent lawsuits under 28 U.S.C. § 1338(a). *See, Gunn v. Minton*, 568 U.S. 251 (2013) (malpractice claim must raise a federal issue, substantially and actually disputed; substantiality term failed as the alleged malpractice is not significant to the overall federal system).

This chapter discusses appropriation of publicly disclosed intangible assets. Chapter 7 reviews trade secret and idea appropriation. As in previous chapters, it will be useful first to identify the trade relations and intangible assets the foregoing bodies of federal and state law protect. The chapter will then review actionable and privileged appropriation of those trade relations and assets.

A. TRADE RELATIONS AND INTANGIBLE ASSETS PROTECTED

This and the following chapter consider existing or prospective trade relations of a party wishing to publicly exploit a product of intellectual effort. The specific concern lies in the laws protecting purely prospective commercial relations of such a party.

Federal laws protect some products of intellectual effort. Examples include some inventions (including ornamental industrial designs and certain asexually reproduced plants), various literary or artistic works, *sui generis* protection of certain plant varieties, "mask works" (templates to create complex electronic circuits on semiconductors chips), and vessel hull designs. Alternatively, a publicly disclosed product of intellectual effort may receive common-law protection against misappropriation unless federal law expressly or impliedly preempts it.

1. PATENTABLE INVENTIONS

Federal patent law requires an inventor to accept the U.S. government's standing contractual offer: exclusive rights to an invention for a limited time in return for its full public disclosure. There are substantive and procedural requirements as well. The substantive requirements specify what constitutes a patentable invention. The procedural requirements specify how patent rights are obtained, transferred, and terminated.

a. Subject Matter Protected

The statutory term "invention" means "invention or discovery" as defined in 35 U.S.C. § 100. This statutory term apparently does not mean the same thing as its constitutional counterparts. Rather, the statutory term references products and processes. To be patentable, the subject matter must (1) fall within a specified protected subject matter class, and (2) meet a general standard of novelty and non-obviousness. In this sense, "novelty" brings to light that which was previously unknown. Beyond these important constitutional requirements, federal patent protection limitations are essentially statutory. Three subject matter types meet these patentability prerequisites: utility, design, and plant patents. Patents may be granted for inventions primarily used for illegal or immoral purposes. *Juicy Whip, Inc. v. Orange Bang Inc.*, 185 F.3d 1364 (Fed. Cir. 1999).

Utility patents are the most frequently sought patent type. They require a further showing that the invention is useful, as well as new and non-obvious. The subject matter classes covered by a utility patent include (1) *a process,* (2) *a machine,* (3) *an article of manufacture,* (4) *a composition of matter,* or (5) *an improvement* of any of the foregoing classifications.

Each patent class excludes certain subject matter types. The "process" classification, for example, was construed to exclude abstract ideas, scientific principles, mental processes, printing systems, and mathematical formulae. *See, e.g., Gottschalk v. Benson,* 409 U.S. 63 (1972); *Parker v. Flook,* 437 U.S. 584 (1978) (mathematical formula used in a computer program is not patentable).

Combining excluded subject matter with patentable subject matter can yield a viable patent. For example, the Supreme Court determined a curing process using mathematical formulae embodied in a computer program for several steps was patentable, and that a claim containing otherwise statutory subject matter does not become non-statutory merely because it uses a mathematical formula, computer program, or digital computer. *Diamond v. Diehr,* 450 U.S. 175 (1981). *See also Arrhythmia Research Tech., Inc. v. Corazonix Corp.,* 958 F.2d 1053 (Fed. Cir. 1992) (products and process claims for signal analysis encompass statutory subject matter); *In re Alappat,* 33 F.3d 1526 (Fed. Cir. 1994) (creating a smooth waveform display in a digital oscilloscope is patentable statutory subject matter).

An "article of manufacture" likewise excludes a mere arrangement of printed matter or an article found in nature. A "composition of matter" excludes materials found in nature. On the other hand, concentrated and purified forms of products of nature are patentable if human intervention created the composition and it does not occur naturally in that form. *Merck & Co. v. Olin Mathieson Chem. Corp.*, 253 F.2d 156 (4th Cir. 1958). A live, human-made micro-organism constitutes a "manufacture" or "composition of matter" by statute. *Diamond v. Chakrabarty*, 447 U.S. 303 (1980). Genetically enhanced seeds receive utility patent protection, despite the *sui generis* protection available under the Plant Variety Protection Act. *See Pioneer Hi-Bred Int'l v. J.E.M. Ag Supply, Inc.*, 200 F.3d 1374 (Fed. Cir. 2000). For design patents, the "article of manufacture" term encompasses both the product sold to the consumer and a single component of a multicomponent product. *See Samsung Elecs. Co. v. Apple Inc.*, 580 U.S. 53 (2016) (damage award for the infringer's total profits under 35 U.S.C. § 289 could be limited to profits from certain components rather than the entire product).

The issue of patent-eligible subject matter became a running dispute between the Federal Circuit and Supreme Court, leading to an unusual concentration of Supreme Court decisions on this matter. The Supreme Court specifically held business methods are patentable subject matter, but only to the extent they are not abstract ideas. *Bilski v. Kappos*, 561 U.S. 593 (2010). The *Bilski* decision also noted business methods patents are subject to a prior use defense enacted by Congress in 1999. Previously, the Court of Appeals for the Federal Circuit (CAFC) upheld a data processing system patent, but rejected a claimed method of competitive bidding due to lack of statutory subject-matter where there was "no transformation or conversion of subject matter representative of or constituting physical activity or objects." *In re Schrader*, 22 F.3d 290 (Fed. Cir. 2009). *See also In re Comiskey*, 554 F.3d 967 (Fed. Cir. 2009) (method and system for mandatory arbitration involving certain legal documents not § 101 patent-protectable subject matter). The *Bilski* decision also rejected the CAFC's attempt to make the machine-or-transformation test (requiring a process be tied to a particular machine or transform matter from one state to another) the only test to determine the patent eligibility of a process under § 101. This ruling thus preserves other tests from previous CAFC cases, such as the "useful, concrete, and tangible result" and the "algorithm applied to physical elements or process steps" tests.

In *Mayo Collaborative Servs. v. Prometheus Labs., Inc.*, 561 U.S. 66 (2012), the Supreme Court reiterated that transforming a law of nature into patent-eligible subject matter requires more than its combination with well-understood, routine, or conventional activities. While a patent claim may contain a law of nature, the claim cannot preempt entire use of the natural law and the additional claim elements must be significant. *Id.* Similarly, while naturally-occurring gene fragments are not patent-eligible by isolating them, artificial complimentary DNA is patent-eligible since it does not occur naturally. *Association for Molecular Pathology v. Myriad Genetics, Inc.*, 569 U.S. 576 (2013). *See also University of Utah Research v. Ambry Genetics Corp.*, 774 F.3d 755 (Fed. Cir. 2014). The AIA specified that the USPTO may not issue patents "directed to or encompassing a human organism" or "reducing, avoiding, or deferring tax liability".

The Supreme Court created a two-part test for patent eligibility in *Alice Corp. v. CLS Bank Int'l*, 573 U.S. 208 (2014). The first step considers whether a claim is "directed to" a patent-ineligible concept such as a law of nature, a natural phenomenon, or an abstract idea. If so, patent eligibility requires an "inventive concept" so an element or combination of elements of the claimed invention "'transform[s] the nature of the claim' into a patent-eligible application." This decision has been particularly damaging to software patents applications that do not improve a particular technology. *See, e.g., Enfish v. Microsoft,* 822 F.3d 1327 (Fed. Cir. 2016); *McRO v. Bandai,* 837 F.3d 1299 (Fed. Cir. 2016).

Inventions falling within (and not judicially excluded from) one or more of the five statutory protectable subject matter classes must meet a general standard of *novelty, utility,* and *non-obviousness* to receive utility patent protection. Novelty exists when an invention is not identically disclosed by "prior art" (information previously available to the public). *See Gayler v. Wilder*, 51 U.S. 477 (1850) (one who rediscovers lost arts would be entitled to a patent). Novelty is negated if prior art "anticipated" the invention. *See Coffin v. Ogden*, 85 U.S. 120 (1873) (patent invalid due to another's prior construction of the invention).

The America Invents Act ("AIA") amended 35 U.S.C. § 102 to define prior art as any disclosure anywhere in the world that is "patented, described in a printed publication, or in public use, on sale, or otherwise available to the public before the effective filing date of the claimed invention". This expanded disclosure rule has certain exceptions, including any publication by the inventor within one year of filing a patent application (thus preserving a grace period allowing the inventor a limited publication window prior to applying for a patent). A publicly disclosed sale is sufficiently "in public use, on sale, or otherwise available to the public before the effective filing date of the claimed invention" to prevent patent registration under 35 U.S.C. § 102(a), even if the invention's details were not publicly disclosed. *Helsinn Healthcare S.A. v. Teva Pharm. USA, Inc.*, 586 U.S. ___, 139 S. Ct. 628 (2019). Section 102 previously defined anticipation to include only those inventions that were known or used by others in a publicly accessible manner in the U.S. or patented or published anywhere in the world prior to a patent applicant's invention date.

The AIA defined prior art to include any U.S. patent applications (including foreign priority applications) effectively filed and published or deemed published by another inventor prior to the claimed invention's effective filing date. This embraced a "first-to-file" priority rule for U.S. patent applications similar to other nations. The previous "first-to-invent" system was much more evidence intensive and allowed inventors to delay filing and still receive patent protection. The tradeoff is that the breadth of disclosures and protections are often more limited when haste influences invention development and application preparation.

Utility exists when an invention has an obvious and direct benefit to mankind. Inventions that are frivolous or injurious to morals, health, or good order negate utility. An invention that has no known use or is useful only in the sense that it may be an object of further scientific research is not patentable. *Brenner v. Manson*, 383 U.S. 519 (1966); *In re Fisher*, 421 F.3d 1365 (Fed. Cir. 2005) (claimed nucleotide sequences a mere "object of use testing" lacked any specific and substantial utility). *But see In re Brana*, 51 F.3d 1560 (Fed. Cir. 1995) (*in vitro* and animal tests can prove utility to treat human disorders when human testing would require government approval).

An invention is non-obvious if the differences between the subject matter and prior art are such that the subject matter as a whole would not have been obvious at the time the invention was made to a person having ordinary skill in the subject matter. *Graham v. John Deere Co.*, 383 U.S. 1 (1966). The AIA repealed 35 U.S.C. § 103(b), which relaxed the non-obvious requirement for biotechnological processes.

In *KSR Int'l Co. v. Teleflex, Inc.*, 550 U.S. 398 (2007), the Supreme Court rejected a rigid application of the CAFC's "teaching, suggestion, or motivation" obviousness test to the extent it assumed a person of ordinary skill attempting to solve a problem will be led only to those elements of art designed to solve the same problem. The Court noted that a design need or market pressure to solve a problem with a finite number of identified, predictable solutions would give a person of ordinary skill good reason to pursue known options within their technical grasp, whether or not they address precisely the same problem. A particular combination that was "obvious to try" might show obviousness under 35 U.S.C. § 103.

To avoid an obviousness determination, an inventor should show an array of possible choices can achieve the inventor's objective, or problems the inventor solved that the prior art did not discuss. *PharmaStem Therapeutics, Inc. v. ViaCell, Inc.*, 491 F.3d 1342, 1364 (Fed. Cir. 2007). The AIA eliminated failure to disclose the best mode of practicing the invention as a ground for invalidity, unenforceability, or cancellation by the USPTO. While the AIA preserved best mode disclosure as a ground for USPTO examination, the USPTO never seriously policed this disclosure requirement in practice. Added time constraints from the first-to-file system supports the punishment's elimination.

The two other statutory patentable subject matter classes—ornamental designs and plants—have slightly different standards than utility patents. Design patents must be shown to be *novel, original,* and *ornamental* as they are based on the article's appearance and not utility. Similarly, plant patents must be a *distinct, new,* and *asexually-reproduced* variety not found in nature. Ornamental designs and asexually reproduced plants must be non-obvious as well as new. *See* 35 U.S.C. §§ 161, 171 ("The provisions of this title relating to patents for inventions shall apply to patents for plants [designs], except as otherwise provided."). *See also Egyptian*

Goddess, Inc. v. Swisa, Inc., 543 F.3d 665 (Fed. Cir. 2008) (Design patent infringement is determined by applying the purchasing care of an "ordinary observer", using prior art as the "frame of reference" for comparison, and discarding "point of novelty" or "nontrivial advance" approaches.)

b. Obtaining a Patent

U.S. patent applications are filed with the U.S. Patent and Trademark Office (USPTO) of the U.S. Department of Commerce. Prior to filing a patent application, inventors should have a patent attorney search USPTO patent records, much as one might search a real property title. This search helps determine whether patentability is probable.

Pursuant to 35 U.S.C. § 112, a patent application must include specifications containing 1) a written description of the invention (the "written description" requirement); 2) the manner and process of making and using the invention in clear, concise, and exact terms that would enable any person skilled in the art to make and use the same (the "enabling disclosure" requirement); 3) a disclosure of the best mode contemplated by the inventor of carrying out the invention (the "best mode" requirement); and 4) one or more claims particularly pointing out and distinctly claiming the subject matter which the applicant regards as their invention. The term "specification" identifies parts of the patent application preceding the claims.

Patent descriptions present a strategic challenge to applicants. Narrowing a description reduces the patent's value, while broadening a description increases the likelihood of rejection. Treating patent applications as an ongoing negotiation, attorneys often make broad initial claims and narrow them based upon the examiner's refusals. That said, "a patent is invalid for indefiniteness if its claims, read in light of the specification delineating the patent, and the prosecution history, fail to inform, with reasonable certainty those skilled in the art about the scope of the invention." *Nautilus, Inc. v. Biosig Instruments, Inc.*, 572 U.S. 898 (2014). A patent claiming an entire class of processes, machines, manufactures, or compositions of matter must enable a person skilled in the art to create or use the full scope of the claimed invention to avoid invalidity, not only a subset. *Amgen Inc. v. Sanofi,* 598 U.S. ___, 143 S. Ct. 1243 (2023).

Patent applications must be filed in the name of the actual inventor or inventors. *See* 35 U.S.C. § 115. The U.S. Constitution restricts federal patent protection to "inventors" and their "discoveries." To be an inventor, a person must contribute to the invention's conception. *See, e.g., Fiers v. Revel*, 984 F.2d 1164, 1168 (Fed. Cir. 1993). This does not require involvement in reducing the invention into practice. *In re DeBaun*, 687 F.2d 459, 463, (CCPA 1982). However, an inventor must contribute "a particular solution to the problem at hand, not just a general goal or research plan" as may occur with managerial involvement. *In re Verhoef*, 888 F.3d 1362, 1366 (Fed. Cir. 2018) The term "inventor" limits protectable subject matter to discoveries of human contrivance. *See, e.g., Thaler v. Iancu*, 1:20–

cv–00903 D.I. 33 (E.D. Va. April 6, 2021) (excluding artificial intelligence); *University of Utah v. Max-Planck-Gesellschaft zur Forderung der Wissenschaften E.V.*, 734 F.3d 1315 (2013) (excluding corporations).

Corporations may apply for patents, but only in the inventor's name. When an inventor assigns or is obligated to assign an invention to a company, the AIA permits the company to file a patent application in the inventor's name even if the inventor refuses to sign the required oath. The Bayh-Dole Act, 35 U.S.C. §§ 201(c), (e), 202(a), gave federal contractors such as universities, small businesses, and non-profit organizations control over the intellectual property created by federally-funded research. However, this Act does not automatically vest an inventor's title to an invention in a contractor or authorize contractors to unilaterally take title to an invention. *Board of Trust. of Leland Stanford Junior Univ. v. Roche Molecular Sys., Inc.*, 563 U.S. 776 (2011).

Unlike most nations, prior to 1994 a U.S. patent protection term was 17 years as measured from the date the patent issued. The Uruguay Round Agreements Act of 1994 amended 35 U.S.C. § 111 to permit filing provisional utility or plant patent applications without accompanying claims. Provisional applications allow U.S. inventors to establish priority without starting the limited patent protection term. Patent protection terms are now measured from the non-provisional application filing date, in accordance with Article 33 of the TRIPS Agreement. A provisional patent application must be replaced by a non-provisional one to avoid abandonment.

The AIA included patent examination improvements. The Act created a prioritized patent examination path at an additional fee. The AIA also codified a process allowing third party submission of potentially relevant prior art to challenge a patent application prior to issuance. It further provided a post-issuance mechanism to cure acts or omissions during the patent application's prosecution.

Historically, U.S. patent applications remained confidential until the USPTO issued a patent. Applicants could maintain trade secret protection for unprotectable inventions, even though this limited publicly-available prior art. The American Inventors Protection Act (AIPA) of 1999 (P.L. 106–113, 113 Stat. 1536, Nov. 29, 1999) (not to be confused with the AIA) required U.S. patent applications be published 18 months from the earliest filing date for which benefit was sought. Exceptions to this publication rule include 1) abandonment; 2) secrecy orders; 3) provisional applications; 4) design patent applications; and 5) an inventor request that the application not be published and certification the invention was not and will not be the subject of a foreign patent application that requires patent application publication 18 months after filing.

Patent applications under the Paris Convention determine priority by the earliest foreign filing date. To receive this priority upon motion, the inventor must file a U.S. patent within 12 months of the foreign filing for utility or plant patents (35 U.S.C.

§ 119), or within 6 months for design patents (35 U.S.C. § 172). The foreign patent filing disclosures must meet U.S. patent law requirements.

When using a U.S. patent application for foreign patent filings (or those based on an international agreement) where the other nation's invention description requirements are less extensive than the U.S. requires, the applicant may redact a U.S. application copy to eliminate parts not required by the foreign nation. *See* 35 U.S.C. § 122(b)(2)(B)(v), as amended by P.L. 106–113 (1999). This meets international treaty obligations for patent disclosures while maintaining confidentiality for purely domestic applications.

Opposers can challenge patent validity on any grounds but must file their opposition within nine months of the patent grant. Opposition and inter partes re-examination procedures cannot be instituted if the petitioner filed a civil action challenging a patent claim's validity. If an opposer subsequently files such a civil action, it will automatically be stayed unless the petitioner moves to dismiss it or the patent owner moves to lift the stay, files a civil action, or files a counterclaim for infringement. *See* 35 U.S.C. § 315.

For patents issued under the first-inventor-to-file rules, the AIA created a new post-grant opposition procedure in addition to existing ex parte and inter partes re-examination procedures. 35 U.S.C. §§ 302, 311. This post-grant opposition procedure allows limited challenges to a patent on §§ 102 or 103 grounds based on prior art from patents or printed publications.

Post-grant oppositions and inter partes re-examinations are heard by a three-judge panel at the Patent Trial and Appeal Board (PTAB). Inter partes re-examination procedures can only be instituted after the post-grant opposition period ends. The standard for opening the former is a reasonable likelihood that the petitioner will prevail with respect to at least one of the claims challenged.

The PTAB may now hear "derivation" proceedings in lieu of the previous interference proceedings. Interference proceedings determined first-to-invent priority. Derivation proceedings determine whether a competing application or prior disclosure was derived from the applicant's own work.

If the USPTO rejects an applicant's claims, the applicant may seek judicial review in the Court of Appeals for the Federal Circuit under 35 U.S.C. § 141 or through civil action against the USPTO's Director in the Eastern District of Virginia under 35 U.S.C. § 145. An applicant may introduce new evidence during the appeal, limited only by the Federal Rules of Evidence and Civil Procedure. *Kappos v. Hyatt*, 566 U.S. 431 (2012). For § 145 lawsuits, the USPTO is not entitled to attorney's fees as part of the applicant's obligation to pay all of the proceeding's expenses. *Peter v. NantKwest, Inc.*, 589 U.S. ___, 140 S. Ct. 365 (2019).

c. Transfer and Termination of Patents

A U.S. patent grants certain rights. The patent holder can exclude others from making, using, offering for sale, or selling the invention in the U.S.; importing the invention into the U.S.; and if the invention is a process, they can exclude making, using, offering for sale, selling, or importing into the U.S. any products made by that process. As a result of amendments made by the Uruguay Round Agreements Act of 1994, the patent protection term is twenty years from the filing date for utility and plant patents, and fourteen years from the date of issuance for design patents. *See* 35 U.S.C. §§ 154, 173. The American Inventors Protection Act (AIPA) of 1999 further amended § 154 to guarantee diligent applicants at least a 17 year protection term by extending the term of any patent not granted within 3 years of filing. *Wyeth v. Kappos*, 591 F.3d 1364 (Fed. Cir. 2009) discusses application of these adjustments for delays.

As with other forms of intellectual property, patent rights may be assigned or licensed. An assignment transfers all or some of the patentee's ownership rights in the invention. A license merely grants the licensee permission to make, use, sell, offer for sale, or import the invention. While patent rights are federally created rights, state contract and property laws largely govern patent assignment or licensing. While patent infringement must be litigated in federal courts, patent assignments and licensing agreements are enforced in state courts unless diversity of citizenship or a federal question exists.

Even so, state law governing patent assignments and licenses must be consistent with federal patent law. Thus, states may not enforce a patent assignment or license that was judicially declared invalid. Nor may contract provisions extend a license or royalty period beyond the patent's expirations. *Brulotte v. Thys Co.*, 379 U.S. 29 (1964).

The common law regulating patent assignments and licenses creates important rights independent of federal patent law. The common-law "shop right" doctrine, for example, treats an employer who can show an employee developed a patentable invention on company time and with company facilities and materials as having an implied, irrevocable, non-assignable, non-exclusive, royalty-free license to use the employee's invention. If an employee is hired specifically for research or development, courts may find an implied agreement that any discoveries made will belong to the employer.

Patent right transfers must comply with federal antitrust law as well. A patent itself is a legal monopoly, which its owner may exploit freely. However, patents cannot be used to create other monopolies or unreasonable restraints on trade. A recurring patent licensing controversy is whether license restrictions are reasonably necessary to reward the patent owner for the invention, or if they constitute "patent misuse" by unreasonably restraining trade. While antitrust principles must be considered, patent licenses are still evaluated based on patent rather than antitrust law principles. *Kimble v. Marvel Ent., LLC*, 576 U.S. 446 (2015) (declining to adopt antitrust "rule of reason" approach to patent license review as contrary to policy and *stare decisis*).

Settlement agreements can be a form of license. *FTC v. Actavis, Inc.*, 570 U.S. 136 (2013) resolved a patent infringement lawsuit between a brand name and generic drug manufacturer. The patent infringement lawsuit resolved through "reverse payment" settlements, where the generic company agreed not to bring its FDA-approved product to market in return for a share of the brand-name manufacturer's monopoly profits. The Court held this arrangement is not *per se* unlawful but must be evaluated under the antitrust "rule of reason" approach even though the reverse settlement's anti-competitive effects could fall within patent law policies. The Court noted the pro-competition objectives of the Hatch-Waxman Act regulating these drug patent disputes, 21 U.S.C. § 355(j)(2)(A)(vii)(IV)), and that antitrust factors should apply when evaluating the scope of monopoly and antitrust immunity a patent can convey.

The Supreme Court held states could no longer apply the common law "licensee estoppel" doctrine in *Lear, Inc. v. Adkins*, 395 U.S. 653 (1969). This doctrine prevented patent validity challenges by a patent licensee. *Lear* further held states could not require ongoing royalty payments by licensees during patent validity litigation. The Court concluded that the licensee estoppel doctrine discouraged legitimate attacks on patent validity by the only parties with sufficient economic incentive to mount the attack.

But cf., *Roberts v. Sears, Roebuck & Co.*, 573 F.2d 976 (7th Cir. 1978) (*Lear* inapplicable and a district court correctly declined to decide patent validity in a suit for fraud, negligent misrepresentation, and breach of a confidential relationship when a company procured patent right assignment of an employee's invention created while off duty).

Where a licensee seeks a declaratory judgment against a patent owner that its products do not infringe the licensed patent, the patent owner must prove the alleged infringement, and the Federal Circuit has subject-matter jurisdiction over the dispute since the cause of action is based in patent law. *Medtronic, Inc. v. Mirowski Family Ventures, LLC*, 571 U.S. 191 (2014).

Federal patent law creates certain procedural formalities for patent transfers. 35 U.S.C. § 261 permits patent and patent application assignments, or fractional interests therein. However, the assignment must be by a written instrument recorded in the U.S. Patent Office to have full legal effect against subsequent bona fide purchasers. Patent licenses have no recording requirements. Oral assignments and unrecorded written assignments function much like a license—they create rights between the parties to the agreement but not rights that are enforceable against third parties.

Classifying an agreement as an assignment or a license is no mere formality. Courts will classify an agreement according to its actual legal effect, regardless of how the agreement is labeled. An exclusive license to make, use, or sell the patented invention with "all substantial rights" (usually patent enforcement) amounts to an assignment despite its label.

Whether an agreement is an assignment or a license has many practical ramifications, such as determining who has the right to sue for infringement in federal court. The right to sue for infringement is an incident of ownership, so it can be transferred under an assignment but not under a (non-exclusive) license. In a licensing arrangement the licensor is, in effect, merely agreeing not to sue a licensee for making specified uses of the patented invention. A non-exclusive licensee has no right to sue others for infringement. The licensee depends on the licensor to protect the patent from infringement.

Patent rights terminate when a patent expires and are retroactively extinguished upon judicial invalidation. Judicial patent invalidation prior to their expiration is a frequent, and to a certain extent, unavoidable federal patent law feature. As the patent application process is confidential and largely non-adversarial, the USPTO has simply been unable to discern whether patent applications in fact disclose novel and non-obvious inventions with a high degree of accuracy.

Prior to the Court of Appeals for the Federal Circuit's creation, the patent viability problem was further exacerbated by the federal court tendency to use a more stringent non-obviousness standard than that the USPTO. Consequently, while the USPTO granted about 60% of all patent applications filed, courts invalidated as much as 60% of all patents granted. Creating the Federal Circuit Court of Appeals, which has exclusive jurisdiction to hear appeals of patent application denials and patent infringement proceedings, brought greater uniformity to non-obviousness tests. *But see KSR Int'l Co. v. Teleflex, Inc.*, 550 U.S. 398 (2007), *supra*, rejecting the lower court's overly rigid approach to non-obviousness.

2. COPYRIGHTABLE LITERARY AND ARTISTIC WORKS

Federal copyright law, like federal patent law, sets substantive and procedural requirements to obtain protection for literary and artistic works. Substantive statutory requirements specify what constitutes a protectable "writing" of an "author," pursuant to Article 1, section 8, clause 8 of the U.S. Constitution. Various procedural requirements specify how a copyright is acquired, protected, transferred, and terminated.

a. Subject Matter Protected

Federal copyright protection requires a literary or artistic work meet the constitutional definition of a "writing", and its creator meet the constitutional definition of an "author." The U.S. Constitution promotes "Science" and the "Useful Arts," as interpreted in their 18th century context to mean knowledge either worthy to be known for its own sake or useful in achieving some end. As the parallel structures of the Patent and Copyright Clauses show, U.S. copyright laws promote the progress of "science" while U.S. patent laws promote the progress of the "useful arts", not the reverse.

Following this constitutional policy, the Supreme Court defined a "writing" as all means by which "ideas in the mind of the author are given visible expression" or as any physical rendering of fruits of creative intellectual or aesthetic labor. *See, e.g., Burrow-Giles Lithographic Co. v. Sarony,* 111 U.S. 53 (1884) (Section 4952 of the Copyright Act of 1865, explicitly extending copyright protection to photographs, was constitutional); *Goldstein v. California*, 412 U.S. 546 (1973). Thus defined, a constitutional "writing" includes virtually any literary or artistic work, including visual works and those created for a purely commercial purpose. Implicit in the court's broad definition is a judicial policy of deferring to Congress as to what works should receive copyright protection. While the constitutional definition of a writing is broad, it arguably limits which works Congress can grant copyright protection. The Court held as a constitutional matter that a "writing" is (1) the fruit of intellectual labor that is (2) reduced to tangible form.

This intellectual labor requirement excludes trademarks (or at least those not inherently distinctive) from copyright protection. In *The Trade-Mark Cases,* 100 U.S. 82 (1879) the Court held expenditure of intellectual labor in creating a trademark (or at least the particular trademarks in question) was too trivial to merit copyright protection. The Court's conclusion is open to criticism to the extent it applies to trademarks that are fanciful, arbitrary, or have some secondary meaning. Still, requiring some minimal degree of intellectual labor is itself sound enough, as it excludes common words and phrases from copyright protection.

Even if there is no constitutional bar to granting copyright protection for fanciful marks or names, policy dictates copyright law must not render superfluous the likelihood of confusion or dilution requirements for federal trademark infringement. In *Feist Publ'ns, Inc. v. Rural Tel. Serv. Co.*, 499 U.S. 340 (1991), the Supreme Court reaffirmed the requirement that a work be "original" is not merely a statutory requirement, but rather a constitutional requirement implicit in the word "writing."

Requiring the product of intellectual labor be reduced to tangible form excludes ephemeral works (i.e., those not fixed in any tangible form) from federal copyright protection. However, Congress provided a federal cause of action against the unauthorized fixation and trafficking in sound recordings and music videos. *See* 17 U.S.C. § 1101.

17 U.S.C. § 201 grants the author of an original work its associated rights. Requiring writings be the works of an "author" limits federal copyright protection to those who expend the intellectual labor to create the writing and imposes a constitutional requirement that the fruits of that labor be original to the author and not mere copies of an earlier work.

A work of authorship must be created by a human being. *Burrow-Giles Lithographic Co. v. Sarony*, 111

U.S. 53, 58 (1884). This excludes protection for works prepared by animals or nature. *See, e.g., Naruto v. Slater,* 888 F.3d 418 (9th Cir. 2018) (animals lack standing to sue for copyright infringement; sections of the Copyright Act imply an author must be human); *Urantia Found. v. Maaherra,* 114 F.3d 955 (9th Cir. 1997) (no protection for a work created by non-human "spiritual beings"). Machine learning, and ultimately artificial intelligence, presents a unique challenge as a created work may originate from software programmed by a human that contributes intervening steps outside human direction. To date, attempts to protect machine-generated works have been rejected. *See, U.S. Copyright Office, Cancellation Decision re: Zarya of the Dawn* (Vau001480196) (Feb. 21, 2023) (protecting human-authored text and selection and arrangement of text and images, but not the machine-generated images); *Thaler v. Perlmutter,* 1:22-cv-01564 (D.D.C. Aug. 18, 2023) (rejecting protection for artwork autonomously created by a computer algorithm).

For most purposes, the 1976 Act operates prospectively from its January 1, 1978 effective date. Certain provisions of its predecessor, the Copyright Act of 1909, remained in force for works created prior to that date. The 1909 and 1976 Acts have both different definitions of what constitutes a copyrightable work and different procedures for obtaining, transferring, and terminating copyrights.

Prior to the 1976 Act, copyright protection came from a dual system of state common-law protection prior to general publication and federal statutory protection after general publication. Unlike the dual trademark law system which provides *concurrent* federal and state protection of trade symbols, common-law and statutory copyright provided *alternative* protection. "General publication" served as the all-important dividing line between the two systems. Common-law copyright was based on the right of the author or originator of a literary or artistic work to keep the work secret or place conditions on its limited publication to others. Federal copyright law, conversely, provided exclusive protection for a work after its unlimited or general publication. Under the 1976 Act, federal copyright protection extends to all otherwise copyrightable literary or artistic works fixed in tangible form, whether generally published or not. This preempts much of what was formerly known as the common law of copyright.

Section 102(a) of the 1976 Act states copyright protection "subsists" (i.e., automatically vests) in original works of authorship fixed in any tangible medium of expression. A work is "fixed" in a tangible medium of expression if and only if its "embodiment . . . is sufficiently permanent or stable to permit it to be perceived, reproduced, or otherwise communicated for a period of more than transitory duration." 17 U.S.C. § 101. *See MAI Sys. Corp. v. Peak Computer Inc.,* 991 F.2d 511 (9th Cir. 1993) (loading a computer program into random access memory, which is erased when a computer is turned off, constitutes fixation). *But cf., Cartoon Network v. CSC Holdings,* 536 F.3d 121 (2d Cir. 2008) (a work momentarily captured in remote storage digital video recorder system buffer was embodied for only a transitory duration and thus not "fixed").

Section 102(a) enumerates eight specific classes included within the statutory term "works of authorship." The statutory definition of the term "including" and the legislative history of the 1976 Act reveal that Congress did not intend this list to be exhaustive. Rather, the classes are merely enumerated to tailor the scope of exclusive right for each specified subject matter class. On the other hand, Congress disclaimed any intent to create an open-ended class of protectable works. For 1976 Act protection, a work must either fall clearly within or be reasonably analogous to one of the following categories of works: (1) Literary; (2) Musical; (3) Dramatic; (4) Pantomimes and choreographic (reduced to tangible form); (5) Pictorial, graphic and sculptural; (6) Motion pictures and other audiovisual; (7) Sound Recordings; and (8) Architectural. Section 101 further defines some categories. Several of these classes, i.e., pantomimes, choreographic works, sound recordings, and architectural works (as opposed to architectural plans), had no counterpart under the 1909 Act.

The 1909 and 1976 Acts both protect compilations and derivative works. Under the 1976 Act, a compilation is a work formed by collecting and assembling pre-existing materials or data. A derivative work is any work based on a pre-existing work. Derivative works may consist of a translation, sound recording, abridgement, condensation, fictionalization, art reproduction, motion picture version, or any other form where the pre-existing work is recast, transformed, or adapted. Any work based on pre-existing material, data, or on a pre-existing work can thus be separately copyrighted. However, the compilation or derivative work must have enough originality to constitute an original work of authorship and cannot infringe any copyright others may have in the pre-existing work. Mere expenditure of time, labor, or money is not sufficient to make a compilation or derivative work original. *See Feist Publ'ns, Inc. v. Rural Tel. Serv. Co.*, 499 U.S. 340 (1991) (phone book lacks the requisite originality for a copyrightable work).

Congress passed the Architectural Works Copyright Protection Act in 1990 to specifically include architectural works in copyright law. This did not affect existing protections for architectural and engineering drawings which have long received copyright protection as pictorial or graphic works. *See, e.g., Del Madera Props. v. Rhodes & Gardner, Inc.,* 637 F.Supp. 262, 263 (N.D.Cal. 1985). Architectural works are distinguished from other structures based on whether they are designed for human occupancy. *See* 37 C.F.R. § 202.11; *Gaylord v. United States,* 595 F.3d 1464 (Fed. Cir. 2010). Exclusive rights in an architectural work do not include the right to prevent others from taking pictures or photographs of a publicly visible architectural work. *See* 17 U.S.C. § 120; *Leicester v. Warner Bros.*, 232 F.3d 1212, 1217 (9th Cir. 2000). A photographer may still secure copyright protection for such images. *Pagano v. Chas. Beseler Co.*, 234 F. 963, 963–64 (S.D.N.Y. 1916). While an artist may have "moral rights" to control the display or destruction of their artwork, copyright law created exceptions allowing a building's owner to alter or destroy the building, including any artwork painted on or otherwise attached to the building.

Certain subject matter classes are expressly or implicitly excluded from federal copyright protection. For example, Congress expressly incorporated a prior 1909 Act judicial exclusion into § 101 of the 1976 Act, stating the design of a useful article shall be considered a "pictorial, graphic or sculptural work" only to the extent that the design incorporates pictorial, graphic, or sculptural features that can be identified separately from the utilitarian features of the work. The legislative history (though not the 1976 Act language itself) indicates distinctive typefaces are excluded from protection.

Section 102(b) expressly excludes copyright protection for any idea, procedure, process, system, method of operation, concept, or discovery. This codifies the separation of protected expression from ideas, allowing instant public availability and enjoyment of ideas, theories, and facts. *Golan v. Holder*, 565 U.S. 302 (2012) (§ 514 of the Uruguay Round Agreements Act, bringing certain public domain works back under copyright, did not exceed Congress's constitutional authority under the Copyright Clause). Similarly, the "scènes à faire" doctrine refuses copyright protection to expressions which are standard, stock, or common treatments within a genre. *See, e.g., Mattel, Inc. v. Azrak-Hamway Int'l, Inc.*, 724 F.2d 357, 360 (2d Cir. 1983).

In the software field, this doctrine excludes protection of features common to many designs, public domain materials, and elements dictated by efficiency or external environmental factors.

The § 102(b) limitations do not exclude copyright protection for computer programs despite the prohibitions against protecting processes, systems, and operation methods. *See Apple Computer, Inc. v. Franklin Computer Corp.*, 714 F.2d 1240 (3d Cir. 1983) (computer programs, whether in object code or source code, are literary works capable of copyright protection even when embedded in an internal permanent memory device incorporated into the circuitry of a computer). *See also* P.L. No. 96–517, Dec. 12, 1980 (amending the Copyright Act of 1976 by adding a definition of a computer program and a new § 117 stating it is not an infringement for a computer program owner to make a copy of it as an essential step in using the program with a machine or for archival purposes). Even so, functional aspects of software cannot be protected. *See, e.g., Sega Enters. Ltd. v. Accolade, Inc.,* 977 F.2d 1510, 1524 (9th Cir. 1992); *Bateman v. Mnemonics, Inc.*, 79 F.3d 1532 (11th Cir. 1996).

By not expressly including literary titles as a class of protectable subject matter, Congress presumably ratified prior case law excluding them from copyright protection under the 1909 Act. *Cf.* 37 C.F.R. § 202.1(a) (Copyright Office rule excluding as not subject to copyright: "words and short phrases, such as names, titles, and slogans").

Works analogous to (and not expressly or impliedly excluded from) one or more of the foregoing statutory protectable subject matter classes must also constitute (1) an original work of authorship (2) reduced to tangible form. 17 U.S.C. § 102. Congress purposely left the phrase "original works of authorship" undefined in the 1976 Act, stating its intention to incorporate without change the standard of originality established by the courts under the 1909 Act. H. Rep. No. 94–1476. Under the 1909 Act, "originality" meant the work originated from the author and was not merely a copy of an earlier work.

Section 103 of the 1976 Act, like the 1909 Act, specifically extends copyright protection to compilations (i.e., collections of preexisting materials or data) and derivative works (i.e., works based upon one or more preexisting works). A work, including a compilation or derivative work, is more than a mere copy of some earlier work only if the author contributes something more than a trivial variation that is recognizably the author's own. *See Meshwerks v. Toyota Motor Sales U.S.A.*, 528 F.3d 1258 (2008) (digital vehicle depictions were copies, not independent creations; the relevant expressive creation occurred outside the modeling process).

Some courts require protectable derivative works be "substantially different" from the underlying work to prevent overlapping claims. *See, e.g., Gracen v. Bradford Exch.*, 698 F. 2d 300 (7th Cir. 1983). Other courts do not find derivative works subject to a more exacting originality requirement that other works of authorship. *See Shrock v. Learning Curve Int'l*, 586

F.3d 513 (7th Cir. 2009) (rejecting both the *Gracen* rule and argument that promotional photographs of children's toys lacked sufficient originality for copyright protection).

This minimal originality requirement markedly contrasts with patent law's non-obviousness requirement for obtaining a utility, design, or plant patent. The difference stems from the difference in the constitutional use of the words "authors" and "writings" on the one hand and "inventors" and "discoveries" on the other. The latter terms imply patent protection requires an element of inventiveness and human manipulation, while the former demand only that the work be original to the author and fixed in a tangible form. Copyright law's lower protection standard explains this, as copyright law only covers original expression and not the facts or ideas expressed.

Distinguishing protected expression from unprotected facts and ideas can be challenging. Courts vary protected expression findings based on a work's originality and creativity. For example, a fictional literary work's author may obtain protection for both the work's literal words and any reasonably-detailed original structural patterns appearing in the work. A factual or utilitarian work's author has a protectable interest in any original expression used to convey facts or ideas, and in any originality in selecting or arranging the facts. *See, e.g., Whelan Assocs., Inc. v. Jaslow Dental Lab., Inc.*, 797 F.2d 1222 (3d Cir. 1986) (computer program copyright protection may extend beyond the programs' literal code to their structure, sequence, and organization). *But cf. Hoehling v. Universal City Studios, Inc.*, 618 F.2d 972 (2d Cir. 1980) (historical interpretation of Hindenburg disaster, even if original, is not protected by copyright); *Computer Assocs. Int'l v. Altai*, 982 F.2d 693 (2d Cir. 1992) (*Whelan*'s general formulation that a computer program's overall purpose equates with the program's idea is descriptively inadequate).

Diminishing originality in an author's expression, selection, or arrangement of facts or ideas reduces copyright protection to mere prohibition against outright copying. Where authors draw identical maps or compile identical information directories, each work can obtain copyright protection and no author can claim infringement against another so long as each work was produced by independent effort. A mere alphabetized directory of names, addresses, and telephone numbers lacks the requisite originality to constitute a protectable work of authorship, notwithstanding the "sweat of the brow" required to compile the directory. *See Feist Publ'ns, Inc. v. Rural Telephone Serv. Co.*, 499 U.S. 340 (1991). *See also Financial Info., Inc. v. Moody's Investors Serv.*, 808 F.2d 204 (2d Cir. 1986) (daily report containing municipal bond information confirmed insufficient evidence of independent creation to render a work of authorship); *Lotus Dev. Corp. v. Borland Int'l*, 49 F.3d 807 (1st Cir. 1995) (computer menu command hierarchy in spreadsheet program not copyrightable subject matter); *Matthew Bender & Co. v. West Pub. Co.*, 158 F.3d 693 (2d Cir. 1998) (copyright does not protect system of volume and page numbering). An idea and its expression will merge and not be protectable if there are a limited number of ways to express an idea and copyright protection could exhaust all possible expressions. *Morrissey v. Proctor & Gamble Co.*, 379 F.2d 675 (1st Cir. 1967) (sweepstakes contest instructions not protectable).

The courts and Congress similarly limited the scope of copyright protection for objects having a utilitarian function. Any discrete literary or artistic features of a useful object are copyrightable. However, purely utilitarian features and aesthetic features not capable of existing independently as a work of art are not copyrightable. *See, e.g., Carol Barnhart, Inc. v. Economy Cover Corp.*, 773 F.2d 411 (2d Cir. 1988) (human torso forms for clothing displays cannot be copyright-protected works as the aesthetic and artistic features are inseparable from their utilitarian function). Utility or design patent protection is available for these features. Thus, while a statuette that happens to serve as a lamp base can receive copyright protection, a lamp itself cannot no matter how aesthetic its design. *See, e.g., Mazer v. Stein*, 347 U.S. 201 (1954); *Esquire, Inc. v. Ringer*, 591 F.2d 796 (D.C. Cir. 1978).

Aesthetic elements of useful articles may receive copyright protection if they are a "work of art separate from the useful article" and would qualify as a protectable pictorial or graphic work "if [they] were imagined separately from the useful article into which [they were] incorporated." *Star Athletica, LLC v. Varsity Brands, Inc.*, 580 U.S. 405 (2017) (copyright protection may be secured even if the design feature makes the article more useful).

Copyright protection is not available to tangible forms of expression that function as identifying trade symbols. *See* 37 C.F.R. § 202.1(a) (Copyright Office rule excluding the following from copyright: "words and short phrases such as names, titles, and slogans; mere variations of typographical ornamentations lettering or coloring; familiar symbols or designs; mere listing of ingredients"). While one may question whether all such symbols should properly be excluded as a constitutional matter, there are persuasive policy reasons for excluding trademarks from copyright protection. The *Sears-Compco* decisions emphasize that the right to identify a product without confusion is not necessarily synonymous with the exclusive right to use a symbol. The USPTO and courts both concluded that trademark and copyright protection should be alternative, not concurrent. Thus, a word, symbol, or slogan functioning as a trademark does not constitute a work of authorship. Commercial prints and labels that do not function as a trademark, however, are copyrightable subject matter. *See, e.g., Drop Dead Co. v. S.C. Johnson & Son, Inc.*, 326 F.2d 87 (9th Cir. 1963) (upholding copyright and trademark infringement finding against copier of a product's laudatory and instructional words and label design).

b. Obtaining a Copyright

Copyright protection did not always occur automatically upon fixing a work in a tangible medium of expression. Federal copyright protection under the 1909 Act required the author publish the work with a copyright notice to receive protection. General publication without the required notice abandoned the author's rights to the work. This draconian rule led courts to distinguish between general and "limited" publication. Displaying a graphic artwork, delivering or broadcasting a lecture or speech, or performing or broadcasting a play, dance, or musical work were all classified as limited rather than general publications and did not require copyright notice. *See, e.g., King v. Mister Maestro Inc.*, 224 F.Supp. 101 (S.D.N.Y. 1963) (Dr. Martin Luther King's famous "I Have a Dream" speech, delivered to 200,000 people, was not a general publication); *Estate of Martin Luther King, Jr. v. CBS, Inc.*, 194 F.3d 1211 (11th Cir. 1999).

Common-law copyright protection formerly held distinct advantages over federal protection. Unlike federal statutory copyrights, common-law protection lasted indefinitely, arose automatically upon creation, extended to all foreign or domestic authors, and excluded any use of the protected work by others (whether for profit or not). Congress preempted common-law copyright protection in the 1976 Act. This was likely to provide more balanced protection for unpublished works, including performances and displays, at least with respect to any federally protected (or clearly unprotected) works of authorship fixed in a tangible medium of expression. *See* 17 U.S.C. § 301. Common-law copyright may continue for unfixed works of authorship. *Cf.*, *Estate of Hemingway v. Random House*, 244 N.E.2d 250 (N.Y. 1968) (assuming without a decision that certain limited kinds of spoken dialogue might be protected, but specifying that the speaker must indicate an intent to exercise control over publication).

Under the 1976 Act, an author obtains federal copyright protection (and presumably loses any common-law protection) automatically upon fixing a work in a tangible medium of expression. Until 1989, maintaining and enforcing a copyright still required certain formalities. Works published without copyright notice, for example, could lose their protection unless relatively few copies were made or certain remedial steps were taken.

The Visual Artists Rights Act of 1990 grants a visual work of art's author an exclusive right to (1) *claim authorship* (the attribution right) and (2) *prevent* any intentional *distortion, mutilation,* or other *modification* of a qualifying work of visual art, or any intentional or grossly negligent *destruction* of a work of recognized stature (the right of integrity). 17 U.S.C. § 106A. Section 301 was amended to preempt equivalent state law rights for visual art works. The § 106A rights are analogous to an author's "moral rights" common in Europe and elsewhere. However, U.S. moral rights are far more limited given § 101's very narrow definition of a "work of visual art."

When the United States joined the Berne Convention for the Protection of Literary and Artistic Works on March 1, 1989, the U.S. had to provide copyright protections for works without imposing any formalities. In implementing the Berne Convention, Congress made copyright notice use optional, though this notice still eliminates an innocent infringement defense. 17 U.S.C. § 401. Copyright registration and deposit became optional for foreign works claiming Berne Convention protection as well. However, these acts are still preconditions to bringing an infringement action against U.S. or other foreign works. The deposit and registration requirements help designate a protected work and develop the Library of Congress' collection.

A copyright term was 28 years under the 1909 Act, with a renewal right for an additional 28 years vesting exclusively in the author or certain of the author's heirs. The 1976 Act provided a single, longer copyright term: the life of the author plus 50 years. This Sonny Bono Copyright Term Extension Act extended the latter term to 70 years. For anonymous or pseudonymous works or works made for hire, the term is 95 years from the publication date or 120 years from creation, whichever expires first. The Supreme Court affirmed the Sonny Bono Copyright Term Extension Act's constitutionality in *Eldred v. Ashcroft*, 537 U.S. 186 (2003).

Existing works still under federal copyright protection in 1976 had their protection extended to the remainder of the initial term and a renewal term of 67 years. Works within their renewal term received protection for a total of 95 years from the date of first publication. For unpublished works created (and subject to common law copyright protection) on the new Act's January 1, 1978 effective date, protection extended until December 31, 2002 if the work remained unpublished or until December 31, 2047 if the work was published prior to December 31, 2002. This rule limits a work's protective term and encourages publication.

Unpublished works receive copyright protection without regard to the author's nationality or domicile under § 104 of the 1976 Act. Published works are protected only if, when first published, either (1) one or more of the authors was either a U.S. national or domiciliary, or a national, domiciliary, or sovereign authority of a treaty party to a relevant international agreement, or were stateless; (2) the work was first published in the U.S. or a foreign nation treaty party on the date of first publication; (3) the work is a sound recording first fixed within a treaty party nation; (4) the work is a pictorial, graphic, or sculptural work incorporated into a building or other structure, or an architectural work embodied in a building or structure located in the U.S. or a treaty party nation; (5) the work was first published by the United Nations, any of its agencies, or the Organization of American States; or (6) the work comes within the scope of a relevant Presidential proclamation.

Section 104A restores copyright protection to certain works not in the public domain in their source country but that are in the U.S. public domain due to (1) noncompliance with U.S. copyright law formalities; (2) lack of subject matter protection for sound recordings fixed before February 15, 1972; or (3) lack of national eligibility. *See Golan v. Holder*, 565 U.S. 302 (2012) (upholding constitutionality of this copyright term restoration); *Dam Things from Denmark, a/k/a/ Troll Co. ApS v. Russ Berrie & Co.*, 290 F.3d 548 (3d Cir. 2002) (while a foreign author has a restored copyright, a derivative work's creator is considered a licensee rather than an infringer under 17 U.S.C. § 104A(d)(3); the trial court erred in granting preliminary injunctive relief by conflating the derivative work originality test with the substantial similarity test for infringement).

While copyright vests initially in a work's author or authors under § 201(a) of the 1976 Act, § 201(b) alters this vestment for works made for hire. Section 101A defines "work made for hire" as either a (1) work prepared by an employee within the scope of employment; or (2) work specially ordered or commissioned and prepared for one or more of nine specified uses, if (but only if) the parties expressly agreed in a written and signed instrument that the work is a work made for hire. These nine use categories (with defined terms appearing in quotes) are as a: 1) contribution to a "collective work"; 2) part of a "motion picture" or other "audiovisual work"; 3) translation; 4) "supplementary work" (including any work prepared for publication as a secondary adjunct to another author's work, such as an introduction or illustration); 5) "compilation"; 6) "instructional text"; 7) test; 8) answer materials for a test; or 9) atlas. When a work is made for hire, the person or entity commissioning the work is considered the work's author and owns all rights to the work unless the parties expressly agreed otherwise in a written and signed instrument.

The creator's employment status may affect a work's copyright ownership. Courts apply common-law agency principles to decide whether a person is an employee or independent contractor. *See Community for Creative Non-Violence v. Reid*, 490 U.S. 730 (1989) (sculptor's independent contractor status meant the sculpture was not a work made for hire as it did not fall within the nine enumerated categories, although dicta indicated contributing the sculpture's base may render it a joint work).

c. Transfer and Termination of Copyrights

Copyright in a work may be transferred in whole or in part throughout the term of the copyright, so long as certain formalities are observed. A copyright owner may license others to copy, distribute, perform, or display the copyrighted work. As with trademarks and patents, common-law property and contract principles largely govern copyright assignment and license validity including the common-law "shop-right" doctrine. *See also Morseburg v. Balyon*, 621 F.2d 972 (9th Cir. 1980) (The 1909 Copyright Act does not preempt the California Resale Royalties Act which requires a royalty payment to the artist when a fine arts work is sold in California or the seller resides in California); *but see Association of Am. Publishers v. Frosh*, 586 F.Supp.3d 379 (D. Md. 2022) (state mandatory license of electronic literary products to

Maryland libraries unconstitutional and preempted by the Copyright Act).

For a valid copyright transfer, federal law requires an assignment or exclusive license be conveyed by written instrument signed by the rights owner or their duly authorized agent. 17 U.S.C. § 204(a). A non-exclusive license, by contrast, may be conveyed orally or by mere conduct. An assignment or exclusive license must be recorded in the Copyright Office to be enforceable against anyone other than the parties to the transfer. 17 U.S.C. § 205.

In addition to allowing for voluntary copyright licensing, the 1976 Act contains many compulsory (i.e., legally mandated) licensing provisions. These include compulsory licensing of: 1) non-dramatic musical works to make and distribute phonorecords or digitally transmissions after a phonorecord of the work was distributed by the copyright owner's authority (§ 115); 2) published pictorial, graphic, sculptural, and non-dramatic musical works for non-commercial broadcasts (§ 118); 3) secondary transmissions of works by cable television systems (§ 111); 4) general and local satellite retransmission of television signals (§§ 119, 122); 5) certain non-interactive digital audio transmissions of sound recordings (§ 114); and 6) certain ephemeral recordings to facilitate digital transmissions permitted under § 114 (§ 112(e)).

Reproduction and distribution rights are subject to compulsory licensing of publicly distributed non-dramatic musical works for other artists to make "cover recordings". 15 U.S.C. § 115. A licensee may also make a musical arrangement of the licensed work to the extent necessary to adapt the work to the style or manner of interpretation of the performance involved. The arrangement cannot, however, change the melody or fundamental character of the work.

Reproduction and distribution rights in a work do not include a right to make adaptations of the work. A copyright owner that licensed a work's reproduction or distribution rights may still sue the licensee for infringement if the licensee makes unauthorized changes to the work. *See, e.g., Gilliam v. Am. Broad. Cos.*, 538 F.2d 14 (2d Cir. 1976) (preliminary injunctive relief upheld against licensee attempting to edit licensed programming).

The § 109 "first sale" doctrine limits distribution and display copyrights, allowing the purchaser of a particular copy or phonorecord embodying a copyright work to sell, dispose of, or publicly display the work to viewers at the purchaser's location. This limits a copyright owner's ability to control the work or purchaser's business conduct after the sale. The first sale doctrine is limited to distribution and display rights and does not permit creation of derivative works. *Mirage Editions, Inc. v. Albuquerque A.R.T. Co.*, 856 F.2d 1341 (9th Cir. 1988). Section 109(a) is silent regarding geography, so the first sale doctrine applies to copies of a work lawfully made abroad as well as domestically. *Kirtsaeng v. John Wiley & Sons, Inc.*, 568 U.S. 519 (2013). Section 109(b) limits the first sale doctrine to exclude rentals or leases of phonorecords or computer software due to the likelihood of unauthorized copying.

As technological progress diminishes the cost of reproducing and distributing many types of works, copyright owners have taken steps to limit even permissible copying of their works. The Audio Home Recording Act of 1992 created Chapter 10 of the Copyright Act, 17 U.S.C. §§ 1001 *et seq.*, providing a statutory scheme for regulating digital audio recording devices. Manufacturers of such recording devices must include controls to manage serial copying and pay royalties to the music industry. The statute is essentially a dead letter as the technology was not widely adopted.

The Digital Performance Rights in Sound Recordings Act amended § 106 of the Copyright Act to provide a limited public performance right for sound recordings through digital audio transmission. Internet broadcasts, or "streaming", have made this right quite valuable. An entity communicating the same perceptible images and sounds to multiple people simultaneously transmits a performance to the public within the meaning of 17 U.S.C. § 106(4) and may be liable for copyright infringement. *Am. Broad. Cos. v. Aereo, Inc.*, 573 U.S. 431 (2014) (service providing television programming over the internet using dedicated antennas performed the works rather than merely supplying equipment).

Software creators frequently assert their works are licensed rather than sold, and therefore not subject to the first sale doctrine. *But see UMG Recordings, Inc. v. Augusto*, 628 F. 3d 1175, 1180 (9th

Cir. 2011) (the transaction's substance, not the label, governs whether software sold or licensed). These "shrink-wrap" licenses were originally imposed within a physical disk's packaging and asserted the purchaser agreed to the contract by opening the disk's wrapper, contract unseen.

Shrink-wrap and related licensing is generally an accepted practice. In *ProCD v. Zeidenberg*, 86 F.3d 1447 (7th Cir. 1996), shrink-wrap licenses were held enforceable under Uniform Commercial Code Art. 2 and not preempted by § 301 of the Copyright Act as the contractual rights involved were not equivalent to any exclusive rights within the general scope of copyright. A federal court held Louisiana's statute codifying shrink-wrap licenses was preempted by § 117 of the Copyright Act, which grants the owner of a software copy the right to make another copy or an adaptation as an essential step to use the program or for archival purposes. *Vault Corp. v. Quaid Software Ltd.*, 847 F.2d 255 (5th Cir. 1988). This decision is criticized since § 117 confers certain rights to software copy owners, not licensees, whereas the contracts enforceable by state law specified the limited license applied both to the computer program's copyright and physical disk containing it.

Digital distribution of software led to "click-wrap" licenses requiring contract acceptance to run a program, with the licensor deciding whether the contract was available prior to purchase. For both "shrink-wrap" and "click-wrap" licenses dependent on a specific user's authorization, challenges arise when dealing with resellers, organizations that may not bound by a non-executive's actions, and hardware device sellers. Website operators often assert "browse-wrap" licenses through terms of service and related agreements.

To improve how Article 2 of the Uniform Commercial Code handled intangibles transactions, the National Conference of Commissioners on Uniform State Laws drafted the model Uniform Computer Information Transactions Act ("UCITA") in 1999. The proposed code strongly favored these "-wrap license" protection measures to the detriment of software users and faced fierce criticism for harshly limiting consumer protections. Versions of UCITA were ultimately only adopted in Maryland and Virginia. Meanwhile, at least five states adopted legislation preventing software owners from applying UCITA laws to state residents. As a result, enforcement of these digital licenses varies appreciably by state.

Under both the 1909 and the 1976 Act, authors (or their heirs) may regain their original rights in a work after an initial transfer of ownership or license of rights. The 1909 Act vested the renewal right exclusively in the author or certain of the author's heirs. Under the 1909 Act, courts held the renewal right, like the copyright itself, could be assigned. The 1976 Act, with its single term, allowed an author or certain of the author's heirs (spouse, children, and grandchildren) to terminate any initial copyright transfer or license at a certain point prior to the end of the copyright term, whether or not a right to terminate was contractually reserved or relinquished in the original agreement. The renewal or termination right is intended to safeguard authors against unprofitable transfers resulting from the author's weak bargaining position or the impossibility of accurately valuing a literary or artistic work prior to its exploitation. If only one of multiple co-authors exercises this termination right, that author becomes a co-copyright owner and may grant non-exclusive licenses letting others use the work. The co-author has a duty to account to the protected work's other co-owners.

Rights in a work made for hire are not subject to termination by the hired author. However, parties may not stipulate in a contract that a work is made for hire simply to extinguish the termination right.

Should an ownership transfer be terminated, a termination notice must be served on the grantee (or the grantee's successor in title) and recorded in the Copyright Office, just like the transfer itself. If the party entitled to terminate an ownership transfer or license fails to serve termination notice within the specified time period or fails to observe the requisite formalities, no termination occurs and the initial grant will continue in force.

3. PLANT VARIETIES, MASK WORKS, AND VESSEL HULL DESIGNS

Congress enacted a variety of *sui generis* intellectual property statutes, such as the Plant Variety Protection Act of 1970 (7 U.S.C. §§ 2401 *et seq.*), the Semiconductor Chip Protection Act of 1984 (17 U.S.C. §§ 901 *et seq.*), and the Vessel Hull Design

Protection Act of 1998 (17 U.S.C. §§ 1301 *et seq.*). Notwithstanding the seeming proliferation of *sui generis* protection, few cases have been brought under any of these statutes.

The Plant Variety Protection Act ("PVPA") of 1970 was amended in 1980 and again in 1994, the latter amendment being designed to fulfill U.S. obligations under the International Union for the Protection of New Plant Varieties (or UPOV, its French-language acronym). The revision covered new plant varieties reproduced sexually, i.e., through seeds. Bacteria, viruses, and related subject matter are excluded. Plant patent protection is available for asexually reproduced plant varieties, and utility patent protection may be available for genetically engineered seeds or plants. To receive a plant variety protection certificate, the variety claimed must meet the statutory requirements of *distinctiveness, uniformity,* and *stability* as well novelty. There is no non-obviousness requirement. Thus, the PVPA creates what amounts to a kind of copyright protection for new sexually-produced plant varieties. The term of protection is 20 years from date of issue, except for trees and vines where the term is 25 years. The U.S. Department of Agriculture administers the PVPA.

The Semiconductor Chip Protection Act ("Chip Act") creates what might best be called a hybrid protection by combining aspects of patent, copyright, and trade secret law to semiconductor chip designs (called "mask works" using terminology from an outdated production method). Rather than focusing on a copy of the full mask work, the trier of fact determines whether a duplicated portion of the chip was "qualitatively important" to the overall chip design. *Brooktree Corp. v. Advanced Micro Devices, Inc.*, 977 F.2d 1555 (Fed. Cir. 1992). Chip Act protection covers a level of abstraction in mask works, such as groupings. *Altera Corp. v. Clear Logic, Inc.,* 424 F. 3d 1079 (9th Cir. 2005). The Chip Act also encourages other countries to provide equivalent legal protections by conditioning U.S. protection of foreign chip designs upon comparable protection for U.S. chip designs in that nation.

The Chip Act's primary purpose was arguably to stimulate international chip design protection. Japan and various European nations enacted a *sui generis* law substantially similar to the U.S. Chip Act. The existing copyright laws of the United Kingdom, Australia, and perhaps the Netherlands and Sweden may protect mask works on substantially the same basis as the U.S. Chip Act. The World Intellectual Property Organization (WIPO) prepared a draft treaty on the Protection of Intellectual Property in Respect of Integrated Circuits (IPIC) in 1985. The TRIPS Agreement requires WTO member countries to comply with most provisions of the (still unratified) IPIC, but also specifies additional minimum standards for the protection of integrated circuit designs. Domestically, the Chip Act may have responded to a non-existent problem. *See* Part B.3, *infra*.

The subject matter and owners eligible for Chip Act protections are defined much like U.S. copyright law. However, definitions of registration, notice, duration, and exclusive rights granted by the Chip Act more closely resemble U.S. patent law than copyright law. The principal reverse engineering limitation of these exclusive rights resembles neither U.S. patent nor copyright law, but rather the common law of trade secrets. *See* Ch. 7 *infra*.

Congress created yet another *sui generis* form of intellectual property protection with the Vessel Hull Design Protection Act, enacted as a part of the Digital Millennium Copyright Act of 1998. This Act protects original vessel hull designs, completing the federal boat hull protection regime process that began with the Supreme Court's preemption of similar state statutory protection in *Bonito Boats v. Thunder Craft Boats*, 489 U.S. 141 (1989). With minor amendments, this statute could be transformed into a full-blown industrial design statute common in Europe and elsewhere (and supposedly mandated by the TRIPS Agreement). The U.S. has no exact counterpart as U.S. design patent protection is limited to original designs that are also non-obvious. Vessel hull design registration is a prerequisite for protection under the Act and must be sought within two years of the design's publication. 17 U.S.C. § 1310 (1998). The protection term is 10 years. 17 U.S.C. § 1305.

Congress periodically considers, but never enacted, yet another form of *sui generis* protection for database content. The European Union began offering legal protection for databases starting in 1996. *See* Directive 96/9/EC of the European Parliament and of the Council, of 11 March 1996.

Existing common-law tort of misappropriation protections (discussed *infra*) and enforceability of "click-wrap" online contracts in the U.S. (discussed *infra*, Part B.2.) arguably makes such *sui generis* protection unnecessary.

4. OTHER INVESTMENTS OF INTELLECTUAL EFFORT: NEWS, DATA, PRIVACY, PUBLICITY, AND EPHEMERAL PERFORMANCES

a. News and Data

The common law protects various publicly disclosed products of intellectual effort that do not receive federal patent or copyright protection. In the seminal case of *International News Serv. v. Associated Press*, 248 U.S. 215 (1918) ("*INS v. AP*"), for example, the Supreme Court held news services have a "quasi-property" interest in the news they gathered and could prevent rival news services from appropriating that news for competitive purposes even after publication. The *INS v. AP* misappropriation doctrine was applied to many other products of intellectual effort that at the time did not qualify for federal patent or copyright protection. *See, e.g., Waring v. WDAS Broad. Station*, 194 A. 631 (Pa. 1937) (protecting musicians from unauthorized phonograph record broadcasts); *Metropolitan Opera Assoc. v. Wagner-Nichols Recorder Corp.*, 279 A.D. 632 (N.Y.A.D. 1 Dept. 1951) (protecting an opera company from unauthorized recording of their radio broadcasts); *Dior v. Milton*, 156 N.Y.S.2d 996 (N.Y.A.D. 1 Dept. 1956) (protecting a designer from unauthorized copying of dress designs).

Justice Brandeis's *INS v. AP* dissent reflected the general mixed response to this decision. The dissent asserted that the common law did not previously treat news as property and did not previously consider appropriation of publicly disclosed information for a competitive purpose as wrongful. Copyright law protects original expression, not mere facts like the news. Similarly, trade secret law only protects facts or ideas not publicly disclosed. The longstanding rule was that unrestricted disclosure meant facts, ideas, and their unpatented or uncopyrighted expression are "free as the air to common use." Brandeis also questioned whether the courts were the right government agency to change that fundamental legal concept.

The misappropriation doctrine received an equally hostile reception in some lower federal courts. The Second Circuit consistently refused to apply *INS v. AP* to facts not substantially similar to it. For example, in *Cheney Bros. v. Doris Silk Corp.*, 35 F.2d 279 (2d Cir. 1929) the court did not apply this doctrine to dress design copying as it would create a common-law intellectual property right and usurp Congress' authority to decide what products of intellectual effort may be protected.

The Supreme Court abandoned the accumulated corpus of federal common law including *INS v. AP* in *Erie R.R. Co. v. Tompkins*, 304 U.S. 64 (1938). The *Erie* decision intimated earlier holdings may have unconstitutionally usurped *state* lawmaking power and directed lower federal courts to apply state substantive law in federal diversity cases. While *INS v. AP* was no longer authoritative federal common law, several state courts still cited *INS v. AP* as an authoritative expression of state common law and had federal courts follow the doctrine even as it forbade using it as an authoritative expression of federal law. *See, e.g., Waring v. WDAS Broad. Station, Metro. Opera Assoc. v. Wagner-Nichols Recorder Corp.,* and *Dior v. Milton, supra.*

Some lower federal courts determined the Supreme Court's *Sears-Compco* decisions preempted the common law of misappropriation when they held (albeit in copyright law dictum) that a state cannot prohibit copying an article which is unpatented and uncopyrighted. *Sears, Roebuck & Co. v. Stiffel Co.*, 376 U.S. 225 (1964); *Compco Corp. v. Day-Brite Lighting, Inc.*, 376 U.S. 234 (1964). In *Columbia Broad. Sys. Inc. v. DeCosta,* 377 F.2d 315 (1st Cir. 1967), for example, the court would not grant common-law protection to a creator to prevent their character's wholesale appropriation by a television series.

Other federal courts disregarded *Sears-Compco,* finding where Congress could protect a work but has not, the courts (or state legislatures) may grant this protection. This view determined federal law only preempted state law where Congress expressly granted protection, or expressly or impliedly proclaimed certain subject matter was not protectable. While federal patent law indicated both what Congress wished to protect and to remain free, federal copyright law left too many areas unattended to be fully preemptive of state law.

The Supreme Court accepted the latter view in *Goldstein v. California*, 412 U.S. 546 (1973). *Goldstein* confirmed that states retain power to protect literary and artistic works so long as that protection does not conflict with federal copyright law. *Goldstein* further held that Congress' mere failure to grant copyright protection to a given class of literary or artistic works did not mean such works were meant for the public domain or that the states could not protect the works. Thus, state record and tape piracy statutes providing criminal penalties for sound recording misappropriation did not conflict with federal copyright laws before their amendment to protect sound recordings. States appeared free to protect any creative effort within the constitutional definition of a writing that was left unprotected by Congress, either by statute or by common law.

In § 301(a) of the Copyright Act of 1976, Congress expressly preempted state laws granting rights equivalent to copyright in works falling within the subject matter of federal copyright protection. Section 301(b) expressly permits state protection for (1) subject matter not covered by the Act; or (2) granting rights not equivalent to those created by the Act.

Illustrating what constitutes non-preempted subject matter, a House Report (on an earlier version of § 301 with specific examples of state laws not preempted by the Act) noted that states retain the power to protect ephemeral performances and the sort of "hot" news addressed in *INS v. AP*. H.R. Rep. No. 94–1476 (1976). The express language of § 301(b) is more equivocal, allowing state protection for not only any subject matter that is not a constitutional "writing," but also any constitutional writing that is excluded from copyright protection purely as a statutory matter. But what about § 102(b)'s exclusion of any idea or discovery, construed to exclude protection of facts? Section 301(b) seems to protect statutorily copyrightable subject matter, so long as the rights extended are not equivalent to those the Act created. Whether something is equivalent to or distinguishable from copyright can be challenging for matters like publicity rights or those rights a "click-wrap contract" creates by controlling access to a work.

To illustrate what constitutes rights not equivalent to those created by the Act, the above-mentioned House Report noted that the common law misappropriation tort is not necessarily synonymous with copyright infringement or the evolving common-law rights of "privacy" and "publicity". The Report also noted the common law of trade secrets, defamation, and fraud remain unaffected so long as the causes of action contain elements different from copyright infringement. Examples include an invasion of personal rights for privacy or a breach of trust or confidentiality for trade secrets. While common law trade secrets, defamation, and fraud clearly meet this standard, the common-law misappropriation tort and common-law rights of privacy and publicity are similar to copyright laws.

During the 1976 Act debates, the Justice Department warned against exempting misappropriation from preemption as it might defeat the purposes of § 301 and encourage states to pass misappropriation laws. *See* 122 Cong.Rec.H. 10910 (Sept. 22, 1976). Based on this objection, all state law illustrations not preempted by § 301 were deleted from § 301(b). Courts must decide what is and is not preempted under § 301. *See, e.g., Financial Info., Inc. v. Moody's Investors Serv.*, 808 F.2d 204 (2d Cir. 1986), holding that while plaintiff's bond card information was not protectable facts under federal copyright law, plaintiff's misappropriation claim was still preempted. Here, the plaintiff "proved neither the quantity of copying nor the immediacy of distribution necessary to sustain a 'hot' news claim", and the House Report stated that as long as the work fits within one of the general subject matter categories of §§ 102 and 103, the Act prevents state protection even if the work fails to achieve federal copyright protection. *See also* H.R. Rep. No. 94–1476 (1976). *But see Feist Publ'ns, supra,* holding Congressional power is constitutionally limited to protecting "original" works of authorship. It remains unclear whether the Congressional power to preempt is broader than the Congressional power to protect.

b. Privacy and Publicity

Privacy and publicity laws provide different solutions to the problem of controlling how others use one's identity. Privacy laws usually apply to use or disclosure of personal information an individual does not intend to widely disclose. Publicity rights focus upon commercializing a celebrity's investment in their persona. Technological progress continues to spur significant challenges in both areas.

Privacy rights, like the misappropriation doctrine, originate in the early twentieth century. Unlike the tort of misappropriation which arose from a federal court decision, the right of privacy was stimulated by a law review article which originated this misappropriation doctrine and was co-authored, ironically, by Louis Brandeis. *See* Warren & Brandeis, The Right to Privacy, 4 Harv.L.Rev. 193 (1890). The article led to widespread judicial and legislative recognition to a right of privacy. *See, e.g., Pavesich v. New England Life Ins. Co.*, 50 S.E. 68 (Ga. 1905) (common-law right of privacy invaded by insurance company using an individual's name, picture, and spurious testimonial in its advertising). *See also* N.Y. Civil Rights Law §§ 50–51 (misdemeanor and tort penalties for using a person's name or picture for "advertising purposes or the purposes of trade" without their written consent).

The invasion of privacy tort evolved into four common-law branches of the right to privacy. Actionable public disclosure of private facts occurs when information that is both highly offensive to a reasonable person and not of legitimate public concern is publicly communicated. Intrusion upon solitude occurs where an activity, considered highly intrusive to a reasonable person, invades a person's solitude or seclusion (i.e., where there is a reasonable expectation of privacy). The intrusion may be physical or electronic. False light privacy invasion is public communication of information the discloser knows or should have known to be false that would be highly offensive to a reasonable person. The information need not be defamatory. Finally, appropriation of a person's name, likeness, or other indicia of personal identity will constitute an invasion of *privacy,* but only where the use of such indicia is for personal gain or commercial advantage and invades the victim's personal right to be free of unwanted publicity. These privacy torts evolved significantly to address factors such as an individual's status (private, government, or public figure), the speaker's status (publisher or distributor of information), and subject matter (public interest and First Amendment concerns apply), among other circumstances.

Contemporary privacy laws expanded in response to personal data's growing importance in the information economy, repercussions for increasingly common and severe data security breaches, and the global patchwork of privacy law regimes. Certain types of sensitive personal data have long received enhanced protections, such as medical and financial records and certain identification information. *But see Dubin v. United States,* 599 U.S. ___, 143 S. Ct. 1557 (2023) (identity theft crimes require use of another person's identifying information as the crux of the criminal activity, so committing healthcare fraud does not also involve aggravated identity theft merely because the fraudulent billing includes patient information). Information about children, as a particularly vulnerable population, is also subject to greater regulation. These laws were largely enforced by government entities and state attorneys.

This left individuals little recourse against companies using their data unless an individual concrete harm could be linked to this use.

Protections for an individual's information have since improved. Led by the European Union, global privacy regimes increasingly scrutinize how personal information is collected, shared, processed, used, stored, and deleted. In the absence of a federal privacy law statute (as of the publication date), a minority of states have promulgated their own privacy regimes. The European Union's controller/processor model is largely a commonality which divides compliance obligations. This model usually requires contracts between companies providing and using data about identifiable individuals from covered persons and sets assistance and other legal obligations between these companies. Most U.S. states passing privacy laws as of the date of publication followed this controller/processor model, although their regimes tend to be much less strict than the E.U.

As the first U.S. state to pass a comprehensive consumer privacy law, California adopted a regime that granted similar consumer rights as the E.U. and later other state laws, but ultimately diverges in its approach to assessing company responsibilities and enforcement. The California Consumer Privacy Act of 2018 (amended by the California Privacy Rights Act of 2020) regulates how companies interact with California resident data, requires substantial compliance activities (including contracts between companies and service providers, individual access, and online privacy statements), and establishes both state and private rights of action for violations. *See* Cal. Civ. Code §§ 1798.100 *et seq*.

This widespread recognition of personal privacy rights was called into question following the U.S. Supreme Court's ruling in *Dobbs v. Jackson Women's Health Org.*, 597 U.S. ___, 142 S. Ct. 2228 (2022) which overruled past decisions that abortion was a constitutionally-protected privacy right derived from the First, Fourth, Fifth, Ninth, and Fourteenth Amendments. While the decision asserts in dicta that it does not affect privacy right precedents outside of abortion, *Dobbs* nevertheless casts doubt upon how other privacy rights may be treated in future decisions. As disparate state laws fill this regulatory vacuum, laws governing access to the personal information of identifiable individuals will likely receive increasing attention. *See, e.g., United States v. Microsoft Corp.*, 584 U.S. ___, 138 S. Ct. 1186 (2018) (vacating and remanding the question of whether a U.S. e-mail services provider must disclose to the federal government electronic communications within the provider's control but stored abroad following amendment of the Stored Communications Act of 1986, 18 U.S.C. §§ 2701 *et seq.*, by the Clarifying Lawful Overseas Use of Data Act, (P.L. 115–141)).

Unlike privacy laws seeking to limit information about personal information, the right of publicity entitles a person exploiting their public persona to protect the pecuniary value of their name, likeness, fictitious personalities, or other indicia of personal identity from unauthorized commercial use. Common defenses to a prima facie misappropriation of another's publicity rights claim include newsworthiness, consent, or incidental use.

Where a person has no interest in exploiting the commercial value of their name, likeness, or identity, the right to prevent others from doing so amounts to a purely personal right to be free of unwanted publicity. Where this interest exists, prohibiting unauthorized commercial exploitation is more appropriately characterized as a right to the publicity value of the name or likeness. This right of publicity is often described as a "property right" and its violation is more akin to the tort of misappropriation than to other privacy invasions. *See, e.g., Zacchini v. Scripps-Howard Broad. Co.*, 433 U.S. 562 (1977) (common-law right of publicity "an entirely different tort" than other invasion of privacy forms, being analogous to and having the same goals as federal patent and copyright laws).

Section 301 of the Copyright Act of 1976 largely did not preempt the right of publicity. Common law and statutory publicity rights are arguably equivalent to the exclusive rights created by the 1976 Act, as they prohibit unauthorized copying of personal names and likenesses. However, personal names and likenesses (as opposed to particular pictorial renditions of a likeness), are generally not recognized as protectable subject matter by the 1976 Act. *See Brown v. Ames*, 201 F.3d 654 (5th Cir. 2000) (misappropriation of one's name or likeness not preempted under either

§ 301 of the 1976 Act or the Supremacy Clause of the U.S. Constitution).

Where the only claimed exploitation of a person's likeness or voice is as part of a copyright-protected work, the right of publicity is likely preempted by federal copyright law. *See Baltimore Orioles, Inc. v. Major League Baseball Players Ass'n*, 805 F.2d 663 (7th Cir. 1986) (baseball telecasts are copyrighted works, made for hire, and owned by baseball clubs; players' publicity rights in their game-time performances are preempted by § 301(a) of the 1976 Act); *Laws v. Sony Music Ent., Inc.*, 448 F.3d 1134 (9th Cir. 2006) (singer's common law and statutory right of publicity claims preempted where defendant was licensed to use a digital sample of singer's recording in a subsequent musical recording). *But cf., Wendt v. Host Int'l, Inc.*, 125 F.3d 806 (9th Cir. 1997), holding that right of publicity claims by actors against robot creator using the actors' likenesses were not preempted, as the actors did not oppose exhibition of copyright protected television programs. This holding is questionable, as the actors arguably sought to prevent exploitation of a derivative work based on their show.

State publicity right protections also face First Amendment scrutiny. In *Zacchini, supra*, the Supreme Court held that the First Amendment provided no defense to a claim that a television station's unauthorized broadcast of an entire performance misappropriated the performer's publicity rights. *But see Cardtoons, L.C. v. Major League Baseball Players Assoc.*, 95 F.3d 959 (10th

Cir. 1996) (Oklahoma right of publicity does not recognize fair use defense for parody, but parody sports cards are protectable speech under the First Amendment); *ETW Corp. v. Jireh Publ'g, Inc.*, 332 F.3d 915 (6th Cir. 2003) (painting honoring golfer's tournament victory not commercial speech and so was fully protected by the First Amendment).

Debate continues over whether and to what extent to recognize a distinct right of publicity as a matter of sound state policy. So long as the common-law right of publicity avoids federal statutory and constitutional preemption, each state makes its own determinations. This may occur through statute or common law and has led to significantly divergent standards. Approximately half of U.S. states recognize a distinct publicity right, although sometimes as part of a person's privacy rights. Other states may protect publicity rights through unfair competition laws, applying the tort of misappropriation to a wrongful attempt to "pass off" a product as endorsed or produced by the celebrity.

Publicity rights may cover a variety of celebrity references. The right of publicity may prevent unauthorized commercial use of: 1) nicknames, *Hirsch v. S.C. Johnson & Son, Inc.*, 280 N.W.2d 129 (Wis. 1979); 2) catchphrases or slogans, *Carson v. Here's Johnny Portable Toilets, Inc.*, 698 F.2d 831 (6th Cir. 1983); 3) voice imitations, *Midler v. Ford Motor Co.*, 849 F.2d 460 (9th Cir. 1988); 4) sports equipment, *Motschenbacher v. R.J. Reynolds Tobacco*, 498 F.2d 821 (9th Cir. 1974) (racecar an attribute of the driver's identity); 5) persona parodies, *White v. Samsung Elecs. Am., Inc.*, 989 F.2d 1512 (9th Cir. 1993) (robot parody of game show celebrity); or 6) artistic renderings of a celebrity's image, *Comedy III Prods., Inc. v. Gary Saderup, Inc.*, 21 P.3d 797 (Cal. 2001) (lack of significant transformative or creative contribution fatal to defense); *In re NCAA Student-Athlete Name & Likeness Licensing Litig.*, 724 F.3d 1268 (9th Cir. 2013) (video game images). Trademark law grants publicity rights to products regardless of whether there is a connection between the goods and the celebrity's fame. *NPG Records and Paisley Park Enterprises v. JHO Intellectual Property Holdings*, 2022 USPQ2d 770 (TTAB 2022).

There are disagreements as to whether the right of publicity should be a descendible property right. Supporters argue recognizing an inheritable property right encourages individual enterprise and creativity. *See, e.g., Price v. Hal Roach Studios, Inc.*, 400 F.Supp. 836 (S.D.N.Y. 1975) (actors' widows' rights invaded by film producers' attempt to assign merchandising rights in the deceased actors' names and likenesses). Some assert the right of publicity should survive the owner's death, even if the owner did not exploit the right during their lifetime. *Martin Luther King, Jr., Center for Soc. Change, Inc. v. American Heritage Prods., Inc.*, 296 S.E.2d 697 (Ga. 1982); Cal. Civ. Code § 3344.1 (1971). While a celebrity's death logically ends use of their persona, their estate often still benefits from merchandizing and sales of unreleased artwork or other possessions. Technological advancements further blur this line as holographic performances and machine-generated artwork utilizing deceased a celebrity's attributes become more common.

Those opposing a descendible right of publicity argue potential conflicts with the First Amendment, problems defining the right's scope and duration, and the likelihood a merely marginal incentive to create threatens countervailing societal interest in the free dissemination of ideas. Some courts either restrict or wholly reject the concept of descendible publicity rights. *See, e.g., Memphis Dev. Found. v. Factors Etc., Inc.*, 616 F.2d 956 (6th Cir. 1980) (no descendible right in Elvis Presley's name and likeness, even if exploited during his lifetime); *Factors Etc., Inc. v. Pro Arts, Inc.*, 652 F.2d 278 (2d Cir. 1981) (*Memphis Dev. Found.* stated controlling Tennessee law); *but see State ex rel. Elvis Presley v. Crowell*, 733 S.W.2d 89 (Tenn. Ct. App. 1987). *See also Lugosi v. Universal Pictures*, 603 P.2d 425 (Cal. 1979) (unexercised opportunity to exploit publicity rights was not descendible); *but see* Cal. Civ. Code § 3344.1 (1971), *supra*.

Those favoring a descendible right of publicity recognize the need for a durational limitation, often long enough to provide for heirs living at the time of the public figure's death. Some propose publicity rights should last for a term equivalent to the 1976 Copyright Act limits—namely life of the creator plus fifty years. *See* Cal. Civ. Code § 990 (1984).

c. Ephemeral Performances

Ephemeral performances present a challenge to copyright law. The work's creators are largely unable to affix the work in a tangible medium while performing, and significant value of the work lies in its live performance. Without additional protections, any observer with recording equipment could seize the fruit of the performers' efforts. Tort and contract laws assist artists and athletes in addressing these challenges. *See, e.g., Zacchini, supra* (unauthorized news broadcast of performer's entire act infringed performer's property interest in the performance); *Facenda v. N.F.L. Films, Inc.*, 542 F.3d 1007 (3d Cir. 2008) (release of deceased announcer's broadcasts required the use "not constitute an endorsement of any product or service", preserving the right of publicity from unauthorized use in a video game).

B. ACTIONABLE AND PRIVILEGED INFRINGEMENT/APPROPRIATION

The Constitution grants authors and inventors "exclusive rights" in their respective works and discoveries. The common law provides analogous rights to certain products of intellectual effort that do not receive federal patent or copyright protection. However, not every use of another's protected work is an infringing one. Nor does every appropriation of another's unpatented or uncopyrighted investment of intellectual effort constitute a misappropriation. To distinguish actionable uses from privileged ones, first the extent and limits of the exclusive rights granted to a given work must be understood. Then the admitted invasions of those rights must be evaluated for privilege. If no privilege exists, remedies are available for the infringement or misappropriation.

1. PATENT INFRINGEMENT

A patent holder has the right to exclude others from making, using, offering for sale, selling, or importing either a patented invention, design, or the product of a patented process. Infringement means violation of another's exclusive intellectual property rights. Patent infringement takes many forms, including direct, contributory, or induced. According to 35 U.S.C. § 271(a)–(c), infringement of a utility patent (and by implication, infringement of a design patent) occurs when anyone either (1) makes, uses, offers for sale, sells a patented invention within the U.S., or imports a patented product into the U.S. during the patent term without authorization; (2) actively induces patent infringement; or (3) contributes to patent infringement by selling a component of a patented machine, manufacture, combination or composition, or material or apparatus for use in practicing a material part of a patented process, knowing it to be specially made or adapted for such use and not a staple article or commodity available for a variety of uses.

Note that the right to exclude others from making, using, offering for sale, selling, or importing an invention is not necessarily the same as having an exclusive right to utilize the patented invention itself. Patented inventions are often improvements to inventions already subject to other patents. In such cases, the inventor's exclusive right only lets them prevent others (including the original inventor) from using the improvement without permission. Cross-licensing agreements between patent owners are common.

Direct infringement occurs when one makes, sells, uses, or otherwise exploits a patented product or process without permission of the patent holder. *See* 35 U.S.C. § 271(a). A patent holder must prove the accused performed these acts willfully and within the United States.

Having another party perform one or more of the protected steps will not avoid direct patent infringement liability. *Shield v. Halliburton Co.*, 493 F.Supp. 1376, 1380 (W.D. La. 1981). Rather, one party must have "direction or control" over all steps of the patented claim or have the steps performed on their behalf. *BMC Resources, Inc. v. Paymentech, L.P.*, 498 F.3d 1373, 1375 (Fed. Cir. 2007); *Muniauction, Inc. v. Thompson Corp.*, 532 F.3d 1318, 1321–22 (Fed. Cir. 2008). Direct infringement requires that the patented system be fully used, and that all the patented steps occurs within the U.S. *NTP, Inc. v. Research in Motion, Ltd.*, 418 F.3d 1282 (Fed. Cir. 2005) (selling a device that performs a patented method is not the same as selling a patented invention).

If patent protection extends to all devices practicing an industry standard and the standard provides sufficient levels of specificity to establish practicing that standard would always result in infringement, a court may rely on this industry standard to find infringement. *Fujitsu Ltd. v. Netgear Inc.,* 620 F.3d 1321 (Fed. Cir. 2010).

Indirect patent infringement may occur when the accused entity is not the original patent violator. 35 U.S.C. § 271(b) prohibits actively inducing patent infringement by others. The violator need not have knowledge that their actions are illegal. However, proof of willful intent can entitle the patent holder to enhanced damages, reasonable royalties, or lost profits. Indirect infringement claims may include contributory infringement or infringement by active inducement.

A defendant is not liable for inducing patent infringement when no party directly infringed the patent. *Limelight Networks, Inc. v. Akamai Techs., Inc.*, 572 U.S. 915 (2014). The Court noted that Congress can impose inducement liability based on non-infringing conduct, and that attempts to prohibit evasion of method patent infringement by separating the steps did not justify judicially rewriting the statute. This reversed the Federal Circuit's determination that induced infringement could arise when no one entity performed all the claimed method steps. *Akami Tech., Inc. v. Limelight Networks, Inc.*, 692 F.3d 1301, 1307 (Fed. Cir. 2012).

Contributory or induced infringement prohibits actions that contribute, or potentially contribute, to another's patent infringement. The long list covers:

> [w]hoever offers to sell or sells within the United States or imports into the United States a component of a patented machine, manufacture, combination or composition, or a material or apparatus for use in practicing a patented process, constituting a material part of the

> invention, knowing the same to be especially made or especially adapted for use in an infringement of such patent, and not a staple article or commodity of commerce suitable for substantial noninfringing use. . .

35 U.S.C. § 271(c). Making and selling items customers will use for patent infringement constitutes contributory patent infringement by the manufacturer, as it would be too burdensome for the patent holder to sue all directly infringing customers. *Aro Mfg. Co. v. Convertible Top Replacement Co.*, 377 U.S. 476 (1964). *See also, Ricoh Co., Ltd. v. Quanta Computer Inc.*, 550 F.3d 1325, 1337 (Fed. Cir. 2008) ("one who sells a component especially designed for use in a patented invention may be liable as a contributory infringer, provided that the component is not a staple article of commerce suitable for substantial noninfringing use"). Meeting an industry standard may comprise contributory infringement where the level of specificity would always result in infringement. *Fujitsu Ltd. v. Netgear Inc., supra.*

Induced infringement constitutes active encouragement of direct infringement, which must occur knowing the encouraged acts constitute direct infringement. 35 U.S.C. § 271(c). Like contributory infringement, induced infringement requires the accused inducer know that a third party's conduct would infringe a patent. A defendant's belief about a patent's validity is not a defense to induced infringement. *Commil USA, LLC v. Cisco Sys., Inc.*, 575 U.S. 632 (2015).

Induced infringement frequently occurs when companies (or their importers) manufacture parts outside the U.S. and encourage customers to use or combine the parts with products in a way that infringes a U.S. patent. However, a manufacturer is not likely to contribute to the infringement if the accused part has other valid uses.

To prove induced infringement, a patent holder must show direct infringement of the patent and both knowing and specific intent to encourage another party's patent infringement. *See, e.g., Broadcom Corp. v. Qualcomm Inc.*, 543 F.3d 683 (Fed. Cir. 2008). Evidence of these activities regularly comes from instruction manuals, advertising materials, labels, or website content. In *Global-Tech Appliances, Inc. v. SEB SA*, 563 U.S. 754 (2011), the Supreme Court determined the "knowledge" requirement includes willful blindness, where the inducing party (1) subjectively believes there is a high probability the patent exists and (2) takes deliberate actions to avoid learning of the patent's existence. This is separate from any intent required to produce the acts themselves (i.e., making, using, offering to sell, selling, or importing of a patented invention). The affirmative inducement act must occur during the six-year damages period established by 35 U.S.C. § 286. *Meso Scale Diagnostics, LLC v. Rochae Diagnostics,* 30 F.4th 1109 (2022).

The Patent Law Amendments Act of 1984 prohibits supply "in or from the U.S. all or a substantial portion of the components of a patented invention . . . in such a manner as to actively induce the combination of such components outside the [U.S.] in a manner that would infringe the patent if such combination occurred within the [U.S.]" 35 U.S.C. § 271(f). This reversed a previous Supreme Court holding that allowed a company to ship all parts of a patented invention abroad for assembly without infringement liability. *See Deepsouth Packing Co. v. Laitram Corp.*, 406 U.S. 518 (1972). *But cf.*, *Microsoft Corp. v. AT&T*, 550 U.S. 437 (2007) (while domestic installation of software would infringe a patent, software copied abroad prior to installation does not since software without an activating medium is an abstraction and not a component). Providing one component of a multi-component system cannot constitute "a substantial portion of the components of a patented invention" for § 271(f)(1). *Life Techs. Corp. v. Promega Corp.*, 580 U.S. 140 (2017) (favoring quantitative component analysis over a qualitative test of a component's importance).

Similar to induced infringement, joint patent infringement occurs when multiple parties cooperatively infringe a claimed method patent. *BMC Resources, Inc. v. Paymentech, L.P.*, 498 F.3d 1373 (Fed. Cir. 2007) (imposing vicarious liability on controlling party's agent through agency principles). An accused infringer must control the other party for joint patent infringement to occur. *Muniauction, Inc. v. Thomson Corp.*, 532 F.3d 1318 (Fed. Cir. 2008).

For § 271(f) patent violations caused by supplying at least a substantial portion of a patented invention's components, the Federal Circuit differentiates between "apparatus" claims requiring physical components, and "method" claims requiring a "series of actions or steps." Selling a device that performs a claimed method is not the same as selling a patented invention. *Joy Techs., Inc. v. Flakt, Inc.*, 6 F.3d 770, 773 (Fed. Cir. 1993). Software is a set of instructions directing hardware to perform a sequence of actions rather a sequence of actions itself, so software sales do not constitute direct patent infringement of a method claim. *Ricoh Co., Ltd. v. Quanta Computer Inc.*, 550 F.3d 1325 (Fed. Cir. 2008). In *Cardiac Pacemakers, Inc. v. St. Jude Medical, Inc.*, 576 F.3d 1348 (Fed. Cir. 2009), the court held method claims lack the physical component element necessary for coverage under § 271(f), overturning *Union Carbide v. Shell Oil Co.*, 425 F.3d 1366 (Fed. Cir. 2005).

The Omnibus Trade and Competitiveness Act of 1988 further amended U.S. patent law to prohibit import into the U.S. or sale or use within the U.S. of a product made outside the U.S. by a process patented in the U.S. 35 U.S.C. § 271(g).

While patent infringement is generally a question of fact decided by the factfinder, patent claim construction is a question of law to be decided by a judge. *Markman v. Westview Instruments, Inc.*, 517 U.S. 370 (1996). *But see Phillips v. AWH Corp.*, 415 F.3d 1303 (Fed. Cir. 2005) where Judge Mayer's dissent argues the CAFC's adherence to the *Markman* rule in the name of promoting uniformity results in " 'interpretive necromancy,' in which rulings resemble reality, if at all, only by chance".

During a *Markman* hearing, judges may interpret patent claims based on their literal meanings, which may include narrowing, amending, or rejecting patent claims. While the ultimate claim construction is a legal conclusion subject to de novo review, fact finding in construing a patent claim (such as background science) is examined for clear error and is not subject to de novo review. *Teva Pharm. USA, Inc. v. Sandoz, Inc.,* 574 U.S. 318 (2015).

For non-statutory intellectual property claims, the accused unfair method or act must have a threat or effect "to destroy or substantially injure an industry in the United States", "to prevent the establishment of such an industry", or "to restrain or monopolize trade and commerce in the United States". 19 U.S.C. § 1337(a)(1)(A). Pursuant to § 337 of the Tariff Act of 1930, 19 U.S.C. § 1337, a U.S. patent owner may petition the International Trade Commission ("ITC") to order, subject to review, exclusion of imports which infringe their patent. The statutory language for § 337 applies to any "unfair methods of competition and unfair acts in the importation of articles." 19 U.S.C. § 1337(a)(1)(A). While ITC cases include patents, trademarks, copyrights, trade secrets, false advertising, antitrust, and contract matters, most are patent claims. *See also* Ch. 8 B(1)(b)(3), *infra.*

Section 337(a)(1)(B) of the Tariff Act of 1930 prohibits "importation into the United States, the sale for importation, or the sale within the United States after importation by the owner, importer, or consignee, of articles that (i) infringe a valid and enforceable United States patent . . . or (ii) are made, produced, processed, or mined under, or by means of, a process covered by the claims of a valid and enforceable United States patent." *See* 19 U.S.C. § 1337(a)(1)(B).

The petitioning party must prove infringement of a valid U.S. patent related to an imported product, and that the cited patent is used in an existing domestic industry. The ITC's patent infringement or invalidity determination does not have preclusive effect in other court proceedings. *Texas Instruments, Inc. v. Cypress Semiconductor Corp.*, 90 F.3d 1558, 1569 (Fed. Cir. 1996). However, federal district courts must stay cases regarding the same issues as the ITC is considering upon a party's motion. 19 U.S.C. § 1337(b)(3). Section 1337(c) lets the ITC terminate an investigation if the parties agree to arbitration.

To demonstrate a domestic industry exists, as required under 19 U.S.C. § 1337(a)(2)–(3), the complainant must satisfy a two-prong test. *See, e.g., Removal Elec. Cards and Elec. Card Reader Devices*, ITC Inv. No. 337–TA–396 (1997). The "technical" prong requires showing "an industry in the United States, relating to the articles protected by the patent . . . concerned, exists or is in the process of being established." 19 U.S.C. § 1337(a)(2) (1994). The "economic" prong of the test considers an industry exists within the United States when there is "with respect to the articles protected by the patent . . . concerned (A) significant investment in plant and equipment; (B) significant employment of labor or capital; or (C) substantial investment in its exploitation, including engineering, research and development, or licensing." *Id.* at § 1337(a)(3).

The domestic industry test is not hard to satisfy. For example, in *Variable Speed Wind Turbines*, ITC Inv. No. 337–TA–376 (1997), the Commission determined the domestic industry requirement was satisfied by an intervening co-complainant whose U.S. operations were limited to licensing significant domestic activities under the patent in suit.

The ITC regulates importation of articles into the U.S., their sale for importation, or their sale within the U.S. after importation. The ITC has full discretion whether to investigate a petition's claims and may initiate an investigation without a petition. ITC cases primarily differ from federal district court claims in their abbreviated time frame, ability to grant general exclusion orders rather than remedies against a particular entity, and the ITC's inability to award damages. An ITC staff attorney may act as a party to the proceeding by engaging in discovery and taking positions on motions.

Since the ITC's jurisdiction is over the accused product (*in rem*) rather than an accused party (*in personam*), ITC claims can address a full range of parties or goods. The ITC regularly construes its powers broadly to address increasingly sophisticated circumvention techniques. For example, the ITC determined it can prevent importation of non-infringing goods that would be modified to infringe intellectual property rights well after their importation. *Suprema, Inc. v. ITC*, 796 F.3d 1338, 1352–53 (Fed. Cir. 2015) ("articles that infringe" covers post-importation modification of imported goods to directly infringe at seller's inducement, in this case post-import software installation); *but see Clear Correct Operating, LLC v. ITC,* 810 F.3d 1283 (Fed. Cir. 2015) (divided panel held the term "articles" in § 337 covers only "material things", so electronic data transmissions alone are not actionable).

After receiving a complaint requesting an investigation, the ITC has thirty days to determine whether to investigate. An administrative law judge manages the investigation similar to an abbreviated bench trial, culminating in an on-the-record evidentiary hearing where the complaining parties, defending parties, and the ITC's own Commission Investigative Attorneys may all present evidence.

After an administrative law judge issues an initial determination on the petition, the ITC automatically adopts it. *See, e.g., Condensers, Parts Thereof, and Products Containing Same, Including Air Conditioners for Automobiles,* ITC Inv. No. 337–TA–334 (1997). The decision may receive further review upon a Commissioner's timely vote, or if the parties successfully petition the ITC. A party to the petition may also file a reconsideration request to discuss new questions raised by the determination or file an appeal to the U.S. Court of Appeals for the Federal Circuit. 19 U.S.C. § 1337(c).

The ITC may grant an exclusion order or cease and desist order following an § 337 violation determination. Monetary damages are not available. For exclusion orders, the ITC directs U.S. Customs and Border Protection to block infringing products from entering the United States. 19 U.S.C. § 1337(d). A limited exclusion order blocks importation of infringing goods from specified manufacturers or importers. A general exclusion order blocks importation of all infringing goods from any source, regardless of whether the investigation included the source. This ensures a losing party does not circumvent an order using a non-party importer. Cease and desist orders prohibit a party from engaging in the proscribed activity. 19 U.S.C. § 1337(f). They prevent a losing party from selling their domestic inventory of infringing products, as a party might otherwise stockpile infringing goods while the case is pending.

Although ITC determinations are subject to review by the President as well as the U.S. Trade Representative and the Court of Appeals for the Federal Circuit, presidential rejection of ITC determinations are rare. For example, a president disapproved the *Dynamic Random Access Memories*, ITC Inv. No. 327–TA–242 (1987) determination, asserting the limited exclusion order threatened potential disruption of the computer industry. In *Duracell, Inc. v. ITC*, 778 F.2d 1578 (Fed. Cir. 1985), the Federal Circuit determined presidential rejection of a "grey market goods" decision was not reviewable. The Federal Circuit also found no § 337 requirement that a President articulate in detail the reasons for rejection. Instead, a disapproval was sufficient for the President's own policy reasons, including the desire to avoid conflicting administrative interpretations of existing laws.

A U.S. patent owner may also petition the U.S. Trade Representative to sanction foreign countries providing inadequate or ineffective protection to the intellectual property of U.S. nationals.

2. COPYRIGHT INFRINGEMENT

Federal copyright law provides the exclusive right to prevent others from reproducing a protected work, preparing derivative works, distributing copies of the work, or publicly perform or display the work within the United States. *See* 17 U.S.C. § 106. Copyright enforcement requires proof of ownership or an exclusive license to the specific enforced right as well as proof of infringement. Federal registration creates a presumption of validity and ownership. 17 U.S.C. § 410. Federal courts have exclusive jurisdiction over copyright claims. 18 U.S.C. § 1338(a). Venue may be the defendant's location or where the allegedly infringing acts occur. 28 U.S.C. § 1400(a).

Section 501 of the Copyright Act states anyone is an infringer of the copyright or author's rights if they violate any of the copyright owner's exclusive rights as provided by §§ 106–122, the author's rights as provided by § 106A, or who imports copies or phonorecords into the United States in violation of § 602. Section 602 states that importation into the U.S. "without the authority of the owner of copyright under this title, of copies or phonorecords of a work that have been acquired outside the United States is an infringement of the exclusive right to distribute copies or phonorecords under § 106, actionable under § 501." The Protecting Lawful Streaming Act of 2020

(PLSA) criminalized engagement in large-scale, for-profit piracy of copyright-protected materials.

Section 501's protection of copyright owners' "exclusive rights" bears emphasis. Copyright protection does not grant a copyright owner complete control over all possible use of their works. *Sony Corp. v. Universal City Studios, Inc.*, 464 U.S. 417, 432 (1984). "An unlicensed use of the copyright is not an infringement unless it conflicts with one of the specific exclusive rights conferred by the copyright statute." *Twentieth Century Music Corp. v. Aiken*, 422 U.S. 151, 154–155 (1975). Unlike exclusive patent rights, copyright law does not include a right to exclude others from making, using, or selling a substantially similar work created without reference to the protected work. As the term "copyright" suggests, infringement generally involves unauthorized copying—though what constitutes copying under the 1976 Act may be broader than the common understanding.

The Copyright Remedy Clarification Act of 1990 (CRCA) amended § 501(a) of the 1976 Copyright Act to clarify that states, state instrumentalities, and state officers or employees acting in their official capacities can be held liable for copyright infringement in the same manner as anyone else. *See* 17 U.S.C. §§ 501(a), 511. Unlike an equivalent patent provision, discussed *infra,* the CRCA has not been overturned based on Fourteenth Amendment Due Process Clause challenges. *See Florida Prepaid Postsecondary Educ. Expense Bd. v. Coll. Sav. Bank,* 527 U.S. 627 (1999) (dissent noted legislative history contains many examples of state copyright infringement). *But see Chavez v. Arte Publico Press*, 204 F.3d 601 (5th Cir. 2000) holding the CRCA is an improper exercise of Congressional power as the CRCA's legislative history does not disclose that Congress responded to the kind of massive constitutional violations that prompted remedial legislation under the Fourteenth Amendment, that it considered state remedy adequacy, or that it sought to limit coverage to constitutional violations.

Copyright infringement required the defendant prove "copying" of the protected work in a manner the plaintiff has a right to prevent, which can be challenging. Often, direct evidence of copying will be introduced, or an inference of copying may be drawn by showing the accused's access to the protected work and the degree of similarity between the accused work and the protected one. Ordinarily, copying may be shown based on "substantial similarity", where an average layperson would recognize the accused work as appropriated from the protected work. *Warner Bros. Inc. v. ABC, Inc.*, 654 F.2d 204,208 (2d Cir. 1981). Where works are compilations or incorporate substantial unprotectable elements, a "virtually identical" test considers whether substantially the entire work was copied. *See, e.g., Apple Computer, Inc. v. Microsoft Corp.,* 821 F.Supp. 616, 623 (N.D. Cal. 1993).

One of the most vexing challenges in copyright law is determining how much similarity constitutes substantial similarity. Substantial similarity may be found even though something less than literal similarity is shown. Either comprehensive non-literal similarity or fragmentary literal similarity may be enough to constitute an infringement.

Where the similarity is literal but fragmentary, the focus lies in whether the segments copied constitute a substantial amount or a substantially important portion of the plaintiff's work. Where the similarity between two works is comprehensive but non-literal, the issue is whether the substantial similarity occurs in protected expression or unprotected facts and ideas. *Compare, Hoehling v. Universal City Studios*, 618 F.2d 972 (2d Cir. 1980) (interpretations of historical event are not copyrightable as a matter of law), *with Saul Steinberg v. Columbia Pictures Indus.*, 663 F.Supp. 706 (S.D.N.Y. 1987) (striking stylistic similarities between myopic map illustrations on magazine cover and film poster). Likewise, more factual or utilitarian works receive a narrower range of non-literal copyright-protected expression. Ultimately, the evaluation parses what constitutes protected expression versus unprotected facts or ideas.

Each individual right granted by copyright ownership exists independently. For example, cutting pictures from a commemorative art book and mounting them on ceramic tiles for sale at retail infringes the adaptation right but not the reproduction right. *Mirage Editions, Inc. v. Albuquerque A.R.T. Co.*, 856 F.2d 1341 (9th Cir. 1988). Similarly, a visual artist's attribution right and right of integrity exist independently of the exclusive rights of copyright owners in § 106.

Direct infringement, an unprivileged violation of any of the exclusive rights copyright law grants, is a strict liability matter so there is no need to prove intent to infringe. Even so, courts require an element of volitional conduct in copying the work to establish direct liability. *See, e.g., Cartoon Network v. CSC Holdings,* 536 F.3d 121 (2d Cir. 2008) (no public performance rights violation by company merely providing online remote storage digital video recorder system to customers who made copies not transmitted "to the public").

Indirect (secondary) liability may be imposed on those assisting another's direct copyright infringement. Of these secondary liability forms, contributory infringement requires proof of intentional or reckless misconduct. Vicarious liability is a form of strict, no-fault liability.

In *Sony Corp. of Am. v. Universal City Studios, Inc.*, 464 U.S. 417 (1984), the Supreme Court held the test for contributory copyright infringement is essentially the same as the statutory test for contributory patent infringement, and that mere sale of copying equipment will not constitute contributory infringement if the equipment is capable of substantial non-infringing uses. *See* § B(1), *supra.* However, one is liable for contributory copyright infringement if, with knowledge or reason to know of the infringing activity, one either induces, causes, or materially contributes to the infringing conduct of another. *A & M Records, Inc. v. Napster, Inc.*, 239 F.3d 1004 (9th Cir. 2001). *See also Metro-Goldwyn-Mayer Studios, Inc. v. Grokster, Ltd.*, 545 U.S. 913

(2005) (liability for active inducement of infringement by a company distributing a device to promote its use for copyright infringement, as shown by clear expression or other affirmative steps taken).

One can also be held vicariously (i.e., strictly) liable for another's direct copyright infringement where one has 1) a right and ability to supervise the direct infringer and 2) an obvious and direct financial interest in the exploitation of the copyrighted material. *See Shapiro, Bernstein & Co. v. H.L. Green Co.*, 316 F.2d 304 (2d Cir. 1963) (department stores vicariously liable for the manufacture and sale of "bootleg records" by an independent "licensee" that operated the stores' record departments).

Since copyright infringement requirements are based upon domestic activities, importation of copyright-protected works creates challenges. The § 602 importation right is subject to limitations on the § 106 exclusive rights of copyright owners, including the "first sale" doctrine codified in § 109(a). *See Quality King Distribs. v. L'Anza Research Int'l,* 523 U.S. 135 (1998) (copyright owner cannot prevent importation of products lawfully sold in foreign markets); *Kirtsaeng v. John Wiley & Sons, Inc.*, 568 U.S. 519 (2013) (first sale doctrine applies to copies of copyrighted works lawfully made abroad). These imported products are generally known as parallel imports or "grey market" goods. *See also* Ch. 4(B)(1)(d), *supra*.

Congress enacted the No Electronic Theft Act ("NET") in 1997, amending § 506 of the Copyright Act. NET criminalized particular willful infringements, even in cases where the infringer was not acting for the purpose of monetary gain. NET responded to *United States v. LaMacchia*, 871 F.Supp. 535 (D.Mass. 1994), (dismissing wire fraud charges against student operating an illegal online software exchange). Monetary gain had theretofore been a required element to establish criminal copyright infringement.

The Copyright Alternative in Small-Claims Enforcement Act of 2020 created a system within the U.S. Copyright Office to resolve copyright disputes under $30,000 (either $15,000 per claim or $30,000 for the entire case) similar to a small claims court system. Board decisions are not precedential. Foreign claimants are permitted, but not foreign respondents. A copyright infringement lawsuit respondent may opt-out of having a claim heard by the Copyright Claims Board, requiring the claim to be brought in an appropriate court. Awards made by the Copyright Claims Board may be appealed to federal courts, but only vacated in exceptional circumstances such as fraud, corruption, misrepresentation, or a Board action exceeding its authority.

3. SUI GENERIS RIGHTS

Certified breeders of any sexually reproduced or tuber propagated plant variety (other than fungi or bacteria) can exclude others from selling the variety, offering it for sale, reproducing it sexually or asexually (unless the latter is pursuant to a plant patent), importing or exporting it, or using it in producing a hybrid or different variety for twenty years (25 years for trees or vines). 7 U.S.C. § 2483. Performing any of these acts (or delivering or shipping the variety, or merely stocking it for any of the foregoing purposes—*see* 7 U.S.C. § 2541) without the certified breeder's authorization will infringe on the patent. There are three exemptions: 1) the so-called farmers' exemption allowing farmers to save seeds produced by or descended from the variety for use or sale for non-reproductive purposes; 2) use or reproduction for research purposes; or 3) transportation by a common carrier in the ordinary course of business. 7 U.S.C. §§ 2543–45. The AIA grants the CAFC exclusive jurisdiction for plant variety protection appeals.

Mask work registration secures for a semiconductor design owner all exclusive rights enumerated in 17 U.S.C. § 905 for the ten year period specified in § 904. Registration grants the right to prohibit others from 1) reproducing the mask work in any form; 2) importing semiconductor chip products embodying the mask work; and 3) distributing semiconductor chip products embodying the mask work. Mask work owners may also prohibit others from inducing or knowingly causing any person to violate any of the owner's exclusive rights. There is a glaring absence of any exclusive adaptation or derivative work right. *But cf.*, *Altera Corp. v. Clear Logic, Inc.*, 424 F.3d 1079 (9th Cir. 2005) (copying transistor grouping placement on a chip violated the Act, as such placement is not an unprotectable system or idea).

There are limitations on the exclusive rights mask work owners receive. Of these, the § 906(a) reverse engineering privilege is most important. This privilege holds no mask work infringement occurs when a person reproduces the mask work solely for teaching, analyzing, or evaluating the concepts or techniques embodied in the mask work or the circuitry, logic flow, or organization of mask work's components. The results of this analysis may be incorporated into an original mask work made for distribution without infringement. The reverse engineering limitation of the Chip Act, together with the absence of any adaptation right, effectively permits derivative works (or, in patent law language, improvements) without authorization or recompense to the original mask work's owner.

Registered vessel hull designs are protected for ten years. During this time, the owner has the exclusive right to 1) make, have made, or import for use in trade, any useful article embodying the design; and 2) sell or distribute for sale or for use in trade any useful article embodying that design. 17 U.S.C. § 1308 (1998). The Act exempts from infringement liability 1) any seller or distributor who sells or distributes a vessel hull embodying the design without knowledge that the design was protected and copied (17 U.S.C. § 1309(b)); 2) any infringing act done without knowledge that the design was protected under the Act (17 U.S.C. § 1309(c)); or 3) any reproduction "solely for the purpose of teaching, analyzing, or evaluating the appearance, concepts, or techniques embodied in the design, or the function of the useful article embodying the design" (17 U.S.C. § 1309(g)).

4. MISAPPROPRIATION

A prima facie common law misappropriation case merely requires proof that the (1) a plaintiff made a substantial investment of time, money, or intellectual effort; (2) the defendant appropriated the product of plaintiff's investment; and (3) the defendant's appropriation injured the plaintiff. These elements, notable chiefly for their vagueness and ambiguity, require considerable qualification due to federal patent and copyright law preemptions. States cannot prohibit others from appropriating a publicly-disclosed product of intellectual effort where it falls within a patentable subject matter class enumerated in the federal patent statute. *See Sears Roebuck & Co. v. Stiffel Co.*, 376 U.S. 225 (1964); *Compco Corp. v. Day-Brite Lighting, Inc.*, 376 U.S. 234 (1964); *Bonito Boats, Inc. v. Thunder Craft Boats, Inc.*, 489 U.S. 141 (1989); Ch. 1 *supra*. Likewise, states cannot prohibit appropriation of products covered by the copyright statute once the product is reduced to tangible form.

The terms "appropriation" and "misappropriation" have not taken a fixed legal meaning, even for products of intellectual effort that states can protect. Instead, these are blanket terms denoting various distinct types of harm to various distinct interests. Some misappropriation cases, for example, simply appear to be palming off cases by another name. The protected intangible business value is a distinctive product, service, or business identifier and the defendant's "misappropriation" makes deceptive use of it. *See, e.g., Chaplin v. Amador*, 269 P. 544 (Cal. App. 1 Dist. 1928) (Charlie Chaplin granted protection from motion pictures starring "Charles Aplin" wearing a similar costume. *See also Metropolitan Opera Assoc. v. Wagner-Nichols Recorder Corp.*, 107 N.Y.S.2d 795 (N.Y.A.D. 1 Dept. 1951) (unauthorized recording of an opera company's radio broadcasts enjoined, inferring an intent to mislead the public even without palming off allegations).

Other misappropriation cases contain elements of commercial privacy invasion, appropriation of trade value prior to unrestricted publication, reverse palming off (*e.g.*, plagiarism), or improper interference with contracts. *International News Serv. v. Associated Press,* 248 U.S. 215 (1918) enjoined a news agency from bribing a competitor's employees or inducing members to breach the association's bylaws and share news before publication. Likewise, *Pittsburgh Athletic Co. v. KQV Broad. Co.*, 24 F.Supp. 490 (W.D. Pa. 1938) enjoined a radio station from broadcasting games viewed from outside the enclosed ballpark when another station held an exclusive broadcasting contract. *See also Bajpayee v. Rothermich*, 372 N.E.2d 817 (Ohio App. 10 Dist. 1977) (laboratory executive's unauthorized use of employee's unpublished article violated employee's recognition rights to their work product, whether in relief for plagiarism, invasion of a right of publicity, or prima facie tort, even though no common-law copyright was claimed and the employer owned the discovery).

INS v. AP made actionable a non-deceptive trade value appropriation following unrestricted publication. The wrong committed was simply diverting profits from the news collector to a competitor that could charge lower prices for the news by avoiding collection costs. Ultimately, the wrong could drive the injured party out of business, with the misappropriating party soon to follow. *See also Southwest Airlines Co. v. Farechase, Inc.*, 318 F.Supp. 2d 435 (N.D. Tex. 2004) (company "scraping" another website's data sufficient for misappropriation claim); *Goldstein v. California*, 412 U.S. 546 (1973) (recording production costs greatly exceed retail costs of producing a record); *but see Ticketmaster Corp. v. Tickets.com, Inc.*, No. CV 99–7654 (C.D. Cal. Mar. 27, 2000)(no copyright infringement by competitor's "deep hyperlinking" [i.e., links to website's interior rather than homepage] since the only copied information was facts not protected by the Copyright Act).

Dastar Corp. v. Twentieth Century Fox Film Corp., 539 U.S. 23 (2003) held publishing public domain videos without attribution to the original producer was not reverse passing off or a false designation of origin in violation of § 43(a) of the Lanham Act. To avoid conflict with federal copyright laws, the § 43(a) "origin of goods" should be construed as the tangible product sold in the marketplace rather than the origin of ideas or communications the goods embody or contain. This focus on tangible rather than intangible origin is supported by *Wal-Mart Stores, Inc. v. Samara Bros., Inc.*, 529 U.S. 205 (2000), holding § 43(a) protection for a product design requires showing the design was distinctive enough to acquire secondary meaning.

When an appropriator does not compete with the business whose intangible assets are appropriated, the only injury would be diversion of a prospective business opportunity. Many courts hold that there cannot be misappropriation without competition. *See, e.g., U.S. Golf Ass'n v. St. Andrews Sys., Data-Max, Inc.*, 749 F.2d 1028 (3d Cir. 1984) (computer program using association's handicap formula not misappropriation as the association governs amateur golf and does not sell the formula); *National Basketball Ass'n and NBA Props., Inc. v. Motorola*, 105 F.3d 841 (2d Cir. 1997) (pager displaying sports scores did not misappropriate "hot news" as NBA's primary business is not disseminating facts and pager service had no competitive effect on the NBA's primary business). *But see Board of Trade of the City of Chicago v. Dow Jones & Co.*, 456 N.E.2d 84 (Ill. 1983) (offering commodity futures contracts based on the Dow Jones Industrial Average without Dow Jones & Co.'s consent would misappropriate a valuable business asset even without competition, and any public detriment from denial of this service is outweighed by encouraging new indexes for commodity futures contracts).

Even a competition requirement may still be too broad if a plaintiff cannot show the competitive conduct actually threatens their profitability. Absent this proof, the misappropriation doctrine may be used to eliminate competition or preserve a monopoly. *See, e.g., Associated Press v. United States*, 326 U.S. 1 (1945) (Bylaws at issue in *INS v. AP* violated the Sherman Antitrust Act); *FTC v. Sperry & Hutchinson Co.*, 405 U.S. 233 (1972) (established trading stamp company's suppression of independent exchanges through misappropriation lawsuits was unfair competition. *But see Bonito Boats, Inc. v. Thunder Craft Boats, Inc.*, 489 U.S. 141 (1989) (state statute prohibiting unauthorized use of direct molding to duplicate boat hulls for sale preempted by federal patent law. *See also, National Basketball Ass'n and NBA Props., Inc. v. Motorola*, 105 F.3d 841 (2d Cir. 1997) (to survive preemption, "hot-news" claims must also show 1) time-sensitive value of the factual information; 2) free-riding by the defendant; and 3) threat to the very existence of the product or service provided by the plaintiff if relief is not granted.

Federal copyright law and First Amendment considerations limit potential abuse of the misappropriation doctrine to curtail free use of knowledge and ideas. The Supreme Court's *Goldstein v. California* decision that a state record and tape piracy statute did not conflict with federal copyright law, *supra*, emphasized the state statute did not restrain use of an idea or concept. Similarly, the First Amendment is no defense for misappropriating an *entire* performance through unauthorized broadcast, rather than making mere incidental use of it. *Zacchini v. Scripps-Howard Broad. Co.*, 433 U.S. 562 (1977). Since the broadcast severely limited the performer's ability to charge admission fees, this was merely damages for the misappropriation. *See also Hoehling v. Universal City Studios*, 618 F.2d 972 (2d Cir. 1980) (states pre-empted from removing historical facts, themes, and research from the public domain as they are deliberately exempted from copyright protection to encourage recorded knowledge contributions).

5. INVASION OF PUBLICITY RIGHTS

Commercial misappropriation of another's publicity rights is a common-law invasion of privacy generally recognized as a distinct cause of action. As with the common-law misappropriation tort, however, expansive interpretation of publicity rights can threaten freedom of expression. *See, e.g., White v. Samsung Elecs. Am., Inc.*, 989 F.2d 1512 (9th Cir. 1993) (robots parodying game show host constituted a misappropriation of host's publicity rights). *Compare, Rogers v. Grimaldi*, 875 F.2d 994 (2d Cir. 1989) (right of publicity not violated by film titled "Fred and Ginger" telling story about actors imitating Ginger Rogers and Fred Astaire, and no false or deceptive advertising under § 43(a) of the Lanham Act as a matter of law where there was no explicit indication that Ginger Rogers produced or endorsed it), *with Parks v. LaFace Records*, 329 F.3d 437 (6th Cir. 2003) (viable § 43(a) and common-law right of publicity action against producer and musicians using civil rights icon's name for a song despite minimal connection). *See also* § A.4. *supra*.

C. AFFIRMATIVE DEFENSES AND REMEDIES

Even a survey of the numerous affirmative defenses and remedies involved in patent and copyright litigation can only touch upon primary elements coherently. In addition to patent and copyright-specific affirmative defenses, invalidity and the equitable defenses of laches, acquiescence, and unclean hands bear scrutiny.

1. PATENTS

a. Patent Infringement Defenses

Section 282 of the Patent Act allows pleading non-infringement or invalidity as patent infringement defenses. Since a non-infringement defense challenges the patent holder's prima facie infringement claim, the patent holder must prove infringement. Many non-infringement defenses are available, including permissible repair, experimental use, rights exhaustion, and certain prior uses.

Patent invalidity is an affirmative defense, so the party challenging the patent's validity bears the burden of proof. Patent invalidity must be proved by clear and convincing evidence. *Microsoft Corp. v. i4i Ltd. P'ship*, 564 U.S. 91 (2011). Assignor estoppel bars a patent infringement defendant that assigned the patent from later asserting a patent invalidity defense if, and only if, the assignor's invalidity claim contradicts explicit or implicit representations the assignor made when assigning the patent. *Minerva*

Surgical, Inc. v. Hologic, Inc., 594 U.S. ___, 141 S. Ct. 2298 (2021).

Non-infringement and invalidity claims may also be affirmatively raised via a proceeding pursuant to the Declaratory Judgment Act. The facts alleged must show a substantial case or controversy between parties having adverse legal interests of sufficient immediacy and reality to warrant relief. In *MedImmune, Inc. v. Genentech, Inc.*, 549 U.S. 118, 127 (2007), the Supreme Court rejected the CAFC's rule that a licensee in good standing cannot establish a case or controversy regarding a patent's validity, enforceability, or scope. The Court instead concluded that all circumstances must be reviewed to determine if "there is a substantial controversy between parties having adverse legal interests of sufficient immediacy and reality to warrant the issuance of a declaratory judgment." The Federal Circuit eroded this broad test in *Association for Molecular Pathology v. USPTO*, 653 F.3d 1329 (Fed. Cir. 2011), establishing an injury traceable to a patent owner requires both 1) an affirmative enforcement act by the owner and 2) meaningful preparation to conduct potentially infringing activity.

Among the most important amendments in the America Invents Act (AIA) expanded the 35 U.S.C. § 273 prior use defense beyond business method patents to any "subject matter consisting of a process, or consisting of a machine, manufacture, or composition of matter used in a manufacturing or other commercial process." The defense applies if an accused infringer makes a good faith commercial use of the subject matter in the U.S. This may be internally, through an arm's length sale, or at an arm's length commercial transfer resulting in commercial use. This prior use must occur at least one year before the earlier of the invention's effective filing date or the date the invention was publicly disclosed as prior art under § 102(b). This personal defense cannot be transferred "except as an ancillary and subordinate part of a good-faith assignment or transfer for other reasons of the entire enterprise or line of business to which the defense relates," and may not apply when federal funding or an institution of higher education is involved.

The equitable defenses of acquiescence and unclean hands are essentially the same as those raised in trademark infringement. *See* Ch. 4 *supra*. Patent statutes exempt certain conduct from the unclean hands defense that do not constitute patent misuse. *See* 35 U.S.C. § 271(d), *Dawson Chem. Co. v. Rohm & Haas Co.*, 448 U.S. 176 (1980) (patented process owner did not commit patent misuse by refusing patent licenses to any company that would not purchase all their requirements of an unpatented substance required for the process, where the only known use of the substance was in the patented method). *But cf. Agfa Corp. v. Creo Prods., Inc.*, 451 F.3d 1366 (Fed. Cir. 2006) (failure to disclose relevant prior art to USPTO during prosecution rendered patents unenforceable due to inequitable conduct); *Belcher v. Hospira,* 11 F.4th 1345 (Fed. Cir. 2021) (same result from inconsistent statements made to the FDA and USPTO).

The laches defense does not apply to patent claims brought during the statutory limitations period. *SCA Hygiene Prods. Aktiebolag, v. First Quality Baby Prods., LLC,* 580 U.S. 328 (2017). The U.S. Patent Act, 35 U.S.C. § 286, sets the statute of limitations for patent actions: "[e]xcept as otherwise provided by law, no recovery shall be had for any infringement committed more than six years prior to the filing of the complaint or counterclaim for infringement in the action." While patent infringement may be considered an ongoing violation as additional infringing units are manufactured or sold, § 286 essentially limits the scope of recovery for earlier activities to six years prior to filing a complaint.

An accused patent infringer may assert the equitable estoppel defense if: (1) the patentee, through misleading conduct (or silence), led the alleged infringer to reasonably infer there is no enforcement intention; (2) reliance on the patentee's conduct; and (3) material prejudice to the alleged infringer if the patentee can proceed with the claim. *Radio Sys. Corp. v. Lalor*, 709 F.3d 1124, 1130 (Fed. Cir. 2013). Equitable estoppel matters are fact-intensive inquiries.

One does not infringe another's patent by studying the patented invention's specifications and designing an invention that accomplishes the same result in a different way. Another invention accomplishing substantially the same result in substantially the same way, however, will result in patent infringement even though the inventions differ in some insubstantial respect and the junior invention was independently derived. *See Warner-Jenkinson Co. v. Hilton Davis Chem. Co.*, 520 U.S. 17 (1997) (upholding the continuing validity of the "doctrine of equivalents"). *See also Festo Corp. v. Shoketsu Kinzoku Kogyo Kabushiki Co., Ltd.*, 535 U.S. 722 (2002) (patentee alleging infringement under the doctrine of equivalents must prove a narrowing amendment made during patent prosecution did not surrender the particular equivalent in question); *Johnson & Johnston Assoc. v. R.E. Serv. Co.*, 285 F.3d 1046 (Fed. Cir. 2002) (*en banc*) (patent drafter who discloses but declines to claim subject matter dedicates it to the public and cannot claim it through the doctrine of equivalents). While completely rebuilding a patented invention constitutes an infringement, merely repairing it is not an infringing activity. *See Jazz Photo Corp. v. ITC*, 264 F.3d 1094 (Fed. Cir. 2001).

While a purely experimental use of a patented invention (as opposed to commercial use) will not constitute infringement, an experiment to determine the commercial feasibility or practicability of the patented invention is an infringing commercial use. A university's non-profit status does not give rise to an experimental use defense, at least where the university is experimenting with, not upon, the patented invention. *Madey v. Duke Univ.*, 307 F.3d 1351 (Fed. Cir. 2002). It is not an infringement, however, to make, use, or sell a patented invention (with certain exceptions) solely for uses reasonably related to developing and submitting information pursuant to a federal law regulating the manufacture, use, or sale of drugs or veterinary biological products. 35 U.S.C. § 271(e); *Merck KGaA v. Integra Lifesciences I Ltd.*, 545 U.S. 193 (2005).

The Hatch-Waxman Act grants safe harbor protections to activities seeking FDA regulatory approval. 35 U.S.C. § 271(e)(1). This Act prevents patent infringement claims "solely for uses reasonably related to the development and submission of information under a Federal law which regulates the manufacture, use, or sale of drugs or veterinary biological products." *See Proveris Scientific Corp. v. Innovasystems, Inc.*, 536 F.3d 1256 (Fed. Cir. 2008) (applying the safe harbor to research tools). The Supreme Court expanded these protections to medical devices in *Eli Lilly & Co. v. Medtronic, Inc.,* 496 U.S. 661, 664 (1990). *See also AbTox, Inc. v. Exitron Corp.,* 122 F.3d 1019 (Fed. Cir. 1997). The user need not actually submit information to the FDA, so long as there was a reasonable activity with a "reasonable basis for believing that a patented compound may work." *Merck KGaA v. Integra Lifesciences I, Ltd., supra,* at 198–99.

States retain sovereign immunity from patent infringement claims. *Florida Prepaid Postsecondary Educ. Expense Bd. v. College Sav. Bank*, 527 U.S. 627 (1999). Congress did pass the Patent and Plant Variety Protection Remedy Clarification Act ("PRCA"), 35 U.S.C. §§ 271(h), 296(a) to remove state sovereign immunity for patent infringement. However, the Supreme Court held this abrogation of sovereign immunity invalid as the legislation could not be sustained as enacted pursuant to the guarantees of the Fourteenth Amendment's Due

Process Clause, the only recognized constitutional basis for such an abrogation. As pointed out in Chapter 4, *supra*, the Court held invalid a similar provision in the Trademark Remedy Clarification Act. The *Florida Prepaid* majority opinion expressed concern about the absence of a pattern of widespread state patent infringement, the states' constitutional rights, and Congress' failure to limit the PRCA to cases where the state refuses to offer any remedy to patent owners. Regardless, government entities may intentionally infringe on patents to develop affordable generic drugs for the public good. 28 U.S.C. § 1498.

An accused patent infringer does not have an affirmative duty of due care to avoid infringement and may avoid enhanced damages as long as the infringing conduct does not meet a minimum standard of objective recklessness. *In Re Seagate Tech., LLC*, 497 F.3d 1360, 1371 (Fed. Cir. 2007). While evaluating this objective recklessness standard, the *Seagate* court further determined an accused patent infringer has no affirmative duty to obtain a patent counsel's advisory opinion and that providing the results of such an advisory opinion at trial does not waive the trial counsel's attorney-client or work product privileges.

The "first sale" of a patented invention generally terminates, or "exhausts", the patent holder's rights to control the post-sale use of the patented article. An article's sale impliedly licenses the purchaser (and successive purchasers) to use the invention. The exhaustion or implied license principle also underlies the repair/reconstruction dichotomy. *See Jazz Photo Corp., supra*. The patent exhaustion doctrine only affects the "particular article" sold, so a patent holder can prevent the purchaser from making new copies of the patent-protected article. *Bowman v. Monsanto Co.*, 569 U.S. 278 (2013) (patent exhaustion doctrine does not permit reproduction of patented seeds through unauthorized planting and harvesting).

In *Quanta Computer, Inc. v. LG Elecs., Inc.*, 553 U.S. 617 (2008), the Supreme Court held the exhaustion doctrine also applies to patented methods and barred an infringement claim where a licensing agreement merely forbade the licensee from selling components that substantially embodied the patents to a third party for combination with other components. *See also Impression Prods., Inc. v. Lexmark Int'l, Inc.*, 137 S. Ct. 1523 (2017) (patent exhaustion prevents a patent holder from suing for patent infringement to prevent post-sale use of the item, even when the use violates a customer contract or the item is imported into the U.S.; contract restrictions on additional sales are enforceable through contract law but not patent infringement).

Lower courts also recognize that private parties retain the freedom to contract concerning a patented product's sale conditions. *See Mallinckrodt, Inc. v. Medipart, Inc.*, 976 F.2d 700 (Fed. Cir. 1992) (upholding a "single use only" limitation on the sale of a patented product); *Arizona Cartridge Remfrs. Assoc., Inc. v. Lexmark, Int'l, Inc.*, 421 F.3d 981 (9th Cir. 2005) (packaging contract terms imposing post-sale conditions on purchasers enforceable as a "box-wrap" license, where a user accepts the contract terms by opening the box).

Determining the proper venue for patent litigation is an ongoing challenge given the perceived advantage certain jurisdictions may offer patent holders. Venue is proper "in the judicial district where the defendant resides, or where the defendant has committed acts of infringement and has a regular and established place of business". 28 U.S.C. § 1400(b). Applying the broad corporate activity standard of 28 U.S.C. § 1391(c) basically allowed infringement lawsuits to be filed anywhere the accused product was sold. The Supreme Court narrowed this jurisdiction in holding "residence" only referenced the state of incorporation for domestic companies. *See TC Heartland LLC v. Kraft Foods Group Brands LLC*, 581 U.S. 258 (2017). Jurisdiction over foreign companies is appropriate in any judicial district. *Brunette Mach. Works, Ltd. v. Kochum Indus., Inc.*, 406 U.S. 706 (1972). For foreign patent holders whose domestic designee cannot be located at the address provided or was never identified, the U.S. District Court for the Eastern District of Virginia will have jurisdiction. 35 U.S.C. § 293. In states with multiple judicial districts, a defendant only resides in the district where it maintains a principal place of business, or if none exists, where its registered office is located. *In re BigCommerce, Inc.*, 890 F.3d 978 (Fed. Cir. 2018).

Following this narrowing of the "residency" definition, patent litigants focused on the other portion of the statute, primarily focusing on the requirement for "regular and established place of business". The Federal Circuit established a three-part test requiring "(1) there must be a physical place in the district; (2) it must be a regular and established place of business; and (3) it must be the place of the defendant." *In re Cray,* 871 F.3d 1355, 1360 (Fed. Cir. 2017). *Cray* went on to provide examples of insufficient jurisdictional ties such as virtual spaces, places of sporadic activity or single actions, and employee home offices. *See also, In re Google LLC*, 949 F.3d 1338 (Fed. Cir. 2020) (a "regular and established place of business" requires regular physical presence of an employee or other agent of the defendant, which is not created by a third-party data center hosting company servers).

When state and federal claims are filed and a federal district court dismisses the federal claims, the court may decline to exercise supplemental jurisdiction over the remaining state law claims under 28 U.S.C. § 1367(c)(3). *Carlsbad Tech., Inc. v. HIF Bio, Inc.*, 556 U.S. 635 (2009). In *Carlsbad Tech.*, the Supreme Court held the United States Court of Appeals for the Federal Circuit may review this dismissal since it is not a remand for lack of subject-matter jurisdiction for which appellate review is barred by 28 U.S.C. §§ 1447(c) and (d).

b. Patent Infringement Remedies

Patent infringement remedies take many forms. Damages must adequately compensate for the infringement at no less than a reasonable royalty rate. 35 U.S.C. § 284. Judicial remedies made statutorily available for patent infringement are likewise similar to those available for trademark infringement (including treble damages in appropriate cases). Awards granted should be consistent with Congress' purpose of offering patent owners complete compensation for the infringement. *General Motors Corp. v. Devex Corp.*, 461 U.S. 648 (1983). Awards may include lost foreign profits when parts are shipped abroad for assembly into an infringing product as a permissible domestic application of 35 U.S.C. § 284 rather than impermissible extraterritorial application of 35 U.S.C. § 271(f)(2). *WesternGeco LLC v. Ion Geophysical Corp.*, 585 U.S. ___, 138 S. Ct. 2129 (2018) (Section 284 focuses on "complete compensation" for infringement). An infringing product may often be only a component of the entire product, further complicating the analysis. *See, e.g., Exmark Mfg. Co. v. Briggs & Stratton Power Prod. Group,* 879 F.3d 1332, 1348–54 (Fed. Cir. 2018) (entire product may define royalty base for a component).

The patent infringement theory applied may affect available damages. For example, indirect or contributory infringement damages must be related to products leading to direct patent infringement. *See, e.g., Golden Blount v. Robert H. Peterson Co.*, 438 F. 3d 1354 (Fed. Cir. 2006) (no direct infringement for products returned before infringing assembly); *Cardiac Pacemakers, Inc. v. St. Jude Med., Inc.*, 576 F.3d 1348 (Fed. Cir. 2009) (damages limited to products actually used to perform the claimed method). *But see Lucent Techs., Inc. v. Gateway, Inc.*,

580 F.3d 1301, 1334 (Fed. Cir. 2009) ("[W]e have never laid down any rigid requirement that damages in all circumstances be limited to specific instances of infringement proven with direct evidence.").

Monetary relief may include compensatory damages, such as covering the patent owner's lost profits or actual money received by the infringer. Lost profits, or money the patent holder could have made if there was no infringement, must be proven with a sufficient causation nexus proving the patent holder suffered specifically due to the infringement. Lost sales, price erosion, increased expenses, and future losses may be asserted.

Fed.R.Civ.P. 65(b) permits temporary restraining orders against further infringement. The plaintiff need not even provide notice to the alleged infringer prior to seeking such a remedy. However, the patent holder must provide specific facts that clearly show immediate and irreparable losses, injury, or damage before the alleged infringer can even be heard in court. The patent holder's attorney must also make certain assertions. Temporary restraining orders usually only last until a preliminary injunction hearing is held.

Injunctive relief prevents the accused from practicing the patent pursuant to 35 U.S.C. § 283. This relief can be available at the beginning of a lawsuit or as part of a judgment. Preliminary injunctions require an accused infringer stop the allegedly harmful actions. This may help prevent irreparable harm to a patent holder's market position during the litigation. However, this can be an extreme remedy since patent infringement is unproven at this point and the injury this would cause the accused makes it ripe for abuse. A plaintiff seeking a preliminary injunction must prove (1) likelihood of success on the merits; (2) irreparable harm without preliminary relief; (3) the balance of equities favors the plaintiff; and (4) an injunction is in the public interest. *Winter v. Natural Res. Def. Council*, 555 U.S. 7 (2008).

Permanent injunctive relief, awarded after the lawsuit concludes, follows a similar test. In *eBay, Inc. v. MercExchange, LLC*, 547 U.S. 388 (2006), the Supreme Court reiterated that courts granting permanent injunctive relief in patent infringement cases must apply the traditional four-factor test rather than automatically awarding it. These factors are: 1) irreparable injury, 2) inadequate legal remedies, 3) a balance of hardships, and 4) whether the award is in the public interest. While rarely successful, non-practicing entities can satisfy the requirements by asserting potential injury to their licensing program. *See Software Research, Inc. v. Dynatrace LLC,* 316 F.Supp. 3d 1112, 38 (N.D. Cal. 2018).

There are several royalty calculation methods available to patent holders, the most common ones being a hypothetical negotiation and an analytical approach. The "hypothetical negotiation" estimates the royalty a willing licensee would pay the licensor when the infringement began, applying fifteen factors to calculate a royalty percentage. *Georgia-Pacific Corp. v. United States Plywood Corp.*, 318

F.Supp. 1116 (S.D.N.Y. 1970). The "analytical approach" calculates damages based on the infringer's internal profit projections at the time the infringement began. *See, e.g., TWM Mfg. Co. v. Dura Corp.*, 789 F. 2d 895 (Fed. Cir. 1986). Other methods include a "25% rule", paying 25% of gross profits before taxes, a "comparable licensure" rule which looks at similar industry licenses, and an "entire market value rule" which considers various market factors such as sales, product timing, and features added by the infringer.

When patent infringement is held willful, the infringer may face up to three times the normal compensatory damages, as well as court costs. 35 U.S.C. § 284. The Supreme Court held a patent holder may recover enhanced damages by showing through a preponderance of the evidence that the infringer's activities were "egregious". *See Halo Elecs., Inc. v. Pulse Elecs., Inc.*, 579 U.S. 93 (2016) (willfulness determinations a matter of court discretion only reviewable for abuse of discretion; the infringer's subjective knowledge at the time of the challenged conduct shown by a preponderance of the evidence). This overruled the Federal Circuit's narrower test requiring objective recklessness and subjective knowledge of wrongdoing, proven by the higher clear and convincing evidence standard. *In re Seagate Tech. LLC*, 497 F.3d 1360 (Fed. Cir. 2007). The Federal Circuit since asserted that willful infringement requires proof of wanton, malicious, and bad faith behavior. *SRI Int'l, Inc. v. Cisco Sys., Inc.*, 918 F.3d 1368 (Fed. Cir. 2019).

Courts may award attorney's fees in exceptional cases. 35 U.S.C. § 285. An exceptional case is "simply one that stands out from the others with respect to the substantive strength of a party's litigating position or the unreasonable matter in which the case was litigated" as decided by a preponderance of the evidence. *Octane Fitness, LLC v. ICON Health & Fitness, Inc.*, 572 U.S. 545 (2014). This rejected the Federal Circuit's standard that exceptional cases required clear and convincing evidence of either material inappropriate conduct or litigation that was both objectively baseless and brought in subjective bad faith. *Brooks Furniture Mfg., Inc. v. Dutailer Int'l., Inc.*, 395 F.3d 1378 (2005). *See also Highmark Inc. v. Allcare Health Mgmt. Sys., Inc.*, 572 U.S. 559 (2014) (exceptional case determinations are discretionary, so district court decisions are only reviewable for abuse of discretion).

2. COPYRIGHTS

The principal affirmative defenses to tortious misappropriation claims are that of federal preemption and First Amendment commercial speech freedoms. Copyright law is not "categorically immune from challenges under the First Amendment." *Eldred v. Ashcroft*, 537 U.S. 186, 221 (2003). However, constitutional matters pose a challenge since both sides may have speech interests, namely the rights to speak or not speak. *See Salinger v. Colting*, 607 F.3d 68, 81 (2d Cir. 2010).

Where neither of these defenses applies, a full panoply of legal and equitable remedies are available. Affirmative defenses specific to copyright infringement frequently challenge copyright ownership claims or the alleged copyright violation. Statutory safe havens limit the scope of individual rights copyright law grants.

a. Copyright Ownership Defenses

Copyright ownership challenges are fact intensive. A copyright is an original work of authorship, requiring the owner show independent creation and at least a minimal degree of creativity to receive copyright protection in the work. Works lacking sufficient originality may not receive protection, such as certain compilations, factual recitations, or reproductions of unprotected works. *See, e.g., Feist Publ'ns. Inc., supra.* An individual actor's film performance is unlikely to constitute a copyrightable work and is even less likely to be considered an exclusive one. *Garcia v. Google, Inc.*, 786 F.3d 733 (9th Cir. 2015).

The merger doctrine prevents copyright protection of specific ideas or ideas that can be expressed in only a limited number of ways. *See, e.g., Affiliated Hospital Prods., Inc. v. Merdel Game Mfg. Co.*, 513 F.2d 1183 (2d Cir. 1975) (no protection for game concepts or rules); *Herbert Rosenthal Jewelry Corp. v. Kalpakian,* 446 F.2d 738 (9th Cir. 1971) (others may make bee-shaped jewel pins).

Similar to the merger doctrine, the scènes à faire ("scenes that must be done") doctrine protects standard or necessary story elements such as common themes, expressions, folklore, and common visual or cultural references. First used in *Cain v. Universal Pictures Co.*, 47 F.Supp. 1013 (S.D. Cal. 1942), a judge held the concept of a couple sheltering from a storm in a church was common and that incidents necessarily associated with such a situation (playing music, praying, experiencing hunger) were inevitable and therefore not protectable. *See also CCC Info. Servs., Inc. v. Maclean Hunter Mkt. Reports, Inc.*, 44 F.3d 61, 68 (2d Cir. 1994) ("expression [that] is essential to the statement of the idea"); *Murray Hill Publ'ns, Inc. v. Twentieth Century Fox Film Corp.*, 361 F.3d 312, 319 n. 2 (6th Cir. 2004) (expression is not protected when non-protectable ideas dominate a combination of idea and expression); *Walker v. Time Life Films, Inc.*, 784 F.2d 44 (2d Cir. 1986).

The scènes à faire doctrine also applies to computer software copyrights. This denies copyright protection to computer program aspects "dictated by practical realities—*e.g.*, by hardware standards and mechanical specifications, software standards and compatibility requirements, computer manufacturer design standards, target industry practices, and standard computer programming practices." *Lexmark Int'l v. Static Control Components, Inc.*, 387 F.3d 522 (6th Cir. 2004). This challenge often arises with security devices intended to prevent access or parts installation from sources other than the manufacturer. *See, e.g., Sega Enters. Ltd. v. Accolade, Inc.,* 977 F.2d 1510 (9th Cir. 1992).

Works by a federal government officer or employee as part of their official duties do not receive domestic copyright protection under 17 U.S.C. § 105, although foreign copyright protection may be possible. Exclusions exist for certain independent agencies and federal subsidiaries such as the U.S. Postal Service (Postal Reorganization Act of 1970 [Pub. L. 91–375]) and the Department of Commerce (15 U.S.C. § 290e). Similarly, the government edicts doctrine precludes copyright protection for laws, judicial opinions, and statutes. *See Wheaton v. Peters*, 33 U.S. 591 (1834), *Banks v. Manchester*, 128 U.S. 244 (1888). This doctrine applies to legal annotations that the state legislature adopts. *Georgia v. Public.Resource.Org, Inc.*, 590 U.S. ___, 140 S. Ct. 1498 (2020).

States have sovereign immunity protecting them from copyright infringement lawsuits, just like patent law. *Allen v. Cooper*, 589 U.S. ___, 140 S. Ct. 994 (2020). This case rejected Congress' unauthorized attempt to remove this right by amendment of 17 U.S.C. § 501(a) through the Copyright Remedy Classification Act of 1990.

A copyright infringement lawsuit may not be brought until the Copyright Office registers the copyright pursuant to 17 U.S.C. § 411(a); merely filing an application is not sufficient. *Fourth Estate Pub. Benefit Corp. v. Wall-Street.com, LLC*, 586 U.S. ___, 139 S. Ct. 881 (2019). There are, however, limited circumstances where a copyright infringement lawsuit may be filed before registration. *See, e.g.*, 17 U.S.C. § 408(f)(2) (compositions vulnerable to pre-distribution infringement such as movies or musicals), § 411(c) (live broadcasts). The 17 U.S.C. § 411(b)(1)(A) safe harbor excuses inaccurate information in a copyright registration certificate so long as the inaccurate information was included without knowledge of the inaccuracy. *Unicolors, Inc. v. H&M Hennes & Mauritz, L.P.*, 142 S. Ct. 941, 951 (2022) (lack of either factual or legal knowledge are excusable inaccuracies in a copyright registration). For greater detail on the limits of copyright protection, *see* § 2(a), *supra*.

There are limitations to the rights copyright owners can claim in contract. Copyright misuse attempts to use copyright protections to secure an exclusive right or limited monopoly not granted by the Copyright Office. *See Lasercomb Am., Inc. v. Reynolds*, 911 F.2d 970,972 (4th Cir. 1990). Examples include requirements not to create or use competing products or limiting licensed software uses to effectively preclude developing non-infringing works. *See, e.g., Practice Mgmt. Info. Corp. v. American Med. Assoc.*, 121 F.3d 516 (9th Cir. 1997); *DSC Commc'ns Corp. v. DGI Techs., Inc.*, 81 F.3d 597, 601 (5th Cir. 1996). Copyright misuse does not invalidate a copyright, but it does render the copyright unenforceable during the misuse period. The defendant's own behavior may affect the outcome. *See, e.g., Alcatel USA, Inc. v. DGI Techs., Inc.*, 166 F.3d 772 (5th Cir. 1999) (party seeking equitable injunction should not have unclean hands).

b. Copyright Exclusivity Defenses

If the copyright's ownership is confirmed, a defendant may contest the ownership's exclusivity. There are defenses for the use or creation of certain types of works. Fair use is the most well-known of these defenses, while independent development applies in much more limited circumstances. Statutory "safe havens" limit the scope of each of the rights granted in a protected work.

(1) Fair Use and Independent Creation

The exclusive rights in all copyrighted works are subject to a broad "fair use" exemption contained in § 107 of the 1976 Act. Section 107 states that it is not infringement to make "fair use" of a copyrighted work for purposes such as criticism, comment, news reporting, teaching (including copying for classroom use), scholarship, or research. Courts consider four primary, non-exclusive factors in fair use cases:

(1) the *purpose* and *character* of the use, including whether the use is commercial or for non-profit educational purposes;

(2) the *nature* of the *copyrighted work,* including its intended purpose and availability to the potential user;

(3) the *amount* and *substantiality* of the portion used in relation to the copyrighted work as a whole; and

(4) the *effect* of the use upon the *potential market* for or *value* of the copyrighted work.

Courts recognized a fair use privilege long before the 1976 Act's passage. In § 107 of the 1976 Act, Congress explicitly recognized and essentially restated the judicially developed fair use privilege. The 1976 Act's safe havens are not intended to curtail the fair use privilege, but rather simply define permissible uses.

While the legislative history describes fair use guidelines as "minimum standards" and not the outer limits of fair use, courts still treat the guidelines as "instructive" for fair use issues. *See, e.g., Google LLC v. Oracle Am., Inc.*, 593 U.S. ___, 141 S. Ct. 1183 (2021) (assuming a software interface may be subject to copyright protection, limited copying of an application programming interface ("API") is fair use as declaring code is functional and using the program on a new platform was transformative); *Marcus v. Rowley*, 695 F.2d 1171 (9th Cir. 1983) (teacher copying from another teacher's book greatly exceeded the "brevity" and "spontaneity" guidelines, although not those concerned with "cumulative effect," committed copyright infringement as a matter of law). *Cf., Encyclopaedia Britannica Educ. Corp. v. Crooks*, 447 F.Supp. 243 (W.D.N.Y. 1978) (noncommercial educational program broadcast copying for school system's permanent retention and use was beyond relevant statutory "safe havens" and too extensive to apply the fair use defense).

While no § 107 factor is determinative, the fourth factor is implicit in the other three. If a particular use of a copyrighted work serves a sufficiently distinguishable function that does not significantly impair the work's value, then using even a substantial portion of the copyrighted work will be deemed a fair use and not an infringement. *See, e.g., Triangle Publ'ns v. Knight-Ridder Newspapers, Inc.*, 626 F.2d 1171 (5th Cir. 1980) (using a protected cover in a comparative advertisement for a competing booklet constituted fair use as it did not by itself affect the value of the plaintiff's copyright); *Solid Oak Sketches, LLC v. 2K Games, Inc.*, 449 F.Supp. 3d 333 (S.D.N.Y. 2020) (portrayal of athletes' tattoos in sports simulation video game was de minimis and fair use, and there is a reasonable inference that tattoo artists grant recipients an implied nonexclusive licenses to use the tattoos as part of their likenesses); *Sega Enters. v. Accolade, Inc.*, 977 F.2d 1510 (9th Cir. 1993) (reverse engineering [i.e., decompiling] a computer program to access unprotected software elements needed to achieve interoperability with an independent program when no other means of access to those elements exists constitutes fair use of the copyrighted work); *Kelly v. Arriba Soft Corp.*, 336 F.3d 811 (9th Cir. 2003) (visual search engine may copy images and photographs online as fair use, but framing or linking to full-sized photos violates public display rights). *But cf., Bowers v. Baystate Techs.*, 320 F.3d 1317 (Fed. Cir. 2003), where Judge Dyk's dissenting opinion concedes states can permit parties to contract away their statutory fair use defense if the contract is freely negotiated, but arguing state laws authorizing shrink-wrap licenses prohibiting reverse engineering should be preempted. *See also Assessment Techs. of WI, LLC v. WIREdata, Inc.*, 350 F.3d 640 (7th Cir.

2003) (software developer abused process and possibly misused its copyright when enforcing a license prohibiting dissemination of data collected by other software users, at least where no trade secret claim was available, when demonstrative software versions revealing the database's structure were freely distributed).

In additional to the four fair use factors, although not codified by § 107, courts consider whether the protected work's use is "transformative". Expressive forms such as burlesque, parody, and satire all involve varying degrees of mimicry that require copying substantial portions of a protected work. Parody, at least, received judicial recognition as deserving protection both as social and literary criticism form and an entertainment form. *See Campbell v. Acuff-Rose Music, Inc.*, 510 U.S. 569 (1994) (parody song may be fair use despite its commercial character); *Suntrust Bank v. Houghton Mifflin Co.*, 268 F.3d 1257 (11th Cir. 2001). *But see Dr. Seuss Enters. v. Penguin Books*, 109 F.3d 1394 (9th Cir. 1997) (satire targeting something other than the original work for mockery is not fair use). Transformative uses of a work that do not support fair use findings "include the translation of a novel into another language, the adaptation of a novel into a movie or play, or the recasting of a novel as an e-book or an audiobook." *Authors Guild, Inc. v. HathiTrust*, 755 F.3d 87, 95 (2d Cir. 2014).

Transformative use considerations remain subservient to the first fair use factor, examining the degree of the new work's further purpose or different character, balanced against the new use's commercial nature. The Supreme Court held that uses that have a further purpose or different character are more likely to be considered transformative and therefore sufficiently distinct from the original work, but these transformative uses must go beyond those that would qualify as a derivative work supporting a fair use finding. *Andy Warhol Found. For the Visual Arts, Inc., v. Goldsmith,* 598 U.S. ___, 143 S. Ct. 1258 (2023).

Similarly, using a relatively small portion of a copyrighted work in another work reflecting the author's substantial independent effort is unlikely to undermine the commercial value of the quoted work, even where the two works compete in the same market. *Cf., Rosemont Enters., Inc. v. Random House, Inc.,* 366 F.2d 303 (2d Cir. 1966) (unauthorized biographer using a copyrighted article was not an infringement even though the article's author and copyright owner was also an authorized biographer).

On the other hand, unauthorized use of even a small part of an unpublished work may be infringing if the author can show an adverse impact on the copyrighted work's marketability. *Harper & Row Publishers Inc. v. Nation Enters.,* 471 U.S. 539 (1985) (unauthorized quotation of 300–400 words of an unpublished 200,000-word autobiography not fair use where another magazine canceled an excerpt publication agreement due to the premature disclosure). *But see Authors Guild, Inc. v. Google, Inc.,* 804 F. 3d 202 (2d Cir. 2015) (scanning libraries of books to create digital copies, enabling search functions, and offering snippet views was fair use despite commercial purpose). A 1992 amendment to § 107 clarified that a work's unpublished nature shall not itself bar a fair use finding made by considering all the foregoing factors.

Copying an entire work for the non-commercial purpose of delayed viewing is not an infringement but rather a fair use, at least without meaningful likelihood of future harm to the copyright owner. *Sony Corp. of Am. v. Universal City Studios, Inc.*, 464 U.S. 417 (1984). The *Sony* court also held selling recording devices does not constitute contributory infringement since the devices are widely used for this legitimate purpose, even though some owners also accumulate copyrighted program libraries. *But see Pacific and S. Co., Inc. v. Duncan*, 744 F.2d 1490 (11th Cir. 1984) (selling copies of TV news broadcasts to report subjects an infringement). Note that while "time shifting" is considered fair use, shifting works by location using digital storage is not. *See, e.g., UMG Recordings, Inc. v. MP3.com Inc.*, 92 F.Supp.2d 349 (S.D.N.Y. 2000).

The mere absence of measurable pecuniary damage does not require finding fair use. Where there is substantial copying for the same intrinsic purpose, even copying for non-profit educational use may constitute copyright infringement as a matter of law. *See Marcus v. Rowley*, 695 F.2d 1171 (9th Cir. 1983).

Library photocopying presents a unique challenge to fair use. In *Williams & Wilkins Co. v. United*

States, 487 F.2d 1345 (Ct. Cl. 1973), the Court of Claims held photocopying entire articles from medical and scientific journals by government entities constituted fair use and was not copyright infringement. Described in the dissent as "the Dred Scott decision of copyright law," the case apparently did not seriously consider the effect of defendants' practices on plaintiff's potential market. Instead, the decision focused exclusively on the role defendants' copying played in advancing medical and scientific research. Later decisions focused more on how the copying affects the marketplace than on scholarly purpose. *See, e.g., American Geophysical Union v. Texaco Inc.*, 60 F.3d 913 (2d Cir. 1994) (photocopying articles from a scientific journal not fair use); *Princeton Univ. Press v. Michigan Document Servs.*, 99 F.3d 1381 (6th Cir. 1996) (copy service preparing university course supplements held liable for infringement); *but see Authors Guild v. Google, Inc., supra.*

Guidelines exist for teacher and classroom copying in not-for-profit educational institutions, drafted by an ad hoc committee of educators, authors, and publishers. Although it only appears in the legislative history of the 1976 Copyright Act and not the Act itself, these guidelines are nearly as important of a reproduction right limitation as the statutory fair use exemption. *See* H.R. Rep. No. 94–1476, 94th Cong., 2d Sess. 68–72 (1976); Conf. Rep. No. 1733, 94th Cong., 2d Sess. 70 reprinted in 1976 U.S. Code Cong. & Admin. News 5810, 5811 (1976). Strongly criticized by the American Association of University Professors and the Association of

American Law Schools as too restrictive, the guidelines specify the quantity and conditions under which both a single copy of a work may be made for teachers and multiple copies may be made for classroom use.

Independent creation is a common law protection for a similar work created without knowledge of the copyright protected work. In such cases, each author owns a copyright in their own work. As recognized in *Feist Pubs., Inc. v. Rural Tel. Svc. Co., Inc.*, 499 U.S. 340 (1991), copyright law protects originality, which does not require novelty. This allows such overlapping authorship to exist. Unlike patent law, independent creation is a complete defense against copyright infringement allegations.

Since it is difficult to directly prove another's copying, a copyright holder creates an inference of copying by establishing reasonable access to the work and substantial similarity between the works which the accused then has the burden to disprove. *See, e.g., Granite Music Corp. v. United Artists Corp.,*532 F.2d 718, 721 (9th Cir. 1976). Courts should not engage in speculations or conjecture to find access to the plaintiff's work. *Alexander v. Irving Trust Co.,* 132 F.Supp. 364 (S.D.N.Y. 1955). Substantial similarity determinations can be made as a matter of law or fact. *Weitzenkorn v. Lesser*, 40 Cal.2d 778 (1953).

A copyright infringement defendant may raise the same equitable defenses of acquiescence and unclean hands as in trademark and patent infringement cases. The laches defense was precluded by *Petrella v. Metro-Goldwyn-Mayer, Inc.*, 572 U.S. 663 (2014), which held the separation-of-powers doctrine precluded this remedy for damage claims brought within the statutory three-year limitations period when a copyright infringement claim accrues.

(2) Safe Havens

Each of the rights in a copyright-protected work have various limitations and qualifications on their scope which collectively serve as "safe havens," defining what is a permissible use and not infringement. "Limitations" safe havens qualify exclusive rights, while "scope" safe havens limit exclusive rights for one or more copyrightable subject matter types as enumerated in § 102. For example, both the reproduction and distribution rights have a limitation enabling libraries and archives with open collections to make or distribute isolated and unrelated single copies of literary, dramatic, or choreographic works, as well as pantomimes and sound recordings. This may be done for noncommercial preservation of an unpublished work, replacing the published work, or meeting a user request for a small part of an available work or a copy of an unobtainable work. 17 U.S.C. § 108.

Congress frequently passes or amends copyright laws, creating a patchwork of rule variations based upon the user's circumstances or the work itself. For example, 17 U.S.C. §§ 121 and 121A limit exclusive rights for and expand authorized reproduction of media works, making them more accessible to those with physical disabilities or other limitations. Orphan works, works where the copyright owner cannot be identified or contacted for permission, are exempt from certain library or archival use limitations. 17 U.S.C. § 108(i).

Distribution, performance, and display rights are limited to *public* distributions, performances, and displays. There is not always a clear difference between public and private performances and displays. For example, the public performance right is infringed by exhibiting copyright-protected video cassettes in private booths on commercial premises devoted to that purpose. *Columbia Pictures Indus., Inc. v. Redd Horne, Inc.*, 749 F.2d 154 (3d Cir. 1984). *See also American Broad. Cos. v. Aereo, Inc.*, 573 U.S. 431 (2014) (service providing television programming over the internet using antennas dedicated to individual subscribers still performed the works rather than merely supplied equipment). However, a hotel may rent videodiscs to guests for viewing in individual rooms without contributory infringement of the public performance right. *Columbia Pictures Indus., Inc. v. Professional Real Estate Inv., Inc.*, 866 F.2d 278 (9th Cir. 1989).

Performance and display rights are also subject to numerous public policy exceptions for activities like classroom instruction, educational broadcasting, religious services, certain non-profit and ancillary commercial activities, and transmissions to blind or deaf audiences. 17 U.S.C. § 110. Various compulsory licensing provisions contained in the Copyright Act also qualify these rights. *See* § A.2.c *supra*.

Sound recording exclusive rights are limited to reproduction, adaptation, and distribution rights.

They do not include a performance or display right. Thus, publicly playing a recording does not infringe a sound recording copyright. If a copyright is infringed, it will be the underlying work's copyright. Likewise, the performance and display royalties collected under the Act's various compulsory licensing systems for public broadcasts go to the owner of the underlying copyrighted work, not the sound recording copyright owner. Public performances via sound recording digital transmissions, however, are now specifically protected under § 106(6) of the Copyright Act. All exclusive rights in published pictorial, graphic, sculptural, and non-dramatic musical works are subject to compulsory licensing for noncommercial broadcasts.

The Digital Millennium Copyright Act (DMCA), enacted in 1998, attempts to recalibrate the copyright regime in response to the Internet's digital distribution capabilities. Title I of the DMCA's five titles purportedly implements (but actually greatly exceeds) WIPO treaty obligations. The new Chapter 12 of the Copyright Act bans circumventing certain technological protection and copyright management systems. Section 1201 specifically prohibits users from circumventing a "technological measure that effectively controls access to a work protected under this title." It also prohibits selling devices that circumvent technological measures controlling access to a work or otherwise protecting a copyright owner's rights. A copyright infringement defense, such as fair use, is not a defense to DMCA violations. The DMCA establishes limited safe havens for non-profit libraries, archives, educational institutions, law enforcement, intelligence, other government activities, reverse engineering for interoperability purposes, and encryption research.

Title II of the DMCA adds a new 17 U.S.C. § 512 to the Copyright Act that provides a series of safe harbors from contributory or vicarious copyright infringement liability for most telecommunications companies, Internet service providers (ISPs), and other online services and content hosts that comply with the section's detailed and complicated provisions. The common element of these safe harbors require the host make reasonable steps to "take down" specific infringing material upon notification and take reasonable measures to prevent repeat infringers from using the host's services. *See In re Aimster Copyright Litig.*, 334 F.3d 643 (7th Cir. 2003); *A&M Records, Inc. v. Napster, Inc.*, 239 F.3d 1004 (9th Cir. 2001). *But cf. Perfect 10 v. CCBill,* 488 F.3d 1102 (9th Cir. 2007) (ISP need not affirmatively police users for evidence of repeat infringement nor respond to copyright owner notifications that do not substantially comply with the notice requirements of § 512(c)(3)(A); an ISP does not have sufficiently direct financial benefit to be vicariously liable under § 512(c)(1)(B) where the infringing activity is simply an added benefit rather than a draw for subscribers); *Viacom Int'l, Inc. v. YouTube,* 676 F.3d 19 (2d Cir. 2012) (§ 512(c) safe harbor requires knowledge or awareness of specific infringing activity to render an ISP liable for contributory infringement, but § 512(c)(1)(B) does not include a specific knowledge requirement for vicarious liability). *See also* Ch. 8, *infra* reviewing the 47 U.S.C. § 230 safe harbor for Internet sites hosting third-party information.

Title III of the DMCA amends § 117 of the Copyright Act to permit a computer owner or lessee's making or authorizing making a copy of certain computer programs to maintain or repair the computer. Title IV makes various Copyright Act amendments, including letting broadcasters make specified "ephemeral" recordings of digital broadcasts as permitted for analog broadcasts under § 112. Title V consists of the Vessel Hull Design Protection Act. *See* Part A.3, *supra*.

c. Copyright Infringement Remedies

Copyright infringement remedies, 17 U.S.C. §§ 501–513, are similar to those available for trademark and patent infringement. They may include damages (including punitive damages) or an accounting of profits, declaratory relief, injunctions, seizure and disposition of infringing articles, costs, and attorney's fees. Criminal penalties are available in some cases if brought within five years of the cause of action. Actual damages may include lost earnings from the infringement and the infringer's profits. Statutory damages may range from $200 to $30,000 per infringement, which can be increased to $150,000 for intentional infringement. Infringing establishment proprietors may owe twice the licensing fees that would have been charged for up to three years previous. Copyright infringement generally presumes irreparable harm, supporting injunctive relief claims. *See, e.g., Apple Computer v. Franklin Computer Co.*, 714 F.2d 1240 (3d Cir. 1983).

Both the 1909 and 1976 Acts specifically provide for a purely discretionary award of attorney's fees, impoundment of allegedly infringing works while infringement proceedings are pending, and statutory damages recovery (in a sum under the 1976 Act of not less than $750 or more than $30,000, as the court considers just), in lieu of actual damages. Willfulness or innocence of the infringement may alter these amounts. If a copyright holder seeks actual damages, the holder must show lost revenue and then the infringer must then prove the loss would have occurred even in the absence of copyright infringement. *Harper & Row v. Nation Enters.*, 471 U.S. 539, 567 (1985).

17 U.S.C. § 505 allows for recovery of full costs by or against any party other than the United States, which includes reasonable attorney's fees to the prevailing party. "Full costs" means the costs available by law as specified in 28 U.S.C. §§ 1821 and 1920 of the general costs statute and does not include non-taxable costs such as expert witness fees, e-discovery expenses, or jury consultant fees; only Congress may award litigation expenses beyond those specified. *Rimini St., Inc. v. Oracle USA, Inc.*, 586 U. S. ___, 139 S. Ct. 873 (2019). When deciding whether to award attorney's fees under § 505, courts must consider all relevant circumstances rather than just whether the losing party advanced a reasonable claim or defense. *Kirtsaeng v. John Wiley & Sons, Inc.,* 579 U.S. 197 (2016) (relevant precedential

factors may include the losing party's motivations and deterrence interests). Like the Lanham Act but unlike the patent statute, both the old and new Acts permit recovery of an infringer's profits.

As with patents, a U.S. copyright holder may petition the ITC to order exclusion of imports that infringe the copyright and may petition the U.S. Trade Representative for sanctions where foreign copyright protections for U.S. nationals are inadequate or ineffective pursuant to § 337 of the Tariff Act of 1930.

CHAPTER 7

APPROPRIATION OF TRADE SECRETS AND IDEAS

Some intangible products of intellectual effort receive legal protection without public disclosure. Trade secrets are:

> [A]ll forms and types of financial, business, scientific, technical, economic, or engineering information, including patterns, plans, compilations, program devices, formulas, designs, prototypes, methods, techniques, processes, procedures, programs, or codes, whether tangible or intangible, and whether or how stored, compiled, or memorialized physically, electronically, graphically, photographically, or in writing if (a) the owner thereof has taken reasonable measures to keep such information secret; and (b) the information derives independent economic value, actual or potential, from not being generally known to, and not being readily ascertainable through proper means by, the public.

18 U.S.C. § 1831. While patents protect inventions for a limited time after public disclosure, trade secret laws may protect an invention as long as it remains a secret. Even so, trade secrets can include a combination of elements in the public domain so long as the "unique combination, affords a competitive advantage and is a protectable secret." *Imperial Chemical Indus., Ltd. v. National Distillers & Chemical Corp.*, 342 F.2d 737 (2d Cir. 1965); *see also*

Rivendell Forest Prods. Ltd. v. Georgia-Pac. Corp., 28 F.3d 1042, 1046 (10th Cir. 1994)

For all practical purposes, American trade secret law began with *Peabody v. Norfolk*, 98 Mass. 452 (1868) where a manufacture sought injunctions against a competitor and a former employee to prevent them from replicating a manufacturing process using the former employer's information. The *Peabody* court held that (1) a person who invents or discovers a manufacturing process and keeps it a secret, whether it is a proper subject for a patent or not, has an assignable property interest in the process which a court of equity will protect against another who undertakes to use the process or to disclose it to third persons in violation of contract and breach of confidence; (2) an employee's promise not to disclose a secret imparted during their employment is binding even beyond their employment term; (3) a trade secret does not lose its secrecy by being confidentially disclosed to agents or servants without whose assistance it could not be utilized; and (4) a third party with notice of a confidential relationship that still arranges to receive a secret may be enjoined from carrying out the arrangement.

There are multiple legal theories granting legal protection to trade secrets. Some courts emphasize that trade secrets are a protectable intellectual property form, influenced no doubt by patent, copyright, and trademark law. *See, e.g., Cincinnati Bell Foundry Co. v. Dodds*, 10 Ohio Dec.Reprint 154 (1887); *Cf., Ruckelshaus v. Monsanto Co.*, 467 U.S. 986 (1984) (a government agency's trade secret use or disclosure is only a taking of property compensable by the Fifth Amendment of the U.S. Constitution where the information is submitted under a confidentiality guarantee, but not where the information is voluntarily disclosed to the agency). For most courts, trade secret laws start with the breach of a confidential relationship. As Justice Holmes noted in *E.I. Du Pont De Nemours Powder Co. v. Masland*, 244 U.S. 100 (1917):

> The word property as applied to trademarks and trade secrets is an unanalyzed expression of certain secondary consequences of the primary fact that the law makes some rudimentary requirements of good faith. Whether the plaintiffs have any valuable secret or not the defendant knows the facts, whatever they are, through a special confidence he accepted. The property may be denied but the confidence cannot be.

Other courts focus on the tortious nature of the methods used to ascertain the secret. For example, in *Tabor v. Hoffman*, 23 N.E. 12 (N.Y. 1889), an inventor whose patent expired enjoined a manufacturer from using certain pump patterns when the patterns remained secret and the manufacturer's agent surreptitiously copied them during repairs. The *Tabor* trial court held a competent engineer could make the patterns from the pump, but the process would be time-consuming and expensive. The *Tabor* appellate court upheld the injunctive relief grant, holding even if copying the patterns was more convenient than necessary, the patterns were nevertheless a secret not disclosed by the pump's "publication". The manufacturer had no right to obtain the patterns by unfair means (i.e., surreptitious copying) or to use them. *See also E.I. DuPont de Nemours & Co. v. Christopher*, 431 F.2d 1012 (5th Cir. 1970) (aerial photography of a factory during construction was an improper means of obtaining another's trade secret).

Inducing another to breach a confidentiality contract can also be a tortious way to obtain a trade secret. As the *Peabody v. Norfolk* court illustrates, however, trade secret misappropriation liability is not limited to those who breach confidential relations or improperly obtain another's trade secret. Rather, liability includes those using a trade secret knowing another improperly disclosed it.

The Supreme Court's *Sears-Compco* decisions, *supra,* which assert federal patent laws prevent states from using unfair competition law to prohibit copying unpatented and uncopyrighted articles, generated considerable debate over whether and to what extent patent law preempted trade secret common law. The Supreme Court purportedly resolved the controversy in *Kewanee Oil Co. v. Bicron Corp.*, 416 U.S. 470 (1974), holding state trade secret law does not undermine federal patent law because an inventor is unlikely to rely on trade secret law and forfeit any right to patent protection after one year. Trade secret law was thus not preempted by patent law even where trade secret protection is granted to a patentable but unpatented invention. *See also Roberts v. Sears, Roebuck & Co.*, 573 F.2d 976 (7th

Cir. 1978) (no error in declining to decide patent validity in a suit for fraud, breach of a confidential relationship, and negligent misrepresentation when a company procured a patent rights assignment from an employee developing a new tool outside of work). The Court's *Kewanee Oil* opinion is criticized because the inventor did exactly what the Court said an inventor was unlikely to do—namely seek trade secret protection over patent protection.

In *Aronson v. Quick Point Pencil Co.*, 440 U.S. 257 (1979), the Court held federal patent law did not preempt state contract law by allowing a royalty agreement that lasted as long as a company sold articles embodying a patent-pending invention, with a reduced rate if the invention did not receive a patent. The *Kewanee* and *Aronson* decisions indicate state trade secret laws still provide legal protection for inventions as an alternative to patent law.

A parallel "law of ideas" emerged at the same time trade secret laws were developing. This body of law provides some protection to those submitting ideas to a business for consideration, regardless of whether the submitter was in business themselves. As with trade secrets, courts occasionally characterize such ideas as a protectable intellectual property form. *See, e.g., Hamilton Nat'l Bank v. Belt*, 210 F.2d 706 (D.C. Cir. 1953) (a person owns sufficient property rights in their idea as to recover damages for its appropriation or use when the idea is original, concrete, useful, and is disclosed in circumstances which reasonably and clearly indicate contemplated compensation for its use). While most courts accepted there may be property rights in an idea, disclosure without a contract often meant the recipient acquired the idea or secret. *See, e.g.*, *Bristol v. Equitable Life Assurance Soc'y of the U.S.*, 30 N.E. 506 (N.Y. 1892).

English courts protected unpublished writings, including those containing trade secrets and ideas, long before the *Peabody v. Norfolk* decision. In *Youatt v. Winyard*, 1 Jac. & W. 394 (1820), the court enjoined use or disclosure of certain veterinary medicine recipes that the defendant surreptitiously copied as an employee. Similarly, in *Abernathy v. Hutchinson*, 3 L.J.Ch. 209 (1825) the court enjoined publication of a distinguished surgeon's unpublished lectures as a breach of confidence, holding lecture attendees may take notes for their own use but could not publish the lectures for profit. This came to be known as common-law copyright.

The federal Copyright Act of 1976, 17 U.S.C. § 301(a), preempts much of the U.S. common law of copyright. On or after January 1, 1978, the 1976 Act exclusively covers all works of authorship fixed in a tangible medium of expression and come within the subject matter of copyright as specified by §§ 102 and 103, whether created before or after that date and whether published or unpublished. Section 106 of the Act specifies all legal or equitable rights equivalent to any of the exclusive rights within the general scope of copyright.

The subject matter classes protected by the 1976 Copyright Act and the exclusive rights it confers on a copyright holder are discussed in Chapter 6, *supra*. The owner of an unpublished copyrightable work embodying a trade secret has access to all federal copyright law rights and remedies to prevent unauthorized copying of the work embodying the trade secret. This understands copyright protection extends only to an author's original expression and not to the idea expressed.

Before an infringement action can be filed, a domestic or non-Berne Convention work must be registered and deposited with the Library of Congress. The Library's records are publicly available. However, the Register of Copyrights may exempt certain works from the deposit requirement, and the Copyright Office has promulgated regulations protecting trade secrets in certain cases. *See* 37 C.F.R. §§ 202.19(e), 202.20(c)(2)(vi)–(vii) (1991) (enabling copyright holders to 1) seek special relief, namely an exemption from deposit requirements with the Library of Congress; 2) obtain the Copyright Office's prompt post-examination return of any "secure test" (such as the LSAT) deposited as a part of registration; and 3) deposit identifying portions, rather than an entire copy, of any computer program sought to be registered and allowing the depositor block out any trade secret material the program contains).

In *General Motors v. Ignacio Lopez de Arriortua*, 948 F.Supp. 684 (E.D. Mich. 1996), the court held that § 44(h) of the Lanham Act, which protects foreign nationals against unfair competition, incorporates substantive Paris Convention provisions. Article 10*bis* of the Convention requires member countries provide effective protection against unfair competition, namely any act of competition contrary to honest practices in industrial or commercial matters. This granted GM and its German subsidiary a federal cause of action for trade secret misappropriation by former employees. *See also* WTO TRIPS Agreement, Article 39 (ensuring effective protection against unfair competition includes protecting undisclosed information and data submitted to governments or governmental agencies against acquisition, use, or disclosure in a manner contrary to honest commercial practices, as provided in Article 10*bis* of the Paris Convention); *BP Chems. Ltd. v. Jiangsu Sopo Corp.*, 285 F.3d 677 (8th Cir. 2002) (Foreign Sovereign Immunities Act's presumed immunity does not bar claims against a foreign sovereign's commercial activities and transactions in the U.S., and a state-owned company's procurement of U.S. engineering know-how protected as a trade secret met the commercial activity exception to foreign sovereign immunity).

This chapter focuses on common law protections for trade secrets and ideas. Trade secret and idea misappropriation liability may be based on: (1) breaching a contract or confidence; (2) improperly ascertaining a secret or idea; or (3) using a trade secret or idea known to have been improperly disclosed by another. This chapter reviews contractual and confidential trade relation types and the kinds of trade secrets and ideas protected by law. This chapter also identifies unauthorized acquisitions, disclosures, or uses of trade secrets that support a claim for relief.

A. TRADE RELATIONS AND TRADE VALUES PROTECTED

1. CONTRACTUAL AND CONFIDENTIAL RELATIONS

Trade secret and ideas laws protect contractual and confidential trade relations. Contractual and confidential relations may both exist between a business and its employees, between business partners, between a corporation and its officers and directors, or between a business and some other commercial or non-commercial party.

Confidential relations may be created by express contract or be implied from existing trade relations. Express contractual provisions can be a mere promise not to use or disclose a trade secret or idea or a covenant not to compete.

Sometimes the only practical method to prevent unauthorized trade secret use or disclosure is for the receiving party to agree not to compete with the disclosing business for a period of time after the trade relation terminates. *See* Ch. 3, *supra*. Courts may enforce an express covenant not to compete as a permissible means of protecting trade secrets, so long as the covenant is no broader than required to protect the trade secret and does not impose undue hardship on the restricted party. However, courts will not imply a covenant not to compete where no express covenant exists. The only implied obligation to protect trade secrets is not to make unauthorized use or disclosure of trade secrets or ideas learned during a confidential relation.

Not every trade relation is necessarily a confidential one. Courts are willing to imply a covenant by a prospective purchaser not to disclose or exploit information disclosed during negotiations should the sale not go through. *See, e.g., Smith v. Dravo Corp.*, 203 F.2d 369 (7th Cir. 1953). *See also Hamilton Nat'l Bank v. Belt*, 210 F.2d 706 (D.C. Cir. 1953) (implying contract for radio program sponsor to compensate program's originator existed although the express contract to purchase the idea and hire the originator ended when it initially appeared the idea could not be implemented); *Landsberg v. Scrabble Crossword Game Players, Inc.*, 802 F.2d 1193 (9th Cir. 1986) (initial manuscript disclosure for the limited purpose of seeking a trademark license was confidential and the author's expressed intent to commercially exploit the manuscript conditioned use of any portion of the manuscript upon payment).

Mere employment does not create a confidential relationship. Courts may imply an employee pledge of secrecy when an employer discloses an identified trade secret to the employee. When an employee develops the trade secret at work, courts are less willing to imply a secrecy pledge. *See, e.g., Wexler v. Greenberg*, 160 A.2d 430 (Pa. 1960). In such cases, courts require something more to imply a confidence obligation, such as employment specifically to develop the information as a trade secret. Employee non-competition agreement legality varies by state, with a few states prohibiting them outright and many other scrutinizing them for reasonable time, place, and manner restrictions and exempting members of certain professions from these requirements. In January 2023, the Federal Trade Commission challenged employment non-compete agreements as unfair competition contrary to Section 5 of the Federal Trade Commission Act. The FTC proposed rules that would prohibit employers from entering into non-compete agreements with employees and rescind existing agreement. *See, Non-Compete Clause Rule,* 88 Fed. Reg. 3482 (proposed Jan. 19, 2023) (to be codified at 16 C.F.R. pt. 910).

Unsolicited idea submissions alone do not create a confidential relationship. *See, e.g., Hisel v. Chrysler Corp.*, 94 F.Supp. 996 (W.D. Mo. 1951) (refusing to imply a relationship of trust and confidence where an idea's originator was told the corporation assumed no obligation for received ideas and submitted the idea anyway). *See also Smith v. Snap-On Tools Corp.*, 833 F.2d 578 (5th Cir. 1987) (trade secret proprietor may not unilaterally create a confidential relationship without the knowledge or consent of the receiving party; reliance on confidentiality must exist at the time of disclosure and may not be established afterwards).

2. TRADE SECRETS AND IDEAS

A trade secret may be any commercially valuable information, whether in the form of an *invention* (such as a machine or process); an abstract *industrial or commercial idea* (such as a new product concept or marketing plans); or a *compilation of data* (such as customer lists, financial information, or pricing or cost information). "Negative know-how", namely learning what will not work, can receive trade secret protection as well. *See, e.g., Metallurgical Industries Inc. v. Fourtek, Inc.,* 790 F.2d 1195 (5th Cir. 1986). *But see SI Handling Sys., Inc. v. Heisley,* 753 F.2d 1244 (3rd Cir. 1985) (an employer cannot keep employee knowledge of past mistakes and failures a trade secret). U.S. trade secret law sources include the Economic Espionage Act of 1996 (EEA), the Defend Trade Secrets Act of 2016 which amended the EEA, and state laws including variations of the Uniform Trade Secret Act (UTSA).

Trade secrets protect broader subject matter than patents and copyrights, as trade secrets may include ideas, lists, and raw data. Other trade secret advantages include indefinite duration, no disclosure requirements, and no filing or maintenance fees. Shortcomings of trade secret reliance include the loss of protection by disclosure, no protection from independent discovery or reverse engineering, and appreciable secrecy maintenance requirements that vary by state.

Where a distinct commercial relationship exists, contracts often include a section describing how confidential information and trade secrets should be treated. Non-disclosure agreements are common where parties begin exploring such relationships. Regardless of form, these agreements should define categories of information considered protected, whether the information must be specifically identified for protection (particularly for oral disclosures), the protection duration for confidential information (with indefinite trade secret protection obligations), and provisions for returning or disposing of the information after the relationship concludes. Some contracts address how a party should respond to government or other regulatory disclosure demands, limit employee solicitation or trade in securities, or set enforcement procedures.

Many courts limit the scope of a "trade secret" to information the business actually uses to obtain an advantage over competitors who do not know or use the secret. Of course, not all information treated as confidential is necessarily a trade secret or a protectable idea. *See, e.g., Religious Tech. Ctr. v. Wollersheim,* 796 F.2d 1076 (9th Cir. 1986) (confidential religious materials do not constitute a trade secret). Protections for other ideas and information, such as ideas submitted by a non-commercial party, are often treated as a separate body of law. *See, e.g., Hamilton Nat'l Bank v. Belt, supra* (protection of ideas treated distinctively differently than the protection of inventions, literary productions, and trade secrets).

Comment (b) to 4 Restatement of Torts (First), § 757 (1939) indicated regular use is a prerequisite to find a protectable trade secret exists. As regular use is not required by either federal patent law or the common law of ideas, however, many courts do not require regular use as a condition of granting relief in trade secret cases. *Accord*: Restatement Third, Unfair Competition § 39, comment d.

Confidential information must be guarded from disclosure to receive protection. This often requires technological and administrative controls to provide adequate physical security and adequate notice of the information's confidential nature. *Compare Incase, Inc. v. Timex Corp.*, 488 F.3d 46 (1st Cir. 2007) (upholding judgment for defendant as a matter of law where there was no evidence supporting plaintiff's claim that it took reasonable steps to protect its proposed package design's confidentiality) *with S. Field Maint. & Fabrication LLC v. Killough,* No. 2:18–cv–581–GMB, 2019 BL 28443 (M.D. Ala. Jan. 29, 2019) (owner took reasonable protective measures even though failing to mark some alleged secrets as confidential).

Matters of public or general knowledge in an industry or trade cannot be protected trade secrets, regardless of the precautions taken. *See BondPro Corp. v. Siemens Power Generation, Inc.*, 463 F.3d 702 (7th Cir. 2006), holding defendant's patent disclosing a similar process to the plaintiff's adequately-protected process was not actionable as the patent application failed to disclose information not previously known to the public. Matters that are completely revealed in a patent or a product design are no longer a protectable secret. No trade secret protection exists once a patent application is published, a patent issued, or a product disclosing the secret is publicly distributed.

Protecting confidential information does not require absolute secrecy. Commercially reasonable privacy measures need only be employed to protect confidential information from espionage that can reasonably be anticipated and prevented. A trade secret or idea may be disclosed to employees and others, so long as the disclosure is designated as confidential. Others may independently discover the trade secret or have the same idea without depriving the secret or idea of protection, so long as the discovering parties also keep the matter secret and are not too numerous.

Trade secret disclosures to a government entity follow this same principle. Freedom of Information Act ("FOIA") Exemption 4 for "trade secrets and commercial or financial information obtained from a person and privileged or confidential" shields from disclosure commercial or financial information that its owner actually and customarily treats as private and provides to the government in return for a privacy promise. *Food Mktg. Inst. v. Argus Leader Media*, 588 U.S. ___, 139 S. Ct. 2356 (2019). A business submitting documents to the government may oppose their disclosure under the Administrative Procedures Act. *Chrysler Corp. v. Brown*, 441 U.S. 281 (1979). Even when a state government responds to FOIA requests by providing information used for commercial purposes, the state may deny an out-of-state business access to this information without violating constitutional rights. *McBurney v. Young*, 569 U.S. 221 (2013).

Where a patent or public product distribution does not reveal everything about a secret or idea, the information remains secret to that extent protectable. *See Tabor v. Hoffman, supra. See also Smith v. Dravo Corp.*, 203 F.2d 369 (7th Cir. 1953) (finding a protectable trade secret in certain blueprints and models of cargo containers, despite 100 containers being in public use, at least where the defendant failed to show it actually inspected any of the available containers before manufacturing similar ones). *But see Van Prods. Co. v. Gen. Welding & Fabricating Co.*, 213 A.2d 769 (Pa. 1965) (no trade secret exists where permissible means could ascertain the information). A patent application (as opposed to the patent itself) is not a general disclosure if the application is not subject to the publication requirements contained in 35 U.S.C. § 122, as amended in 1999. *See* Ch. 6 *supra*.

Several courts require a trade secret possess some element of novelty, although it need not amount to an invention in a patent law sense. Similar requirements apply to business ideas. *See, e.g., Hamilton Nat'l Bank v. Belt, supra* (business ideas must be concrete as well as new, novel, or original, and concrete). As a practical matter, however, such a requirement seems only to be another (misleading) way of requiring the information or idea not be common knowledge. An idea's novelty, usefulness, originality, or concreteness are also relevant to determining if there is an implied understanding that compensation exists and is contemplated if the idea is accepted and used. *Compare, Murray v. Nat'l Broad. Co.*, 844 F.2d 988 (2d Cir. 1988) (an idea must be original or novel for protection as property, and no promise to pay for an idea may be implied absent novelty and originality) *with Landsberg v. Scrabble Crossword Game Players, Inc.*, 802 F.2d 1193 (9th Cir. 1986) (breach of contract claim rests not upon a protectable property interest's existence but upon the implied promise to pay the reasonable value of the material disclosed, and no contract will be implied if disclosure occurs before compensation is a known condition of the idea's use). *See Nadel v. Play-by-Play Toys & Novelties, Inc.*, 208 F.3d 368 (2d Cir. 2000) (novelty finding provides sufficient consideration to support a designer's contract claims against a manufacturer, where the idea must be original or novel to support an alternate tortious misappropriation claim).

Trade secrets and ideas may be assigned or licensed, just like distinctive trade symbols, patents, copyrights, and other investments of intellectual effort. The transaction does not change the need to maintain the trade secret or idea's confidentiality. Loss of secrecy results in a loss of rights, except as against those who have expressly agreed to pay royalties for so long as an invention, idea, or information is used. *See, e.g., Aronson v. Quick Point Pencil Co., supra.*

The Uniform Trade Secrets Act (UTSA) defines a trade secret as information, including a formula, pattern, compilation, program, device, method, technique or process, that 1) derives independent actual or potential economic value from not being generally known or readily ascertainable by proper means and 2) is the subject of reasonable efforts to maintain its secrecy. Excepting the UTSA's failure to specify the relevant information must actually be a secret, the UTSA mirrors much of Article 39 of the WTO Agreement on Trade-Related Aspects of Intellectual Property Rights (TRIPS), implementing Article 10*bis* of the Paris Convention (1967).

Nearly all states have adopted some form of the UTSA, but with appreciable variances. *See, e.g., Learning Curve Toys, Inc. v. Playwood Toys, Inc.*, 342 F.3d 714 (7th Cir. 2003), noting Illinois trade secret laws adopted the UTSA trade secret definition, but state courts frequently use a six-factor list to determine if a trade secret exists that are derived from § 757 of the Restatement (First) of Torts. *See also Burbank Grease Serv. LLC v. Sokolowski*, 717 N.W.2d 781 (Wis. 2006) (Wisconsin trade secret laws provide the statute "displaces conflicting tort law, restitution law, and any other law of this state providing a civil remedy for misappropriation of a trade secret," but does not preclude these civil remedies where the information does not meet the statutory trade secret definition).

The lack of state trade secret law uniformity leads to varying outcomes, making forum shopping inevitable. Geographic nuances can affect how a trade secret owner can prosecute trade secret theft. Trade secrets may need to be plead with "reasonable particularity" before discovery in states like California, while other states postpone disclosure requirements to later in the litigation process. In some states a trade secret owner must show the confidential information is not "readily ascertainable by proper means." Some states provide a right of action against an innocent acquirer, while others limit recovery to the source of the theft. Some courts presume "inevitable harm" from a trade secret's loss, while other require proof of harm.

The "inevitable disclosure" doctrine is among the more controversial of these geographic variances. This doctrine asserts a former employee cannot work with certain of the former employer's competitors as the employee cannot help but use their previous employer's trade secrets to help their new employer "achieve a substantial advantage" and "respond strategically" to certain business activities. *See, e.g., PepsiCo, Inc. v. Redmond,* 54 F.3d 1262 (7th Cir. 1995). While protective of company inside information, these cases are regularly criticized as assigning an involuntary non-compete agreement against employees and enabling abusive lawsuits against former employees regardless of actual evidence.

The Defend Trade Secrets Act of 2016 ("DTSA") amended the Economic Espionage Act of 1996 to provide a general private right of action in federal courts for trade secret claims. The DTSA disfavors the inevitable disclosure doctrine, as it expressly disallows injunctions that "prevent a person from entering into an employment relationship" and prohibits any conditions placed on a person's employment in an injunction based "merely on the information the person knows." 18 U.S.C. § 1836(b)(3)(A)(i).

The DTSA provides whistleblower immunity in certain circumstances. *See* 18 U.S.C. § 1833(b), *Christian v. Lannett Co., Inc.*, No. CV 16–963 (E.D. Pa. Mar. 29, 2018) (disclosure made pursuant to a court order must be consistent with DTSA's immunity provision allowing a whistleblower to disclose trade secrets "in confidence. . . to an attorney . . . solely for the purpose of reporting or investigating a suspected violation of law.").

The DTSA does not preempt state trade secret laws. Federal and state claims may be filed in parallel. Where state trade secret laws are unfavorable, solely filing a federal claim can avoid state law requirements. Pursuing federal or state claims affect the available remedies as well. This includes possible exemplary (i.e., punitive) damages for willful and malicious trade secret misappropriation, and the applicable damage multiplier. Likewise, the DTSA permits collection of attorney's fees while some states such as Missouri do not.

B. ACTIONABLE AND PRIVILEGED APPROPRIATION

Not every appropriation of another's trade secret or commercially valuable idea is actionable. As we have seen, liability rests on breach of contract or confidence in using, disclosing, or improperly acquiring a secret or idea. Liability may also apply to those using a trade secret knowing a third party improperly acquired or disclosed it.

1. IMPROPRIETY IN THE METHOD OF ACQUIRING A TRADE SECRET OR IDEA

Certain methods of acquiring another's trade secret or idea are clearly improper. Industrial espionage, bribing another's employees, and surreptitious copying as in *Tabor v. Hoffman, supra,* may expose one to civil or criminal liability. Likewise, inducing former employees to breach an express or implied contract not to disclose their former employer's trade secrets is just as actionable as interference with any other type of express or implied contract. (*See* Ch. 3, *supra.*) The Uniform Trade Secrets Act states that "improper means" includes theft, bribery, misrepresentation, breach or inducement of a breach of duty to maintain secrecy, or espionage through electronic or other means.

Impropriety in the method of acquiring a trade secret may be found even without evidence of trespass, illegal conduct, or interference with another's contractual relations. For example, taking aerial photographs of a factory construction site warranted an injunction compelling disclosure of the photographer's client, even though the plane stayed in public airspace. *See E.I. duPont deNemours & Co. v. Christopher*, 431 F.2d 1012 (5th Cir. 1970). *See also BC Ziegler & Co. v. Ehren,* 414 N.W.2d 48 (Wis. App. 1987) (business records purchased from scrap paper company remained trade secrets). The *duPont* court concluded discovery of another's trade secret by any means other than one's own independent research efforts or inspection and analysis of a publicly distributed product (i.e., reverse engineering) is improper unless the other party voluntarily discloses the secret or fails to take reasonable precautions to protect the secret. Apparently considering a cost-benefit analysis on security precautions, the *duPont* court emphasized judicial tolerance of espionage must cease when the cost to prevent another's spying is so high as to dampen the inventive spirit.

The *duPont* case also suggests, through dictum, what would constitute privileged appropriation of another's trade secret. Reverse engineering, independent discovery, and surveilling operations not reasonably shielded from public view are all characterized as permissible. *See also Chicago Lock Co. v. Fanberg*, 676 F.2d 400 (9th Cir. 1982) (no impropriety in procuring and publishing serial number and key code correlations from various locksmiths who had reverse engineered the locks).

2. UNAUTHORIZED USE OR DISCLOSURE OF A TRADE SECRET OR IDEA

One of the most difficult questions plaguing trade secret law is whether there is an actionable trade secret appropriation when a former employee uses knowledge or skills gained during their previous employment. Approaches vary widely by state. Courts generally allow employees to carry away their own faculties, skills, and experiences. However, employees may not reveal information gained solely through their employment. Sadly, the two are often intertwined.

When deciding employment-based trade secret cases, courts consider the limitations a former employee will experience when seeking new employment if the person cannot use certain knowledge. Courts also consider whether the employee developed the protected information at their own initiative. As with patents and copyrights, information an employee specifically develops as their job generally belongs to the employer.

Otherwise, the employee could claim the information as a product of their own knowledge and skill. This would only be subject to an employer's common-law "shop right" (i.e., an implied, irrevocable, non-exclusive, non-assignable, royalty-free license) for secrets or ideas developed using company time or materials. However, *Wexler v. Greenberg*, 160 A.2d 430 (Pa. 1960) found no breach of a confidential relationship when a former employee disclosed or used reverse engineering formulas the employee developed as a routine part of their previous employment. Regardless, employees without knowledge of or a meaningful ability to use competitive knowledge should not be restrained by non-competition covenants.

The employer's actions notifying employees of restrictions on information disclosure are also relevant. Courts generally hold that an employer bears the burden of making such restrictions explicit. Restrictions must be reasonably limited in duration, geographic scope, and manner. The extent of an employer's investment in developing the protected information may also be probative.

Where a former employee with access to confidential customer lists solicits former customers, many courts allow the former employee to use any part of the lists they remember, so long as there was no deliberate effort to memorize or copy the lists. *See, e.g., Leo Silfen, Inc. v. Cream*, 278 N.E.2d 636 (N.Y. 1972) (employer's lawsuit failed where former employee's solicitation of the employer's customers was at most a product of casual memory).

Express covenants not to compete may offer an employer better protection from trade secret theft. Such covenants may be appropriate to protect the employer's goodwill but will be voided as an unreasonable restraint on trade where their scope is greater than necessary to protect the employer's goodwill or imposes undue hardship on the employee. *See* Ch. 3, *supra; PepsiCo, Inc. v. Redmond*, 54 F.3d 1262 (7th Cir. 1995) (upholding injunction delaying employment where an employee would inevitably disclose knowledge of former employer's strategic plans for the year).

3. KNOWING USE OF AN IMPROPERLY DISCLOSED TRADE SECRET OR IDEA

Receipt and subsequent use of another's trade secret may be improper, even where the recipient did not engage in espionage or induce a breach of contract to obtain the secret. Some states consider whether a recipient knows certain information is confidential. This commonly arises when an employee voluntarily discloses information acquired during their previous employment. Where a former employee's use of confidential information is not privileged, their new employer that did not know the information was confidential may still be liable for knowingly receiving or continuing to use the information after learning its trade secret status.

Some courts presume the recipient knows protected information was confidential merely from the act of hiring a former employee. This implies the new employer has some reason to know their new hire had a duty of non-disclosure and was likely to breach that duty. In *Carter Prods., Inc. v. Colgate-Palmolive Co.*, 130 F.Supp. 557 (D.Md. 1955), the court imposed liability without any direct evidence that a competing business induced an employee to disclose their former employer's trade secrets when hiring them to reverse engineer a product the former employee helped develop. The *Carter Prods.* court concluded the new employer must have known that the employee was bound by a non-disclosure agreement and was obligated to do more to ascertain what the employee could disclose before assigning him work known to directly compete with the work he had done for his former employer. This decision implies either negligent or reckless interference with another's contractual relations.

The Uniform Trade Secrets Act specifies a party must have "had reason to know" the information received was another's trade secret, requiring proof of a reckless, rather than a merely negligent, disregard of another's trade secrets.

C. AFFIRMATIVE DEFENSES AND REMEDIES

1. AFFIRMATIVE DEFENSES

A trade secret's existence is generally a question of fact that the owner must prove. Technological and other advancements in knowledge can extinguish a trade secret. Likewise, information that is readily ascertainable through proper means cannot be protected. Such proper means can include independent invention, reverse engineering, disassembly or decompiling, product observation when in public use or display, or receiving the information from a source not obliged to keep it confidential (such as a mutual customer).

Many trade secret disputes hinge on the information asserted to be a trade secret. Frequently the complaining party will resist defining the scope and extent of the information allegedly receiving trade secret protection while the defending party will insist on prompt disclosure. A trade secret owner faces a dilemma when pursuing litigation as disclosing too much of their trade secret may amount to forfeiture of it, especially if the judge will not seal the evidence. Commercial trade secret information such as customer lists or business plans may require fewer specific disclosures than complex technical trade secrets. *See AlterG Inc. v. Boost Treadmills LLC,* No. 18–cv–07568–EMC (N.D. Cal. Sep. 5, 2019).

Trade secrets only retain their status as such so long as they are kept confidential. Trade secrets may be lost when previously secret information becomes generally known, the owner publicly released them, or the owner does not adequately protect the secret. Examples include publishing white papers, giving public presentations, or broadly sharing alleged trade secrets with customers, suppliers, or other business entities without proper protections. A trade secret owner that does not take prompt action to protect its secrets or alert good-faith acquirers to their existence may lose their ability to assert trade secret claims against a third party. *Cypress*

Semiconductor Corp. v. Superior Ct. 163 Cal.App.4th 575 (2008).

The reverse engineering defense against trade secret misappropriation asserts that information is not a secret if it is readily ascertainable from a product obtained through proper means. A protectable trade secret cannot be fully disclosed by a marketed product susceptible to reverse engineering, namely "starting with the known product and working backward to divine the process which aided in its manufacture." *Kewanee Oil Co. v. Bicron Corp.*, 416 U.S. 470, 476 (1974). However, the trade secret must be "readily ascertainable" for this defense. The more difficult, time consuming, and costly the discovery process, the less likely the process will be considered reverse engineering. *See, e.g., Zotos Int'l, Inc. v. Young,* 830 F.2d 350 (D.C. Cir. 1987).

States may not prohibit reverse engineering of products that are not protected under patent or copyright law. *Bonito Boats, Inc. v. Thunder Craft Boats, Inc.*, 489 U.S. 141 (1989). Actual reverse engineering of the product may not be required, so long as reverse engineering was possible. *See, SI Handling Sys., Inc. v. Heisley,* 753 F. 2d 1244 (3d Cir. 1985); *but see Pioneer Hi-Bred Intern. v. Holden Found. Seeds, Inc.,* 35 F. 3d 1226 (8th Cir. 1994) (mere ability to lawfully obtain a trade secret is not a defense if the accused does not actually use a proper means to acquire the information). Trade secret owners often address this defense through contractual restrictions, triggering breach of contract claims when a product user exercises their reverse engineering right.

The independent development defense precludes misappropriation liability where a trade secret is readily ascertained independently and without improper means. Some states hold the party asserting independent development bears the burden of proof, while others require a trade secret owner must prove misappropriation when the accused can independently develop the secret. *Compare Moore v. Kulicke & Soffa Indus., Inc.,* 318 F. 3d 561 (3d Cir. 2003) (Pennsylvania trade secret owner must prove independent development did not occur) *with Bolt Assocs., Inc. v. Alpine Geophysical Assocs., Inc.,* 365 F.2d 742 (3d Cir. 1966) (New Jersey trade secret recipient bears a heavy burden of persuasion to show independent development through a third party customer's specifications rather than from trade secret information received under a protective agreement).

Venue for trade secret theft can be a challenging issue that may not be decided prior to holding a trial. For example, *Smith v. United States*, 22 F.4th 1236 (11th Cir. 2022) involved a person residing in Alabama who took data from servers in central Florida from a business in northern Florida. The court vacated a Northern District of Florida jury verdict, finding the defendant's residence was a proper venue and refrained from determining whether the Middle District of Florida was also a proper venue. In so holding, the court found the location of the crime's effects are irrelevant to venue as no part of the trade secret theft statute states any essential conduct element in terms of effects of the trade secret owner.

To access the Defend Trade Secrets Act, a plaintiff must allege the trade secret theft occurred after May 11, 2016. *See, e.g., Attia v. Google LLC*, 983 F.3d 420 (9th Cir. 2020); *Magnesita Refractories Co. v. Tianjin New Century Refractories Co., Ltd.*, No. 1:17–CV–1587, 2019 WL 1003623 (M.D. Pa. Feb. 28, 2019) (RICO Act complaint using DTSA violations dismissed as two or more trade secret theft acts must occurred after May 11, 2016, but DTSA claims continued due to alleged ongoing use of trade secrets).

The DTSA specifies that a trade secret "owner" may bring claims under this statute. However, the term "owner" may include non-owners having legal rights to possess the trade secret. *Advanced Fluid Sys., Inc. v. Huber*, 958 F.3d 168 (3rd Cir. 2020).

The statute of limitations for trade secret misappropriation usually starts once the trade secret owner knows or has reason to know of the misappropriation. The federal three-year statute of limitations begins to run after a trade secret owner has notice that the trade secrets were misused. *CMI Roadbuilding, Inc. v. Iowa Parts, Inc.*, 920 F.3d 560 (8th Cir. 2019). However, states disagree as to whether trade secret misappropriation is a single continuing tort or multiple torts. This disparity affects the statute of limitations for bringing certain claims. *Compare Ashton-Tate Corp. v. Ross*, 916 F.2d 516, 523–24 (9th Cir. 1990) (continuing misappropriation constitutes a single claim, and the statute of limitations that began running upon improper disclosure does not restart if the accused later begins using the trade secrets), *with Heraeus Medical GMBH v. Esschem, Inc.*, 927 F.3d 727 (3d Cir. 2019) (While the Uniform Trade Secrets Act treats continuing misappropriations as a single claim, Pennsylvania treats them as multiple discrete claims with each misappropriation act having its own limitations period under "the separate accrual rule"). Regardless, a trade secret owner's research efforts to disprove a potential defense such as independent development do not toll the statute of limitations period. *Chasteen v. Unisia Jecs Corp.*, 216 F. 3d 1212 (10th Cir. 2000).

The DTSA also added an affirmative defense for whistleblowers disclosing trade secret information "solely for the purpose of reporting or investigating a suspected violation of law" or when opposing retaliation thereof. 18 U.S.C. § 1833. *Compare Christian v. Lannett Co.*, No. CV 16–963 (E.D. Pa. Mar. 29, 2018) (dismissing trade secret theft counterclaim to employment discrimination lawsuit), *with Unum Group v. Loftus*, 220 F.Supp. 3d 143 (D. Mass. 2016) (insufficient evidence available to establish affirmative defense for motion to dismiss).

The Supreme Court eliminated a primary trade secret misappropriation affirmative defense when it held that state trade secret laws do not undermine federal patent law and are thus not preempted by it, even where the trade secret may be patentable. *See Kewanee Oil Co. v. Bicron Corp., supra*. While federal patent law does not preempt any of the substance of state trade secret laws, however, it arguably limits the scope of remedies available for trade secret misappropriation.

2. REMEDIES

There are numerous civil and criminal remedies available for trade secret theft victims. Of these, injunctive relief receives great attention since it can limit further disclosure or ongoing capitalization of the secrets. Other remedies include compensation for actual loss, unjust enrichment, reasonable royalties, punitive damages, or attorney's fees.

When awarding damages, courts often require a causal relationship between the misappropriated trade secret and the damages sought. Remedies for anticipated future use of misappropriated trade secrets are not available as they are not ripe for adjudication. *Steves and Sons, Inc. v. JELD-WEN, Inc.*, 988 F.3d 690 (4th Cir. 2021). While there is an established Seventh Amendment right to a jury trial for legal remedies such as reasonable royalty awards, such a right for equitable remedies such as unjust enrichment is no longer certain. *Compare TCL Commc'n Tech. Holdings v. Ericsson*, 943 F.3d 1360 (Fed. Cir. 2019) (applying case precedent *Dairy Queen, Inc. v. Wood*, 369 U.S. 469 (1962) to patent lawsuit and holding legal claims sharing common issues with equitable claims create a constitutional jury trial right) *with Texas Advanced Optoelectronic Sols., Inc. v. Renesas Elecs. Am., Inc.*, 895 F.3d 1304 (Fed. Cir. 2018) (denying a constitutional jury trial right for trade secret equitable remedy claims by historical construction of 1791 laws, although noting jury trial is likely available for legal remedies).

Prior to the *Sears-Compco* decisions, courts would grant permanent injunctive relief in trade secret cases as a matter of course, without limiting the prohibition against further trade secret use. *See, e.g.*, *Shellmar Prods. Co. v. Allen-Qualley Co.*, 87 F.2d 104 (7th Cir. 1936) (refusing to modify an injunction against further trade secret use, even after the secret became public). Even before *Sears-Compco,* however, at least one lower court determined injunctive relief is precluded once a trade secret becomes public, and thereafter monetary relief is the only appropriate remedy (i.e., damages or an accounting). *See Conmar Prods. Corp. v. Universal Slide Fastener Co.*, 172 F.2d 150 (2d Cir. 1949), holding that a patent issuance, subsequently declared invalid, precluded injunctive relief against a defendant who came into possession of the invention prior to its public disclosure. The *Conmar* court held that the innocent user of a machine, before learning it is protected by a trade secrecy agreement between the developing employee and their former employer, is excused from liability for the period of innocent use.

After the *Sears-Compco* decisions, some lower courts concluded that avoiding undermining federal patent law meant injunctive relief in trade secret cases must be limited to the time needed to discover the trade secret by proper means, such as reverse engineering or independent discovery. *See, e.g.*, *Hampton v. Blair Mfg. Co.*, 374 F.2d 969 (8th Cir.

1967) where a former employee who surreptitiously obtained blueprints and would not turn them over to the court could not be permanently enjoined from copying unpatented farm implements, only enjoined for such time as would be required to reproduce the implements without wrongful use of the blueprints.

While the Supreme Court did not discuss relief in *Kewanee Oil,* it did reinstate the trial court's injunction prohibiting disclosure or use of a trade secret until either the trade secret was publicly released, had otherwise become publicly available, or the defendant obtained the information from sources with a legal right to convey it. The injunctive relief grant let the restrained party use the secret once it became public or was independently discovered by a third party, but did not explicitly limit the injunction period to the time the *defendant* would have taken to independently discover the secret. *See also K-2 Ski Co. v. Head Ski Co.,* 506 F.2d 471 (9th Cir. 1974) (potential reverse engineering or independent development does not excuse wrongful receipt of trade secrets, they merely limit the owner's protectible interest and the appropriate scope of relief).

In *Aronson v. Quick Point Pencil Co.*, 440 U.S. 257 (1979), the Supreme Court held federal patent law does not preclude state enforcement of a royalty contract lasting so long as the contracting party sells articles embodying a patent-pending invention, even if no patent ultimately issues. Implicit in that holding is that contract liability for royalties may continue even after an unpatented invention is publicly disclosed. Without a contractual obligation to pay royalties, however, monetary liability arguably should be limited to the plaintiff's losses or the defendant's profits during the period of wrongful use. This rule excludes damages for innocent use or use after the secret becomes public.

In *DVD Copy Control Assoc. v. Bunner,* 75 P. 3d 1 (Cal. 2005), the court found no unconstitutional prior restraint violating the First Amendment where a preliminary injunction prohibited a web site operator from disclosing computer code known to have been acquired by others through improper means (i.e., in violation of a license prohibiting reverse engineering of an encryption system for protecting copyrighted digital content). Although the court concluded that such an injunction is subject to First Amendment scrutiny, the injunction did not involve government censorship or unconstitutionally restrict computer code dissemination based on its expressive content. Significant government interests were therefore served by prohibiting trade secret disclosure acquired by improper means, encouraging invention, and upholding commercial ethics standards maintained by trade secret law. The concurrence argued the encryption system was not demonstrably secret when the defendant published it, as it was available on many websites and the defendant was neither the original misappropriator nor in privity with them.

In addition to the foregoing private judicial remedies, trade secret holders may petition the International Trade Commission to prevent importation of goods that misappropriate a trade secret. The ITC has authority, subject to review by the President, to issue cease and desist or exclusion orders barring unfair competition methods through imports. The Omnibus Trade and Competitiveness Act of 1988 declared one primary objective of U.S. international trade law and policy to be ensuring adequate trade secrets protection in foreign countries.

While still minimal compared to intellectual property cases, trade secret misappropriation claims before the ITC have increased since *TianRui Group Co. v. ITC,* 661 F.3d 1322 (Fed. Cir. 2011). In *TianRui Group,* the Federal Circuit affirmed the ITC could consider extraterritorial conduct to protect a domestic industry since § 337 restricts unfair acts and competition methods in the importation of goods. *See also Certain Carbon and Alloy Steel Prods.* (Inv. No. 337–TA–1002) (trade secret theft claim based on computer hacking survived early challenges prior to withdrawal).

There are few other venues available in the U.S. to challenge foreign misconduct other than the ITC. However, a growing number of courts construe the Defend Trade Secrets Act as reaching foreign conduct. *See Motorola Solutions, Inc. v. Hytera Commc'ns Corp. Ltd.*, 436 F.Supp.3d 1150 (N.D. Ill. 2020) (the DTSA allows recovery of damages incurred from foreign misappropriation acts outside the U.S. so long as "an act in furtherance" of the misappropriation occurred in the United States); *vPersonalize Inc. v. Magnetize Consultants Ltd.*, 437

F.Supp. 3d 860, 878 (W.D. Wash. 2020) ("18 U.S.C. § 1837 authorizes civil enforcement actions against foreign entities to the same extent as criminal actions").

As an extraordinary remedy under the DTSA, a court may order infringing goods seized without prior notice to the defendant to prevent further misappropriation. Case law continues to develop this extraordinary remedy. *Compare, Mission Capital Advisors LLC v. Romaka,* No. 16–cv–5878 (S.D.N.Y. July 29, 2016) (DTSA seizure authorized as a Fed. R. Civ. P. 65 order was insufficient when a former employee did not acknowledge receipt of court orders and evaded personal service), *with, OOO Brunswick Rail Mgt. v. Sultanov,* No. 5:17–cv–00017 (N.D. Cal. Jan. 6, 2017) (DTSA seizure unnecessary as Fed. R. Civ. P. 65 order sufficient). *See also Amimon, Inc. v. Shenzhen Hollyland Tech Co. Ltd.,* No. 20–cv–9170 (S.D.N.Y Mar. 13, 2023) (no irreparable harm presumption, injunctive relief is not appropriate without evidence the accused is disseminating trade secrets to a wider audience, irreparably damaging the trade secrets, or is damaging the trade secret owner's reputation).

Congress enacted the Economic Espionage Act of 1996 (EEA), 18 U.S.C. §§ 1831 *et seq.* to make trade secret theft a federal crime under certain circumstances. These circumstances include domestic misappropriations and appropriation for a foreign government, instrumentality, or agent. *See, e.g., United States v. Martin,* 228 F.3d 1 (1st Cir. 2000) (evidence arising out of an e-mail relationship between a dissatisfied employee and a competing company's executive was sufficient to sustain conviction of conspiracy to steal trade secrets in violation of the EEA, as well as interstate transport of stolen property, wire fraud, and mail fraud). Penalties are capped at the greater of $5,000,000 or three times the stolen secret's value. 18 U.S.C. § 1832(b).

Other federal crimes may include the Racketeer Influenced and Corrupt Organizations Act (18 U.S.C. §§ 1961–68), mail and wire fraud (18 U.S.C. §§ 1341, 1343), and various statutes involving unauthorized computer access or use. The wire fraud statute only protects individual property rights. *McNally v. United States,* 483 U.S. 350 (1987). *See also, Ciminelli v. United States,* 598 U.S. ___, (2023) (the wire fraud statute only reaches traditional property interests, not intangible interests unconnected to property).

Various state criminal statutes apply to trade secret misappropriation as well. In addition to direct misappropriation, criminal penalties may apply to unauthorized access of computer information or software, general computer crimes, and receiving stolen property in general.

PART 4

INJURIOUS PROMOTIONAL PRACTICES

CHAPTER 8

INJURIOUS PROMOTIONAL PRACTICES

Marketing campaigns can be severely hampered when other businesses engage in false or deceptive advertising, or other forms of unfair product or service promotion. Obtaining legal redress for such practices remains a challenge. At common law, a business attempting to stop another's deceptive or unfair promotional practices must establish it has or is likely to suffer a specific injury, even if the challenged practice undermines the bargaining or competitive processes as a whole. Due to this hurdle, state and federal statutes provide the principal legal redress for many deceptive or unfair promotional practices. These statutes either relax the common-law requirements for obtaining private relief or provide for public regulation of injurious promotional practices.

Pricing practices are also subject to state and federal legislation. While pricing can promote a product or service, some pricing practices are unfair because they seek an illicit objective. Injurious pricing practices are considered separately in Chapter 9. This chapter focuses on business practices promoting a product or service that are deemed deceptive or otherwise unfair.

A substantial body of law governing deceptive promotional practices—namely trademarks, trade names, and laws governing product substitution and alteration—was already introduced in Part II. Those laws provide private remedies to protect existing business goodwill against deceptive diversion or reputational injury. This chapter reviews laws protecting prospective and existing trade relations from unfair or deceptive promotional practices and the accompanying remedies.

A. TRADE RELATIONS PROTECTED

This chapter mainly considers laws protecting a company's prospective or existing trade relations. These trade relations include a company's relationships with its employees, commercial customers, general consumers, and others. Common law defamation and trade disparagement, for example, protect businesses against injurious falsehood regardless of whether the falsehood interferes with an existing or purely prospective relationship. Likewise, a large statutory body of law prohibits other deceptive or unfair advertising and promotional practices to protect existing or prospective relationships.

Federal and state laws protect trade relations. State statutes modeled on the Uniform Deceptive Trade Practices Act and the Unfair Trade Practices and Consumer Protection Law codify common law prohibitions against trademark and trade name infringement, palming off, and trade disparagement. They also prohibit other types of false advertising practices not regulated by common law. Similarly, § 43(a) of the Lanham Act (15 U.S.C. § 1125) provides a private remedy for any person likely to be damaged by another using false designations of origin or factually false or misleading descriptions or representations for any goods or services put into commerce. The Supreme Court confirmed competitors may bring a Lanham Act claim challenging deceptive or misleading food or beverage labels regulated by the Food, Drug, and Cosmetic Act ("FDCA"). *POM Wonderful LLC v. Coca-Cola Co.*, 573 U.S. 102 (2014) (the Lanham Act protects commercial interests against unfair competition, while the FDCA protects public health and safety).

As discussed in Chapter 4, *supra*, §§ 43(c) and (d) of the Lanham Act respectively provide relief against non-deceptive trademark "dilution" and "cybersquatting" (using another's trademark as a domain name). The Federal Trade Commission Act and other state and federal statutes provide public remedies for virtually all forms of false or misleading advertising and product labeling.

Federal and state laws also provide various public and private remedies for unfair consumer relations practices such as bribing a competitor's employee, unsolicited automated communications, or using lotteries or certain games, contests, giveaways, or premiums.

B. ACTIONABLE AND PRIVILEGED PROMOTIONAL PRACTICES

A promotional practice causing only private economic injury is only actionable if it undermines bargaining or competition on the merits. Actionable promotional practices may be divided into those based on deception and those deemed unfair for undermining bargaining or competitive processes.

Before evaluating the different harms that come from tortious content, the acceptable parameters of commercial speech bear consideration. Purely commercial advertising was originally considered outside First Amendment protections. Judicial unwillingness to enjoin libel took constitutional significance in *Near v. Minnesota*, 283 U.S. 697 (1931), where the Supreme Court struck down as unconstitutional a statute authorizing injunctions against defamatory publications. *Near* established that the Constitution protects free dissemination of ideas and forbids prior restraints on speech as a broad First Amendment principle.

The Supreme Court held the First Amendment protects truthful commercial speech in *Virginia State Bd. of Pharmacy v. Virginia Citizens Consumer Council, Inc.*, 425 U.S. 748 (1976). A footnote in the opinion and subsequent cases clarified that this protection is limited. For example, *U.S. Healthcare, Inc. v. Blue Cross of Greater Philadelphia*, 898 F.2d 914 (3d Cir. 1990) held comparative advertising raising community health issues of public concern was still commercial speech which did not require the *New York Times* "actual malice" protections standard because it was less likely to be chilled by legal liability threats than other forms of speech. The court went on to hold that, notwithstanding *Gertz*, companies engaged in advertising were not public figures and that the *Gertz* test is simply "not helpful in the context of a comparative advertising war."

Rather, the First Amendment requires no higher liability standard for comparative advertising than what substantive defamation, commercial disparagement, or unfair competition laws mandate.

The *Virginia State Bd. of Pharmacy* prohibition against prior restraints on speech, which forbids certain types of expression or subject matters, was held inapplicable to commercial speech. Ultimately, the Court foresaw no obstacle to a state dealing effectively with deceptive or misleading commercial speech. *See, e.g., Proctor & Gamble Co. v. Haugen*, 222 F.3d 1262 (10th Cir. 2000) (commercial advertising and promotions alleging a competitor supported the Church of Satan was sufficiently related to plaintiff's "commercial activities" to be actionable under Lanham Act § 43(a)(1)(B)). The *Virginia State Bd.* Court held only that a state may not forbid *truthful* price information. Corporations later received full free speech rights in *Citizens United v. FEC*, 558 U.S. 310 (2010) which reversed established campaign finance restrictions by prohibiting government restriction of independent political campaign expenditures for corporations and other associations.

Commercial speech requires some protection, although less than other forms of speech. *Central Hudson Gas & Elec. v. Public Serv. Comm'n*, 447 U.S. 557 (1980). *Central Hudson Gas* created a four-part test for constitutional government regulation of commercial speech: (1) whether the commercial speech concerns lawful activity without being misleading; (2) whether there is a substantial government interest in regulating the speech; (3) whether the regulation directly advances the asserted government interest; and (4) whether the regulation is more extensive than necessary to serve the government interest. This rubric lets states regulate commercial speech. *See, e.g., Zauderer v. Office of Disciplinary Counsel*, 471 U.S. 626 (1985) (state may require advertisers to disclose certain information based on the state's interest in preventing consumer deception); *but see Expressions Hair Design v. Schneiderman,* 581 U.S. 37 (2017) (state law regulating pricing by prohibiting credit card surcharges implicates the First Amendment by regulating price communication).

While the *Central Hudson* test imposed an intermediate scrutiny standard for commercial speech, subsequent judicial decisions shifted this standard to strict scrutiny with ideological variance. In *Reed v. Town of Gilbert,* 576 U.S. 155 (2015), the Court held any content-based signage restrictions violate First Amendment strict scrutiny requirements by targeting specific subjects, regardless of viewpoint neutrality. *See also, City of Austin, Texas v. Reagan Nat'l Advertising of Texas Inc.,* 596 U.S. ___, 142 S. Ct. 1464 (2022) (city may prohibit digitizing signs for goods or services sold off-premises while allowing digitized on-premises signs as the restriction is content neutral and survives strict scrutiny under the First Amendment).

Mandatory health and safety disclosures are particularly contentious subject matter. *See, e.g., Sorrell v. IMS Health Inc.,* 564 U.S. 552 (2011) (statute preventing prescription history sale or marketing use without the doctor's consent rejected for content and speaker restrictions on speech); *National Inst. of Family & Life Advocates v. Becerra*, 585 U.S. ___, 138 S. Ct. 2361 (2018) (states cannot require a clinic to state if it is licensed or provide information about available state services since the strict scrutiny exemption to content-based speech laws are limited to factual, non-controversial information in commercial speech and professional conduct that only incidentally involves speech).

Since commercial speech receives constitutional protections, the law tolerates some derogatory statements about another's trade or business so long as they are not defamatory or disparaging. For example, general statements unfavorably comparing products or services or which "puff" or exaggerate the quality of one's own products or services are not ordinarily actionable. Such statements are treated as mere expressions of opinion, the truth or falsity of which cannot be ascertained.

1. DECEPTIVE PROMOTIONAL PRACTICES

Deceptive promotional practices threaten harm to deceived businesses or consumers as well as businesses where the deception unfairly denies an opportunity to bargain or compete. Even so, private legal redress for such competitive harms is limited. For example, the common law provides remedies for commercial victims of consumer-aimed false advertising (such as palming off, defamation, or trade disparagement) only where the commercial victim is specifically identified. Other types of false advertising are only actionable at common law in unusual cases where a business can show its customers were or will be diverted by another company's false claims about its own product, service, or business.

State and federal statutes broadened the private relief available for this kind of deceptive advertising or promotional activity, as public regulation is often the most effective remedy. This is not to diminish the Better Business Bureau's National Advertising Division, an independent industry self-regulatory system that reviews truth-in-advertising disputes between businesses. However, participation in this dispute resolution process is voluntary and companies that refuse to participate in the process or to follow Division recommendations are merely referred to the appropriate government regulatory agency. Given the government's role in establishing guidelines and available relief, it is helpful to review the established privately or publicly actionable deceptive promotional practices (outside trademark infringement and palming off).

a. Privately Actionable Deceptive Practices

(1) Defamation

Defamation is communication of an untrue statement, as fact, to a third party, that harms the statement's subject and is not otherwise privileged. Reputational injury may lower the victim's community reputation or deter third parties from associating or dealing with the victim. The generic term "defamation" references the common law torts of libel and slander. Slander is an ephemeral (usually oral) defamation, while libel is written or otherwise tangibly transcribed.

Libels were presumed to have a greater capacity to do harm than slanders, or at least *per se* libels whose defamatory meanings are apparent on the face of the statement. As such, libels were traditionally actionable even without proof of special (i.e., actual pecuniary) damages. Slander actions, on the other hand, generally required proof of special damages. Derogatory oral statements about another's trade or business were an exception to the special damages requirement. When such slanders were defamatory on their face, the slanders were presumed to cause harm like libels. *But cf., Proctor & Gamble Co. v. Haugen,* 222 F.3d 1262 (10th Cir. 2000) (representation that plaintiff financially supported the Church of Satan and placed the Devil's mark on its product held a disparagement of a general character rather than slander *per se* since it did not pertain to a quality that was peculiarly valuable in plaintiff's business).

Not every derogatory statement is defamatory. Truth is a complete defense to all defamation claims. There may also be an absolute or qualified privilege to make defamatory statements. Absolute privilege has a common law basis and protects political speech, advertisements, statements and reports made by lawmakers during deliberation, witness statements made at trial, and communications between spouses.

See also, Houston Cmty. Coll. Sys. v. Wilson, 595 U.S. ___, 142 S. Ct. 1253 (2022) (elected body's purely verbal censure of a member was not a materially adverse action and did not give rise to a First Amendment claim). Qualified privilege protects a speaker from lawsuits in situations where the speaker can show a good faith belief the statement was true when made and an absence of malice. Examples include news reports on public controversies, regulatory agency proceedings, and warnings of danger. Opinion statements are not factual statements and so are rarely defamatory. Courts do consider a statement's context and whether a reasonable person would understand the statement as asserting a fact or opinion.

A statement disparaging a product or service's quality does not necessarily defame its producer. *See National Refining Co. v. Benzo Gas Motor Fuel Co.*, 20 F.2d 763 (8th Cir. 1927) (claim that gasoline mixture would corrode engines was not libelous as it did not assert the producer knowingly manufactured an unfit product). Defamation requires the statement impute fraud, deceit, dishonesty, or morally reprehensible conduct to the product or service's producer by fair construction of the statement and without extrinsic evidence. Trade disparagement, discussed *infra*, addresses derogatory statements made about a product or service. State laws may find statements defamatory that others would not. *See, e.g., Texas Beef Group v. Winfrey,* 201 F. 3d 680 (5th Cir. 2000) (television broadcast taped in Illinois not liable for business disparagement under Texas False Disparagement of Perishable Food Products Act).

Before 1964, the First Amendment did not limit defamation laws, so state law was the only source for protecting such speech. This changed when the U.S. Supreme Court effectively rewrote common law defamation for public figures in *New York Times v. Sullivan*, 376 U.S. 254 (1964), and *Gertz v. Robert Welch, Inc.*, 418 U.S. 323 (1974). In *New York Times v. Sullivan,* the Court held the First Amendment prohibits recovering damages for a defamatory statement relating to a public official's conduct without proof of "actual malice"—which the Court defined as knowledge or reckless disregard of the statement's falsity. *See also Curtis Publ'g Co. v. Butts,* 388 U.S. 130 (1967) (expanding protection to criticism of public figures); *Philadelphia Newspapers, Inc. v. Hepps,* 475 U.S. 767 (1986) (overturning common law falsity presumption for defamatory speech by media defendant about a matter of public concern); *Hustler Magazine, Inc. v. Falwell,* 485 U.S. 46 (1988). Constitutional "actual malice" is thus a narrower standard than that of common law. The *New York Times* Court expressly held its rule applied to defamation actions brought against non-media as well as media defendants. Later cases held the *New York Times* rule applied to lawsuits brought by public figures as well as public officials. Intervening cases indicated anyone who found themselves involved in a matter of public interest was a public figure.

In *Gertz v. Welch,* the Court confirmed the *New York Times* standard applied to actions "public figures" brought but limited the "public figures" definition to those who thrust themselves to the forefront of particular public controversies to influence the issue. In *Gertz,* a lawyer was not considered a public figure merely for representing a client involved in a matter of public interest. The policy behind this distinction is that public individuals who deliberately seek attention must accept the accompanying risks, and that these public figures likely have greater media access to address defamatory statements than others might.

The *Gertz* Court held that states could define their own appropriate liability standards for defamation actions brought by persons who were not public figures, either by statute or judicial decision. The *Gertz* Court did place limits on state discretion, however. Under *Gertz,* states (1) could not impose liability without fault, which required at least a showing of negligence by the defendant, and (2) must limit damages to the actual injury sustained in any case establishing liability on a standard less exacting than the *New York Times v. Sullivan* "actual malice" standard.

Unlike the *New York Times* decision, *Gertz* did not indicate whether these limits on defamation actions brought by private individuals applied only to media industry defendants or to all defamation cases. Later cases held the *Gertz* restrictions do not apply to defamation cases brought by private individuals against non-media defendants, at least where the defamation did not involve a matter of public concern. *See Dun & Bradstreet, Inc. v. Greenmoss Builders, Inc.,* 472 U.S. 749 (1985) (recovering presumed and punitive damages does not violate the First Amendment when a company's defamation claim against a credit reporting agency's false report of a bankruptcy filing was a purely private matter rather than one of public concern); *TransUnion LLC v. Ramirez*, 594 U.S. ___, 141 S. Ct. 2190 (2021) (credit reporting agency's failure to follow reasonable procedures to ensure information accuracy created concrete reputational harm to only those class members whose misleading credit reports were provided to third-party businesses rather than to all affected class members).

At least one state supreme court (believing *Gertz* required the first part of its decision) abolished the common-law rule allowing defamation liability without regard to fault or injury. Instead, this court required both a negligence showing and, where the speaker enjoyed a conditional privilege as the defamed person's former employer, a reckless disregard of the truth. *Compare Jacron Sales Co., Inc. v. Sindorf*, 350 A.2d 688 (Md. 1976), *with Dairy Stores, Inc. v. Sentinel Pub. Co.*, 516 A.2d 220 (N.J. 1986) (actual malice standard should apply to both media and non-media defendants). *But see Turf Lawnmower Repair, Inc. v. Bergen Record Corp.*, 655 A.2d 417 (N.J. 1995) (same court as *Dairy Stores* held that while negligence is the appropriate standard in defamation actions involving businesses whose activities do not concern public health or safety, do not constitute consumer fraud, and are not subject to substantial government regulations, a news article raised sufficient evidence of consumer fraud to require plaintiff to prove actual malice). Ultimately, defamation liability for private non-media industry remarks about another's trade or business varies by state and could require showing the defendant's fault or the plaintiff's actual damage.

Defamation laws built a "fair comment" affirmative defense into the common law to avoid stifling public debate. This principle grants legal immunity for honest expression of opinion on matters of legitimate public interest when based upon a true or privileged factual statement. *See Milkovich v. Lorain Journal Co.,* 497 U.S. 1 (1990).

A defamatory statement must refer to a particular plaintiff to be actionable. For example, an article disparaging local cab drivers' honesty and including a picture of one of plaintiff's taxis did not defame taxi cab company owners (since it did not imply they were dishonest) nor any particular taxi cab driver (since it referred to them as a group). *Fowler v. Curtis Publ'g Co.*, 182 F.2d 377 (D.C. Cir. 1950).

Repeating or republishing defamatory matter subjects the publisher to defamation liability if they knew or had reason to know of the defamation. Some states grant additional protection to publishers who later retract the allegedly defamatory statement. Conversely, fair and accurate reliance on a public document or statement by a public official providing incorrect information, properly attributed to the source, gives rise to a fair report privilege. *But see, e.g., Burke v. Sparta Newspapers, Inc.,* 592 S.W.3d 116, 124 (Tenn. 2019) (fair report privilege does not apply to phone conversation with a police officer). Similarly, republishing an unaltered news item from a reputable news agency, not knowing or having reason to know the information was false, grants a wire service defense in some states. Some states also offer a neutral reporting privilege allowing the press to report accusation made by one public figure against another. *See, e.g., Edwards v. National Audubon Soc.*, 556 F.2d 113 (2d Cir. 1977); *McCracken v. Gainesville Tribune, Inc.*, 146 Ga. App. 274 (1978).

A speaker's defamation liability does not always apply to the entity publishing the defamatory statement. In *Smith v. California*, 361 U.S. 147 (1959), the Court limited print material distributors' liability as the distributors were not able to read everything they printed. As "republishers" or "disseminators", those distributing a defamatory statement without knowledge or reason to know the material's defamatory nature are free from defamation liability. The emphasis is on whether the entity takes a passive role in publishing a defamatory statement rather than an active speaking or editing role.

A 1996 amendment to the (largely unconstitutional) Communications Decency Act provides a safe harbor for certain communications services providers, both on and off the Internet. *See* 47 U.S.C. § 230. Section 230(c)(1) holds "[n]o provider or user of an interactive computer service shall be treated as the publisher or speaker of any information provided by another information content provider." This provision may be considered a pillar of Internet communications as it shields all intermediary service providers from liability for the individual comments and discussions of its users.

Section 230 codified this limited defamation immunity granted to certain communications services providers posting content from others, so long as they comply with the Act and do not act as a "publisher" or "speaker". *See* Ch. 6.2.b, *supra; Cubby, Inc. vs. CompuServe Inc.,* 776 F.Supp. 135 (S.D.N.Y. 1991); *Dyroff v. Ultimate Software Grp., Inc.*, 934 F.3d 1093 (9th Cir. 2019)(testing whether the accused is an interactive computer service provider or user, being treated as a publisher or speaker of information from another information content provider). However, this immunity does not apply if an online service directly involves itself in creating content that violates civil law. For example, a website requiring user profile information on gender and race for housing matches violated the Fair Housing Act as a content provider. *Fair Hous. Council of San Fernando Valley v. Roommates.com, LLC,* 521 F.3d 1157 (9th Cir. 2008).

Section 230(c)(2) protects these communications service providers for good faith removal of third-party material they deem obscene or offensive, although the "good faith" term is frequently disputed. Third-party content protections cannot be eliminated even if the provider makes editing or publishing decisions (including removal), or through notice by demand letters. *Zeran v. America Online, Inc.*, 129 F.3d 327 (4th Cir. 1997). The protection applies to contractors and commissioned content, not just users, and permits significant editorial privileges. *Blumenthal v. Drudge*, 992 F.Supp. 44 (D.D.C. 1998) (protection for writer paid for use of their statement). Section 230 also provides limited protection for certain editorial activities to encourage removal of unfavorable material. *See, e.g.*, *Batzel v. Smith*, 333 F.3d 1018 (9th Cir. 2003) (immunity for selection, editing, and publishing emails to museum website).

The broad scope of § 230 immunity does have limitations, the list of which continues to expand. Content violating other laws must still be removed. Exceptions to § 230 include materials that violate criminal laws, intellectual property laws, certain other state laws, and privacy laws. *See* 47 U.S.C. § 230(e). *See also Perfect 10 v. ccBill,* 488 F.3d 1102 (9th Cir. 2007); *FTC v. Accusearch,* 570 F.3d 1187 (10th Cir. 2009) (service provider specifically encouraging illegal content is responsible for it); *Lemmon v. Snap, Inc.*, 995 F.3d 1085 (9th Cir. 2021) (negligent software design encouraging dangerous behavior); *Doe v. Internet Brands, Inc.,* 824 F.3d 846 (9th Cir. 2016) (permitting tortious duty to warn claim); *Barnes v. Yahoo!, Inc.,* 570 F.3d 1096 (9th Cir. 2009) (promissory estoppel made provider a party to a contract rather than a publisher); *Malwarebytes Inc. v. Enigma Software Group USA, LLC,* 946 F.3d 1040 (2019) (while the intellectual property exclusion does not apply to false advertising claims, there is no CDA immunity for blocking content for anticompetitive reasons). *But see, Twitter, Inc. v. Taamneh,* 598 U.S. ____, (2023) (social media platforms did not "aid and abet" an international terrorist organization's attack pursuant to 18 U.S.C. § 2333 merely by creating their platforms or having algorithms suggest content to users. In 2018, Congress amended § 230 to exclude immunity for materials that either knowingly or recklessly violate federal and state sex trafficking laws. 47 U.S.C. § 230(e)(5).

The Internet's elimination of geographic communications limitations can complicate matters. State online speech limitations may unconstitutionally restrict interstate commerce. *See, e.g., American Library Ass'n v. Pataki*, 969 F.Supp. 160 (S.D.N.Y. 1997). Merely maintaining a website or posting Internet content alone should not be sufficient to establish general or specific jurisdiction over a defendant. *uBID, Inc. v. GoDaddy Grp. Inc.*, 623 F.3d 421, 425–26 (7th Cir. 2010); *but see Lang Van, Inc. v. VNG Corp.*, No.19–56452 (9th Cir. 2022). The situs of the plaintiff's injury is relevant, but not sufficient to establish this minimum contact. *Walden v. Fiore*, 571 U.S. 277 (2014) (defendant must create the contacts with the forum state itself, not the state's residents).

Foreign nations apply their own defamation standards to Internet communications outside their borders as well. For example, the High Court of Australia allowed an Australian citizen to sue and recover damages from an author posting an article on a New Jersey (USA) magazine's website that questioned the Australian's business dealings with religious charities. *Dow Jones and Co. Inc. v. Gutnick* (2002) 210 CLR 575. The High Court determined the defamation cause of action arose in Australia where the article was downloaded and where the reputational damage occurred. The High Court also held defamation of an identifiable individual puts a publisher on notice of which nation's defamation laws apply. Article 17 of the United Nations' International Covenant on Civil and Political Rights also supports a general right to freedom from unlawful attacks on a person's honor or reputation. GA res. 2200A (XXI), 21 UN GAOR Supp. (No. 16) at 52, UN Doc. A/6316 (1966).

The common law did not significantly burden victims of any facially defamatory oral or written derogatory statements about their trade or business. Rather, the speaker had to prove either that the defamatory statement was true or that the speaker had a good faith belief in the statement's truth plus some justification for making the statement. Justifications included self-defense, defense of another, or defense of the public interest.

These rules practically held speakers liable for facially defamatory statements about another's person or business without justification, regardless of the speaker's actual fault or the victim's actual injury. Even where a statement could be shown to defend some legitimate private or public interest, defamation victims could still recover damages where the defendant published the statement more widely than was necessary or acted out of "actual malice." At common law, "actual malice" was defined as either desire to cause injury or a knowing or reckless disregard of the statement's truth or falsity. Proof of actual malice defeated defamatory statement justifications and made punitive damages available to plaintiffs.

Common law privilege rules may protect what would otherwise be actionable defamatory statements. For example, a patent holder is privileged to publish its reasonable belief that another has infringed its patent so long as the patent holder acted without actual malice, even if no infringement is ultimately found. *Kemart Corp. v. Printing Arts Research Labs. Inc.*, 269 F.2d 375 (9th Cir. 1959).

(2) Trade Disparagement

Trade disparagement, or trade libel, is communication of a false, negative, malicious statement to a third party about a company to discourage business dealings with that company and causes the company financial harm. Unlike defamation which attacks a person's reputation, trade disparagement attacks a company's financial reputation.

Trade disparagement claims require proof of (1) the disparaging statement's falsity, (2) common-law "actual malice" by the defendant (i.e., desire to cause injury or knowing or reckless disregard of falsity of a statement), and (3) special damages resulting from the disparagement. *See e.g. Hurlbut v. Gulf Atl. Life Ins. Co.*, 749 S.W.2d 762 (Tex. 1987); Restatement, Second, of Torts, § 623A, comment g (1977). To prevail, the statement must be shown to be untrue; communicated to someone other than the victim; clearly disparage the product, service, or business; be made with malice; and result in actual harm to the victim. Burdensome pleading and proof requirements severely limit trade disparagement actions. Instead, companies try to characterize disparaging statements as defamatory or to invoke another recovery theory such as prima facie tort. (*See* Ch. 1, *supra*.)

It is not always easy to distinguish statements that impute fraud, deceit, dishonesty, or morally reprehensible conduct from those merely disparaging a product or service's quality. In the early English case of *Dickes v. Fenne*, 82 Eng.Rep. 411 (1639), proof of special damage would be required for the following statement by one brewer of another's product to be actionable: "he would give a peck of malt to his mare, and she should pisse as good beare as Dickes doth Brew." *See also National Refining Co. v. Benzo Motor Fuel Co., supra* (statement that gasoline mixture would corrode automobile engines not libelous); *Hurlbut v. Gulf Atl. Life Ins. Co., supra* (false and malicious denial that former employees were authorized to sell group insurance for defendant treated as a slander claim, barred by the statute of limitations; an alternate trade disparagement claim failed without proof of special injury through specific lost sales). *But see Meyerson v. Hurlbut*, 98 F.2d 232 (D.C. Cir. 1938) (oral statement that plaintiff was cutting prices and selling below cost slanderous *per se* because it implied the plaintiff violated statutes prohibiting such conduct and engaged in conduct the industry widely disapproved); *Harwood Pharmacal Co. v. National Broad. Co.*, 214 N.Y.S.2d 725, 174 N.E.2d 602 (N.Y. 1961).

Some disparaging statements are clearly not defamatory. For example, it is disparaging but not defamatory *per se* to falsely state a person has gone out of business or to falsely imply that a music publisher's songs are not hits. *Cf. Advance Music Corp. v. Am. Tobacco Co.* in Ch. 1, *supra*. For these types of statements, there can be no monetary recovery without proof of "special" damages.

While some courts require a plaintiff show loss of particular customers by name, others allow evidence of a general diminution in business and extrinsic facts showing the business losses resulted from the false statement. *See, e.g., Porous Media Corp. v. Pall Corp.*, 110 F.3d 1329 (8th Cir. 1997). Where there are multiple explanations for a diminution in business, a plaintiff must prove what injuries the disparagement specifically caused. *See, e.g., Houston Chronicle Publ'g Co. v. Martin*, 64 S.W.2d 816 (Tex. Civ. App. 1933).

Time and money spent counteracting disparagement and mitigating losses are not recoverable without evidence that sales were in fact lost or threatened. *See Advanced Training Sys. v. Caswell Equip. Co.*, 352 N.W.2d 1 (Minn. 1984) ("Plaintiff cannot create a cause of action in disparagement through his own conduct where defendant has otherwise failed to provide him with one.")

As previously mentioned, the *Gertz v. Welch* decision narrowed the "public figure" definition to those who put themselves at the forefront of a public controversy. Ordinary businesses are therefore less likely to need to prove a media defendant's disparaging statement was made knowingly or with reckless disregard of the truth. *But see U.S.*

Dominion, Inc. v. Fox News Network LLC, C.A. N21C–03–257 EMD (Del. Super. Ct. Jan. 27, 2023) (voting machine manufacturer alleging defamation considered a limited purpose public figure). *Gertz* also prohibits imposing liability without fault and limits damages to the actual injuries sustained in cases where liability is based on a standard less exacting than that of *New York Times*. These restrictions apparently apply to disparagement as well as defamation actions, at least where the claim is brought against a media defendant. The common law limits disparagement actions even further, requiring proof of both common-law actual malice and actual pecuniary injury.

Where a disparaged business does come within the *Gertz* definition of a public figure, the business must prove by clear and convincing evidence that the disparager acted with a knowing or reckless disregard of the disparaging statement's falsity. *See Bose Corp. v. Consumers Union of the U.S., Inc.*, 466 U.S. 485 (1984) (where a challenged statement borders fact and opinion, review of a trial court's actual malice determination is not limited to the clearly erroneous standard of Federal Rule of Civil Procedure 52(a); de novo review is the appropriate standard, independently examining the record to ensure the lower court properly applied the governing constitutional law and that the plaintiff satisfied its burden of proof through clear and convincing evidence). *But see Suzuki Motor Corp. v. Consumers Union of the U.S., Inc.*, 330 F.3d 1110 (9th Cir. 2003), holding (albeit against vigorous dissent) the evidence raised a genuine issue of material fact as to the defendant's high degree of awareness of the probable falsity of its statements. *See also U.S. Healthcare, Inc. v. Blue Cross of Greater Philadelphia*, 898 F.2d 914 (3d Cir. 1990) (the *Gertz* public figure test does not apply to comparative advertising disputes as they do not need a higher liability standard than defamation, disparagement, or unfair competition).

While plaintiffs seeking damages for derogatory statements about their products, services, or business prefer defamation claims, disparagement claims are better for seeking injunctive relief. Equity courts have historically been extremely reluctant to enjoin libels. Refusals to grant injunctive relief are based on equitable maxims such as equity's refusal to protect purely personal rights or to grant equitable relief where legal remedies (i.e., damages) are adequate.

For a time, equity courts declined to enjoin commercial disparagement. *See, e.g., Kidd v. Horry*, 28 F. 773 (C.C.E.D. Pa. 1886); *Marlin Firearms Co. v. Shields*, 64 N.E. 163 (N.Y. 1902). Some courts granted injunctive relief where disparagement was part of a broader course of tortious misconduct. *See, e.g., Emack v. Kane*, 34 F. 46 (C.C.N.D. Ill. 1888) (injunction against campaign to intimidate rival's customers with patent infringement threats).

Some courts eventually determined injunctive relief should protect product, service, or business goodwill in disparagement cases just like trademark infringement. *See, e.g., Black & Yates v. Mahogany Ass'n*, 129 F.2d 227 (3d Cir. 1941) (property disparagement is not a mere branch or special variety of personal reputation defamation or deceit). *See also Perma-Maid v. FTC*, 121 F.2d 282 (6th Cir. 1941) (upholding FTC order forbidding steel cooking utensils distributor from disparaging aluminum ones). *But see Scientific Mfg. Co. v. FTC*, 124 F.2d 640 (3d Cir. 1941) (FTC Act does not enable the FTC to prohibit a business unconnected to cooking utensil manufacture or distribution from publishing or distributing pamphlets disparaging aluminum cooking utensils); *Organization for a Better Austin v. Keefe*, 402 U.S. 415 (1971) (invalidating as a prior restraint an injunction prohibiting a racially integrated community organization from distributing leaflets accusing a real estate broker of "panic peddling" and "blockbusting.").

To be actionable, disparagement requires the unfavorable comparison assert specific facts. *See, e.g., Testing Sys., Inc. v. Magnaflux Corp.*, 251 F.Supp. 286 (E.D. Pa. 1966) (statement that a product "is no good" and that "the government is throwing them out" was actionable). Moreover, one may be privileged, purely as a matter of common law, to make what would otherwise be disparaging statements. *Cf., Kemart Corp. v. Printing Arts Research Lab., Inc.*, 269 F.2d 375 (9th Cir. 1959) (patent holder charged with "trade libel" was privileged to publish its reasonable belief that another infringed their patent, even if no infringement is ultimately found, so long as the patent holder acted without common-law actual malice); *Flotech, Inc. v. E. I. Du Pont de Nemours & Co.*, 814 F.2d 775 (1st Cir. 1987) (company's good faith statement that it views its own product as ineffective for a particular purpose held privileged, even though it could be understood to comment on the effectiveness of a third party's product).

Courts tend to be solicitous of opinions expressed by consumer testing and rating organizations. Courts often will not enjoin unfavorable rating publications. Further, courts even grant rating organizations injunctive relief to prevent businesses from publishing misleading or exaggerated reports of favorable ratings. *See, e.g., Consumers Union of the U.S., Inc. v. Theodore Hamm Brewing Co.*, 314 F.Supp. 697 (D. Conn. 1970) (temporary injunction to brewer advertising it was rated "top beer in the country" by "Consumer Reports" when it only had a first class rating). Even here, some puffing of a favorable rating may be permissible in advertising. Rating organizations may still be liable for recklessly disregarding facts, no less than businesses puffing their own product. *See, e.g., Advance Music Corp. v. Am. Tobacco Co.*, Ch. 1 *supra* (upholding a complaint alleging radio program song ratings were based on "caprice.").

The Supreme Court held the First Amendment also protects anonymous and pseudonymous speech to encourage expression or discussion of unpopular or uncomfortable ideas with less fear of reprisal. *See, e.g., McIntyre v. Ohio Elections Comm'n.*, 514 U.S. 334, 342 (1995). Such protection challenges businesses disputing criticism of their products or services.

Internet "gripe sites" present an increasing challenge to companies as consumers and others (including surreptitious competitors) can criticize various aspects of a particular product, service, or business. These anonymous websites or messages may be false or highly injurious to a company's reputation. *See* Ch. 4.B.2 *supra*. However, the Supreme Court held anonymous and pseudonymous speech on the Internet receives the same First Amendment protection as it does elsewhere. *Reno v. ACLU*, 521 U.S. 844, 868 (1997). Businesses may attempt to circumvent these protections through claims such as defamation, trademark infringement and dilution, trade disparagement, or copyright infringement.

Threats of costly and time-consuming lawsuits may be used to intimidate or silence criticism by those appropriately exercising First Amendment speech rights. "Strategic Lawsuits Against Public Participation", or "SLAPP" lawsuits, create a chilling effect on news reporting or other participation in public discourse such as reporting legal violations, filing government complaints, public interest litigation, or participating in public hearings. Such lawsuits may be filed by public servants against citizens lodging complaints or criticism as well. In the commercial sector, trade organizations may secure legislation lowering defamation standards for disparaging certain industries or products and use it to attack such speech.

Some states have anti-SLAPP legislation to protect against such abuses. Anti-SLAPP laws can apply to any lawsuit filed to gain subpoena power sufficient to compel identification of an anonymous critic where the claimant has little hope to prevail on the merits of their claim. Such lawsuits are often brought against online forum operators in attempts to reveal an anonymous or pseudonymous critic's identity. Such attempts to silence criticism are contrary to the constitutionally preferred remedy for combating false or deceptive anonymous speech, as well as falsehoods and fallacies more generally, which apparently is "more speech, not enforced silence." *See Whitney v. California,* 274 U.S. 357, 377 (1927) (Brandeis, J., concurring).

Anti-SLAPP laws frequently provide for a discovery stay pending a dismissal motion and allow successful defendants recovery of attorney's fees and costs in defending a frivolous lawsuit. Other counterclaims against a SLAPP may include malicious prosecution or common law abuse of process.

Petitions to the government for a redress of grievances receive strong First Amendment protection and opposition to such cases are frequently dismissed. *See Eastern R.R. Presidents Conference v. Noerr Motor Freight, Inc.,* 365 U.S. 127 (1961) (Sherman Antitrust Act cannot be used to penalize railroad operators for a publicity campaign to influence passage or enforcement of a law). The target of an anti-SLAPP claim must prove the petition was objectively baseless and was not genuinely intended to attain a favorable government action or inaction. *United Mine Workers v.*

Pennington, 381 U.S. 657 (1965); *City of Columbia v. Omni Outdoor Advertising*, 499 U.S. 365 (1991) (limiting the "sham" exception to cases where the government process is used as a weapon rather than the outcome of the process).

(3) Other Deceptive Advertising and Promotional Practices

(a) Common Law Remedies for False Advertising

At one time, common-law courts held the absence of evidence of palming off, defamation, or disparagement meant businesses simply had no cause of action for a rival's consumer-aimed false advertising. *See, e.g., American Washboard Co. v. Saginaw Mfg. Co.*, 103 F. 281 (6th Cir. 1900) ("It is doubtlessly morally wrong and improper to impose upon the public by the sale of spurious goods, but this does not give rise to a private right of action unless the property rights of the plaintiff are involved. There are many wrongs which can only be righted through public prosecution, and for which the legislature, and not the courts, must provide a remedy."). Common-law false advertising cases are rarely successful. *But see Electronics Corp. of Am. v. Honeywell, Inc.*, 428 F.2d 191 (1st Cir. 1970).

Ely-Norris Safe Co. v. Mosler Safe Co., 7 F.2d 603 (2d Cir. 1925) created a narrow exception to the common-law rule. Here, a tradesman that falsely provided their customers a substitute good could be prosecuted when only the plaintiff could supply the original and an informed customer would have sought the original. The Supreme Court (which included all three judges deciding the conflicting *American Washboard* case) later reversed the *Ely-Norris* "single source" requirement as lacking a cause of action since other products had features similar to the patented one at issue. *Mosler Safe Co. v. Ely-Norris Safe Co.*, 273 U.S. 132 (1927).

Geographic considerations apply when a seller falsely advertises goods as coming from an origin known for superior quality. *See, e.g., Pillsbury-Washburn Flour-Mills Co. v. Eagle*, 86 F. 608 (7th Cir. 1898); *Grand Rapids Furniture Co. v. Grand Rapids Furniture Co.*, 127 F.2d 245 (7th Cir. 1942) (preliminary injunctive relief for class action). However a court refused class action certification to a trade association and numerous California apparel manufacturers against three New York apparel companies using "California" with their goods in *California Apparel Creators v. Wieder of Cal., Inc.*, 162 F.2d 893 (2d Cir. 1947). The *California Apparel* court distinguished *Grand Rapids,* noting the greater number of potential California plaintiffs and lack of any obvious connection between the products and locality, or relevant apparel quality or grading standards in California. The plaintiffs also could not show injury among many California manufacturers or a likelihood of proving specific customers were diverted from specific plaintiffs by the defendants' actions.

Article 22 of the TRIPS Agreement (*see* Ch. 1) requires WTO members to protect geographic indications identifying a good's origin in a particular territory, region, or locality against misleading suggestions of the good's origin to the public. Article 22 caused a Lanham Act amendment prohibiting registration of primarily geographically misdescriptive trademarks. *See* 15 U.S.C. § 1052(e)(3); *In re Cal. Innovations, Inc.*, 329 F.3d 1334 (Fed. Cir. 2003), discussed in Ch. 4 *supra*. TRIPS Article 23 requires additional protections for geographical wines and spirits indications, and Articles 23 and 24 go on to require WTO members enter international negotiations to facilitate and strengthen geographical indication protections. These negotiations are complicated by complaints from developing nations over the preferred position the TRIPS Agreement grants wines and spirits over other agricultural or location-specific products.

(b) State Deceptive Trade Practices Statutes

Dissatisfaction with common law false advertising remedies led to state legislation granting companies a private right of action against other businesses for consumer-aimed deceptive practices. Many states enacted a version of the Uniform Deceptive Trade Practices Act ("UDTPA"). The primarily UDTPA's protects the consuming public by granting a private cause of action against unfair or deceptive business practices. *Food Lion, Inc. v. Capital Cities/ABC, Inc.*, 194 F.3d 505, 519 (4th Cir. 1999). Any person likely to be damaged by another's deceptive trade practices may obtain relief under the Act, although not all states provide individual causes of action.

The UDTPA is comprehensive in its substantive coverage but limited in available relief. The UDTPA codifies common law prohibitions against trademark and trade name infringement, palming off, and trade disparagement. It also prohibits false or deceptive advertising and other deceptive trade practices misleading or misinforming the recipient of goods or services. These behaviors are generally not actionable at common law. The UDTPA does not require proof of monetary damage, lost profits, or intent to deceive. Federal or other state laws may preempt the UDTPA in the absence of an additional element supporting the claim. *See, e.g., Balsamo/ Olson Group, Inc. v. Bradley Place Ltd. P'ship,* 950 F.Supp. 896, 898 (C.D.Ill. 1997) (copyright infringement inherently misrepresents the author's identity, so there was no distinguishing deception element from the federal Copyright Act).

The UDTPA applies to a broad range of claims. Covered business activities may include unfair contract provisions, coercive sales practices, fictious testimonials, or advertising goods or services without intending to offer them as advertised. While a remedy in tort, the UDTPA has contract dispute applications too. *See, e.g., Makadia v. Continental Waste Mgmt., LLC,* No. 5:16–cv–00257 (E.D.N.C. Nov. 7, 2016) (lender may maintain tort action for contract breach against borrower where the property conversion was sufficiently deceptive); *Sibley v. Nat'l Union Fire Ins. Co. of Pittsburgh,* 921 F.Supp 1526 (E.D. Tex. 1996) (insurance coverage); *Faucette v. 6303 Carmel Rd., LLC,* 775 S.E.2d 316 (N.C. Ct. App. 2015) (condominium dues dispute).

Injunctive relief is the primary remedy available under the UDTPA. Courts may award the prevailing party attorney's fees if the party bringing the claim knew it was groundless, or if the accused is shown to have willfully engaged in an unfair trade practice knowing the practice was deceptive. Some states adopting the UDTPA authorize damages for violation of the Act, including statutory and punitive damages as well as damage multipliers for extreme cases.

The Unfair Trade Practices and Consumer Protection Law ("UTPCPL") provides a much broader array of public and private remedies against deceptive and other unfair practices. These remedies are available to consumers and commercial parties. Enforcement is contemplated by a state attorney general or through private action. State statutes modeled on the UTPCPL are often called "Little FTC Acts" for two reasons. First, the FTC proposed the UTPCPL for state adoption. Second, its provisions generally parallel the Federal Trade Commission Act. The provisions frequently require states to give great weight to federal court opinions and FTC unfair and deceptive acts definitions under the FTC Act. The latter provision effectively incorporates FTC law [see Part B)(1)(B), *infra*] into the substantive law of each state.

(c) Federal Statutory Remedies: § 43(a) of the Lanham Act

To recover damages and injunctive relief for deceptive practices aimed at consumers, businesses increasingly rely on the once obscure § 43(a) of the

Lanham Act, 15 U.S.C. § 1125(a). As amended by the Trademark Revision Act of 1988, § 43(a) applies to statements that are either 1) likely to cause confusion, mistake, or to deceive as to the relationship between the person making the statement and another person or their goods, services, or commercial activities; or 2) misrepresent in commercial advertising or promotion the nature, characteristics, qualities, or geographic origin of the goods, services, or commercial activities of either the person making the statement or of another person. There are four types of proscribed statements—namely 1) any word, term, name, symbol, device, or any combination thereof; 2) any false designation of origin; 3) any false or misleading description of fact; or 4) any false or misleading representation of fact.

The two misconduct types defined by the amended § 43(a) include 1) any form of product, service, or business misidentification based on trademark infringement or passing off; and 2) any other form of false or misleading advertising, whether disparaging another's products, services, or business, or falsely describing or representing one's own. These substantive prohibitions differ significantly from the original § 43(a). Understanding the 1988 amendment to § 43(a) requires review of the interpretive problems arising both before and after the amendment.

Courts originally viewed § 43(a) merely as codification of the common law rule that a commercial plaintiff complaining of false advertising must be either the 1) victim of palming off; 2) "single source" of the falsely advertised goods or services; or 3) producer of goods or services in a limited geographic area whose designation was being misused. *See, e.g., Chamberlain v. Columbia Pictures Corp.*, 186 F.2d 923 (9th Cir. 1951). The prevailing view, however, came to be that § 43(a) created a *sui generis* federal statutory tort not limited by common law. *See, e.g., L'Aiglon Apparel v. Lana Lobell, Inc.*, 214 F.2d 649 (3d Cir. 1954) ("Congress has defined a statutory civil wrong of false representation of goods in commerce and has given a broad class of suitors injured or likely to be injured by such wrong the right to relief in the federal courts").

The principal interpretive problems arising under § 43(a) have been over 1) who has standing to sue, 2) what constitutes actionable misconduct, and 3) what circumstances justify monetary or injunctive relief. The original § 43(a) protected two classes of plaintiffs against two types of misconduct. The original section prohibited (1) false designations of origin for goods or services and (2) false descriptions or representations of the same. It created a federal statutory cause of action for (1) any person doing business in the locality falsely indicated; and (2) any person who believes they have been or are likely to be damaged by any such false description or representation.

Actionable misconduct under the original § 43(a) fell into two broad groups: 1) false designations of origin and 2) false descriptions or representations. The initial interpretive question for false designations of origin was whether § 43(a) extended to all false designations of origin or merely those of *geographic* origin. Section 43(a) was held not limited to false designations of geographic origin in *Federal-Mogul-Bower Bearings, Inc. v. Azoff*, 313 F.2d 405 (6th Cir. 1963) (permitting action for deceptive imitation of product and packaging). Critics fault this case for ignoring that § 43(a) defined the class of plaintiffs who may sue for false designations of origin as those doing business in the specified region. This limiting language suggested the original § 43(a) merely codified a specific line of common law cases [namely the geographic origin cases discussed in § B(1)(a)(3)(a) *supra*] rather than engulfing the entirety of unfair competition law.

On the other hand, § 43(a) specified that false descriptions or representations included "words or other symbols tending falsely to describe or represent" goods or services. Therefore, an action for such false descriptions or representations could be maintained by any person who believes they have been or are likely to be damaged by the false description or representation. This language, together with the § 45 statement that the Lanham Act is intended to protect persons engaged in commerce against unfair competition indicated the purpose of § 43(a) was not as narrow as critics of the *Federal-Mogul-Bower Bearings* case suggested.

Following a broad circuit split in determining who as "any person" had standing to sue for false advertising under the Lanham Act, the Supreme Court developed a new standing test for false advertising cases in *Lexmark Int'l, Inc. v. Static Control Components, Inc.*, 572 U.S. 118 (2014). The

Lexmark court determined a § 43(a) cause of action extends to any plaintiff (not just a direct competitor) who experienced an economic or reputational injury proximately caused by the false advertisement's deception. Consumers or suppliers who purchased inferior products based on the deception lack the economic or reputational interest § 43(a) protects. Proximate cause of an economic or reputational injury exists where consumers withhold trade from the plaintiff due to deceptive advertising. The Court emphasized the "zone of interests" test and proximate cause requirement adequately limited standing and rejected all other existing tests.

The original § 43(a) was broadly construed to grant relief for a wide variety of common-law palming off claims. These claims included deceptive product imitation, deceptive packaging and trade dress, deceptive imitation of unregistered marks and names, deceptive association of non-competing products, and deceptive literary and artistic titles. Section 43(a) was also used to assert more novel claims. *See e.g. Exxon Corp. v. Humble Exploration Co., Inc.*, 695 F.2d 96 (5th Cir. 1983) (dictum) (former owner of abandoned trademark claimed another used it as a "false designation of origin"); *Manhattan Indus., Inc. v. Sweater Bee by Banff, Ltd.*, 627 F.2d 628 (2d Cir. 1980) (dictum). *See also Gilliam v. American Broad. Co., Inc.*, 538 F.2d 14 (2d Cir. 1976) (television show writers and performers are entitled to preliminary relief under § 43(a) to prevent licensee from broadcasting edited versions of the show as a deceptive mutilation of an artistic work). *But cf., Girl Scouts of the U.S.A. v. Personality Posters Mfg. Co.*,

304 F.Supp. 1228 (S.D.N.Y. 1969) (no § 43(a) claim against unauthorized poster using Girl Scout uniform and motto without evidence of customer confusion as to the origin of the goods). *See also U.S. Golf Ass'n. v. St. Andrews Sys., Data-Max, Inc.*, 749 F.2d 1028 (3d Cir. 1984) (sale of computer using U.S.G.A. golf handicap formula did not employ a false designation of origin since the formula was "functional").

By retaining the original § 43(a) "false designation of origin" language but omitting "any person doing business in the locality falsely indicated" as a specific class of persons entitled to sue, the amended § 43(a) effectively codifies the earlier cases broadly construing the original § 43(a) as reaching all forms of palming off. In addition, by extending the prohibition's scope to reach misleading statements about one's own or another's "goods, services or *commercial activities*," the amended § 43(a) appears to provide a federal remedy for trade name infringement.

Section 43(a)'s original prohibition against "any false description or representation" of goods or services was also used to bring a wide variety of false advertising claims for which there may have been no common-law remedy. In some of these cases the defendant's false description or representation appropriated the results of the plaintiff's capital and labor investments. In other cases, the defendant simply claimed its own product had attributes it did not actually possess.

Included in the first type of false description or representation were cases such as *L'Aiglon Apparel, Inc. v. Lana Lobell, Inc., supra*, confirming a cause of action against a defendant who allegedly used an image of the plaintiff's expensive dress to advertise the defendant's inferior, less expensive dress. *See also Boston Prof'l Hockey Ass'n, Inc. v. Dallas Cap and Emblem Mfg., Inc.*, 510 F.2d 1004 (5th Cir. 1975) (duplicating a sports team's symbol on clothing patches for public sale amounted to a false representation under § 43(a)).

The § 43(a) prohibition against false descriptions or representations was construed to cover misleading as well as demonstrably false statements. *See, e.g., Mutation Mink Breeders Ass'n v. Lou Nierenberg Corp.*, 23 F.R.D. 155 (S.D.N.Y. 1959). The amended § 43(a) codifies these cases by extending the prohibition's scope to reach "false or *misleading*" descriptions or representations.

If an advertisement is proven demonstrably false, either explicitly or by necessary implication, extrinsic evidence showing consumer confusion is not required as it is for deceptive advertisements. *Compare, Time Warner Cable, Inc. v. DIRECTV, Inc.*, 497 F.3d 144 (2d Cir. 2007) (claim that a viewer cannot "get the best picture" without DIRECTV is likely literally false after considering the ad in its entirety and not engaging in "disputatious dissection", but reversing rejection of a puffery defense where comparative images in another advertisement were so grossly distorted that no reasonable purchaser would consider them accurate depictions), *with Pizza Hut,*

Inc. v. Papa John's Int'l, Inc., 227 F.3d 489 (5th Cir. 2000) (the slogan "Better Ingredients. Better Pizza." alone is not a statement causing justifiable consumer reliance, but its use with advertising specifically comparing ingredients conveyed "objectifiable" and misleading facts).

Comparative advertising often includes false or misleading representations. *Bernard Food Indus., Inc. v. Dietene Co.*, 415 F.2d 1279 (7th Cir. 1969) determined a § 43(a) claim requires false representations about the advertiser's own product, not just disparagement (i.e., false or misleading representations) of the plaintiff's product. Section 43(a) states a false description or representation must be made in connection with goods or services which the advertiser caused to enter into commerce. *See also American Home Prods. Corp. v. Johnson & Johnson*, 436 F.Supp. 785 (S.D.N.Y. 1977) (comparative ad claiming one product worked faster and better than another is actionable under § 43(a)).

The amended Lanham Act § 43(a)(1)(B) explicitly prohibits "commercial advertising or promotion" that misrepresents "the nature, characteristics, qualities or geographic origin of his or her or *another person's* goods, services, or commercial activities" (emphasis added). Thus amended, § 43(a) apparently provides a federal cause of action for commercial disparagement, presumably shorn of common-law malice and special damages requirements. *See Proctor & Gamble Co. v. Haugen*, 222 F.3d 1262 (10th Cir. 2000) (competing distributor's claims that plaintiff financially supported the Church of Satan and placed satanic marks on its products did not relate to plaintiff's products or services, but was actionable under § 43(a) as it related to plaintiff's "commercial activities" and constituted "commercial advertising and promotion"). *But cf., The Freecycle Network, Inc. v. Oey*, 505 F.3d 898 (9th Cir. 2007) (the amended § 43(a) disparagement prohibition does not extend to trade*mark* disparagement claims, preventing a claim against a former employee who encouraged others to make generic use of the plaintiff's mark). *See also Fashion Boutique of Short Hills, Inc. v. Fendi USA, Inc.*, 314 F.3d 48 (2d Cir. 2002) (salespersons' allegedly disparaging statements to undercover investigators were not "commercial advertising or promotion" under § 43(a)(1)(B)).

Just as the original § 43(a) did not extend to disparaging statements, so it was held not to prohibit truthful comparative claims. *See, e.g., Societe Comptoir De L'Industrie Cotonniere Establissements Boussac v. Alexander's Dep't Stores, Inc.*, 299 F.2d 33 (2d Cir. 1962) (truthful assertion that one's dresses are copies of the original not actionable under § 43(a)). Notwithstanding the 1988 amendment, the line between truthful and misleading claims can be exceedingly fine. *See, e.g., Johnson & Johnson * Merck Consumer Pharm. Co. v. Smithkline Beecham Corp.*, 960 F.2d 294 (2d Cir. 1992) (plaintiff failed to show injury from an advertisement whose claims were literally true but preyed upon a misperception about competitor's product).

An advertiser making no affirmative representations but failing to disclose an arguably material fact cannot be held liable under § 43(a). In *Alfred Dunhill Ltd. v. Interstate Cigar Co., Inc.*, 499 F.2d 232 (2d Cir. 1974) the court held § 43(a) applied only to actual representations, reversing a lower court finding that sales of a damaged product in original trademarked tins without adequate customers warnings was a false representation of their quality. *Accord: Universal City Studios, Inc. v. Sony Corp. of Am.*, 429 F.Supp. 407 (C.D. Cal. 1977) (failure to warn customers that using recorder to copy television programs could violate copyright laws did not state a § 43(a) claim). *See also Zauderer v. Office of Disciplinary Counsel*, 471 U.S. 626, 651–52 (1985) (the interest in preventing deceptive or misleading commercial speech is sufficient to support reasonable disclosure requirements). In *Bohsei Enter. Co. v. Porteous Fastener Co.*, 441 F.Supp. 162 (C.D. Cal. 1977), on the other hand, failure to name an imported product's nation of origin could violate § 43(a). *See also, Boston Prof'l Hockey Ass'n v. Dallas Cap & Emblem Mfg., Inc., supra* (mere unauthorized duplication of a sports team's logo on a clothing patch for public sale was a false representation under § 43(a)).

Even after the 1988 amendment, § 43(a) liability for deceptive nondisclosures remains unsettled. Regardless, § 43(a) should probably be interpreted similarly as extending only to omission of those facts necessary to make an express or implied representation not "misleading". The FTC also contests advertisements with materially deceptive nondisclosures. *See* Part B(1)(b)(1), *infra*.

Section 43(a) is silent about what remedies are available for advertising violations. Other Lanham Act remedy provisions were originally concerned exclusively with remedies for infringement of registered federal trademarks. Courts were thus left to formulate their own remedial guidelines.

To obtain injunctive relief, a plaintiff only needed to show a likelihood of damage due to a materially false representation (i.e., a false representation that was likely to deceive consumers). This "likelihood" test was similar to the injunctive relief granted for trademark infringement.

Damages required proof of deception and loss based on this deception. Proof of loss was not limited to proof of specific lost sales like in common law false advertising cases. For example, *L'Aiglon Apparel, Inc. v. Lana Lobell*, 214 F.2d 649 (3d Cir. 1954) permitted a compensatory damages claim for alleged loss of goodwill and a forced apparel sale when the defendant's deceptive acts caused abandonment of a product line. At least one court referenced antitrust cases, where courts do not require as high a degree of proof of the *extent* of damages as they do of the *existence* of damage. *See Bangor Punta Operations, Inc. v. Universal Marine Co., Ltd.*, 543 F.2d 1107 (5th Cir. 1976) (upholding the jury verdict for a common law copyright infringement and § 43(a) violation). In *Rickard v. Auto Publisher, Inc.*, 735 F.2d 450 (11th Cir. 1984) the court held the Lanham Act's express purpose and intent was best served by permitting all

§ 35 remedies, including attorney's fees, in § 43(a) cases.

The 1988 amendment to the Lanham Act codified the foregoing view by amending §§ 34(a), 35(a), and 36 to clarify the remedies that apply for § 43(a) cases, namely injunctions, profits, damages (including possible treble damages as a form of liquidated damages), costs, attorney's fees in exceptional cases, and destruction of infringing articles. *See, e.g., ALPO Petfoods, Inc. v. Ralston Purina Co.*, 913 F.2d 958 (D.C. Cir. 1990) (profits may be awarded in § 43(a) registered trademark infringement case with proof of bad faith or willful misconduct; damages can include plaintiff's lost profits on sales actually diverted or sales at reduced prices resulting from the false ads, cost of counter-advertising, and quantifiable harm to goodwill). Monetary relief for a successful § 43(a) claim can be extensive. *See, e.g., ALPO Petfoods, Inc. v. Ralston Purina Co.*, 997 F.2d 949 (D.C. Cir. 1993) (Over $12 million in damages awarded for false advertising claim, including $3.5 million in counter advertising and $4.5 million in lost income).

Even if a plaintiff proves the false advertising created actual confusion or demonstrable damage in the marketplace, they can only recover reasonable damage control expenses by showing a likely confusion. Proof of literal falsity with either willfulness or bad faith is not sufficient to award monetary damages. Market injuries such as harm to goodwill require substantial indications showing these injuries actually occurred. Likewise, receiving the defendant's profits in such cases requires some proof either that the plaintiff lost sales or profits, or that the defendant inequitably gained profits. *See Balance Dynamics Corp. v. Schmitt Indus.*, 204 F.3d 683 (6th Cir. 2000).

Similar to the § 43(a) prohibitions against false descriptions, 35 U.S.C. § 292(a) prohibits markings or advertising falsely designating an item as patent-protected. Examples include items not protected by a granted or pending patent and counterfeit items. Persons using false patent markings with intent to deceive the public are subject to a fine of up to $500 for each offense per § 292(a). Knowledge of inaccurate marketing creates a rebuttable presumption of intent to deceive rather than irrefutable proof. *Clontech Labs., Inc. v. Invitrogen Corp.*, 429 F.3d 1052 (Fed. Cir. 2005).

The Federal Circuit holding that each falsely-marked product distributed constitutes an individual "offense" in *Forest Group, Inc. v. Bon Tool Co.*, 590 F.3d 1295 (Fed. Cir. 2009) created a wave of § 292(b) qui tam lawsuits. Qui tam lawsuits are private actions brought on the federal government's behalf in return for a share of any recovery. Mass-produced products with expired patents were the primary target of these lawsuits. *See, e.g., Pequignot v. Solo Cup Co.*, 608 F.3d 1356 (Fed. Cir. 2010). The America Invents Act ("AIA") overruled *Bon Tool* by exempting expired patents from § 292 marking requirements and requiring proof of a competitive injury to bring a private action for compensatory damages.

Section 287 specifies the marking and notice requirements patent holders must follow to receive infringement damages. As amended by the AIA, § 287 recognizes that certain Internet postings with labeling may provide notice, legislatively overruling CAFC decisions holding patent marking requirements do not apply when seeking damages for method or process patent infringement. *See Bandag, Inc. v. Gerrard Tire Co.*, 704 F.2d 1578 (Fed. Cir. 1983); *Crown Packaging v. Rexam Beverage Can,* 559 F.3d 1308 (Fed. Cir. 2009).

Victims of deceptive promotional practices once sought relief through the Racketeer Influenced and Corrupt Organizations Act ("RICO"), 18 U.S.C. §§ 1961–1968. RICO allows recovery of treble damages by any person injured in his business or property as a result of certain activities constituting "*a pattern of racketeering activity*", defined to include (among other things) two or more acts violating federal mail fraud or wire fraud statutes. 18 U.S.C. §§ 1341, 1343. Virtually any false communication, including false advertising or deceptive promotional practices, could violate the literal language of the federal mail and wire fraud statutes and give rise to a RICO claim. The case so holding, *Sutliff v. Donovan Co.'s, Inc.*, 727 F.2d 648 (7th Cir. 1984), was subsequently overruled. *See, e.g., Hammes v. AAMCO Transmissions, Inc.*, 33 F.3d 774 (7th Cir. 1994). For now, Lanham Act § 43(a) serves as the primary source of private judicial remedies for deceptive promotional practices. In addition to private judicial remedies, both federal and state laws allow public regulation of deceptive promotional practices.

(d) National Advertising Division of the Council of Better Business Bureaus

Outside the legal system, advertisers can use the self-regulating organization National Advertising Review Council ("NARC") to voluntarily resolve advertising disputes. NARC sets advertising standards for truth and accuracy. The National Advertising Division of the Council of Better Business Bureaus ("NAD") is the investigative branch of NARC that monitors advertisements for compliance with NARC standards. The Better Business Bureau administers the NAD to add credibility and impartiality to the review process. While most cases are brought by competitors, consumers and the NAD can bring claims as well. NAD decisions usually take thirty to sixty days, but a new Fast-Track SWIFT process ("Single Well-defined Issue Fast Track") can cut this down to twenty when the issue does not require complex substantiation. Examples include disclosure prominence and sufficiency, misleading pricing or sales claims, and accuracy of certain express claims.

After reviewing submitted evidence and arguments (there is no compulsory discovery), the NAD makes non-binding recommendations. Noncompliant parties may refer the dispute to the courts or a government agency. Unlike false advertising litigation, the NAD accepts challenges to merely unsubstantiated claims as well as claims that can be proven false. NAD decisions are not publicized broadly beyond a press release. The National

Advertising Review Board ("NARB") may review NAD reports.

While the NAD applies § 5(a) of the FTC Act, these proceedings have limited legal value. NAD and NARB findings are likely inadmissible hearsay in court proceedings. *In re Processed Egg Prods. Antitrust Litig.*, No. 08–md–2002 (E.D. Pa. October 22, 2019); *Rexall Sundown, Inc. v. Perrigo Co.*, 651 F.Supp.2d 9 (E.D.N.Y. 2009); *Cytosport, Inc. v. Vital Pharm., Inc.*, 894 F.Supp.2d 1285 (E.D. Cal. 2012) (FTC and FDA referrals are not a government agency decision). However, NAD proceedings may support other case elements. *See, e.g., Greifenstein v. Estee Lauder Corp.*, No. 12–cv–09235, 2013 WL 3874073 (N.D. Ill. July 26, 2013) (NAD findings incorporated into Illinois Consumer Fraud and Deceptive Practices Act claim); *Russian Std. Vodka v. Allied Domecq Spirits*, 523 F.Supp.2d 376 (S.D.N.Y. 2007) (NAD proceeding was evidence of a substantial controversy between the parties, and the case was stayed pending NAD findings to benefit from industry expertise). Courts will enforce agreements between litigations to use NAD as an alternative dispute resolution mechanism. *See, e.g., AMF Inc. v. Brunswick Corp.*, 621 F.Supp. 456 (E.D.N.Y. 1985).

b. Public Regulation of Promotional Practices

Public regulation of promotional practices may take the form of criminal legislation or legislation creating a special government regulatory agency. While criminal statutes modeled on the Printers Ink Model Statute (so named because it was drafted for an advertising industry trade journal named "Printers Ink") are widely adopted, they have generally been ineffective. This is partly due to the courts' strict construction of these laws based on their penal nature, and partly as public prosecutors rarely enforce them. State and federal regulatory agencies, by contrast, perform extensive and wide-ranging enforcement. The Federal Trade Commission is the most prominent of these government agencies, having broad authority to challenge unfair competition methods and deceptive or unfair acts or practices in or affecting commerce. *See* 15 U.S.C. § 45. The International Trade Commission has narrower authority to regulate unfair competition methods and unfair acts for U.S. imports. *See* 19 U.S.C. § 1337.

Congress created the Federal Trade Commission (FTC) in 1914 as a part of a two-pronged effort to improve antitrust law enforcement. The Clayton Antitrust Act of 1914 prohibited certain specified types of anticompetitive conduct and provided a broad range of public and private judicial remedies, including private treble damages actions. To enforce this, the FTC Act (15 U.S.C. §§ 41–58) broadly prohibited "unfair methods of competition in commerce" and created a specialized agency empowered to issue administrative cease and desist orders as the exclusive device for its enforcement. Federal courts have federal-question jurisdiction to hear constitutional challenges to the FTC's structure, existence, and administrative proceedings. *Axon Enter., Inc. v. FTC*, 598 U. S. ___, 143 S. Ct. 890 (2023).

The FTC Act's prohibition against "unfair methods of competition in commerce" (15 U.S.C. § 45) became the linchpin of the FTC's authority to regulate promotional practices. The Supreme Court initially declared the judiciary and not the FTC should state what constitutes an "unfair method of competition". The Court later recognized Congress delegated this ability, and reserved for the courts the right to determine whether the decision is properly based in law and fact. *Atlantic Refining v. FTC*, 381 U.S. 357 (1965). The Court made it clear that it would give considerable weight to the FTC's views. *FTC v. Cement Inst.*, 333 U.S. 683 (1948).

For practical purposes, the FTC has the power not only to prevent "unfair methods of competition" but also to define the phrase. The FTC does this through administrative adjudication and promulgating administrative rules. The International Trade Commission's authority is more limited, allowing it to issue exclusion or cease and desist orders (subject to review by the U.S. Trade Representative and the President) to prevent unfair competition methods in the U.S. import trade. Other agencies hold limited authority in this subject as well. *See, e.g.*, 49 U.S.C. § 41712 (Department of Transportation).

In 1938, the Wheeler-Lea Act amendments to § 5 of the FTC Act greatly extended the FTC's authority to prohibit "unfair or deceptive acts or practices in commerce". They mainly granted the FTC specific authority to protect consumers from deceptive acts or practices, and to do so without having to show any simultaneous threat to competitors. These amendments also legislatively confirmed prior case law that held business methods need not threaten a reduction in competition to be "unfair methods of competition" within the meaning of the FTC Act. These cases held methods that tend to eliminate honesty in competition just as anti-competitive as those tending to eliminate competition itself.

The Wheeler-Lea Act also added a new § 12, specifically empowering the FTC to prevent false advertisement in food, drug, therapeutic device, or cosmetic promotions. The Act complements Food and Drug Administration's (FDA) regulatory authority over *labeling* these products. In 1962, the FDA received exclusive authority to regulate *prescription* drug advertising and labeling. The FDA's authority does not preempt state law claims for failure to warn consumers about drug risks without clear evidence the drug manufacturer fully informed the FDA of the state law warning requirements and the FDA refused to approve a change to the drug's label to include the warning. *Merck Sharp & Dohme Corp. v. Albrecht*, 587 U.S. ___, 139 S. Ct. 1668 (2019).

Subsequent legislative enactments granted the FTC specific authority over certain product labeling (i.e., wool, fur, and textile fiber products) and a variety of consumer product packaging. It also allowed FTC regulation of many other consumer-related practices (*e.g.*, credit and debt collection practices, credit reporting, and consumer warranty practices).

Section 5 of the FTC Act remains the FTC's core regulatory authority. The Magnuson-Moss

Consumer Warranty/Federal Trade Commission Improvement Act (FTC Improvement Act of 1975) was the single most significant expansion of the FTC's powers. This Act extended the FTC's § 5 authority to include prevention of "unfair methods of competition in *or affecting* commerce and unfair or deceptive acts or practices in *or affecting* commerce." This amendment brings within the FTC's jurisdiction essentially local commercial practices that adversely impact interstate commerce. Prior to the FTC Improvement Act of 1975, the interstate commerce requirement constituted a significant jurisdictional limitation on the FTC's power. In the 1975 Act's legislative history, Congress stated this jurisdictional expansion did not in any way preempt state law.

Subsequent case law suggests the FTC has authority to administratively preempt contracts or state laws conflicting with its enforcement efforts under the FTC Act. *See American Fin. Serv. Ass'n v. FTC*, 767 F.2d 957 (D.C. Cir. 1985) (affirming rules preventing wage assignments for default in consumer loans and certain nonpossessory security interests in household goods). However, a federal agency may not exercise authority over U.S. states as sovereigns without unambiguous authority, which the FTC Act lacks. *California State Bd. of Optometry v. FTC*, 910 F.2d 976 (D.C. Cir. 1990) (rule that certain state optometry restrictions were unfair acts or practices exceeded the FTC's authority).

State laws more often augment rather than undermine the FTC's enforcement efforts. *See*

§ B(1)(a)(3)(b), *supra*. Unlike the FTC Act, state laws generally provide consumers (and sometimes competitors) with a private right of action for damages and injunctive relief. *See, e.g., Committee on Children's Television v. General Foods Corp.*, 35 Cal.3d 197 (1983) (reversing dismissal of a class action complaint alleging the defendant cereal company engaged in deceptive advertising to children).

A public interest requirement is the second ostensible jurisdictional limitation on the FTC's power, in addition to the interstate commerce limitation. Requirements that prosecuting an act, practice, or method of competition must be "in the public interest" means the FTC lacks jurisdiction over private controversies. Thus, the FTC's jurisdiction over unfair trade practices arguably extends only to those practices that pose a substantial threat to the competitive process or the consuming public. The courts, however, show great deference to the FTC's public interest determinations and rarely reverse an FTC decision on this basis. *See FTC v. Klesner*, 280 U.S. 19 (1929).

The FTC's power to promulgate substantive rules took time to establish. This power allows the FTC to create rules having the force of law as opposed to merely interpreting rules and stating the FTC's understanding of its statutory mandate. The courts officially recognized the FTC's power to promulgate substantive rules that define unfair or deceptive acts or practices in *National Petroleum Refiners Ass'n v. FTC*, 482 F.2d 672 (D.C. Cir. 1973) (the "*Octane*

Posting" case). Congress confirmed this in the FTC Improvement Act of 1975, which added a new § 18 to the FTC Act detailing specific rulemaking procedures for defining unfair or deceptive acts or practices. *See* 15 U.S.C. § 57a.

The *Octane Posting* case indicated that the FTC also has power to promulgate substantive rules defining unfair competition methods though the informal rulemaking procedures of the Administrative Procedure Act, 5 U.S.C. § 553. The elaborate § 18 procedures presumably need not be followed. Unsurprisingly, the FTC proliferated trade regulation rules for a variety of trade practices after 1975, including ophthalmic practices, consumer loans, and franchising agreements.

For violations of an FTC rule or the underlying statute, enforcement procedures take the form of a formal adjudicatory hearing conducted pursuant to the procedures of the Administrative Procedure Act and the FTC Act itself. Neither pre-complaint assurances of voluntary compliance nor post-complaint consent orders are obtained during these procedures.

Various remedial tools are available for FTC Act or FTC rule violations. For most of its history, the FTC was limited to issuing cease and desist orders. The terms of these orders were largely within the FTC's discretion. Orders were only enforceable in civil proceedings brought by the Justice Department in federal court, with a maximum civil penalty of $5,000 per violation. In 1973 the FTC received self-representation power, and the civil penalty rose to $10,000 per violation.

The FTC Improvement Act of 1975 authorized the FTC to seek civil penalties in federal court for trade regulation rules violations and for conduct that the defendant had actual or imputed knowledge to be unfair or deceptive as determined in a previous cease and desist proceeding (whether or not the defendant participated).

The FTC has long sought equitable monetary relief in federal court, but these abilities are presently diminished. The FTC's ability to seek monetary relief for original conduct required the FTC to issue a final cease and desist order and show the court "the act or practice to which the cease and desist order relates is one which a reasonable man would have known under the circumstances was dishonest or fraudulent". *See* 15 U.S.C. § 57b(a)(2). Consumer redress could take the form of consumer refunds or actual damages. Section 13(b) grants the FTC authority to sue in federal court when the accused is either violating or about to violate the law and enforcement would be in the public interest. It also allows the FTC to seek a temporary restraining order, preliminary injunction, or permanent injunction. 15 U.S.C. § 53(b); *see also FTC v. Shire ViroPharma, Inc.*, 917 F.3d 147, 161 (3d Cir. 2019) (FTC cannot challenge conduct that solely occurred in the past).

However, the FTC cannot secure equitable monetary relief such as restitution or disgorgement through the courts under § 13(b), only injunctive relief. *AMG Capital Mgmt., LLC, v. FTC,* 591 U.S. ___, 141 S. Ct. 1341 (2021). Here, the Court concluded monetary relief "necessary to redress injury to consumers" against those engaged in unfair or deceptive acts or practices may be possible under § 19 but requires prior use of traditional § 5 administrative proceedings, namely an FTC administrative law judge's ruling, appealable to the Commission and then a court of appeals.

The FTC Improvement Act also authorized the FTC to seek various forms of consumer redress in state or federal court. Still, the cease and desist order remains the FTC's chief administrative remedy to prevent unfair methods of competition and unfair or deceptive acts or practices. It can be used to order corrective advertising where needed to eliminate the lingering effects of past deceptions. *See* Ch. 4, § C.2.b., *supra*.

The FTC's exercise of its expanded enforcement powers under the FTC Improvement Act of 1975, together with its decision to review the fairness of advertising aimed at children, precipitated an almost immediate Congressional reaction. After twice allowing funding for the FTC briefly to run out, Congress for the first time placed significant legislative limitations on the FTC. The FTC Improvement Act of 1980 required that Congress have an opportunity to legislatively veto a proposed final FTC rule by concurrent resolution within 90 days of its submission; required the FTC to prepare a detailed cost/benefit analysis for every proposed and final rule; required the FTC to publish agendas listing rules it expected to propose or issue; provided the FTC with only limited authority to investigate and promulgate rules concerning children's advertising, the funeral home industry, and the insurance industry; and denied the FTC authority for the next three years to petition for cancellation of a trademark on grounds that it has become generic. The latter provision temporarily halted the FTC's attempt to promote competition among synthetic surface manufacturers by having the trademark "Formica" declared a generic term.

Congress first used its legislative veto to overturn the FTC's controversial proposed rules governing used car sales. The legislative veto was itself declared unconstitutional as it did not require submission to the President for signature. *Consumers Union v. FTC*, 691 F.2d 575 (D.C. Cir. 1982). The FTC ultimately adopted a watered-down version of these original rules, as well as for rules governing the funeral industry.

Notwithstanding the foregoing limitations on the FTC, the FTC's core substantive mandate remains intact. That mandate, as we have seen, may be divided into the FTC's authority to prevent deceptive acts and practices and its authority to prevent other unfair acts or practices and unfair methods of competition.

(1) Federal Trade Commission Regulation of Deceptive Acts or Practices

The FTC's authority over deceptive acts or practices encompasses promotional activities capable of deceiving consumers and materially affecting their purchasing decisions. These two elements comprise the FTC's entire burden of proof in a deceptive practice proceeding.

(a) The Capacity to Deceive. The "capacity to deceive" element of promotional activities is as significant for what it omits as for what it includes. Neither knowledge that an act or practice is deceptive nor intent to deceive need be shown. The FTC need not even show the challenged act or practice actually deceived consumers. *Charles of the Ritz Distrib. Corp. v. FTC*, 143 F.2d 676 (2d Cir. 1944). (An act or practice, taken as a whole, need only have a capacity to deceive the ordinary consumer). The deceptiveness test thus bears a strong resemblance to the "likelihood of confusion" test for trademark infringement. *See* Ch. 4, *supra*.

Courts and the FTC understandably vacillate as to whether an ordinary consumer should be deemed distracted and gullible or reasonably prudent and alert. Stronger protections for vulnerable consumers are more likely to stifle commercial speech through excessive qualifications and thus hamper competition. However, limiting legal prohibitions against acts or practices that would deceive a reasonably prudent and alert consumer allows unscrupulous businesses to prey on consumers that most need protection. A real tension exists between the FTC's mandate to protect the competitive process and its mandate to protect the consumer.

While the *Charles of the Ritz* court held the FTC should have discretion to protect even "wayfaring fools" if it so chose, the FTC eventually shifted to progressively narrower tests for what constitutes deceptive acts or practices. In a 1983 letter to the chairman of a congressional oversight committee, the FTC stated its test for deceptive acts or practices was whether a representation, omission, or practice is *likely* to mislead a *reasonable* consumer or a reasonable or ordinary member of an audience whose capacity to reason may be impaired, such as children, the elderly, or the terminally ill. The FTC first applied this test in *Cliffdale Assocs., Inc.*, 103 F.T.C. 110 (1984), which reprints the 1983 letter as an appendix.

Acts or practices with the requisite capacity to deceive are generally either: (1) direct representations; (2) implied representations; or (3) material nondisclosures. Vague or abstract direct claims (*e.g.*, "New!") as well as the latter present challenges. Courts often defer to FTC "expertise" in resolving these questions.

The FTC found implied misrepresentations in cases involving deceptive trademarks, service marks, trade names, trade dress, product configurations, illustrations, demonstrations, and mockups. Implied misrepresentations were also found in inconspicuous or obtuse qualifying statements, ambiguous advertising claims, and even technically true statements whose overall implication was nevertheless misleading. The FTC's broadest finding was that *any* advertising claim carries an implicit representation that the claimant has a reasonable basis for making the claim. If the claim lacked factual substantiation *at the time it was made*, the claim is deceptive by definition (regardless of later justification).

The FTC used this reasonable basis for implicit advertising claims theory, together with its power to prohibit unfair but non-deceptive trade practices, as the basis for its advertising substantiation program. *See, e.g., Pfizer, Inc.*, [1970–73 Transfer Binder] CCH Trade Reg.Rep. ¶ 20056 (1972) (affirmative product claims without a reasonable basis an unfair practice). *See also American Home Prods. Corp. v. FTC*, 695 F.2d 681 (3d Cir. 1982) (for comparative advertising where a medicine's superiority is in question, the FTC may require at least two well-controlled clinical studies to substantiate the claim); *Thompson Medical Co. v. FTC*, 791 F.2d 189 (D.C. Cir. 1986) (substantiation of a non-comparative efficacy claim for a non-prescription drug required at least two well-controlled clinical studies). *But see* FTC Policy Statement Regarding Advertising Substantiation, 49 Fed.Reg. 31000 (1984), stating future FTC advertising substantiation investigations would proceed on a case-by-case basis rather than as industry-wide "rounds" and would not be publicized before completion. The FTC also emphasized that post-claim evidence of a product claim's truth, while no substitute for pre-claim substantiation, remained relevant when considering whether the public interest supports prosecution and the appropriate scope of an order against an advertiser lacking pre-claim substantiation.

Deceptive nondisclosures generally are omissions of facts necessary to ensure other express or implied representations are not misleading. However, the FTC never placed an affirmative duty on advertisers to "tell all." An FTC deceptive nondisclosure finding basically states another express or implied representation in an advertisement is deceptive. For example, the FTC found material nondisclosures where advertisements held express or implied half-truths, where well-known products were changed in a significant yet non-obvious way, and where a product's appearance was inherently deceptive (*e.g.*, it appeared new or composed of a certain material but was already used or an imitation). These cases complement the FTC's explicit authority to require affirmative information disclosures on various consumer product labels and packaging under the Wool, Fur, and Textile Labeling Acts and the Fair Packaging and Labeling Act.

The FTC has a longstanding view that foreign goods that are not so marked deceptively fail to disclose a material fact. The conclusion rests on two increasingly questionable assumptions—that ordinary consumers believe goods sold in the U.S. were manufactured domestically, and that ordinary consumers prefer domestic goods. Many signatories to the General Agreement on Tariffs and Trade ("GATT") objected that the FTC's position facilitates discrimination against foreign goods which violates GATT's Article IX. Later FTC rulings suggest the FTC will recognize an exception to its rule where there is evidence the public has no preference for domestic goods. However, the Tariff Act of 1930 (19

U.S.C. § 1304) still requires every article of foreign origin imported into the U.S. be labeled with its country of origin, albeit subject to an increasing variety of statutory and administrative exceptions.

The FTC requires at least limited disclosure of any potential dangers to consumer health or safety posed by a product or service (and not merely on its label), apparently exceeding mere prevention of implicit marketing deception. Simply marketing a product or service could implicitly represent that the product or service poses no danger to consumers. A Uniform Commercial Code implicit warranty provision certainly supports this. However, the FTC's concern is not that consumers will be deceptively induced to purchase unsafe products or services. Rather, the FTC is concerned that consumers may not receive information needed to safely use the product or service after it is bought.

The FTC's authority to require disclosure of potential dangers in advertisements is as much a function of its power to prevent "unfair" acts or practices as it is a function of its power to prevent deception. *See, e.g., In the Matter of Int'l Harvester Co.*, 104 F.T.C. 949 (1984), holding the FTC's deceptiveness authority is but a subset of its jurisdiction over unfairness; that not every undisclosed safety problem constitutes a deceptive breach of an implied warranty of fitness; that unfair acts, unlike deceptive acts, must be shown to risk a substantial consumer injury not outweighed by any offsetting consumer or competitive benefit and not reasonably avoided by consumers; and that a manufacturer's failure to effectively warn tractor operators of a small risk that hot fuel would "geyser" when the fuel cap was loosened was not a deceptive breach of an implied warranty of fitness as a matter of law, but was an unfair act since the failure to disclose risked substantial consumer injury, provided no offsetting benefits, and created a risk that tractor operators could not reasonably anticipate and avoid.

The FTC's unfairness authority assertion may complement other legislative and administrative efforts requiring warning labels for potentially dangerous products. For example, the Federal Cigarette Labeling and Advertising Act, 15 U.S.C. §§ 1331 *et seq.*, requires warnings be placed on cigarette packages. At the administrative level, the Consumer Products Safety Commission requires warning labels on a variety of consumer products, and the Food and Drug Administration has authority to prevent misbranding or adulteration of foods, drugs, and cosmetics.

Where federal laws such as the Food, Drug, and Cosmetic Act ("FDCA") conflict with other labeling laws, such as state laws, these other laws are preempted. The FDCA may also supersede some federal laws, known as preclusion. At minimum, the FDCA does not preclude a competitor's private right of action under the Lanham Act. *Pom Wonderful LLC v. Coca-Cola Co.*, 573 U.S. 102 (2014). While courts often interpret the *Pom Wonderful* decision to create a general presumption against preclusion, claims where the Lanham Act or other sources of law implicate FDA judgment still favor preclusion. *See, e.g., JHP Pharm., LLC v. Hospira, Inc.*, 52 F.Supp. 3d 992 (C.D. Cal. 2014); *Exela Pharma Scis., LLC v. Sandoz, Inc.*, 486 F.Supp.3d 1001 (2020). Note that FDCA unfair competition actions cannot be enforced through private action. *Amarin Pharma, Inc. v. ITC*, 18–1247 (Fed. Cir. March 26, 2018).

(b) Materiality. A deceptive act or practice is "material" if it can affect a consumer's purchasing decisions. To be material, a misrepresentation "involves information that is important to consumers and, hence, likely to affect their choice of, or conduct regarding a product." *Kraft, Inc. v. FTC*, 970 F.2d 311, 322 (7th Cir. 1992) (citations omitted). The materiality definition is not limited to actions designed to deceive a rational consumer regarding the inherent qualities of a product, service, or business. Instead, the materiality definition addresses the various functions deceptive acts or practices play in affecting consumer choices.

Whatever their form, the FTC prohibits two broad functional categories of deceptive acts and practices: (1) deceptive representations about the product, service, or business itself and (2) deceptive representations regarding "extrinsic" matters in promoting a product, service, or business. The rationale for prohibiting these two types of deception differs significantly.

The most frequent and least controversial act or practice type deceptively describes a product's content, quality, or effectiveness. The deceptive description may be a direct misrepresentation in advertising or an implied misrepresentation such as a deceptive or misleading trademark. *See, eg., FTC v. Algoma Lumber Co.*, 291 U.S. 67 (1934) (deceptive to advertise one type of pine is superior to another); *Charles of the Ritz Distrib. Corp. v. FTC*, 143 F.2d 676 (2d Cir. 1944)(deceptive to sell "Rejuvenescence" brand skin cream that does not rejuvenate skin).

The FTC also prevents deceptive descriptions of services and business opportunities. Franchising operations and both correspondence and vocational schools are subject to extensive FTC rules designed to prevent consumer deception regarding available services and opportunities. This protects commercial and consumer interests. *See Branch v. FTC*, 141 F.2d 31 (7th Cir. 1944) (§ 5 of the FTC Act and the Webb-Pomerene Act, 15 U.S.C. §§ 41–46 grant the FTC authority to prohibit unfair competition methods in the export trade). *Branch* let the FTC issue a cease and desist order prohibiting a correspondence school operating in the U.S. from soliciting students in Latin American countries using fraudulent methods. The consumer deception in *Branch* occurred abroad and was thus beyond the FTC's consumer protection jurisdiction. Even so, *Branch* held the potential detriment to other U.S. businesses competing in the same market was substantial enough to give the FTC jurisdiction over the school's fraudulent practices as unfair competition methods.

It is a deceptive act or practice to misrepresent, either directly or implicitly, a product or service's origin, composition, or price where a particular consumer preference exists, even without a real defect in the inherent quality of the product or service offered. *See, e.g., FTC v. Mary Carter Paint Co.*, 382 U.S. 46 (1965).

The FTC prohibits false or deceptive endorsements, certifications, or testimonials as a deceptive act or practice. *See, e.g.*, FTC Guides Concerning Use of Endorsements and Testimonials, 16 C.F.R. § 255.1 (requiring that where an ad "represents that the endorser uses the endorsed product, then the endorser must have been a bona fide user of it at the time the endorsement is given"). *But see FTC v. Garvey,* 383 F.3d 891 (9th Cir. 2004) (FTC failed to show a spokesperson was recklessly indifferent to the truth of his statements or aware of a high probability of fraud and intentionally avoided the truth, but judicially declining to decide what degree of deference FTC guides should receive or whether they can form an independent basis for spokesperson liability).

Social media and influencer advertising has increased the deceptive endorsements challenge due to a net decrease in spokesperson sophistication and platform-based limitations. The FTC may regulate those failing to disclose a material connection to a business through financial (including receipt of free or discounted products), employment, personal, or family relationships with a brand. *See* 16 C.F.R. § 255.0. However, the FTC has only taken minimal action in this area. *But see In re CSGO Lotto, Inc.*, F.T.C. File No. C–4632 (Nov. 28, 2017) (settling first FTC complaint against social medial influencer).

Deceptive businesses descriptions may misrepresent how a company functions in the distribution chain, a company's size, or the company's length of operation. The FTC determined consumers prefer to deal directly with manufacturers (expecting lower prices and greater assurance of high-quality goods) and to deal with businesses whose operations are on a larger scale or well-established. Trade names that falsely suggest a connection with an established business, a government agency, or other respected organization are likewise materially deceptive.

Some misrepresentations about goods or services bear no relationship to the quality of goods or services at all. Even if they do, the consumer may learn the truth before making a purchase. Bait-and-switch advertising, fictitious consumer surveys, and fictitious pricing or discounts are all classic examples of wholly extrinsic misrepresentations. *See e.g. All-State Indus. of N.C., Inc. v. FTC*, 423 F. 2d 423 (4th Cir. 1970); *FTC v. Bay Area Bus. Council, Inc.*, 423 F.3d 627 (7th Cir. 2005).

Extrinsic misrepresentations erode consumer resistance more than they mislead the consumer as to whether the product or service, when purchased, will meet the consumer's expectations. Like product, service, or business misrepresentations, extrinsic misrepresentations do not misrepresent the inherent quality of a product, service, or business. Unlike product, service, or business misrepresentations, however, extrinsic misrepresentations merely establish initial contact with the consumer and do not consummate a sale. Accordingly, these misrepresentations are often characterized as creating initial interest confusion. Use of another's trademark to create initial interest confusion is an actionable trademark infringement under the Lanham Act. *See* Ch. 4 B(1), *supra*. These deceptive tactics are a way of overcoming the goodwill of established products, services, or businesses. Extrinsic misrepresentations may overcome consumer buying habits or skepticism. Permitting their practice jeopardizes established business goodwill and would pressure other companies to adopt these tactics.

The FTC prohibits undisclosed simulations when used in place of actual demonstrations. A demonstration carries an implied assertion that the consumer may witness a product's capabilities first-hand and need not rely on the advertiser's claims. As such, demonstrations likely have a material effect on a consumer's purchasing decision. *See FTC v. Colgate-Palmolive Co.*, 380 U.S. 374 (1965) (upholding FTC order prohibiting an advertisement simulating a test it claimed to display).

(2) Federal Trade Commission Regulation of Unfair Acts or Practices and Unfair Methods of Competition

When deceptiveness by advertising or other promotional activities appears attenuated, the FTC may always fall back on its authority to identify and prohibit a practice as "unfair". As we have seen, the courts give great weight to FTC unfairness findings. Courts also hold the terms "unfair acts or practices" and "unfair methods of competition" include, but are not limited to, either deceptive practices or practices likely to have anticompetitive consequences within the letter or spirit of the antitrust laws. *See, e.g., FTC v. R.F. Keppel & Bro., Inc.*, 291 U.S. 304 (1934) (upheld FTC finding that selling candy to children by the "break-and-take" lottery method was an unfair competition method even though there was no deception and competitors could maintain their market positions by adopting similar practices); *Orkin Exterminating Co. v. FTC*, 849 F.2d 1354 (11th Cir. 1988) (breach of over 200,000 lifetime guarantee contracts with stated annual renewal fees an unfair practice).

A practice which does not violate antitrust laws and is not deceptive may nonetheless be unfair. In such cases, the FTC considers (1) whether the practice *offends public policy* as established by *statutes*, the *common law*, or *otherwise* [i.e., whether the practice is within at least the penumbra of some common law, statutory, or other established concept of unfairness]; (2) whether it is *immoral, unethical, oppressive,* or *unscrupulous;* and (3) whether it causes *substantial injury* to *consumers* or *other businessmen*. *See* 29 Fed.Reg. 8324, 8355 (1964), cited with approval in *FTC v. The Sperry & Hutchinson Co.*, 405 U.S. 233 (1972). *But see* Letter of FTC, 5 CCH Trade Reg.Rep. ¶ 50,421 (Dec. 17, 1980), stating the second test is largely duplicative, the FTC has never relied on it as an independent basis for an unfairness finding, and the FTC will only act on the other two tests going forward.

Determining what constitutes an unfair act or practice or unfair method of competition within the meaning of the FTC Act invokes the larger question of what promotional practices have been declared unfair, whether by statute, common law, or otherwise. *See* Part B. 2., *infra*. Regardless, practices will be found unfair if they cause substantial consumer injury and are either not reasonably avoidable by consumers or outweighed by countervailing benefits to consumers or competition. *See In re Int'l Harvester Co., supra* and *Orkin Exterminating Co. v. FTC, supra. Cf., Mainstream Mktg. Serv., Inc. v. FTC,* 358 F.3d 1228 (10th Cir. 2004) (the FTC's national do-not-call registry, which prohibits calls from most commercial telemarketers (excluding charitable or political organizations), is valid commercial speech regulation because it directly advances the government's important interests in safeguarding personal privacy and reducing the danger of telemarketing abuse without burdening an excessive amount of speech).

(3) International Trade Commission Regulation of Unfair Methods of Competition in the Import Trade

The International Trade Commission (ITC) may issue exclusion or cease and desist orders to prevent "unfair methods of competition and unfair acts in the importation of articles" connected with imports claimed to injure established or developing domestic industries or violating intellectual property rights. The ITC derives this authority from § 337 of the 1930 Tariff Act, 19 U.S.C. § 1337. The Tariff Act does not specifically define an "unfair act" or "unfair method of competition," but the ITC interpreted these terms to include conduct that violates the Lanham Act's false advertising provisions. *See Certain Insulated Sec. Chests,* Inv. No. 337–TA–244 (June 17, 1986).

In addition to the intellectual property right violations that comprise most of its caseload, the ITC investigates antitrust violations and a variety of common law acts of unfair competition such as passing off and trade secret misappropriation. *See, e.g., Certain Periodontal Laser Devices,* Inv. No. 337–TA–1070, and *Certain Clidinium Bromide & Products Containing Same,* Inv. No. 337–TA–1109 (investigating unfair acts of false advertising for unapproved drugs and medical devices).

Section 337 complaint investigations often proceed faster than ordinary federal court actions. As a result, businesses seeking redress for trade injuries often file concurrent claims in federal court and the ITC. *See* Ch. 6, *supra* for more detail on ITC procedures.

Trade secret misappropriation claims before the ITC increased following the Federal Circuit's decision in *TianRui Group Co. v. ITC*, 661 F.3d 1322 (Fed. Cir. 2011) (trade secret misappropriation occurring entirely outside the U.S. led to an exclusion order for a reasonable research and development period of ten years). *TianRui Group* held the Commission could consider extraterritorial conduct when necessary to protect a domestic industry as importation is inherently international. Prior to the Defend Trade Secrets Act, § 337 presented one of the few domestic ways to oppose this type of foreign misconduct. Section 337 retains importance since it does not require a domestic act furthering the misappropriation. *See also Certain Carbon and Alloy Steel Prods.*, ITC Inv. No. 337–TA–1002 (2016) (trade secret theft claim based on computer hacking by Chinese government survived early challenges before withdrawal).

2. UNFAIR PROMOTIONAL PRACTICES

Many promotional practices that neither violate the antitrust laws nor are deceptive have nevertheless been widely condemned as unfair. These practices may be divided into two groups: (1) purely commercial marketing practices and (2) consumer-aimed promotional practices.

Unfair commercial marketing practices generally involve either coercive use of economic power or bribery. Bribery and coercion amount respectively to "carrot" and "stick" attempts to subvert the competitive process. Actionable and non-actionable coercion was reviewed in Ch. 2 *supra*. Commercial bribery in competitive (i.e., horizontal) relations was discussed with trade secret misappropriation in Ch. 7, *supra*. This section reviews bribery as an unfair promotional practice in commercial bargaining (i.e., vertical) relationships.

a. Bribery in Commercial Bargaining Relations

Commercial bribery involves surreptitious payments to another's agent or employee to induce an act or forbearance in the briber's favor. The briber may be a competitor, customer, or supplier of the targeted business. The crime of honest services fraud, namely a scheme or artifice to deprive another of the intangible right to honest services, may be used against bribes paid to public servants or for breach of a fiduciary duty in the private sector. *See* 18 U.S.C. § 1346. While technically not a "commercial" action, bribing a government official often has commercial purposes and so is included in this analysis. The government may be a purchaser (government contract) or a supplier (business license or franchise). A difference is that bribery of a government official induces betrayal of a *public* (rather than a *private*) trust.

Bribery of a competitor's agent or employee frequently occurs when a competitor seeks the target's trade secrets. *See* Ch. 7, *supra*. Those bribing a non-competitor's agent or employee generally seek to either establish or improve their treatment in a commercial relation. Frequently the bribe is paid by a supplier seeking to make a sale to a customer's purchasing agent. Where a supplier's goods or services are scarce or unique, a purchaser may try to bribe the supplier's agent or employee to either make a purchase or block a competitor's purchase. There are also forms of commercial bribery to procure favorable promotion of one's product or service (i.e., "payola") or to influence a contest or other game of skill.

Originally, mail and wire fraud statutes proscribed schemes to defraud others of tangible property, financial interests, or honest services. 18 U.S.C. §§ 1341, 1343. The Supreme Court ended this practice by limiting the scope of these statutes to only protecting property rights. *McNally v. United States*, 483 U.S. 350 (1987). Congress tried to legislatively overrule this decision by including in the mail and wire fraud statutes an intangible right of honest services. 18 U.S.C. § 1346. To avoid finding the statute unconstitutionally vague, the Court limited the honest services fraud definition to "offenders who, in violation of a fiduciary duty, participated in bribery or kickback schemes" and did not include "undisclosed self-dealing by a public official or private employee". *Skilling v. United States,* 561 U.S. 358 (2010).

Economic concentration and integration affects commercial bribery opportunities. Early in the 20th century, large business enterprises relied extensively on sales and purchasing agents. Struggles to establish and maintain trade relations led to widespread commercial bribery. Domestic instances of commercial bribery are still common where distribution chains are not integrated (*e.g.*, the beer and liquor industries). Concerns about commercial bribery in foreign markets grew as more of the domestic economy became dependent upon international trade.

Commercial bribery of domestic and foreign government officials became a particular concern as the public sector consumes an increasing supply of U.S. products and services. Questionable corporate payments to government officials range from perfectly legal political contributions to clearly illegal under-the-table payments. Under the Hobbs Act in the United States, a challengeable official act by a government entity requires decision or action on a "question, matter, cause, suit, proceeding or controversy" through formal exercise of government power to further an objective more specific and concrete than general business and economic development in the state. *McDonnell v. United States*, 579 U.S. 550 (2016) (setting meetings, hosting events, or calling other officials are activities too expansive to be an "official act").

All commercial bribery forms covertly undermine existing business relationships, injuring the bribe recipient's employer and the bribe payer's competitors. Employers may experience two types of harm: deprivation of loyal and unbiased service by the agent or employee, and financial injuries by either paying a higher sales price or receiving poorer quality goods or services due to the bribe. The bribe payer's competitors lose an opportunity to compete on equal terms, compelling them to resort to bribery as well. In addition to these purely private injuries, commercial bribery ultimately harms the consuming public by subjecting it to potentially higher prices or inferior goods and services.

Those who uncover bribery have private and public remedy options. An employee accepting a bribe breaches a fiduciary obligation to the employer by failing to remain loyal and by not disclosing the bribe. State equity courts grant employers a right to recover the bribe to prevent the employee's unjust enrichment. A bribe payer induces the employee to breach their fiduciary obligation, comparable to an implied employment contract term. An employer has a common-law right to recover from the bribe payer any damages resulting from the induced breach of that implied contract. *See* Ch. 3, *supra*. Bribes arguably constitute improper interference with the purely prospective relations of the bribe payer's competitors, which would create a common-law relief claim. *See* Ch. 2, *supra*. Recovery under this theory is challenged by requiring establishing that, but for the bribe, a specific competitor and plaintiff would have made the sale.

While § 2(c) prohibits price discrimination disguised as brokerage fees (*See* Ch. 9, *infra*), courts also held § 2(c) prevents undermining public confidence in brokers. Bribes occurring in commerce subject to federal regulation create a cause of action under §§ 2(c) and 4 of the Clayton Act for employers of bribed employees and, more importantly, competitors of the bribe payer. *Environmental Tectonics v. W.S. Kirkpatrick, Inc.*, 847 F.2d 1052, 1066 (3d Cir. 1988); *Genesco, Inc. v. T. Kakuichi & Co.*, 815 F.2d 840, 853 (2d Cir. 1987). This safeguards the role of brokers as a valuable market mechanism. Treble damages are available under § 4(a) of the Clayton Act when a private plaintiff can show a bribe undermines the broker relationship, gives one seller an unfair advantage over a competing seller, and is associated with the evils antitrust laws are designed to prevent. *See, e.g., Brunswick Corp. v. Pueblo Bowl-O-Mat, Inc.*, 429 U.S. 477, 489 (1977). These "evils" include restraint of trade, monopolization, or price discrimination.

As amended by the Robinson-Patman Act, the Clayton Act prohibits payment or receipt of unearned commissions, brokerage, or compensation. *See, e.g., Fitch v. Ky.-Tenn. Light & Power Co.*, 136 F.2d 12 (6th Cir. 1943) (treble damage award upheld for a company whose president took bribes when selecting a supplier). *But see Stephen Jay Photography, Ltd. v. Olan Mills, Inc.*, 903 F.2d 988 (4th Cir. 1990) (rival company did not violate § 2(c) by donating money to schools while seeking a photographer position).

Unlike the Robinson-Patman Act provision prohibiting price discrimination *per se*, the Act's false brokerage provision is not limited to transactions involving goods intended for domestic resale. Instead, the Act's false brokerage provision applies to bribes in foreign as well as interstate commerce. *See, e.g., Canadian Ingersoll-Rand Co. v. D. Loveman & Sons*, 227 F.Supp. 829 (N.D. Ohio 1964) (foreign company stated a § 2(c) cause of action against its chief purchasing agent and a U.S. corporation for allegedly conspiring to extract exorbitant prices); *W.S. Kirkpatrick & Co., Inc. v. Environmental Tectonics Corp., Intern.*, 493 U.S. 400 (1990) (§ 2(c) action stated against a competitor that allegedly bribed Nigerian officials to secure contracts). The only limitation for a Robinson-Patman Act bribe claim is that the bribe must affect U.S. foreign commerce.

The FTC declared commercial bribery an unfair competition method in violation of the FTC Act. Most of the FTC's § 5 proceedings against commercial bribery in domestic trade occurred in the early 1920's before the Robinson-Patman Act was enacted. The FTC has since used both the FTC Act and the Robinson-Patman Act to challenge bribery in U.S. foreign trade where the alleged effect excluded other U.S. companies from the foreign market. *See, e.g., In the Matter of Lockheed, Boeing and McDonnell Douglas Corp.*, 43 Fed.Reg. 36,973 (1978) (proposed FTC consent order where three of the nation's largest aircraft manufacturers agreed not to make payments to commercial customers or foreign governments). In contrast to the Foreign Corrupt Practices Act of 1977, 15 U.S.C. §§ 78 *et seq.*, the FTC Act and Robinson-Patman Act apply to payments made to private commercial parties as well as foreign government officials. The Acts also provide civil liability and criminal sanctions against violators. For analysis of relief from foreign government involvement in or inaction regarding foreign trade activities and limitations thereon (i.e., the act of state doctrine), *see* Ch. 1, § A.2.c.(2) *supra*.

After years of complaints that U.S. anti-bribery law disadvantage U.S. businesses in international trade, the U.S. position was vindicated by the Organization for Economic Co-operation and Development (OECD), an international organization of 29 industrialized countries. The OECD negotiated the 1997 Convention on Combating Bribery of Foreign Public Officials in International Business Transactions. All 29 OECD member countries and several non-member countries joined this

Convention. Still, bribery of government officials remains rampant in many parts of the world.

b. Consumer-Aimed Promotional Practices

Many non-deceptive consumer-aimed promotional practices are condemned as unfair because they constitute "lures to improvidence." These practices could be divided into two groups: the use of lotteries, games, and contests, on the one hand, and the use of giveaways, premiums, and trading stamps on the other. Both practices play on the desire to get something for nothing, while some prey on gambling appetites as well. More recently, automated promotional practices (such as automated telephone and e-mail solicitations) emerged as an unfair practice. Like deceptive bait-and-switch tactics, automated promotional practices may be deemed unfair as they impose undue burdens on consumers.

(1) Lotteries, Games, and Contests

Various games of chance and skill exist, often categorized by the roles played by consideration, prize, and chance. Each state has different laws regarding gambling and related gaming, often permitting some forms of these games with state registration. Without an express statutory prohibition, certain games and contests are permitted so long as no false representations are made in promoting them.

Consideration involves payment for participation. This consideration may be monetary or involve participants expending substantial time or effort.

Many states focus on a pecuniary or economic value approach to this consideration element. Others view any consideration sufficient to support a contract as adequate to meet the element, while a few find any economic benefit received by the sponsor is sufficient. *See, e.g., Wash. v. Safeway Stores, Inc.*, 450 P.2d 949 (Wash. 1969) Consideration may be found, for example, where a customer must complete extensive surveys or be present at a particular location to win a drawing.

Gambling is the unity of consideration, prize, and chance. The federal government criminalizes illegal gambling businesses through a number of statutes including the Illegal Gambling Business Act (18 U.S.C. § 1955) (conducting illegal gambling business), Wire Act (18 U.S.C. § 1084) (using telecommunications to conduct illegal gambling business), Travel Act (18 U.S.C. § 1952) (using interstate commerce to conduct illegal gambling business), and Unlawful Internet Gambling Enforcement Act (31 U.S.C. §§ 5361–67) (accepting payment for illegal internet gambling). Anti-money laundering statutes and RICO, *supra*, may also apply. *See* 18 U.S.C. §§ 1956–57, 1962. However, the U.S. Constitution limits the federal government's regulatory rights in this area. For example, the anti-commandeering rule (preventing the federal government from requiring states to act or refrain from acting in certain ways) prevented a legislative ban on sports betting. *See Murphy v. NCAA*, 584 U.S. ___, 138 S. Ct. 1461 (2018) (prohibition against state-sponsored sports betting violated the 10th Amendment); *Greater New Orleans Broad. Ass'n v.*

United States, 527 U.S. 173 (1999) (federal law prohibiting broadcasted advertisements for gambling casinos violated the 1st Amendment).

States may regulate gambling and other games of chance, including advertising for them, without violating the U.S. Constitution. *Posadas de P.R. Assocs. v. Tourism Co.*, 478 U.S. 328 (1986). Private gambling is illegal in most states, although many operate their own lotteries and allow various related games subject to restrictions by statute and regulatory agencies. Running luck-based games frequently requires attention to restrictions on permitted games, prize sizes, use of proceeds, timing, location, and compliance with comprehensive filing and reporting requirements.

Applying gaming law restrictions to tribal lands presents additional challenges as state laws may be applied to tribal Indians or their reservations where Congress expressly consents. The Court once held that states could enforce bans on particular games through their right to enforce criminal laws which are fully applicable to tribal lands, but a state that merely regulates a game's availability cannot enforce its rules on tribal lands as the state's civil jurisdiction is much more limited. *California v. Cabazon Band of Mission Indians*, 480 U.S. 202 (1987) (Regulatory law with criminal and civil enforcement does not become prohibitory).

In 1988, Congress legislatively modified this decision through the Indian Gaming Regulatory Act, 25 U.S.C. §§ 2701 *et seq.*, which created the National Indian Gaming Commission and a regulatory structure for such gaming in the United States that differentiated certain types of permissible and restricted gaming. Following this statute, gaming activities prohibited by state laws are prohibited on tribal lands as a matter of federal law and those regulated by state laws must conform to federal terms and conditions but are not subject to state gaming regulations. *Ysleta del Sur Pueblo v. Texas*, 596 U.S. ___, 142 S. Ct. 1929 (2022).

While statutory definitions vary from state to state, a lottery may generally be thought of as the non-gratuitous distribution of prizes by lot or chance. A lottery includes all three elements of consideration, chance, and prize and is a type of gambling. While states frequently permit themselves to run lotteries for consideration, private lotteries are often prohibited by criminal statutes to protect the public welfare. *Cf., Phalen v. Va.,* 49 U.S. 163 (1850) (condemning lotteries over other gambling forms). Nevertheless, many states permit charitable lotteries and "bingo" games if properly registered and administrated.

Courts let businesses bring private actions for injunctive relief against competitors violating criminal statutes against private lotteries. *See, e.g., United Stations of N.J. v. Kingsley*, 99 N.J. Super. 574 (1968) (gas station operator may sue oil distributors and retail dealers to prevent certain giveaways allegedly violating a statute prohibiting lotteries and "other games of chance"). Likewise, *FTC v. R.F. Keppel & Brother, Inc.*, 291 U.S. 304 (1934) upheld the FTC's authority to prohibit the "break and take" lottery method of promoting candy sales to children as an unfair method of competition, even without fraud, deception, or conduct likely to trigger the Sherman Act. In so holding, the Court noted this practice exploited a class of consumers who are unable to protect themselves and that the common law and criminal statutes have long treated such practices as contrary to public policy.

States frequently permit sweepstakes and contests, so long as the proper licenses are secured. Event holders must clearly establish the game rules, how a winner is chosen, and the actual prize values. Violations of sweepstakes and contest laws may be prosecuted by states and various government entities including the Federal Trade Commission, Federal Communications Commission, and the U.S. Postal Service.

Sweepstakes are random drawings for a prize without the element of consideration. They are regulated by state and federal law. Many states allow sweepstakes entries through activities such as mailing forms, completing simple surveys, viewing media, or visiting a store. These actions require minimal effort by participants and do not impart great benefit to the promoter. Requiring substantial endeavors from a participant or deriving significant economic benefits from the contest may constitute consideration and therefore risk classification as illegal gambling.

Companies often mitigate the threat of varying state consideration standards rendering their sweepstakes illegal by offering a free alternative method of entry ("AMOE") that allows sweepstakes participation without exchanging anything of value. *But see Barber v. Jefferson County Racing Ass'n*, 960 So. 2d 599, 604–05 (Ala. 2006) (Internet time sold on cards with encoded sweepstakes entries held incidental to game purchase and therefore an illegal lottery despite AMOE). AMOE entrants must receive the same treatment as other entrants for this to be an acceptable alternative. Note that consideration may be unlawfully received after the sweepstakes concludes, such as conditioning a prize award on the winner making a purchase, paying a fee, or attending a sales presentation.

Contests are games that may combine a prize and consideration but lack the element of chance. The role of ability, effort, skill, or judgment in these competitions are frequently scrutinized, as the contest organizer's behavior to influence the results can render a contest unlawful. Sports and arts are common contest types. Trivia and reality television programs also fall into this category so long as they are not rigged to favor a contestant. *See FCC v. American Broad. Co., Inc.*, 347 U.S. 284 (1954) ("giveaway" shows not a form of gambling); *but see* 47 U.S.C. § 509 (amending Communications Act of 1934 to prohibit quiz show fixing in response to extensive gameshow rigging).

Predicting future outcomes is often not acceptable as a contest given the element of chance involved. *See Stevens v. Cincinnati Times-Star Co.*, 73 N.E. 1058, 1060–61 (Ohio 1905) (predicting future events a factor of luck rather than skill, rendering election return guessing contest illegal gambling); *compare, Indoor Recreation Enters. v. Douglas,* 235 N.W.2d 398, 400 (Neb. 1975) (chess a game of skill) *with Boardwalk Regency Corp. v. Attorney Gen. of N.J.,* 457 A.2d 847, 848–51 (N.J. 1982) (backgammon a game of chance). While disputed by enthusiasts, poker's combination of random card draws with skill in statistics and bluffing does not meet contest requirements. *See Charnes v. Central City Opera House Ass'n.,* 773 P.2d 546, 551 (Colo. 1989).

Other games may include the combination of consideration and chance, without a prize. This type of "amusement gambling" is frequently held illegal by courts finding additional playing time to be a sufficient prize. *See e.g. United States v. Sixteen Elec. Gambling Devices,* 603 F.Supp. 32 (D. Haw. 1984) (electronic video games illegally duplicated casino games, where the prize was more playing time); *Kater v. Churchill Downs Inc.,* 886 F.3d 784 (9th Cir. 2018) (electronic casino game held illegal gambling where tokens to continue play could be won or purchased are "a thing of value").

Video game "loot boxes" present a challenge, as they offer random chances to win digital assets of varying scarcity. Loot boxes may be received for free or purchased. They may also be traded for in game currency and sometimes sold to other players. *See Coffee v. Google LLC,* No. 20–cv–03901–BLF (N.D. Cal. Jan. 10, 2022) (application marketplace did not engage in illegal gambling as plaintiff received the virtual currency purchased, and neither a free video game download nor a virtual currency is considered a sale of goods or services sufficient to create an economic injury; platform provider receives § 230 immunity as its role is limited to publishing third-party applications and processing purchases). While outlawed as illegal gambling in some foreign nations and subject to many domestic lawsuits, no U.S. state or federal bill specifically regulating loot boxes has yet become law. However, failure to provide accurate and non-misleading odds regarding outcome probabilities may violate § 5 of the FTC Act.

(2) Premiums and Trading Stamps

Several states adopted various "anti-premium" statutes outlawing use of free goods, premiums, or trading stamps as a promotional device. Customers received trading stamps as an incentive for paying cash rather than credit. The stamps could be exchanged for merchandise, similar to current loyalty cards. Among the rationales given for such criminal prohibitions was that premiums, like lotteries, are a lure to improvidence. *See, e.g., State v. Wilson,* 101 Kan. 789, 168 P. 679 (Kan. 1917) (trading stamp tax a valid police power exercise as it reasonably prevented "evil consequences to the public"). Such lures appeal to a desire to get something for nothing. They may force competing sellers to offer similar premiums, resulting in an overall increase in business and consumer costs. Much of this legislation has since been repealed.

Some states adopted statutes prohibiting sales below cost, and a few remain on the books. *See* Ch. 9, *infra*. Courts consider premiums when calculating whether a sale is below cost. However, trading stamps were not considered when calculating the cost of an item. The U.S. Supreme Court held this distinction is not an arbitrary discrimination in violation of the equal protection clause. *See Safeway Stores, Inc. v. Okla. Retail Grocers Ass'n, Inc.*, 360 U.S. 334 (1959) (rational distinction between an across-the-board trading stamp offer as a cash discount for prompt cash payment and selective below-cost price cuts—i.e., "loss leader" selling—and that the latter was the specific evil that the statute was designed to prevent). Why below-cost pricing (i.e., loss leader selling) is an evil to be prevented is addressed in the next chapter.

(3) Unsolicited Automated Communications

The Telephone Consumer Protection Act of 1991 (TCPA), 47 U.S.C. § 227, amends the Communications Act of 1934 to restrict a variety of unsolicited commercial communications through an automated telephone dialing system ("ATDS"). These restrictions include using an ATDS to call a residential or mobile phone without prior consent; using a prerecorded voice message to call a residential phone line without prior consent; sending an unsolicited advertisement to a fax machine; and using an ATDS to simultaneously engage at least two of a company's telephone lines. To be an ATDS under 47 U.S.C. § 227(a)(1)(A), the automatic dialer device definition is limited to those that use a random or sequential number generator to store or produce telephone numbers rather than all equipment that stores and dials phone numbers. *Facebook, Inc. v.*

Duguid, 592 U.S. ___, 141 S. Ct. 1163 (2021) (sending automated text messages from a stored phone number database was not operating an ATDS as the stored numbers were not randomly or sequentially generated). Unwanted calls burden a consumer's privacy, require no further injury be shown. *Krakauer v. Dish Network LLC*, 925 F.3d 643 (4th Cir. 2019) (class action correctly held a principal liable for agent's willful TCPA violations).

There is a circuit split regarding unwanted text messages. *Compare Melito v. Experian Mktg. Solutions, Inc.*, 923 F.3d 85 (2d Cir. 2019) (unsolicited text messages without other injury is sufficient to show injury-in-fact under the TCPA as they create the same nuisance and privacy invasion); *with Salcedo v. Hanna,* 936 F. 3d 1162 (11th Cir. 2019) (while the FCC's rulemaking authority expands the TCPA voice call provision to text messages, historical analysis and silence by Congress does not justify expanding federal jurisdiction over a new harm).

While consumers can revoke consent to receive calls through any reasonable means, courts split as to how contracts affect this right. *ACA Int's v. FCC*, 885 F. 3d 687 (D.C. Cir. 2018); *compare, Gager v. Dell Fin.,* 727 F.3d 265 (3d Cir. 2013) (consumers may revoke consent implied by credit applications) *with Reyes v. Lincoln Auto. Fin. Serv.*, 861 F.3d 51, 56 (2d Cir. 2017) (consumers cannot revoke consent when it is bargained-for consideration to a contract). When a phone number transfers to a third party, permission to receive automated calls does not follow. *Soppet v. Enhanced Recovery Co.*, 679 F. 3d 637 (7th Cir. 2012).

Exemptions to mass communications prohibitions exist for emergency purposes and those made with the prior express consent of the called party. Healthcare and financial emergencies are included. Congress made another exemption for federal debt collectors in 2015, which was held an unconstitutional content-based restriction of free speech. *Barr v. American Ass'n of Political Consultants*, 591 U.S. ___, 140 S. Ct. 2335 (2020). Federal and state courts may adjudicate private TCPA lawsuits. *Mims v. Arrow Fin. Servs., LLC*, 565 U.S. 368 (2012).

The Federal Communications Commission ("FCC") administers the TCPA and regulates many aspects of unwanted communications, including acceptable times, content, techniques, and technology. The FCC's TCPA rulings receive a high level of deference from the courts, which is essentially any permissible construction of a statute if the issue was not directly addressed by Congress. *See, Chevron v. NRDC*, 467 U.S. 837 (1984); *Satterfield v. Simon & Schuster, Inc.*, 569 F. 3d 946 (9th Cir. 2009). Even so, appellate courts have "exclusive jurisdiction to enjoin, set aside, suspend . . . or to determine the validity of" certain FCC final orders under the Hobbs Act, 28 U.S.C. § 2342(1). *PDR Network, LLC v. Carlton Harris Chiropractic, Inc.*, 588 U.S. ___, 139 S. Ct. 2051 (2019). The FCC eliminated the "established business relationship" exception previously sufficient to avoid TCPA liability, so prior express consent requires a signed writing specifically agreeing to receive automated telemarketing calls or text messages. 27 FCC Rcd. 1830 (2012).

The Do-Not-Call Implementation Act of 2003 (15 U.S.C. §§ 6101 *et seq.*) established the Federal Trade Commission's national registry of phone numbers that may not be contacted for commercial calls. The Do-Not-Call Improvement Act of 2007 eliminated a five-year renewal requirement. Some unsolicited communications are exempted from the Act, such as communications from political or non-profit organizations, surveys, and bill collectors.

Federal measures also exist to limit unsolicited emails. The CAN-SPAM (i.e., Controlling the Assault of Non-Solicited Pornography and Marketing) Act of 2003, 15 U.S.C. §§ 7701 *et seq.*, created a U.S. standard for bulk transmission of commercial email. The Act also prevents states from enacting stronger anti-spam protections and prohibits individuals who receive spam from suing spammers except under laws not specific to e-mail. This Act allows people to unsubscribe from future emails, sets content standards, and makes the Federal Trade Commission responsible for enforcing these requirements. The FTC's enforcement of the Act has been limited, and the Act itself is highly criticized.

In at least two cases, private companies have successfully mounted various Lanham Act § 43 claims against bulk e-mailers. In *America Online, Inc. v. LCGM, Inc.*, 46 F.Supp.2d 444 (E.D. Va. 1998), for example, a company whose domain name was forged as a return address by an adult website in a bulk email successfully sued the website for Lanham Act § 43(c) dilution by tarnishment. In *CVent Inc. v. Eventbrite, Inc.*, 739 F.Supp.2d 927 (E.D. Va. 2010), an event planning website owner stated a § 43(a) claim of reverse passing off against a competing website that had allegedly "scraped" information from the plaintiff's website, reformatted it, and posted it as its own. For dilution by tarnishment, *see* Ch. 4.B.2. For reverse passing off, *see* Ch. 5(B)(1).

CHAPTER 9

INJURIOUS PRICING PRACTICES

A free-market economy presumes prices should not be fixed by private agreements among competitors or the government. Instead, the unencumbered trade relations underlying the economy should prevail as the "law of supply and demand". Price fixing prevention in a free market is largely an antitrust law matter, as competition law is known in the U.S. Only the government can fix prices, and only where natural monopolies exist or unregulated price competition harms the public interest.

Following these economic principles, the common law generally takes a hands-off approach to pricing practices. Running a business at a loss (i.e., selling below cost) may be evidence of a predatory (i.e., anticompetitive or malicious) purpose, but it is not conclusive evidence. *See* Ch. 2, *supra*. Without an improper business objective, traders have the right to sell goods or services at any price. Businesses that enjoy a natural monopoly or provide essential public services are subject to regulations requiring reasonable prices be made equally available to all customers. Even then, "reasonable prices" could mean prices having a reasonable relation to costs or merely prices that do not vary across similarly situated customers. The standards are unclear.

The common-law distinction between purely private enterprises and enterprises "affected with the public interest" acquired constitutional significance after *Munn v. Ill.*, 94 U.S. 113 (1876). Per *Munn*, imposing price regulations on businesses not affected with the public interest is an impermissible deprivation of a constitutionally-protected liberty. The *Munn* economic liberty theory ultimately gave way to the view that there is no closed business class or category affected with the public interest that would be immune to price regulation. This erosion began with *Nebbia v. N.Y.*, 291 U.S. 502 (1934). In *Wickard v. Filburn*, 317 U.S. 111 (1942), the Court conceded that Congress has broad authority to regulate economic matters, and the legislative branch rather than the judiciary must balance the needs for price freedom and price stability.

The Supreme Court did significantly restrict congressional power to regulate commerce until the 1990's. Even so, none of these restrictions prohibited federal regulation of pricing practices. For example, when the Court rejected an argument that Congress had Commerce Clause power to require citizens to buy health insurance, it still held this requirement was a constitutional exercise of Congress' taxing power. *National Fed'n of Indep. Bus's v. Sebelius,* 567 U.S. 519 (2012). Thus, while Congress apparently cannot force individuals to engage in commerce, it can tax them if they choose not to.

The Court did reserve an important, albeit more limited, pricing practice role for itself. A state statute banning truthful prescription drug price advertising was held an impermissible abridgement of constitutionally protected speech. *Virginia State Bd. of Pharmacy v. Virginia Citizens Consumer Council*, 425 U.S. 748 (1976). While the decision favors price freedom over price stability, it merely limits state powers to regulate price *advertising* and not their powers to regulate pricing itself.

State or federal legislatures principally regulate pricing to promote price stability. Legislative powers to regulate pricing practices primarily prevent private price fixing by competitors or regulate natural monopolies. Legislatures might also use this power for wage and price controls or to combat inflation.

Many states previously had "Fair Trade" laws, ironically allowing manufacturers and wholesalers to pursue vertical resale price maintenance. Resale price maintenance means the manufacturer and distributors could set certain minimum or maximum prices for selling goods. Courts found contracts prescribing resale prices violate the Sherman Antitrust Act. However, the 1937 Miller-Tydings Amendment to the Sherman Act legalized vertical minimum resale price maintenance contracts for branded commodities sold in any state allowing such intrastate sales contracts.

The McGuire Act of 1952 expressly lets states enact laws enforcing contracts prescribing stipulated as well as minimum prices. The Act also lets companies enforce these contracts against non-signatory parties. These state statutes make the price agreement a covenant that runs with the branded goods. "Fair Trade" statutes theorized that price cutting could injure a trademarked product's goodwill, so resale price maintenance agreements were a legitimate means of protecting that goodwill.

The interest in trade relations stability purportedly outweighed the interest in price freedom.

Congress ultimately recognized state Fair Trade laws undermined the economic policies federal antitrust laws promoted. Thus Congress repealed the Miller-Tydings Amendment and the McGuire Act in the Consumer Goods Pricing Act of 1975, P.L. 94–145 (Dec. 12, 1975) and removed the antitrust exemption for resale price maintenance agreements. *See California Retail Liquor Dealers Ass'n v. Midcal Aluminum, Inc.*, 445 U.S. 97 (1980) (State wine pricing system constituted resale price maintenance violating the Sherman Act).

State Fair Trade law preemption raised questions about other state and federal price regulation statutes. State and federal statutes prohibiting price cutting (i.e., sales below cost or sales at unreasonably low prices) and price discrimination bore particular scrutiny. The rationale behind these statutes and the pricing practices the statutes try to prevent can differ from the common law's prohibition against predatory pricing. Understanding these statutes begins with the trade relations each body of law protects and the particular types of interference that each address.

A. TRADE RELATIONS PROTECTED

The common law forbids running a business at a loss with no intention of continuing the business after another targeted business is destroyed. Public policy disfavors such actions to injure or destroy another business as this reduces competition. *See* Ch. 2 *supra*. By contrast, state and federal statutory prohibitions against price cutting and price discrimination seem to protect specific classes of trade relations. These statutory schemes regulate two prohibited pricing practice types.

B. ACTIONABLE AND PRIVILEGED INTERFERENCE

Price cutting and price discrimination are two groups of pricing practices made actionable at common law or by statute. Price discrimination can be considered a form of price cutting for a select group. Price cutting and price discrimination are actionable where they further a predatory purpose. Such purposes include lessening competition or the purely malevolent injury or destruction of another business. However, some price cutting and price discrimination forms may be actionable even if there is no predatory objective. In these forms, the practice itself is unfair, not the objective.

1. PRICE CUTTING

Price cutting is only actionable under common law where the sole purpose is to injure or destroy another business. Price cutting to eliminate competition may violate antitrust laws. *See* Ch. 2, *supra*. State statutes prohibiting sales below cost and prohibiting sales at unreasonably low prices, through § 3 of the Robinson-Patman Act ostensibly supplement these two bodies of law.

a. Sales Below Cost

Some statutes prohibit sales below cost, or "loss leader" selling. This promotional practice can be unfair as a destructive means of competition that often leads to price wars. The practice also plays on customer gullibility by falsely creating expectations that a business offering one amazing bargain must have more.

Most states enacted "sales below cost" statutes. *See generally,* Annotation, Francis M. Dougherty, *Validity, Construction, and Application of State Statutory Provision Prohibiting Sales of Commodities below cost—Modern Cases*, 41 A.L.R. 4th 612 (1985) . While widely disregarded by businesses, many of these statutes remain in force and occasionally come to the public's attention. For example, short term promotional events such as "back to school" and "Black Friday" sales apparently violate the literal language of Oklahoma Unfair Sales Act, 15 O.S. 2001, § 598.1. *See* Opinion of the Oklahoma Attorney General, 2011 OK AG 24 (Dec. 13, 2011) (prohibiting certain sales below cost that do not fall within the statute's limited exceptions).

Sales-below-cost statutes vary widely from state to state, but often forbid sales below cost where there is intent to destroy competition or to injure a competitor. Some statutes forbid sales below cost where either the intent or effect destroys competition or injures a competitor. A few statutes claim to forbid all sales below cost regardless of intent, competition, or competitors involved. These prohibitions may apply to all sellers or only those at specified distribution chain levels and may extend to all types of commodities or services sales; to sales of commodities alone; or to sales of selected commodities such as alcohols, cigarettes, and gasoline. *See, e.g.*, Francis M. Dougherty, *Validity, Construction, and Application of State Statutory Provisions Prohibiting Sale of Gasoline Below Cost*, 26 A.L.R. 6th 249 (2007). For example, the Wisconsin Unfair Sales Act applied to a sale below cost even though it met a competitor's price across a state line where gasoline taxes are lower. *See Go Am. LLC v. Kwik Trip, Inc.*, 292 Wis. 2d 795 (2006), holding the sale below cost was exempted, as the price was lowered in good faith to meet, not beat, a competitor's lawful price.

Virtually all states explicitly permit below cost sales designed to meet a competitor's lawful price. States also exempt certain transactions such as clearances, close-outs, judicial sales, damaged or deteriorated goods sales, or sales of perishable goods forced by the threat of spoilage.

Sales-below-cost statute enforcement may involve criminal penalties, civil actions for damages, or injunctions. The statutes frequently allow "any person" to bring civil actions. This can mean virtually anyone may seek to enjoin violations, not merely competitors threatened with injury. *See, e.g., Catalina, Inc. v. P. Zwetchkenbaum & Sons, Inc.*, 267 A.2d 702 (R.I. 1970) (product manufactures may challenge below-cost retail sales). Some courts require the plaintiff be a competitor and suffer actual injury due to the alleged sale below cost. *Heiden v. Ray's Inc.*, 150 N.W.2d 467 (Wis. 1967).

Violations require a nonexempt sale below cost. As many statutes are limited to wholesaler and retailer sales, these statutes generally define "cost" as invoice or replacement cost plus overhead costs. Where a statute applies to manufacturers, the cost is usually computed as raw materials, labor, and all overhead expenses.

There is inherent difficulty in computing what share of overhead an item bears. Statutes usually either create a rebuttable presumption that overhead costs are a certain percentage of the invoice or material and labor costs or permit trade association costs surveys as prima facie evidence of overhead costs. Regardless, the end result is likely an arbitrary estimate of a particular company's overhead costs. One could believe the prohibition against sales below such "costs" is little more than a legislatively-prescribed mandatory markup—that is, a crude form of government-sponsored minimum price fixing. *Cf.*, *Kentucky Milk Mktg. v. Kroger Co.*, 691 S.W.2d 893 (Ky. 1985) (sales below cost statute unconstitutional in defining "cost" to include not only the direct product acquisition costs, but also all overhead expenses).

Including a statutory provision requiring intent to injure competition or a competitor does not resolve this suspicion. Most sales-below-cost statutes include such a provision, and those that do not are frequently struck down as a matter of state constitutional law—at least where criminal penalties for statutory violations exist. Even statutes containing an "intent to injure" requirement do not require a purely malicious intent to injure the competitor. Many statutes hold evidence of a sale below cost is presumptive evidence of intent, burdening the seller with proving a lack of intent to injure a competitor. Since one normally sells below cost specifically to divert customers from a competitor, that burden is nearly impossible to carry.

This statute-based evidentiary presumption of intent is frequently held unconstitutional as well. *But see McLane Co. v. Weiss*, 965 S.W.2d 109 (Ark. 1998) and *McLane S., Inc. v. Davis*, 233 S.W.3d 674 (Ark. 2006) (upholding the statutory constitutionality of presumed intent and a subsequent amendment prohibiting cigarettes sales below cost as well, as the act specifically excluded below-cost sales for reasons other than injuring a competitor). In states where the evidentiary presumption of intent survived constitutional attack, violations often rest either solely on a presumed intent to injure or on evidence of nothing more than a company's competitive purpose to attract a marginal number of a competitor's customers. In contrast to the common law's limited prohibition against predatory price cutting, sales-below-cost statutes practically prohibit purely competitive price cutting.

The Federal Trade Commission asserts that state sales-below-cost legislation regulating retail gasoline prices is not only unnecessary but potentially harmful to consumers. FTC News Release, (FTC File

No. V030011), dated May 21, 2003, stated a proposed amendment to North Carolina's Motor Fuel Marketing Act making it applicable to a single inadvertent sale below cost was unnecessary and could cause higher gas prices for North Carolina consumers.

b. Unreasonably Low Prices

While the Robinson-Patman Act (RPA) focuses on price discrimination, one of its provisions specifically addresses price cutting. Section 3 of the Act, 15 U.S.C. § 13a, prohibits sales "at unreasonably low prices for the purpose of destroying competition or eliminating a competitor. . ." The federal approach to price cutting in the RPA differs substantially from state sales-below-cost statutes. Section 3 of the RPA prohibits sales "at unreasonably low prices for the purpose of destroying competition or eliminating a competitor." There are two elements to the offense: (1) a sale at an unreasonably low price and (2) an intent to destroy competition or injure a competitor. While each element bears separate examination, the absence of *either* element is a complete defense.

The RPA only permits criminal prosecutions, limiting it as an enforcement tool. Section 3 was further held not to be an "antitrust law" whose violation will give rise to a private treble damage action under § 4 of the Clayton Act. *See Nashville Milk Co. v. Carnation Co.*, 355 U.S. 373 (1958). Unsurprisingly, § 3 is used against price cutting even less frequently than state sales-below-cost statutes. Its prohibited price cutting definition bears mentioning as a useful contrast to state sales-below-cost statutes approach.

Section 3 is constitutional despite the general language defining criminal conduct. *United States v. National Dairy Prods. Corp.*, 372 U.S. 29 (1963). Here, the prohibition against "unreasonably low prices" was not impermissibly vague where an indictment specifically alleged a predatory purpose. The Court held § 3 required a specific intent to destroy competition or injure a competitor accompanying an unreasonably low price. The required specific intent apparently does not differ from the predatory intent common law requires for actionable price cutting. So § 3 simply appears to provide a federal criminal remedy for common-law predatory price cutting. Overall, the generality of § 3 appears to be its chief virtue in comparison with the rigid specificity of state sales-below-cost statutes.

Section 3 of the RPA is unlike state sales-below-cost statutes because it does not prohibit sales below cost, only sales at unreasonably low prices. Theoretically, a sale below cost might be reasonable or a sale at a slight profit unreasonable depending on whether there is a legitimate commercial justification for the price. *National Dairy Prods.* clarified that since companies exist to produce a profit, a profitless sale will be deemed unreasonable unless a legitimate commercial objective justifies it. Such justifications include disposing of perishable or outdated goods or meeting a competitor's prices. Similarly, sales prices producing a profit, however slim, will likely be found reasonable. However, the profit from all like sales could consistently be so minuscule compared to the investment as to call into question whether a legitimate commercial objective exists. The true index for price reasonability is the seller's intent or purpose in setting it, not its relation to a given cost definition.

2. PRICE DISCRIMINATION

The Robinson-Patman Act (RPA), 15 U.S.C. §§ 13 *et seq.*, is basically an amendment of § 2 of the Clayton Antitrust Act. While the RPA is technically an antitrust law, both its legislative history and subsequent judicial construction reflect as much of a concern with protecting businesses from injurious pricing practices as with protecting the competitive process. The Act's legislative history reveals congressional concern with protecting independent retailers and wholesalers from price concession coercion by chain retailers or from being completely bypassed by them. Virtually all states enacted statutes prohibiting price discrimination in certain industries. Some states also enacted statutes of general applicability. *See, e.g.,* Cal. Bus. & Prof. Code §§ 17040–41 (1996).

The Clayton Act's original § 2 forbade the localized form of predatory price cutting. Large nationwide suppliers may use this tactic to force small competitors out of a local market. The amended § 2(a) indirectly limits this practice and discourages large volume *buyers* from forcing price concessions. The Act forbids sellers from engaging in price discrimination between different purchasers of commodities having similar grade and quality where the discriminatory effect may lessen, injure, destroy, or prevent competition. Section 2(a)'s indirect approach was apparently chosen to comply with the Supreme Court's restrictive views on when a buyer, as opposed to a seller, engaged in commerce that Congress could regulate.

Section 2(a) expressly excepts from its general prohibition any price concession reflecting a cost saving or changing condition. Section 2(b) allows any price concession that is a bona fide attempt to meet a competitor's price. Section 2(c) prohibits granting or receiving a price concession in the guise of brokerage, commissions, or discounts in lieu thereof to the buyer or its agent. Sections 2(d) and 2(e) prohibit sellers from paying for or providing promotional services in lieu of a price concession. Finally, § 2(f) forbids a buyer from knowingly inducing or receiving a price concession prohibited by §§ 2(a)–(e). Section 3 of the RPA, which cannot be amended by the Clayton Act, provides criminal sanctions for three pricing practices: (1) knowingly discriminating in price by such covert means as discounts, rebates, allowances, or advertising service charges; (2) predatory geographic price discrimination; and (3) predatory price cutting.

The Robinson-Patman Act's civil provisions (§§ 2(a)–2(f)) may be enforced either by the federal government or by private parties injured in their business or property from violations of the Act. The Federal Trade Commission (FTC) and the Department of Justice (DOJ) have concurrent power to enforce these civil provisions. The DOJ largely defers to the FTC, which applies the Act through administrative cease and desist orders enforceable by the courts. The Justice Department retains exclusive power to institute the relatively few criminal proceedings brought under § 3 of the Act. RPA enforcement by the government has been virtually non-existent for the past two decades. However, the RPA may be privately enforced for treble damages or injunctive relief, and these lawsuits continue to proliferate.

While the Robinson-Patman Act's statutory language is complex, it basically defines three distinct types of price discrimination: (1) price discrimination per se, (2) price discrimination as brokerage fees, and (3) price discrimination through promotional allowances and services. Defenses vary with the type of misconduct alleged.

a. § 2(a) Price Discrimination

(1) The Prima Facie Case

A prima facie price discrimination case under § 2(a) of the Clayton Act, as amended by the Robinson-Patman Act (RPA), requires the Federal Trade Commission or a private litigant to show:

(1) a person engaged in commerce

(2) discriminated in price in the course of such commerce

(3) between different purchases of

(4) commodities

(a) of like grade and quality

(b) for use, consumption, or resale within the United States

(5) where one or more of the purchases was in commerce, and

(6) the substantial effect of the discrimination is to either

(a) lessen competition

(b) create a monopoly, or

(c) injure, destroy, or prevent competition with

[1] the person granting the discrimination,

[2] the person who knowingly receives it, or

[3] either of their customers.

Each of these elements can be subject to considerable litigation. As an example, the seller, the discrimination, and at least one of the purchases must be "in commerce"—i.e., be involved with a commodity's physical movement in interstate or foreign commerce. *See, e.g., Lucas v. Citizens Commc'ns Co.*, 244 Fed.Appx. 774 (9th Cir. 2007) (summary judgment upheld for defendant where the company granting selective rebates operated exclusively in the State of Hawaii).

A "discrimination in price" consists of nothing more than charging different prices to at least two contemporaneous purchasers. One does not discriminate, however, by periodically changing prices uniformly available to all purchasers. *See also Volvo Trucks N. Am. v. Reeder-Simco GMC, Inc.*, 546 U.S. 164 (2006) (manufacturer selling through dealers via a customer-specific competitive bidding process was not liable for secondary-line price discrimination [*see* § (b)] without proof the manufacturer discriminated between dealers competing to resell its product to the same retail customer; merely selectively increasing a discount once one dealer wins the competitive bid does not constitute price discrimination); *Smith Wholesale Co. v. R.J. Reynolds, Tobacco Co.*, 477 F.3d 854 (6th Cir. 2007) (upholding a market share incentive discount program where the distributors' ability to obtain the best prices depended on their own marketing decisions); *Freightliner of Knoxville v. DaimlerChrysler Vans*, 484 F.3d 865 (6th Cir. 2007) (same holding as *Smith*).

"Price" is the ultimate cost the purchaser pays, including any discounts, rebates, or allowances. "Purchasers" are limited to those who actually purchase (as opposed to lease or rent) a commodity. A "commodity" is a tangible article of merchandise. Where both commodities and services are involved, the dominant part of the transaction governs. *See, e.g., First Comics, Inc. v. World Color Press*, 884 F.2d 1033 (7th Cir. 1989) (printing contract predominantly for services). Commodities are of "like grade or quality" if they have identical physical qualities. Identical products packaged in different quantities constitute goods of like grade and quality.

Section 2(a) requires commodities be intended for consumption or resale in the United States, in addition to requiring discrimination in commerce. This language permits price discrimination by exporters. It likewise allows importers to "dump" commodities in the U.S. (i.e., selling at lower prices than are charged in other countries) since a § 2(a) violation requires both the compared sales be commodities for use or resale in the U.S. However, other Robinson-Patman Act provisions prohibit certain price discrimination forms by exporters and other U.S. laws explicitly prohibit dumping.

The final element to understanding how § 2(a) of the amended Clayton Act functions as unfair competition legislation is likely the most important. This element is the actionable price discrimination limitation to those causing one of three competitive injury types. The first two competitive injury types (lessening competition and monopoly creation) carry over from the original § 2 of the Clayton Act and reflect the Act's original antitrust goals. The third competitive injury type (injuring, destroying, or preventing competition), however, reflects the RPA's broader concern with preventing injury to individual competitors.

Since an individual competitor's injury generally occurs well before any overall lessening of competition or tendency toward monopoly, Robinson-Patman Act litigation largely focused on this third injury type. As the statutory language indicates, this injury type can occur at the seller level of competition (i.e., primary line injury), at the buyer level of competition (i.e., secondary line injury), or the favored purchaser's customer level (i.e., third line injury). The Supreme Court even extended § 2(a) to a fourth line injury, which is injury to competitors of the customers of the favored purchaser's customers, where the favored purchaser's customers resold the commodity to their own subsidiaries. *See Perkins v. Standard Oil Co.*, 395 U.S. 642 (1969).

The courts and the FTC must decide what the Act considers a competitive injury for all these levels. Early Supreme Court dicta suggested the RPA intended to equate "injury to competition" with "injury to a competitor disadvantaged by the discrimination". The lower courts and the FTC since held the Act intends to preserve competition and only incidentally protects individual competitors. The statutory language seems to contemplate a uniform competitive injury standard, regardless of the level where the competitive injury allegedly occurred. The courts and FTC have varied competitive injury proof requirements depending on whether a primary line or a second, third, or fourth line injury was alleged.

(a) Primary Line Injury. Price discrimination may be a form of predatory price cutting—i.e., pricing designed to drive the seller's competition out of business. Proof the discriminating seller had predatory intent establishes a prima facie case of primary line competitive injury. Where price discrimination results from predatory intent, competitive injury is highly likely. Intent may be

established by direct documentary or testimonial evidence. Intent may also be inferred from circumstantial evidence such as sudden and unexplained price cuts, continuous sales below cost, severe and prolonged undercutting of a competitor's prices, the discriminator's greater competitive strength, or proof the discriminator engaged in other anticompetitive or otherwise unfair trade practices.

While proof of predatory intent is sufficient to establish a prima facie case of first line injury, it is not an essential element of the prima facie case. Price discrimination can also be established by proving the discrimination adversely impacted competitive conditions in the seller's market. Thus, a seller who simply accedes to a buyer's price concession request violates the Act if the price concession had a provable adverse impact on the seller's market.

At one time it appeared merely establishing a sales diversion from one seller to another was sufficient proof of impact. Today, trade diversion is no longer sufficient evidence of first line competitive injury. Trade diversion remains a relevant factor in determining whether the price discrimination adversely impacted the discriminating seller's market. Other relevant factors for first line competitive injury inquiries include the discriminating seller's market dominance, the extent and duration of the seller's price cuts, evidence of offsetting price increases in other markets, the seller's competitors' overall health, and the relative ease of entry into the market.

A growing number of courts and the FTC were influenced by an article claiming predatory pricing is irrational and thus will not likely occur unless the predator has superior financial resources and the predator's market has substantial barriers to entry. *See* Areeda and Turner, Predatory Pricing and Related Practices Under Section 2 of the Sherman Act, 88 Harv.L.Rev. 697 (1975). The FTC adopted a set of presumptions Areeda and Turner suggested: 1) sales at prices that equal or exceed average variable cost should be strongly, even conclusively, presumed to be legal; 2) sales at prices below average variable cost for a significant time should be rebuttably presumed anticompetitive; and 3) sales at prices that equal or exceed average total cost should be conclusively presumed legitimate. *See Matter of Int'l Tel. & Tel. Corp.*, 104 F.T.C. 280 (1984); *see also William Inglis & Sons Baking Co. v. ITT Cont'l Baking Co., Inc.*, 668 F.2d 1014 (9th Cir. 1981); (citing and somewhat relying on the Areeda & Turner article, holding the principles governing proof of predatory intent in an attempt to monopolize claim under § 2 of the Sherman Act are equally applicable to proof of predatory intent in a primary-line RPA claim). *But see A.A. Poultry Farms v. Rose Acre Farms*, 881 F.2d 1396 (7th Cir. 1989) (courts need only examine the cost and price relationships where the market structure makes price cut recoupment feasible for a Sherman Act § 2 claim; intent plays no useful role in Sherman Act predatory price cases, but noting in dictum that until the Supreme Court overrules an earlier holding that the RPA prohibits some primary-line discrimination that the Sherman

Act permits, "predatory intent" coupled with proof of erosion of price levels continues to sufficiently state a RPA § 2(a) claim); *accord, Brooke Group, Ltd. v. Brown & Williamson Tobacco Corp.*, 509 U.S. 209 (1993).

(b) Second, Third, and Fourth Line Injury. The RPA principally prevents price discrimination induced by a favored buyer. Not surprisingly, most litigation under the Act involved second line competitive injuries. Primary line injury cases now require a detailed showing of substantial adverse impact on competitive conditions in the discriminating seller's market. Second line injury, however, merely requires showing a permanent and substantial price differential in a standardized product's sales to two or more purchasers.

Under these conditions the courts and FTC are apparently willing to assume likelihood of private injury and an adverse competitive effect at the purchaser level of competition. *But cf. Volvo Trucks, supra* (in a competitive bidding market, when competition between purchasers occurs before goods are purchased from the seller, there is no showing of competing purchasers); *Toledo Mack Sales & Serv., Inc. v. Mack Trucks, Inc.*, 530 F.3d 204 (3d Cir. 2008) (dealers' competitive bidding process caused competition for customers before the dealers bought from a manufacturer, so the two-purchaser requirement cannot be satisfied at the time of the manufacturer's sale); *Feesers, Inc. v. Michael Foods, Inc.*, 591 F.3d 191 (3d Cir. 2010) (same outcome as *Mack Trucks, Inc.* for the food industry).

The Supreme Court determined an alleged price discrimination victim is not entitled to the price discrimination amount as "automatic damages", but instead must show actual injury attributable to a harm antitrust laws were designed to prevent. *J. Truett Payne Co., Inc. v. Chrysler Motors Corp.*, 451 U.S. 557 (1981). Here, a plaintiff could utilize the relaxed antitrust proof of causation standard, but evidence of little more than a temporary market share decline was insufficient to meet even this standard of proof for causally related injury. *See also Boise Cascade Corp. v. FTC*, 837 F.2d 1127 (D.C. Cir. 1988) (while inference of competitive injury may be drawn from substantial price discrimination between competing purchasers over time, the FTC erred in rejecting as irrelevant the favored purchaser's evidence suggesting absence of competitive injury or reasonable possibility thereof).

In *Texaco, Inc. v. Hasbrouck*, 496 U.S. 543 (1990), the Supreme Court held a supplier need not satisfy rigorous cost justification defense requirements to prove reasonable functional discounts to dual distributor/retailers. There is no diminished competition between the dual distributor's customers and the supplier's direct customers. However, functional discounts must constitute reasonable reimbursement for the dual distributor's actual marketing functions. The functional discounts in *Hasbrouck* did not meet the latter requirement since the dual distributors received a full discount on all purchases, even when most of the volume was sold directly to consumers.

A price differential is deemed substantial when it is likely to influence the favored customer's resale prices or where it occurs in a market having low profit margins and vigorous competition. Only where price differences are insubstantial in amount or temporary in duration have the courts and the FTC examined the actual competitive effect of the price difference on the market in which the favored purchaser operates.

Prima facie cases for third line competitive injury (i.e., injury at the customers of the favored purchaser level) are essentially the same as a second line injury case. However, the favored purchaser must have provably reduced their resale prices due to the discrimination.

The prima facie case of fourth line injury is essentially the same as in a third line injury case. Fourth line cases merely add an intermediate customer between the favored purchaser and the customer with whom the disfavored purchaser or its customers compete. Third or fourth line injury cases are rarely litigated, further underscoring the Act's preoccupation with second line injury.

(2) § 2(a) Price Discrimination Defenses

A discriminating seller may raise three affirmative defenses to rebut a prima facie § 2(a) price discrimination case. Cost justification and changing conditions defenses are provided in § 2(a). The meeting competition defense is separately provided in § 2(b). A discriminating seller avoids liability by establishing any of these defenses, even if the price difference causes competitive injury.

The challenged seller bears the burden of proof for each defense. This burden of proof allocation requires a second line injury case seller to justify any permanent and substantial price differential. It opposes the common-law view presuming lawful pricing and requiring proof the pricing decision was motivated by predatory intent to be unlawful. All three statutory defenses are narrowly interpreted by the Federal Trade Commission and the courts, making it more difficult to justify a substantial price differential. *But see Texaco, Inc. v. Hasbrouck, supra*, stating a supplier need not satisfy the defense's rigorous cost justification requirements to prove discounts to a dual distributor/retailer is reasonable and thus do not cause any competitive injury.

(a) Cost Justification. The RPA's prohibition against price discrimination implicitly holds arbitrary price differentials unfair. These price differentials likely result from a seller's predatory intent or a buyer's coercive use of bargaining power. Accordingly, price differences that are not arbitrary, but merely reflect differences in the seller's costs, are not actionable discrimination. Section 2(a) specifically recognizes evidence of cost differences justifies a price differential.

For cost justification to be more than a purely illusory defense, there must be tolerance for a degree of approximation in price setting and cost calculation. A business cannot be expected to have a cost justification for every price difference, whether before or after the fact. Businesses necessarily deal in averages—the average cost to manufacture and distribute goods to various classes of customers. Classifications that cost-justify a particular price difference are likely acceptable when they are sufficiently homogeneous. This makes the average cost of selling products to a class of customers reasonably approximate to the cost of dealing with each class member for each product sold. Evidence a classification obscures significant cost differences among customers, however, vitiates a proffered cost justification defense.

(b) Changing Conditions. The changing conditions defense in § 2(a) reassures sellers of perishable or seasonal goods that they may reduce prices to dispose of such goods. To establish the defense, there must be some change in either the goods themselves or in market conditions causing the responsive price change. Evidence indicating the compared purchases were not in fact "contemporaneous" provides a basis for negating the prima facie claim that price discrimination occurred. Section 2(a)'s express proviso on changing conditions thus appears merely to emphasize that even relatively contemporaneous price differences may not necessarily constitute price discrimination.

(c) Meeting Competition. Just as a seller may cost-justify a price difference or show that changing conditions made it necessary, so the seller may show that the price difference is not being used aggressively but defensively. Section 2(b) allows a seller to avoid liability for price discrimination by

showing that the lower price was extended in good faith to meet a competitor's equally low price.

The good faith requirement prevents a discriminator who fortuitously meets another's price while attempting to undercut it from escaping liability for price discrimination. On the other hand, the meeting competition defense will not necessarily be defeated because one fortuitously beats a competitor's price during a good faith effort to meet it. Some margin for error in the effort to meet a price is necessary because a seller cannot be sure their information concerning a competitor's price is accurate, especially when a buyer provides it. The margin for error, however, is small and is subject to a good faith effort to verify competitive pricing information of questionable accuracy.

A difficulty arises when the only way to verify a price is to contact the competitor whose price is being met. Businesses accused of collusive price fixing in violation of the Sherman Act often defend price information sharing as necessary to avoid RPA violations. Consequently, courts limit the circumstances where a seller may lawfully contact a competitor to verify a competitor's price. In *United States v. Container Corp. of Am.*, 393 U.S. 333 (1969), the Supreme Court held that even an infrequent and irregular pricing information exchange was illegal under the Sherman Act. The Court also cautioned that any exchange of price information—even when putatively for RPA compliance purposes—must remain subject to close scrutiny under the Sherman

Act. *See United States v. United States Gypsum Co.*, 438 U.S. 422 (1978).

A defendant establishing the "meeting competition" defense need not show that the price being met was itself a legal (as opposed to a discriminatory) price. However, the courts clearly established that the meeting competition defense cannot justify copying a competitor's recognizably illegal discriminatory pricing scheme. In *FTC v. A.E. Staley Mfg. Co.*, 324 U.S. 746 (1945), the Supreme Court emphasized that § 2(b) was not intended to legalize a company's otherwise illicit conduct just because another business had done it first. On the other hand, the meeting competition defense is available where, in response to competitive price increases, a brewer *raises* prices in one state that statutorily requires brewers to sell to wholesalers at a single price throughout the state, while not changing prices to wholesalers in adjoining states. *Falls City Indus. Inc. v. Vanco Beverage, Inc.*, 460 U.S. 428 (1983) (Supreme Court reversal of a ruling that the meeting competition defense is available only if the defendant sets its lower price on a customer-by-customer basis and creates the price discrimination by lowering rather than by raising prices).

b. Unearned Brokerage

Section 2(c) of the amended Clayton Act prohibits (1) a person engaged in commerce (2) from paying or receiving a commission, brokerage fee, compensation, or an allowance or discount in lieu thereof (3) except for services actually rendered in connection with a sale of goods (4) where the person paid is not under the direct or indirect control of the entity making the payment. The provision was principally designed to outlaw arrangements whereby buyers exacted price concessions disguised as brokerage commissions to their agents or to themselves. As discussed in Ch. 8, *supra*, § 2(c) was also held to prohibit commercial bribery in bargaining relations.

Unlike § 2(a), § 2(c) extends liability to the payment or discount recipient as well as to the seller offering it. Section 2(c) applies to exporters as well as importers and domestic businesses. Further, the language of § 2(c) does not require showing price discrimination (i.e., two or more sales) or injury to competition. Nor does the Act allow for cost justification or meeting competition defenses. The only expressly available defense is that the brokerage fee was for services rendered. The courts apparently retreated from their early position that a broker not under the payor's control is inherently incapable of rendering the services contemplated by the statute. However, courts still insist that brokerage fees must be for services *actually* rendered. To date no broker outside the paying company's control has succeeded in establishing that such services were rendered.

Allowances and discounts in lieu of brokerage present a more difficult case. While § 2(c) does not expressly require proof of discrimination (sales at different prices to two or more customers), such evidence may in fact be required in allowance and discount cases to show that the allowance or discount was in fact "in lieu of" brokerage and not simply the result of lower costs. Even so, not all cost savings can be passed along to a purchaser. In *FTC v. Henry Broch & Co.*, 363 U.S. 166 (1960) the Supreme Court held that a cost justification defense based on saved brokerage was unavailable under § 2(c). The legislative policy of preventing coerced price concessions apparently outweighed the uncoerced seller's interest in passing along such cost savings.

c. Discriminatory Promotional Allowances and Services

Sections 2(d) and 2(e) of the amended Clayton Act forbid a seller engaged in commerce from (1) granting promotional payments, services, or facilities (2) to or for a customer's benefit (3) unless they are made available on proportionally equal terms to all customers who compete in reselling the seller's goods. The purpose of these two sections, like that of § 2(c), is to prevent disguised price discrimination. Despite textual differences between §§ 2(d) and 2(e), courts consider them to be companion provisions. Thus, both sections are held to require that the persons and transactions involved be in commerce even though only § 2(d) so specifies. Unlike § 2(c), §§ 2(d) and 2(e) normally require showing discrimination as a part of the prima facie case. Courts occasionally require a seller charged with a § 2(d) or 2(e) violation to prove this conduct is not discriminatory. Unlike § 2(a) price discrimination, however, discriminatory promotional allowances and services are unlawful per se without any need to show competitive injury. *But see World of Sleep, Inc. v. La-Z-Boy Chair Co.*, 756 F.2d 1467 (10th Cir. 1985), questionably citing § 2(a) case *J. Truett Payne Co., Inc. v. Chrysler Motors Corp.*, 451 U.S. 557 (1981) to assert a § 2(e) plaintiff must show that not receiving a promotional allowance affected their ability to compete and favored their competitors. The only affirmative defense available for §§ 2(d) and 2(e) claims is the § 2(b) meeting competition defense. The § 2(a) cost-justification defense is not available.

The effect of §§ 2(d) and 2(e) is to flatly prohibit a business from designing a promotion that excludes certain customers or attempts to cost-justify offering promotional allowances or services only to certain customers, where the customers compete with each other. *See, e.g., Freightliner of Knoxville v. DaimlerChrysler Vans*, 484 F.3d 865 (6th Cir. 2007) (reversing a trial court's dismissal of §§ 2(d) and 2(e) claims by a van dealer against a distributor for allegedly incorporating Dodge versions of a certain van into a program that gave van owners priority when receiving services at Dodge dealers, while not offering a similar service to Freightliner dealers for the same type of van, and holding that under a liberal standard of review for motions to dismiss the court could not exclude a possibility that the distributor somehow tied the van's distribution to this incentive which could be incidental to the van's resale). On the other hand, promotional allowances, services, and facilities need only be made available on proportionally equal terms. Normally this means some relation can be drawn between the volume of goods purchased and the allowance granted.

The FTC issued guidelines (called the Fred Meyer Guidelines) on §§ 2(d) and (e) compliance. While the guidelines do not have legal effect, they offer insights into the FTC's interpretation of these requirements.

d. Buyer Liability for Price Discrimination

While the principal impetus behind the Robinson-Patman Act (RPA) was to prevent chain stores and other large volume buyers from using economic coercion to exact price concessions, the Act primarily focuses on the discriminating seller's liability and only secondarily on the favored buyer's liability. This is because the Supreme Court took a restrictive view on the extent to which a buyer is engaged in commerce that Congress can regulate at the time the RPA was enacted. Thus, only two sections of the RPA apply to a buyer. Section 2(c) makes it unlawful for a buyer to receive unearned brokerage or an allowance in lieu thereof. The other, § 2(f), makes it unlawful: (1) for a buyer engaged in commerce (2) knowingly to induce or receive (3) a discrimination in price prohibited by § 2 of the Act. The FTC and courts concluded that § 2(f) prohibits the knowing inducement or receipt not only of a per se discriminatory price (i.e., a price violating § 2(a)) but also of those forms of disguised price discrimination prohibited by §§ 2(d) and 2(e). In the alternative, such conduct is held to be an unfair method of competition within the meaning of § 5 of the FTC Act.

Subjecting a buyer to liability requires the FTC or a private plaintiff first prove that the seller violated the Act, and then prove the buyer had reason to know that the seller's price was illegal. Thus, if a seller seeks to meet competition in good faith within the meaning of § 2(b) of the Act, a buyer will not be liable under § 2(f) even though the buyer knows the seller is in fact *beating* the competition. *See Great Atl. & Pac. Tea Co., Inc. v. FTC*, 440 U.S. 69 (1979). However, the buyer may not induce the price concession by misrepresenting competitive price information to the seller. *See Kroger Co. v. FTC*, 438 F.2d 1372 (6th Cir. 1971).

3. PRICE DISCRIMINATION AND PREDATORY PRICING IN INTERNATIONAL TRADE ("DUMPING")

Section 2(a) of the amended Clayton Act does not prohibit price discrimination by exporters since it is limited to price discrimination connected with commodities sold for use, consumption, or resale within the United States. Sections 2(c), 2(d), 2(e), and 3 of the Robinson-Patman Act (RPA), on the other hand, contain no analogous limitation. Instead, they extend to any payment or acceptance of unearned brokerage, discriminatory payment, discriminatory furnishing of promotional services, covert or predatory geographic price discrimination, or predatory price cutting so long as the act occurs "in commerce". These provisions apply wherever the prohibited conduct adversely affects U.S. foreign commerce.

Price discrimination in the import trade is of far greater domestic concern than price discrimination in the export trade. The RPA is not the only statute prohibiting an importer from discriminating among U.S. purchasers. Many other federal statutes provide relief against a special form of import price discrimination known as "dumping."

Dumping occurs when a foreign manufacturer sells goods in the United States for less than fair value—i.e., less than it charges for the same goods at home or in other markets. *See* 19 U.S.C. § 1673. This prohibition against selling goods for less than their fair value does not apply to the sale of services, leading to inevitable disputes over how particular contracts should be characterized. *See, e.g., United States v. Eurodif SA,* 555 U.S. 305 (2009) (the Commerce Department's characterization of a disputed transactions as sales of goods rather than uranium enrichment services reflected a permissible interpretation and application of 19 U.S.C. § 1673). The U.S. anti-dumping provision is designed to conform to standards set by the WTO Agreement on the Implementation of Article VI of GATT 1994 (i.e., the WTO Antidumping Agreement). This only permits a WTO member action against dumping where there is genuine ("material") injury to a competing domestic industry. To establish dumping under U.S. law, the government must 1) show that dumping is taking place; 2) calculate the extent of dumping (i.e., how much lower the export price is compared to the exporter's home market price); and 3) prove this dumping is causing or threatening to cause injury. Section 1673 assesses a special antidumping duty on product imports that are or are likely to be dumped in the United States and are either retarding establishment of a U.S. industry or causing or threatening material injury to a U.S. industry.

The Omnibus Trade and Competitiveness Act of 1988 added 19 U.S.C. § 1677k, allowing a U.S. party to challenge so called "input" dumping occurring in a foreign country that is a GATT signatory. Input dumping occurs where the goods being dumped are incorporated into a product that is then exported to the United States. Section 1677k authorizes domestic producers of "like product" in the U.S. to petition the Office of the U.S. Trade Representative for remedial action against the importing country, utilizing the Dispute Settlement Body of the World Trade Organization.

The International Trade Administration (ITA) of the U.S. Department of Commerce, acting on behalf of the Secretary of Commerce, is responsible for determining whether a product is being dumped on the U.S. market. If the Secretary so finds, the International Trade Commission (ITC) must then determine whether the dumping is causing or threatening a material injury to or retarding establishment of a U.S. industry. A finding of such injury or threat results in the assessment and collection of a special duty on the challenged goods. The duty is the difference between the home market price (or the price at other foreign markets) and the price at which the goods are sold in the United States. Any interested party involved in the ITC's administrative proceedings may seek judicial review before the Court of International Trade (formerly the U.S. Customs Court). Such interested parties may include a foreign government or business, or a U.S. business, labor union, or trade association. Final decisions may be appealed to the Court of Appeals for the Federal Circuit.

Price discrimination in the import trade may also occur indirectly when a foreign government subsidizes certain exports. If the ITA determines such anticompetitive actions exist and the ITC determines there is a threat or actual material injury to an existing or developing U.S. industry, the Department of Commerce may issue an antidumping duty or countervailing duty order to offset the government subsidy. *See* 19 U.S.C. §§ 1671 *et seq.* These orders are reviewed every five years for likelihood of continuing or recurring injury.

Section 337 of the Tariff Act of 1930, 19 U.S.C. § 1337, forbids unfair competition methods or unfair acts in the import trade. This provision mainly prevents importation of articles that infringe U.S. intellectual property rights. However, the ITC also asserts jurisdiction over various types of antitrust claims such as predatory pricing. Where such conduct threatens an existing domestic industry or prevents establishment of one, the ITC may exclude the article from the U.S. or issues a cease and desist order. Either action by the ITC may be overturned by the President within 60 days. However, the ITC may not use its authority under § 1337 to address dumping or countervailing duty cases as such.

The difficulty with all legislation aimed at unfair pricing practices in international trade is that—like domestic sales below cost and price discrimination statutes—it lacks a firm economic foundation. As discussed in § B.2.a.(1)(a), *supra*, economists demonstrated that predatory pricing accusations—including predatory dumping—are almost always wrong, since predatory pricing is irrational in all but the most exceptional circumstances. *See, e.g.*, Areeda & Turner, Predatory Pricing and Related Practices Under Section 2 of the Sherman Act, 88 Harv.L.Rev. 697 (1975). Thus, predatory pricing practices simply cannot explain the sheer number of antidumping proceedings brought in the U.S. To the suspicious eye, U.S. antidumping legislation may very well protect from foreign competition the few large domestic companies that perennially file most U.S. dumping complaints.

Indeed, the WTO Antidumping Agreement's purpose is not so much to curb the practice of dumping as it is to rein in worldwide antidumping legislation. Unfortunately, the Uruguay Round of multilateral trade negotiations did little to reduce, and may even have exacerbated reliance on, antidumping legislation as a means of responding to competitive pressures. After all, the WTO prohibits "voluntary export restraints" to settle incipient trade disputes.

A primary accomplishment of the Uruguay Round was said to be inclusion of a "sunset" provision in the WTO Antidumping Agreement. This requires member states to terminate antidumping measures not later than five years from their imposition (or most recent review) unless local authorities initiate a review before that date and determine the measure's expiration would likely lead to a continuation or recurrence of injury. The Uruguay Round Agreements Act, 19 U.S.C. § 1675, duly implements this requirement in the U.S. As a practical matter, however, the sun is unlikely to set on anti-dumping duties unless and until the duties succeed in extinguishing the price competition that gave rise to the initial dumping complaint.

INDEX

References are to Pages